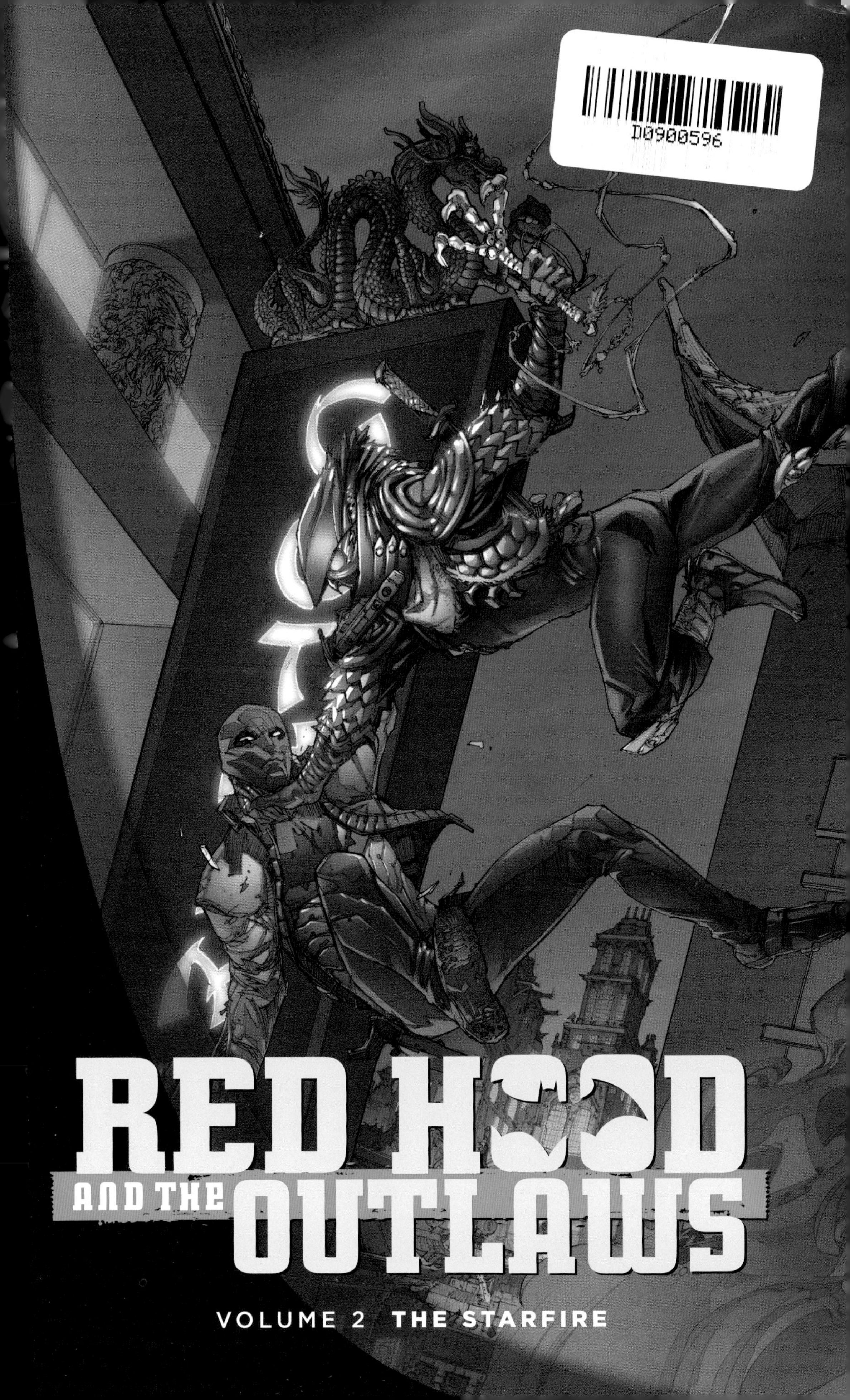

RED HOOD AND THE OUTLAWS

VOLUME 2 THE STARFIRE

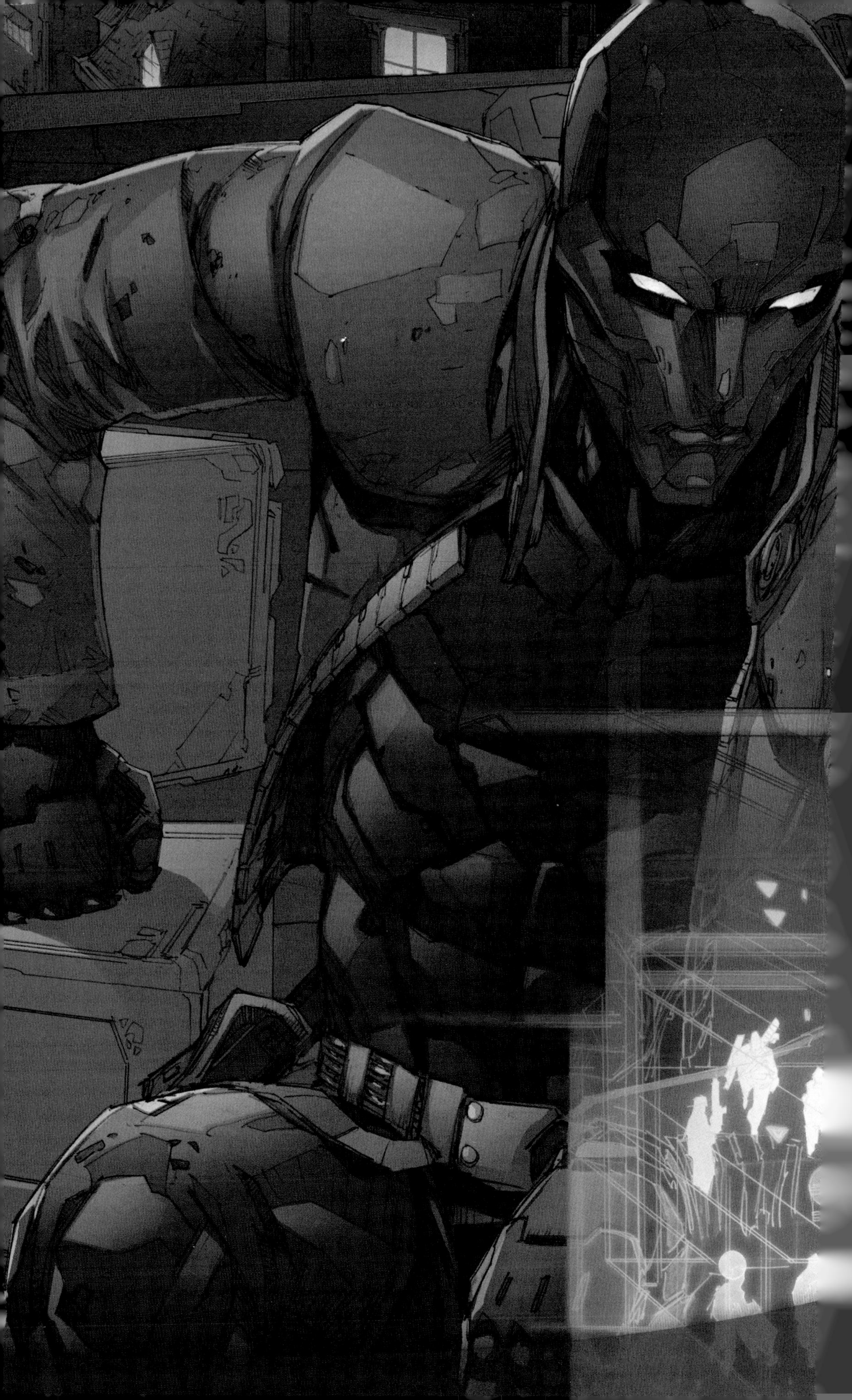

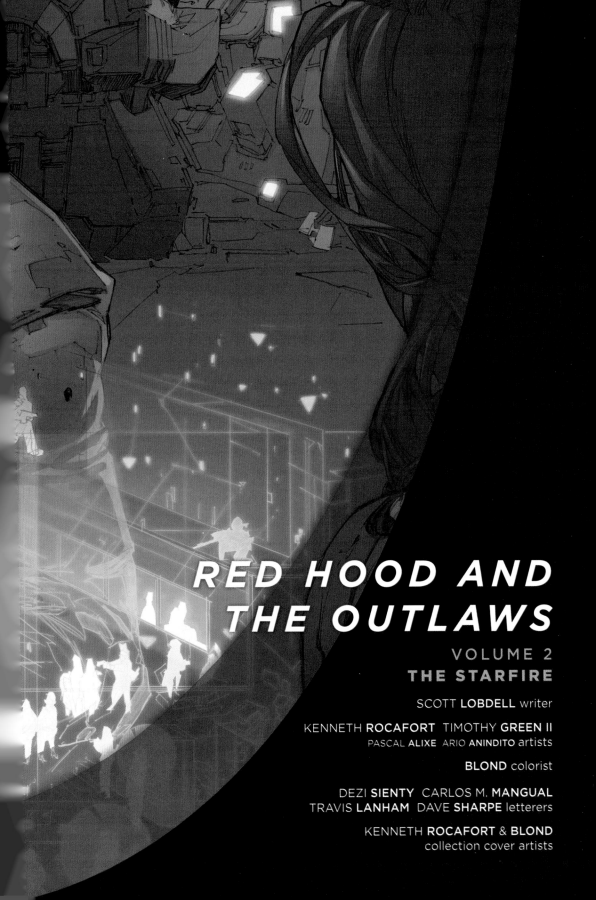

RED HOOD AND THE OUTLAWS

VOLUME 2
THE STARFIRE

SCOTT **LOBDELL** writer

KENNETH **ROCAFORT** TIMOTHY **GREEN II**
PASCAL **ALIXE** ARIO **ANINDITO** artists

BLOND colorist

DEZI **SIENTY** CARLOS M. **MANGUAL**
TRAVIS **LANHAM** DAVE **SHARPE** letterers

KENNETH **ROCAFORT** & **BLOND**
collection cover artists

BOBBIE CHASE EDDIE BERGANZA Editors – Original Series DARREN SHAN KATIE KUBERT Assistant Editors – Original Series
RACHEL PINNELAS Editor ROBBIN BROSTERMAN Design Director – Books
ROBBIE BIEDERMAN Publication Design

BOB HARRAS Senior VP – Editor-in-Chief, DC Comics

DIANE NELSON President DAN DIDIO and JIM LEE Co-Publishers
GEOFF JOHNS Chief Creative Officer
AMIT DESAI Senior VP – Marketing & Franchise Management
AMY GENKINS Senior VP – Business & Legal Affairs NAIRI GARDINER Senior VP – Finance
JEFF BOISON VP – Publishing Planning MARK CHIARELLO VP – Art Direction & Design
JOHN CUNNINGHAM VP – Marketing TERRI CUNNINGHAM VP – Editorial Administration
LARRY GANEM VP – Talent Relations & Services ALISON GILL Senior VP – Manufacturing & Operations
HANK KANALZ Senior VP – Vertigo & Integrated Publishing JAY KOGAN VP – Business & Legal Affairs, Publishing
JACK MAHAN VP – Business Affairs, Talent NICK NAPOLITANO VP – Manufacturing Administration
SUE POHJA VP – Book Sales FRED RUIZ VP – Manufacturing Operations
COURTNEY SIMMONS Senior VP – Publicity BOB WAYNE Senior VP – Sales

RED HOOD AND THE OUTLAWS VOLUME 2: THE STARFIRE

DC Comics, 1700 Broadway, New York, NY 10019
A Warner Bros. Entertainment Company.
Printed by RR Donnelley, Owensville, MO, USA. 8/8/14. Second Printing.

ISBN: 978-1-4012-4090-5

SUSTAINABLE
FORESTRY
INITIATIVE

Certified Chain of Custody
20% Certified Forest Content,
80% Certified Sourcing
www.sfiprogram.org
SFI-01042
APPLIES TO TEXT STOCK ONLY

Library of Congress Cataloging-in-Publication Data

Lobdell, Scott, author.
Red Hood and The Outlaws. Volume 2, The starfire / Scott Lobdell, Kenneth Rocafort.
pages cm
"Originally published in single magazine form in Red Hood and The Outlaws 8-14."
ISBN 978-1-4012-4090-5
1. Graphic novels. I. Rocafort, Kenneth, illustrator. II. Title. III. Title: Starfire.
PN6728.R4385L64 2013
741.5'973—dc23
2013010697

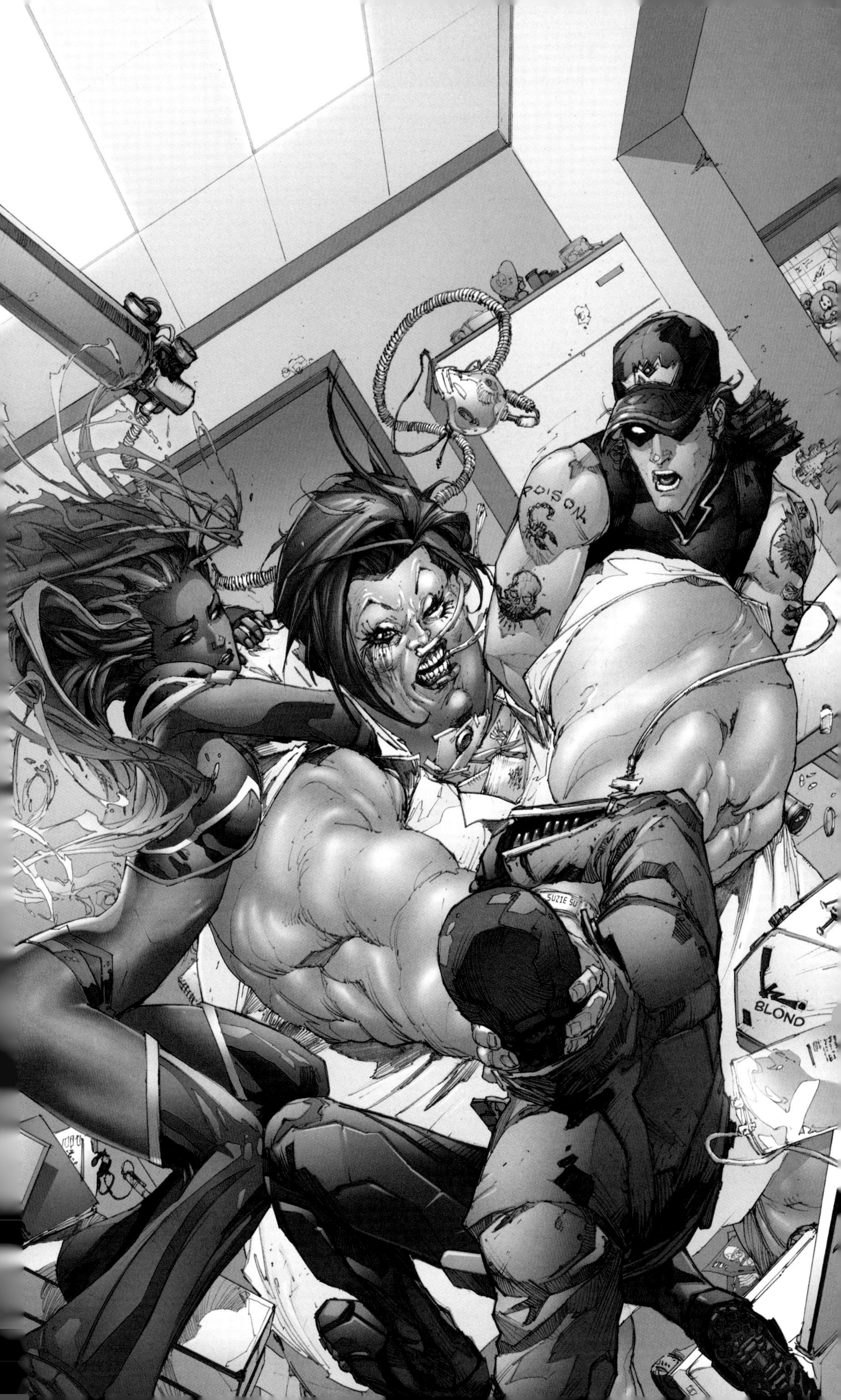
POISON
SUZIE SU
BLOND

SCOTT LOBDELL writer **KENNETH ROCAFORT** artist cover art by **KENNETH ROCAFORT & BLOND**

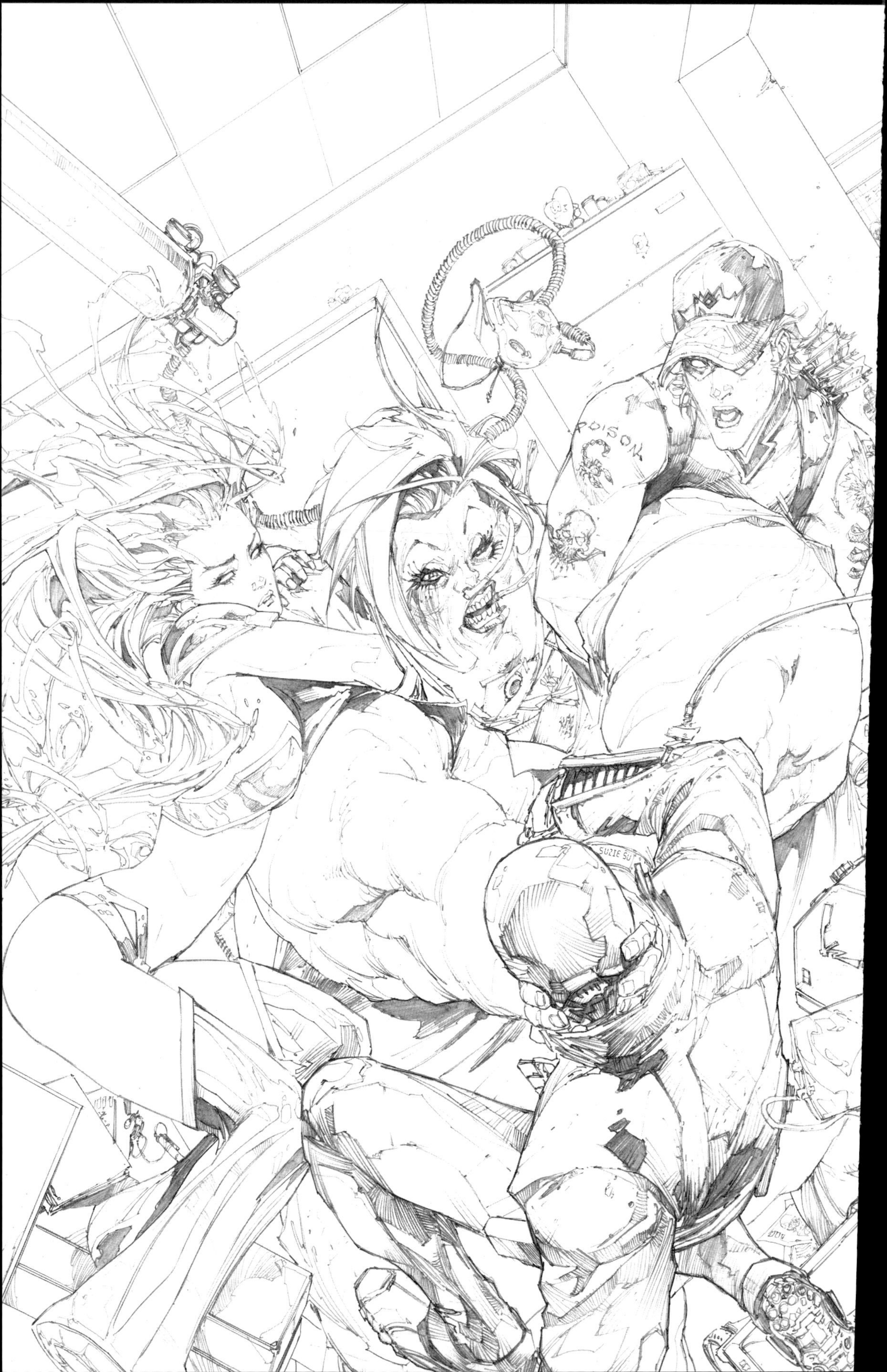
POISON
SUZIE SU

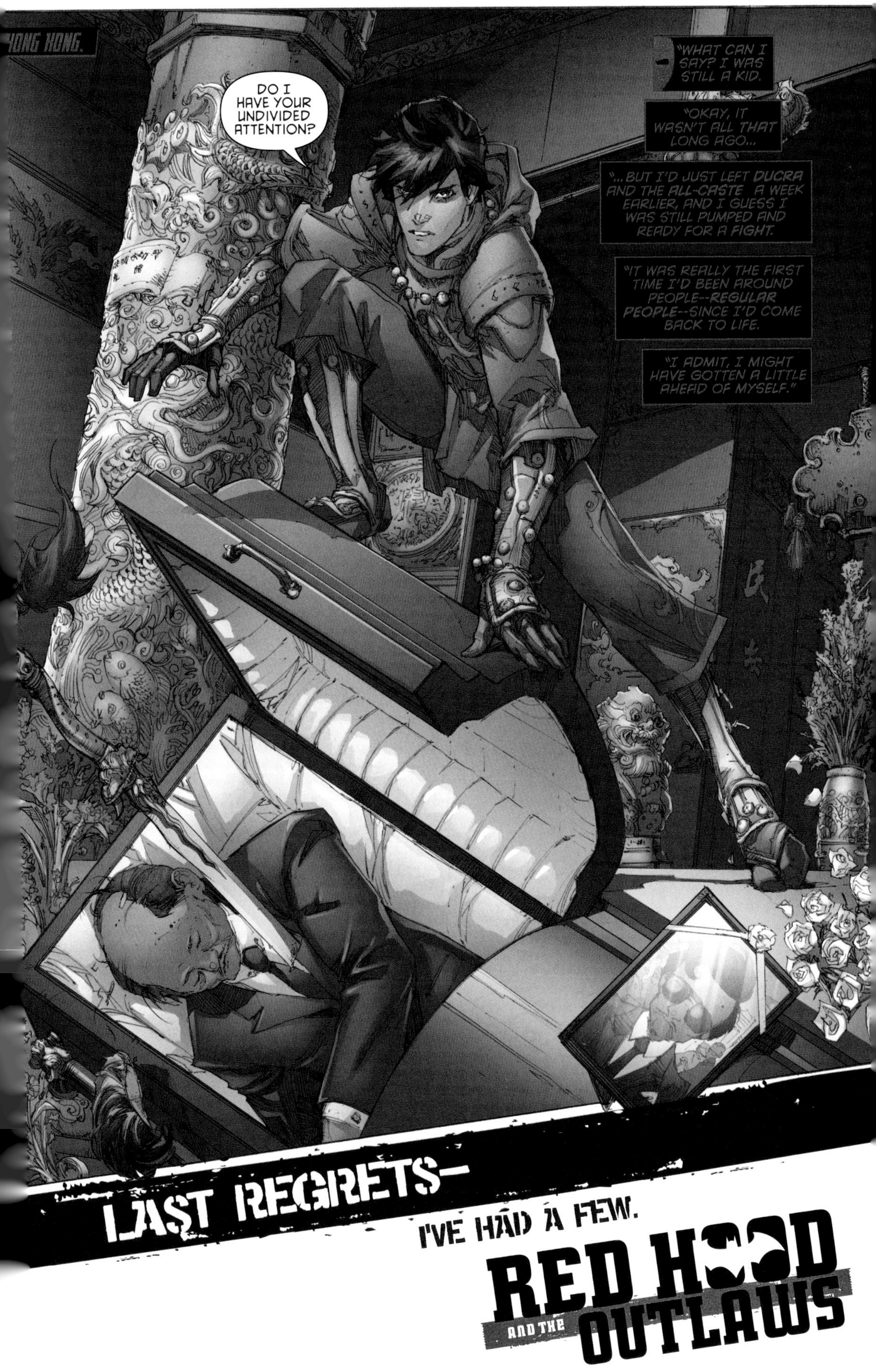

HONG KONG.
DO I HAVE YOUR UNDIVIDED ATTENTION?
"WHAT CAN I SAY? I WAS STILL A KID.
"OKAY, IT WASN'T ALL THAT LONG AGO...
"...BUT I'D JUST LEFT DUCRA AND THE ALL-CASTE A WEEK EARLIER, AND I GUESS I WAS STILL PUMPED AND READY FOR A FIGHT.
"IT WAS REALLY THE FIRST TIME I'D BEEN AROUND PEOPLE--REGULAR PEOPLE--SINCE I'D COME BACK TO LIFE.
"I ADMIT, I MIGHT HAVE GOTTEN A LITTLE AHEAD OF MYSELF."
LAST REGRETS--
I'VE HAD A FEW.
RED HOOD AND THE OUTLAWS

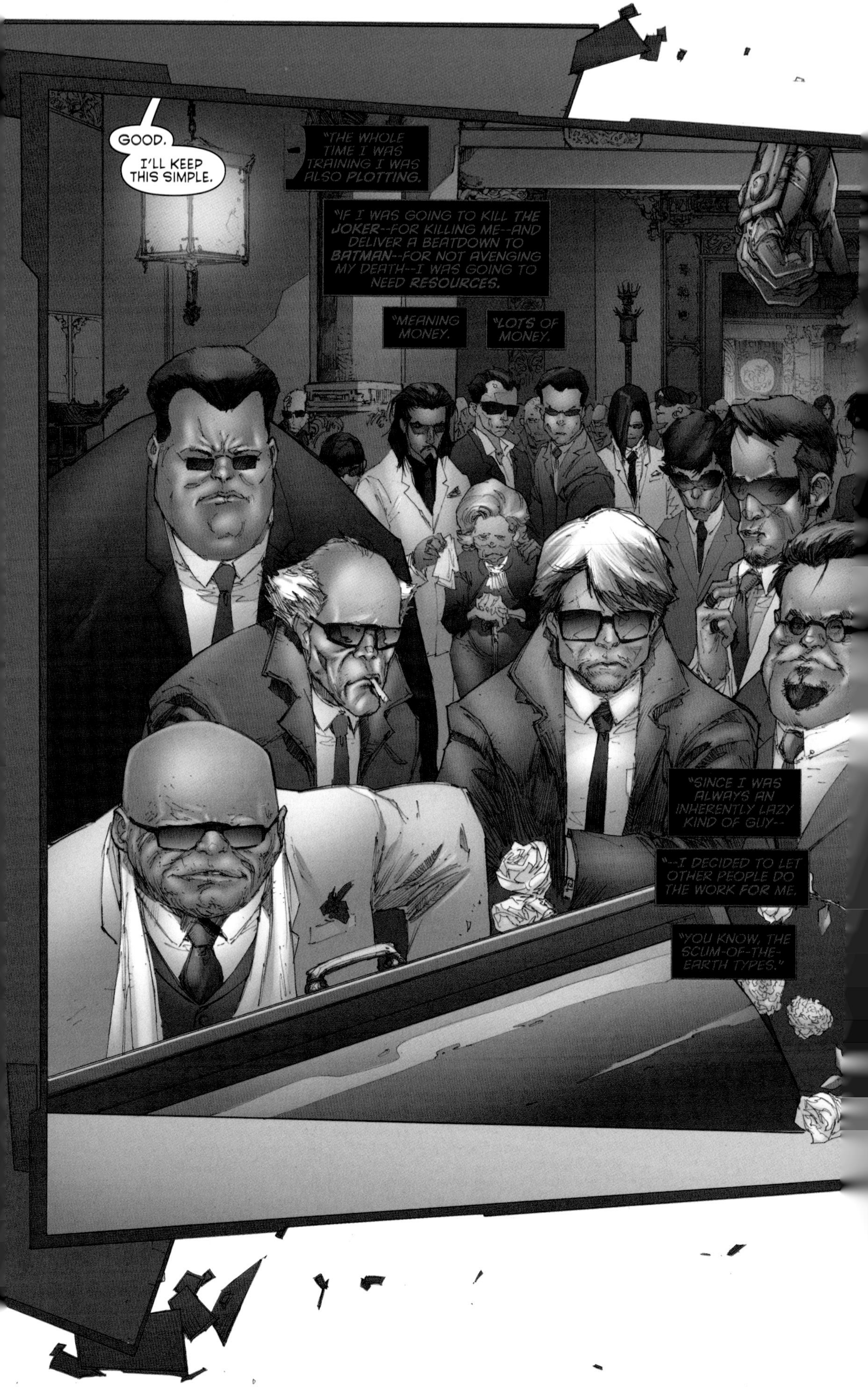
GOOD. I'LL KEEP THIS SIMPLE.
"THE WHOLE TIME I WAS TRAINING I WAS ALSO PLOTTING.
"IF I WAS GOING TO KILL THE JOKER--FOR KILLING ME--AND DELIVER A BEATDOWN TO BATMAN--FOR NOT AVENGING MY DEATH--I WAS GOING TO NEED RESOURCES.
"MEANING MONEY.
"LOTS OF MONEY.
"SINCE I WAS ALWAYS AN INHERENTLY LAZY KIND OF GUY--
"--I DECIDED TO LET OTHER PEOPLE DO THE WORK FOR ME.
"YOU KNOW, THE SCUM-OF-THE-EARTH TYPES."

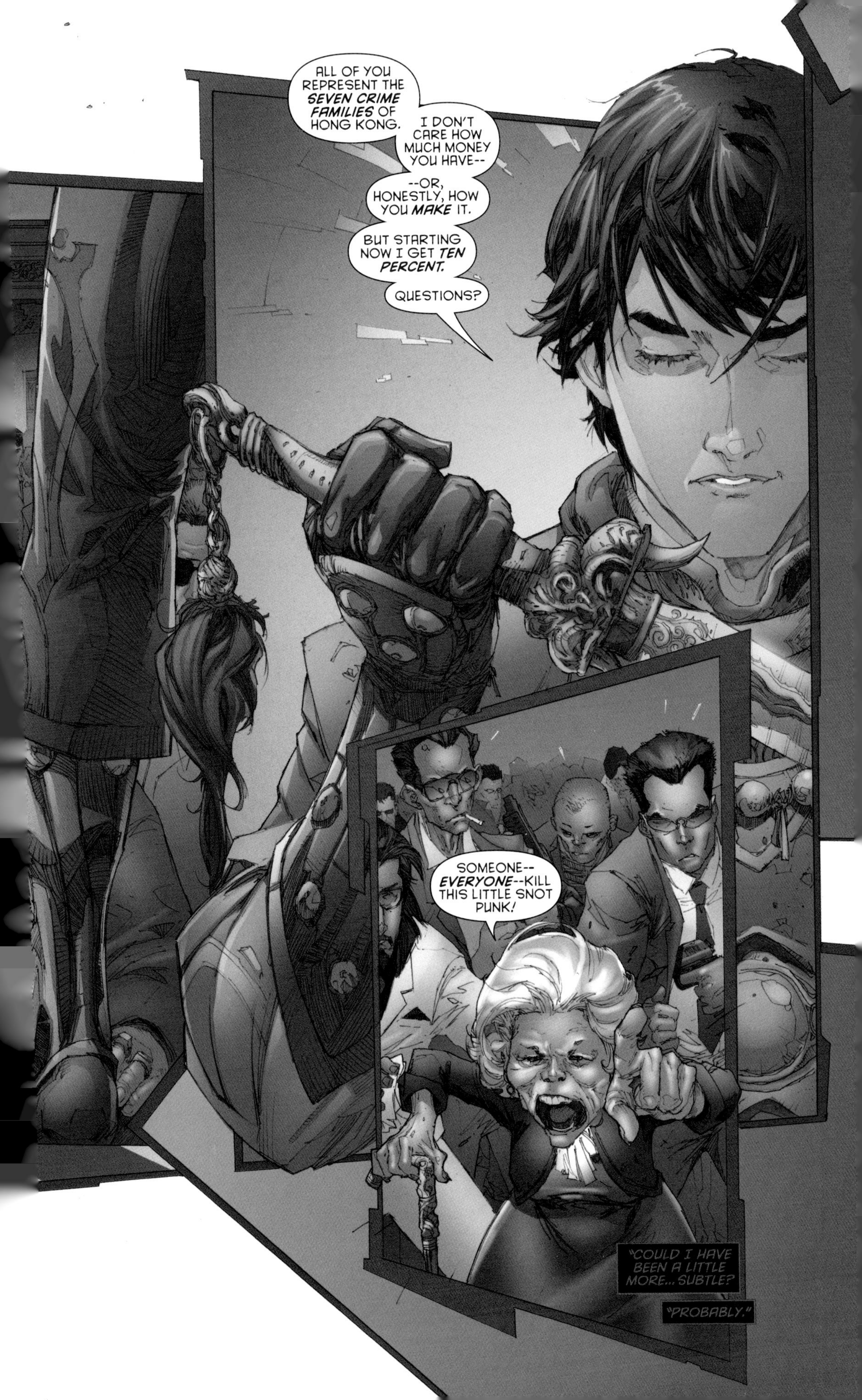
ALL OF YOU REPRESENT THE SEVEN CRIME FAMILIES OF HONG KONG.
I DON'T CARE HOW MUCH MONEY YOU HAVE--
--OR, HONESTLY, HOW YOU MAKE IT.
BUT STARTING NOW I GET TEN PERCENT.
QUESTIONS?
SOMEONE--EVERYONE--KILL THIS LITTLE SNOT PUNK!
"COULD I HAVE BEEN A LITTLE MORE... SUBTLE?
"PROBABLY."

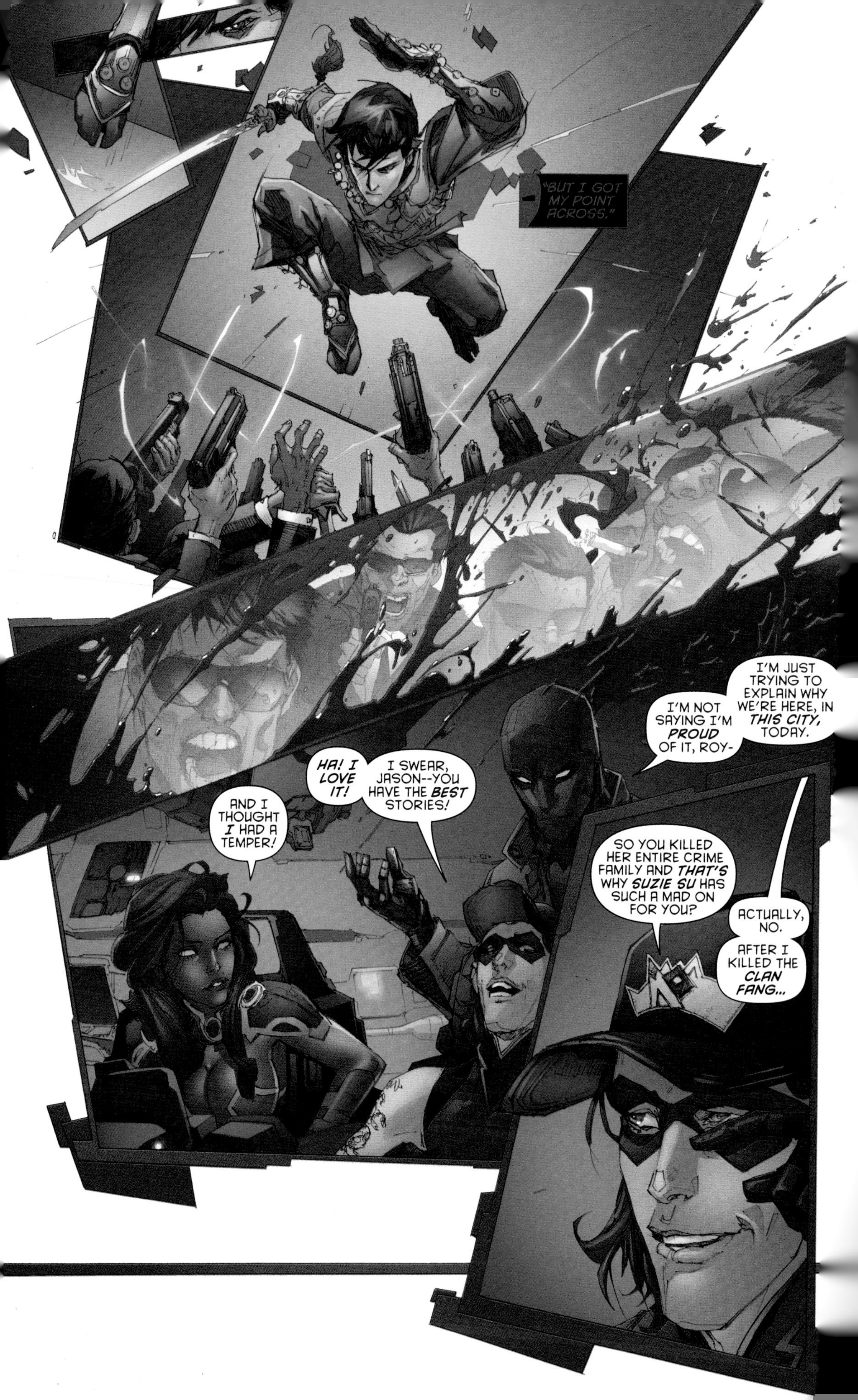

"BUT I GOT MY POINT ACROSS."
I'M NOT SAYING I'M PROUD OF IT, ROY-
I'M JUST TRYING TO EXPLAIN WHY WE'RE HERE, IN THIS CITY, TODAY.
HA! I LOVE IT!
I SWEAR, JASON--YOU HAVE THE BEST STORIES!
AND I THOUGHT I HAD A TEMPER!
SO YOU KILLED HER ENTIRE CRIME FAMILY AND THAT'S WHY SUZIE SU HAS SUCH A MAD ON FOR YOU?
ACTUALLY, NO.
AFTER I KILLED THE CLAN FANG...

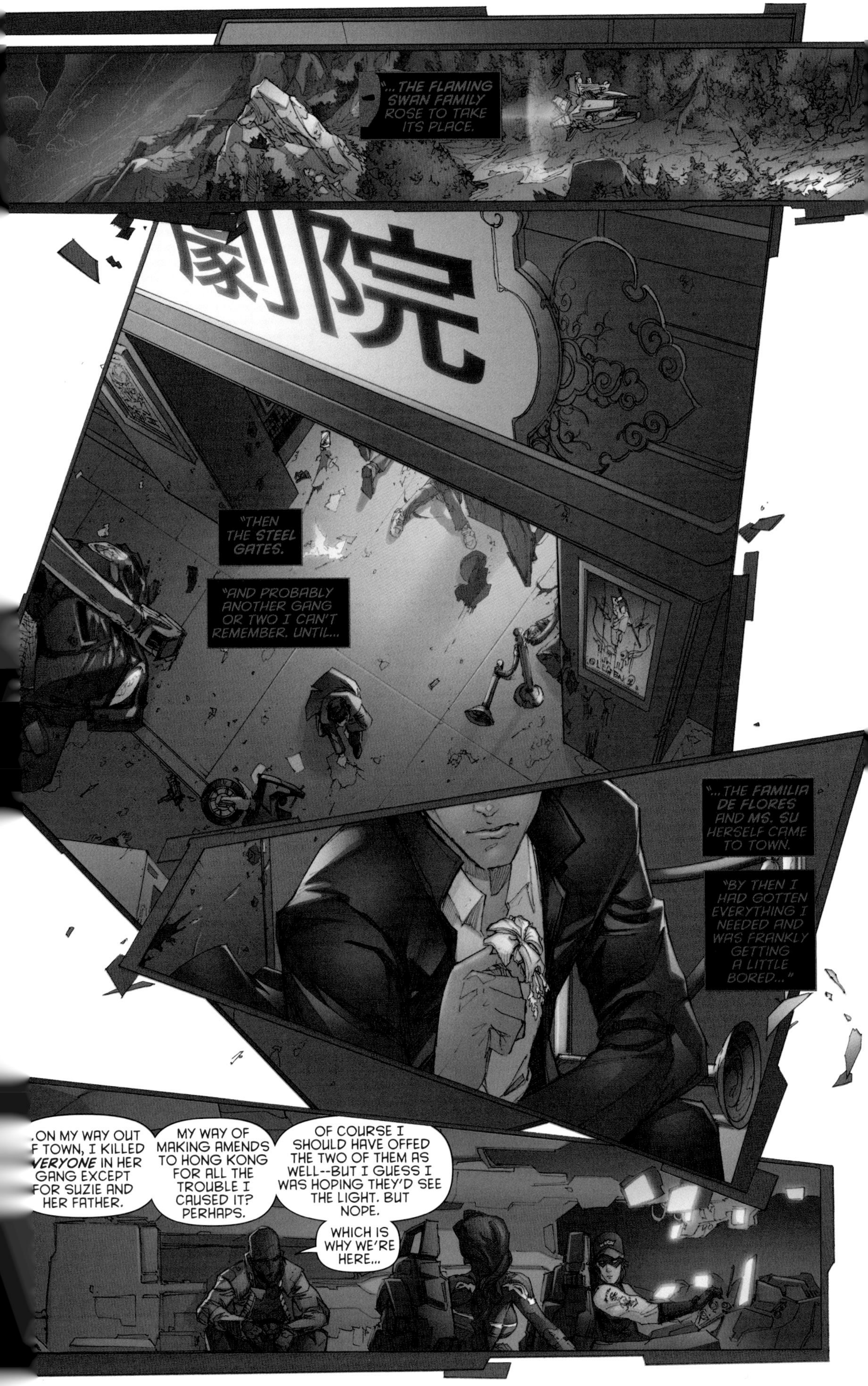
"...THE FLAMING SWAN FAMILY ROSE TO TAKE ITS PLACE.
劇院
"THEN THE STEEL GATES.
"AND PROBABLY ANOTHER GANG OR TWO I CAN'T REMEMBER. UNTIL...
"...THE FAMILIA DE FLORES AND MS. SU HERSELF CAME TO TOWN.
"BY THEN I HAD GOTTEN EVERYTHING I NEEDED AND WAS FRANKLY GETTING A LITTLE BORED..."
.ON MY WAY OUT F TOWN, I KILLED VERYONE IN HER GANG EXCEPT FOR SUZIE AND HER FATHER.
MY WAY OF MAKING AMENDS TO HONG KONG FOR ALL THE TROUBLE I CAUSED IT? PERHAPS.
OF COURSE I SHOULD HAVE OFFED THE TWO OF THEM AS WELL--BUT I GUESS I WAS HOPING THEY'D SEE THE LIGHT. BUT NOPE.
WHICH IS WHY WE'RE HERE...

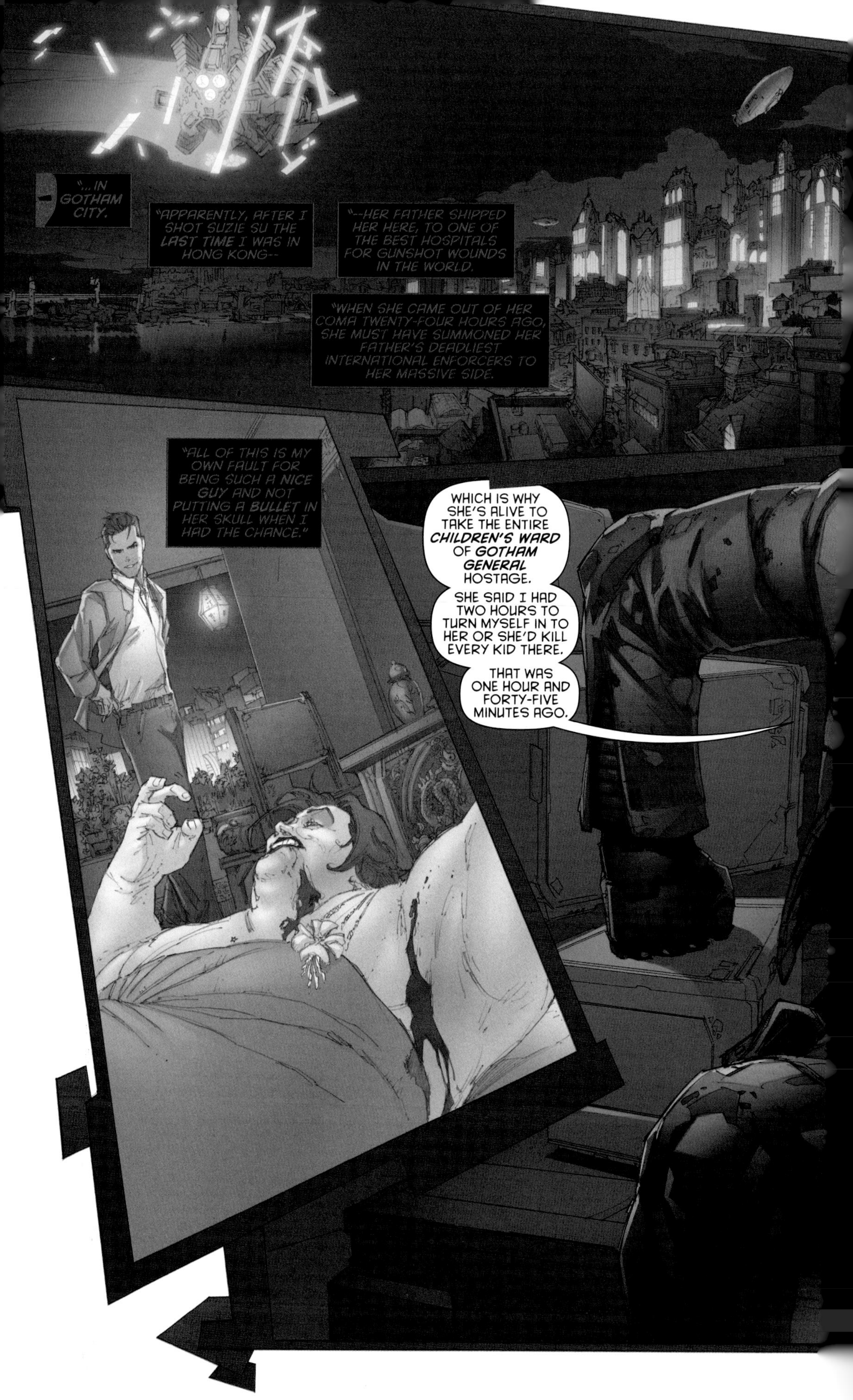
"...IN GOTHAM CITY.
"APPARENTLY, AFTER I SHOT SUZIE SU THE LAST TIME I WAS IN HONG KONG--
"--HER FATHER SHIPPED HER HERE, TO ONE OF THE BEST HOSPITALS FOR GUNSHOT WOUNDS IN THE WORLD.
"WHEN SHE CAME OUT OF HER COMA TWENTY-FOUR HOURS AGO, SHE MUST HAVE SUMMONED HER FATHER'S DEADLIEST INTERNATIONAL ENFORCERS TO HER MASSIVE SIDE.
"ALL OF THIS IS MY OWN FAULT FOR BEING SUCH A NICE GUY AND NOT PUTTING A BULLET IN HER SKULL WHEN I HAD THE CHANCE."
WHICH IS WHY SHE'S ALIVE TO TAKE THE ENTIRE CHILDREN'S WARD OF GOTHAM GENERAL HOSTAGE.
SHE SAID I HAD TWO HOURS TO TURN MYSELF IN TO HER OR SHE'D KILL EVERY KID THERE.
THAT WAS ONE HOUR AND FORTY-FIVE MINUTES AGO.

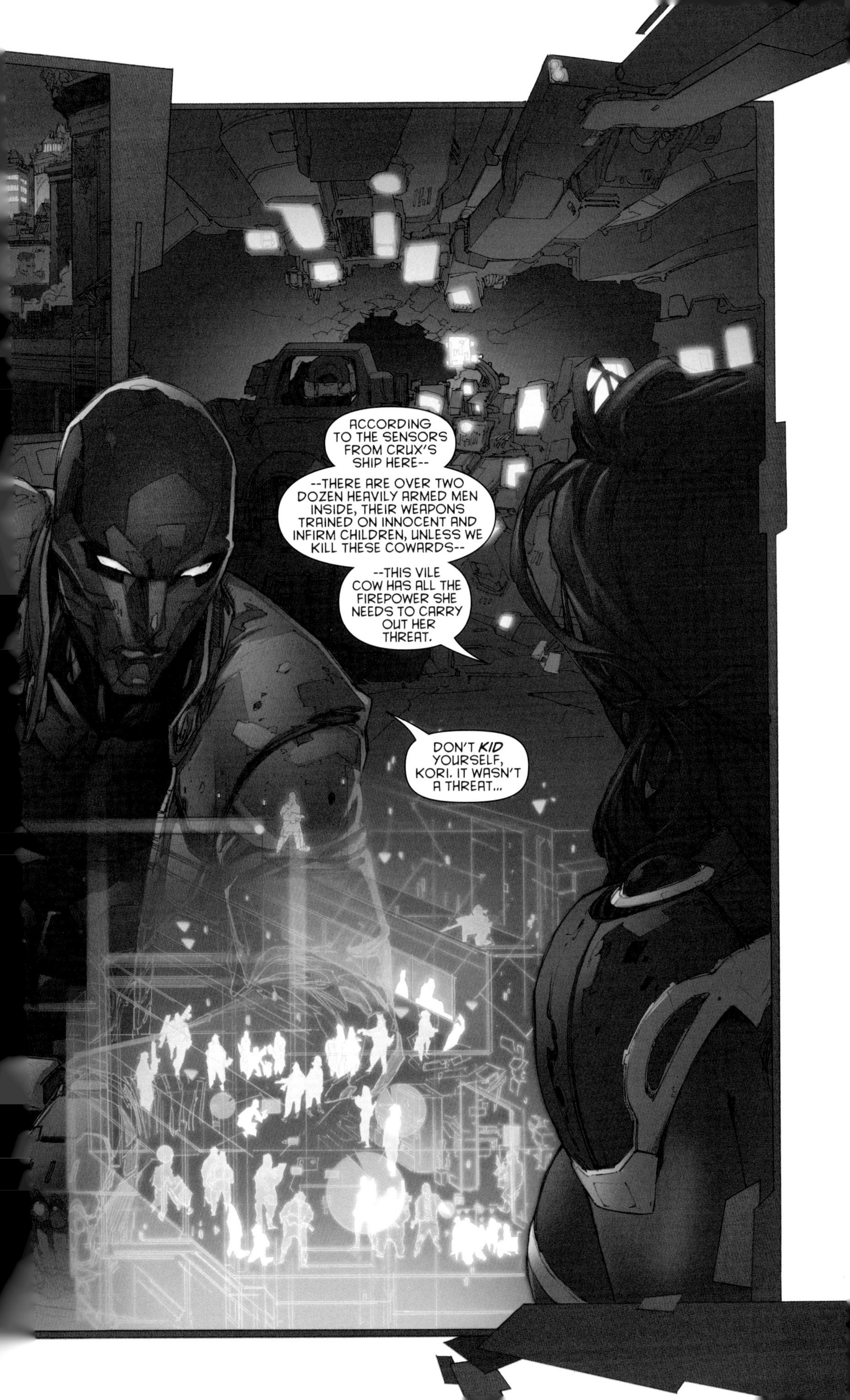
ACCORDING TO THE SENSORS FROM CRUX'S SHIP HERE--
--THERE ARE OVER TWO DOZEN HEAVILY ARMED MEN INSIDE, THEIR WEAPONS TRAINED ON INNOCENT AND INFIRM CHILDREN, UNLESS WE KILL THESE COWARDS--
--THIS VILE COW HAS ALL THE FIREPOWER SHE NEEDS TO CARRY OUT HER THREAT.
DON'T *KID* YOURSELF, KORI. IT WASN'T A THREAT...

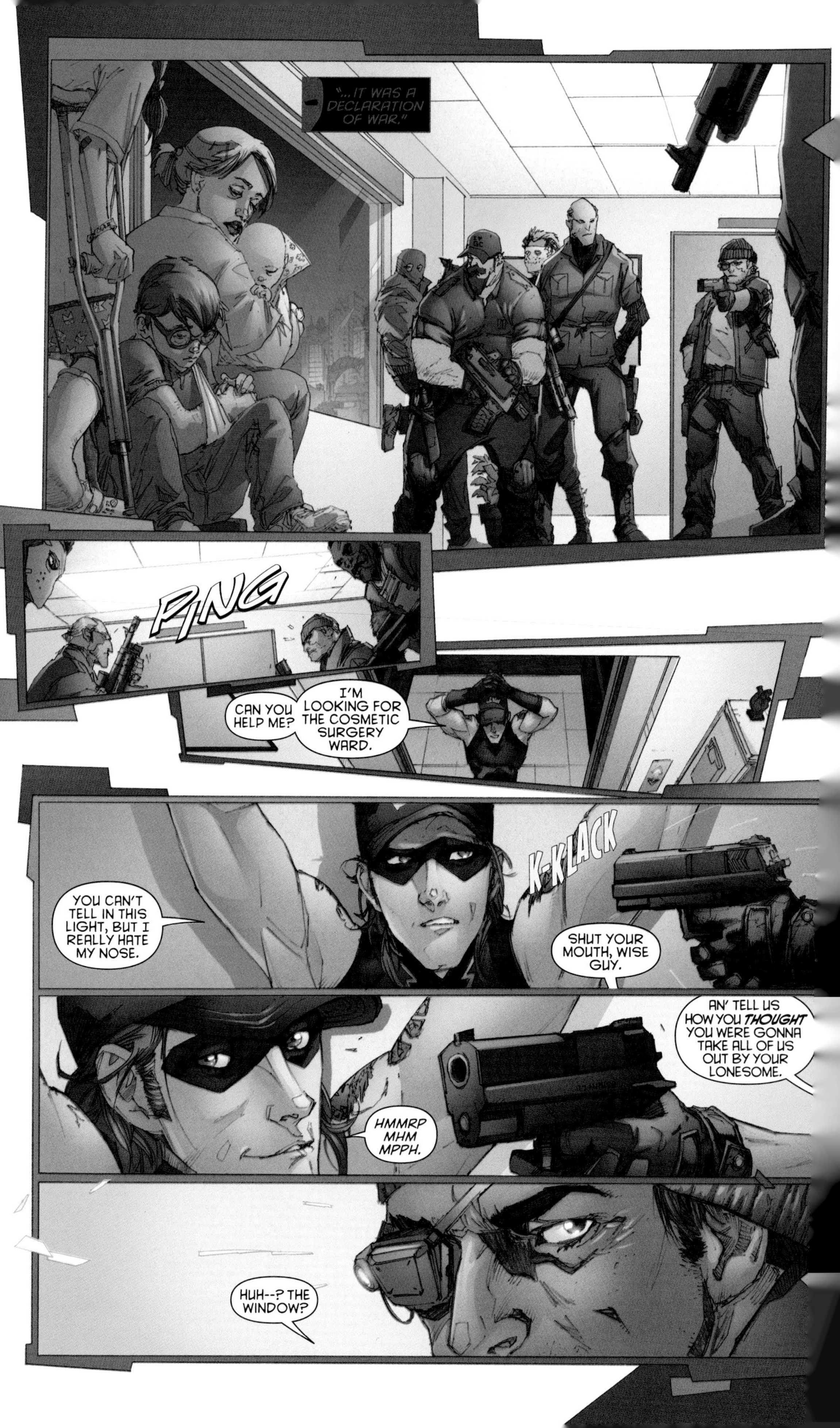
"...IT WAS A DECLARATION OF WAR."
PING
CAN YOU HELP ME?
I'M LOOKING FOR THE COSMETIC SURGERY WARD.
K-KLACK
YOU CAN'T TELL IN THIS LIGHT, BUT I REALLY HATE MY NOSE.
SHUT YOUR MOUTH, WISE GUY.
AN' TELL US HOW YOU *THOUGHT* YOU WERE GONNA TAKE ALL OF US OUT BY YOUR LONESOME.
HMMRP MHM MPPH.
HUH--? THE WINDOW?

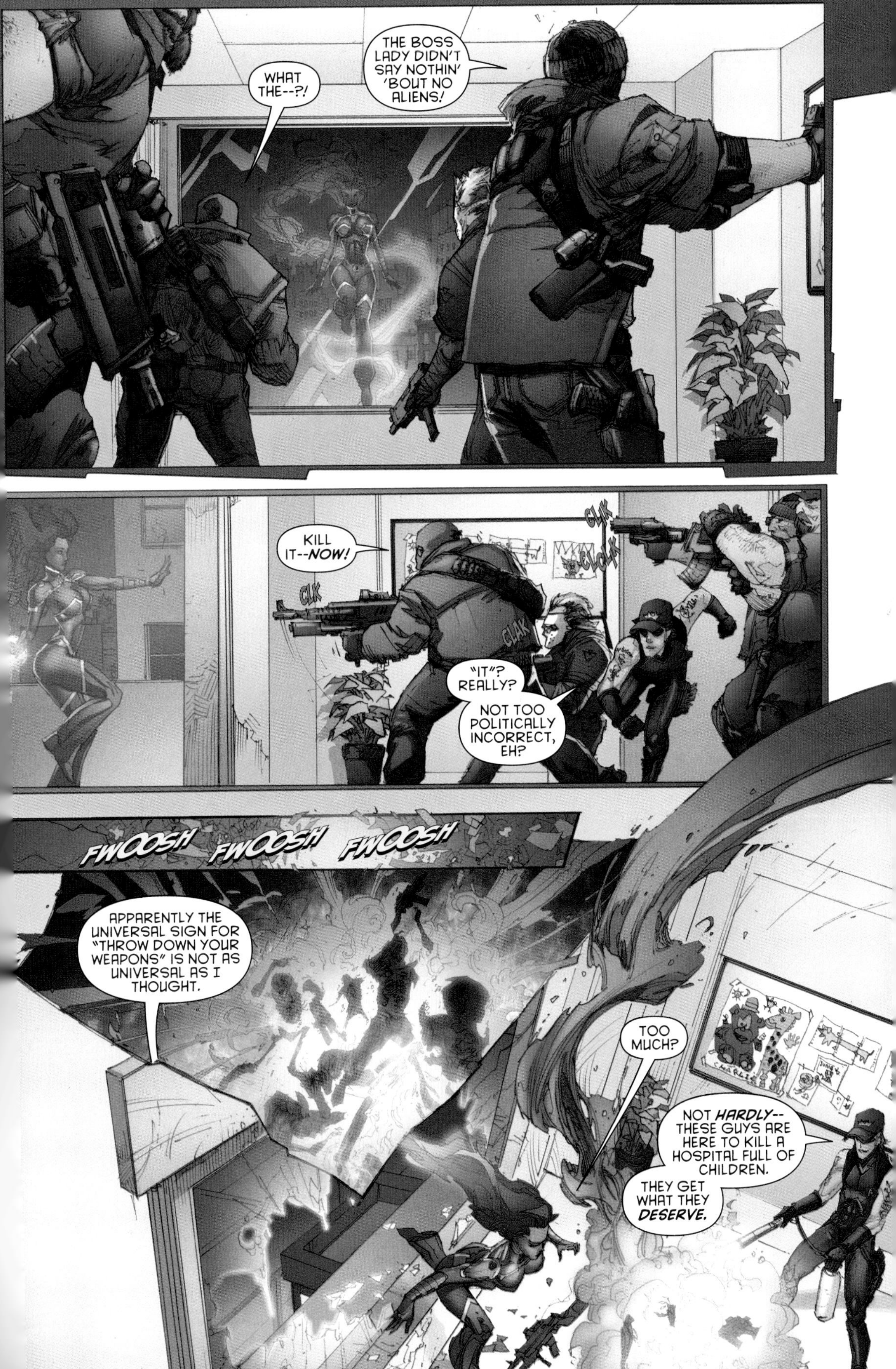

WHAT THE--?!
THE BOSS LADY DIDN'T SAY NOTHIN' 'BOUT NO ALIENS!
KILL IT--*NOW!*
CLK
CLAK
"IT"? REALLY?
NOT TOO POLITICALLY INCORRECT, EH?
FWOOSH FWOOSH FWOOSH
APPARENTLY THE UNIVERSAL SIGN FOR "THROW DOWN YOUR WEAPONS" IS NOT AS UNIVERSAL AS I THOUGHT.
TOO MUCH?
NOT *HARDLY*-- THESE GUYS ARE HERE TO KILL A HOSPITAL FULL OF CHILDREN.
THEY GET WHAT THEY *DESERVE.*

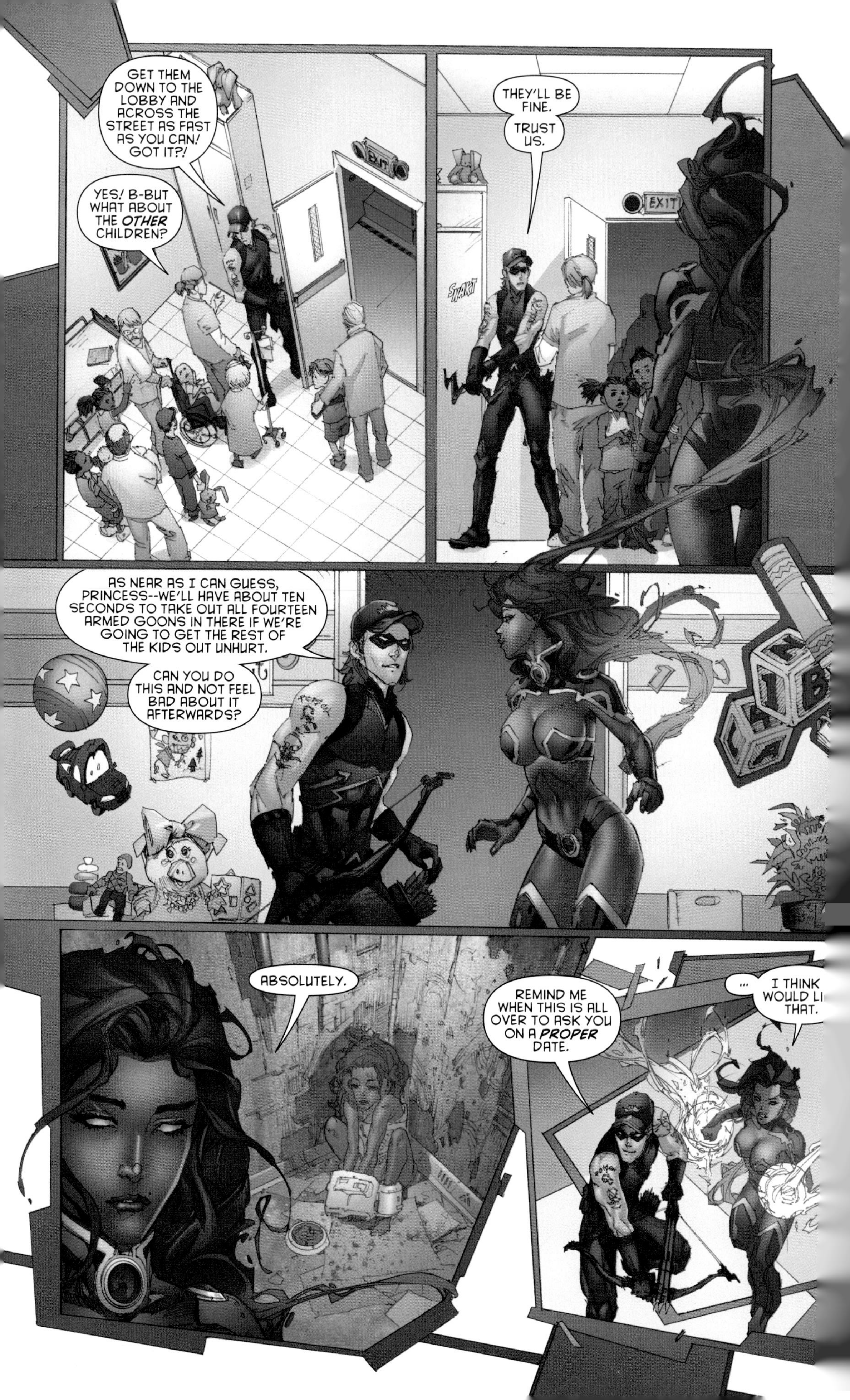
GET THEM DOWN TO THE LOBBY AND ACROSS THE STREET AS FAST AS YOU CAN! GOT IT?!
YES! B-BUT WHAT ABOUT THE OTHER CHILDREN?
EXIT
THEY'LL BE FINE.
TRUST US.
EXIT
SNAKT
AS NEAR AS I CAN GUESS, PRINCESS--WE'LL HAVE ABOUT TEN SECONDS TO TAKE OUT ALL FOURTEEN ARMED GOONS IN THERE IF WE'RE GOING TO GET THE REST OF THE KIDS OUT UNHURT.
CAN YOU DO THIS AND NOT FEEL BAD ABOUT IT AFTERWARDS?
ABSOLUTELY.
REMIND ME WHEN THIS IS ALL OVER TO ASK YOU ON A PROPER DATE.
... I THINK WOULD LI THAT.

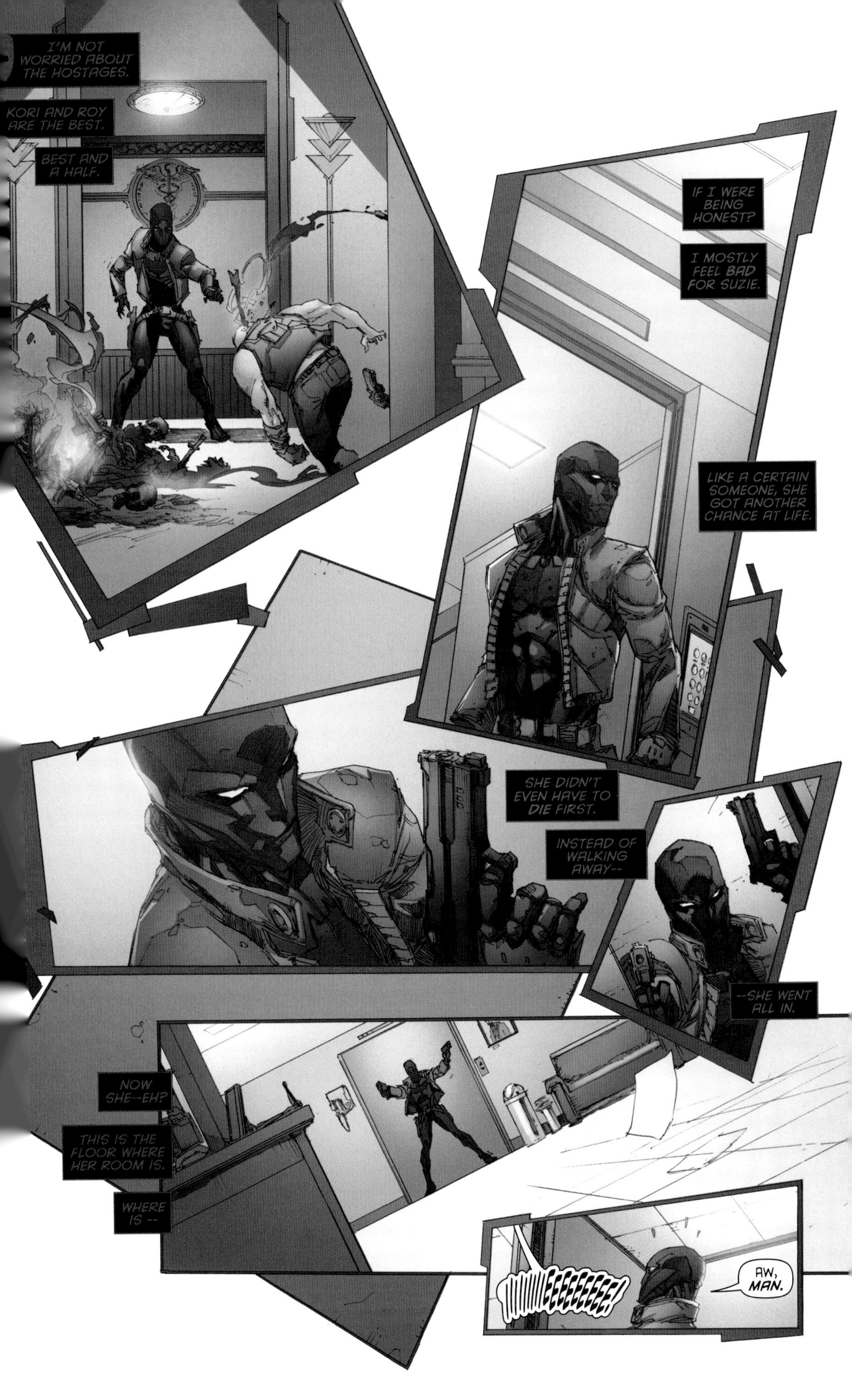
I'M NOT WORRIED ABOUT THE HOSTAGES.
KORI AND ROY ARE THE BEST.
BEST AND A HALF.
IF I WERE BEING HONEST?
I MOSTLY FEEL BAD FOR SUZIE.
LIKE A CERTAIN SOMEONE, SHE GOT ANOTHER CHANCE AT LIFE.
SHE DIDN'T EVEN HAVE TO DIE FIRST.
INSTEAD OF WALKING AWAY--
--SHE WENT ALL IN.
NOW SHE--EH?
THIS IS THE FLOOR WHERE HER ROOM IS.
WHERE IS --
IIIIIIIIEEEEEEEEE!
AW, MAN.

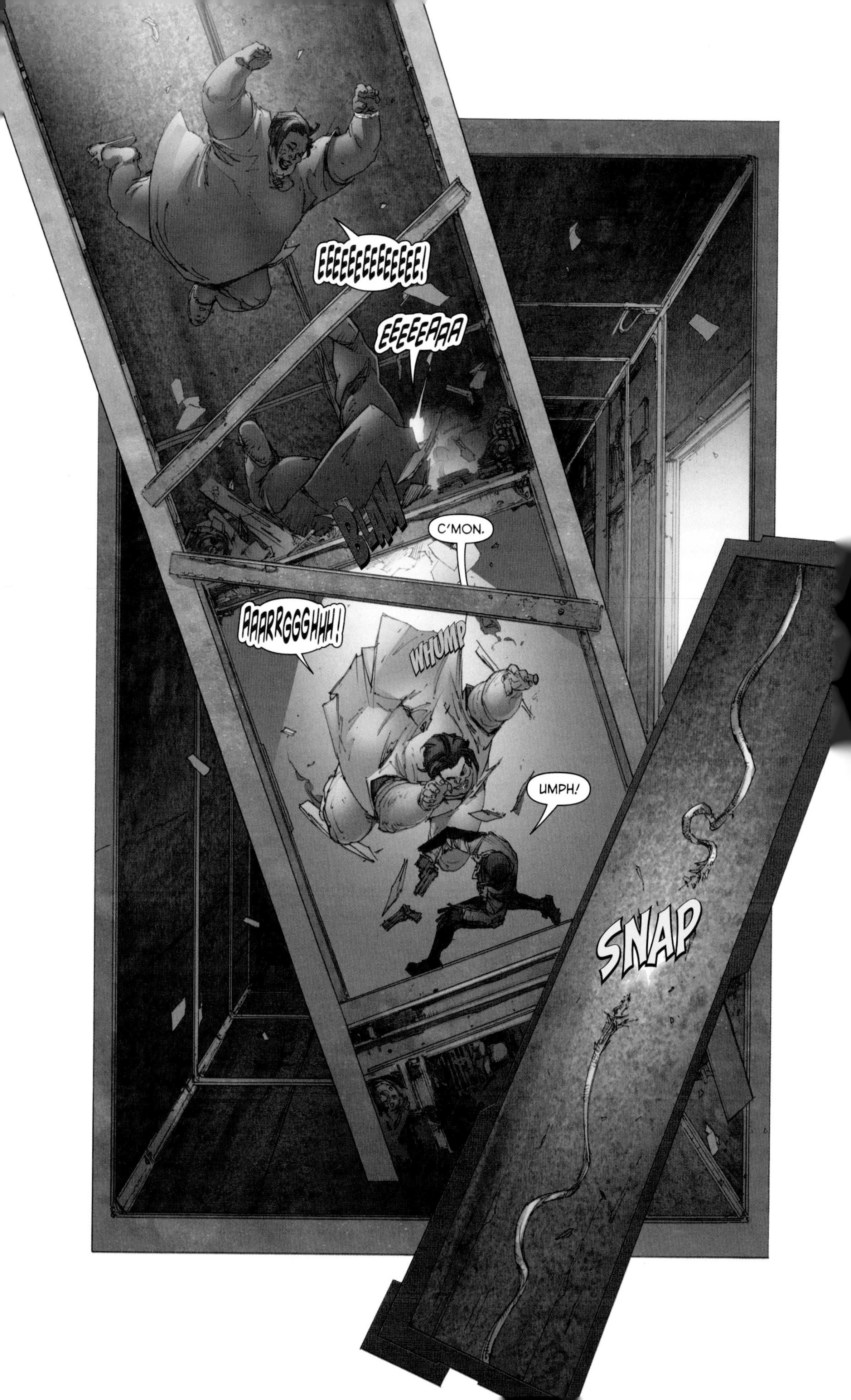
EEEEEEEEEEEEEE!
EEEEEAAA
BLAM
C'MON.
AAARRGGGHHH!
WHUMP
UMPH!
SNAP

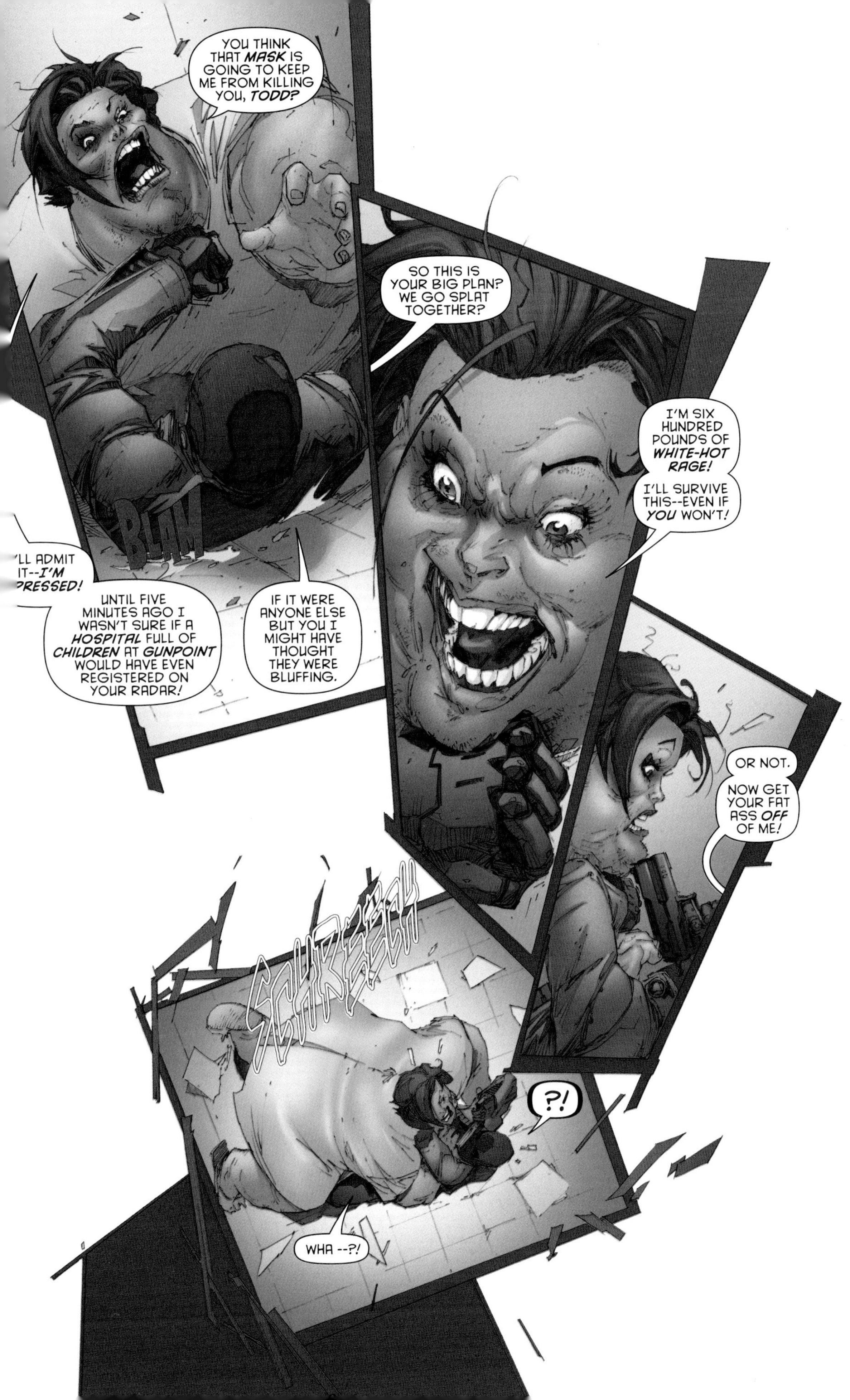
YOU THINK THAT MASK IS GOING TO KEEP ME FROM KILLING YOU, TODD?
BLAM
'LL ADMIT IT--I'M PRESSED!
UNTIL FIVE MINUTES AGO I WASN'T SURE IF A HOSPITAL FULL OF CHILDREN AT GUNPOINT WOULD HAVE EVEN REGISTERED ON YOUR RADAR!
IF IT WERE ANYONE ELSE BUT YOU I MIGHT HAVE THOUGHT THEY WERE BLUFFING.
SO THIS IS YOUR BIG PLAN? WE GO SPLAT TOGETHER?
I'M SIX HUNDRED POUNDS OF WHITE-HOT RAGE!
I'LL SURVIVE THIS--EVEN IF YOU WON'T!
OR NOT.
NOW GET YOUR FAT ASS OFF OF ME!
SCHREECH
?!
WHA --?!

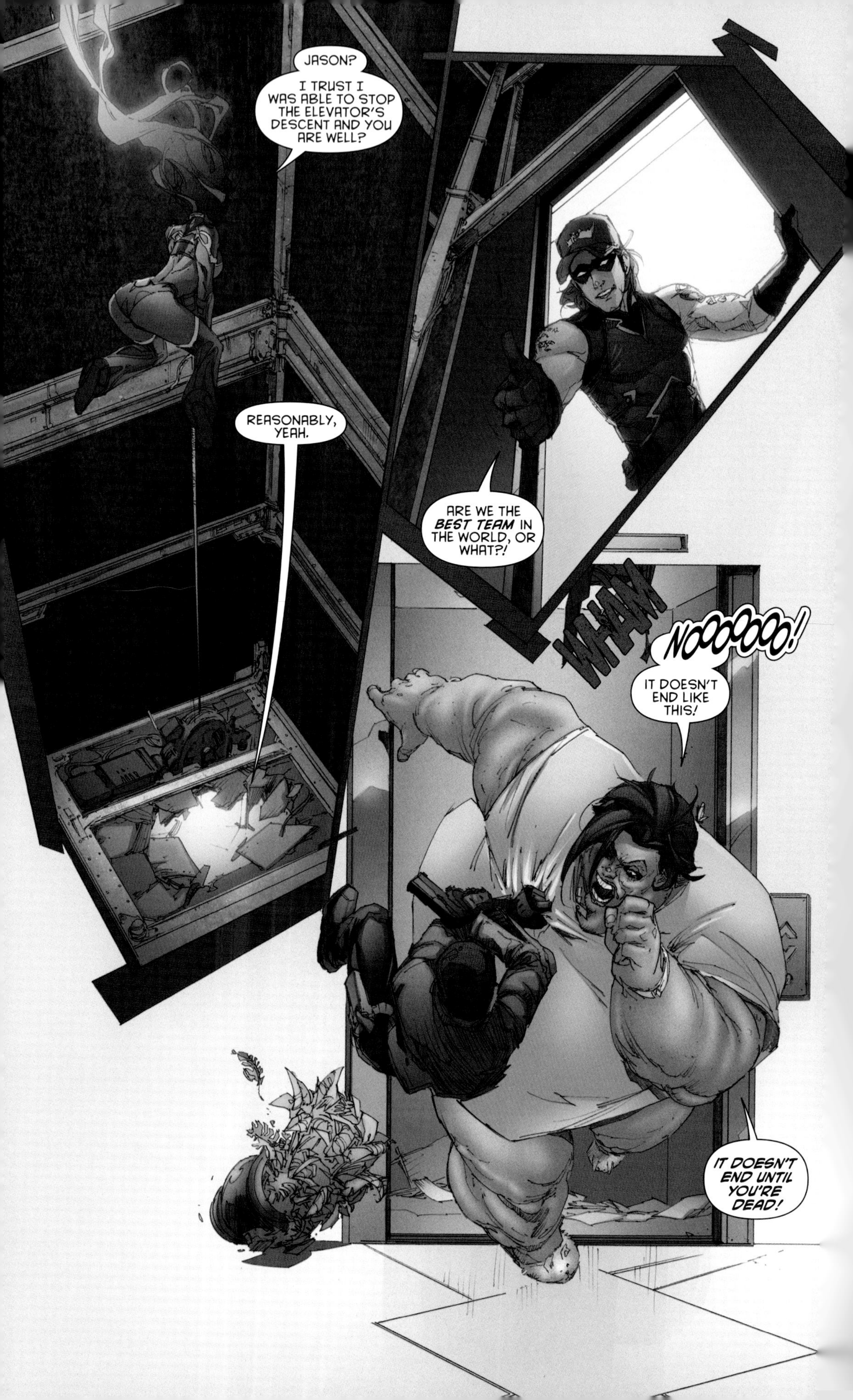
JASON? I TRUST I WAS ABLE TO STOP THE ELEVATOR'S DESCENT AND YOU ARE WELL?
REASONABLY, YEAH.
ARE WE THE BEST TEAM IN THE WORLD, OR WHAT?!
WHAM
NOOOOOOO!
IT DOESN'T END LIKE THIS!
IT DOESN'T END UNTIL YOU'RE DEAD!

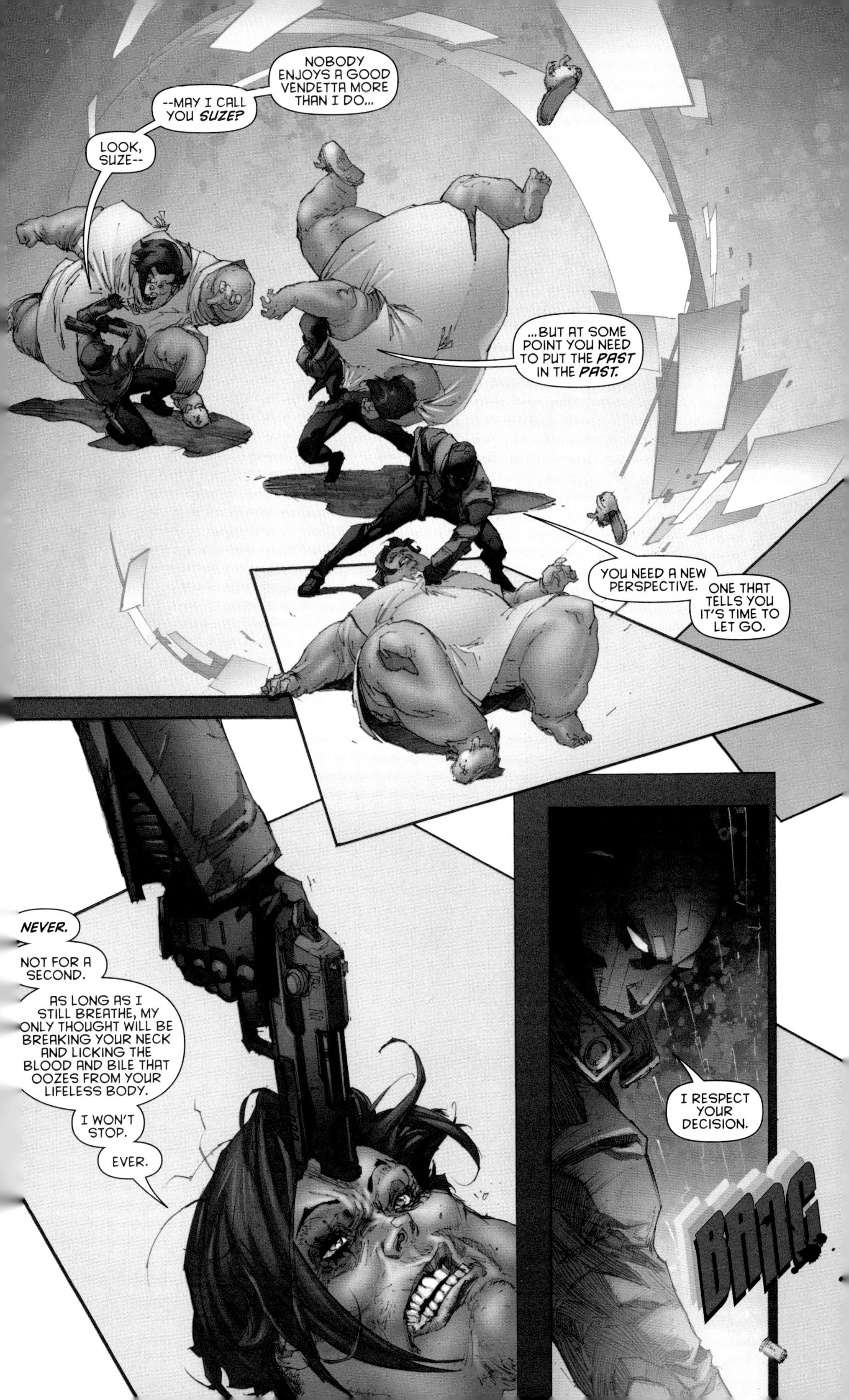

NOBODY ENJOYS A GOOD VENDETTA MORE THAN I DO...
--MAY I CALL YOU SUZE?
LOOK, SUZE--
...BUT AT SOME POINT YOU NEED TO PUT THE PAST IN THE PAST.
YOU NEED A NEW PERSPECTIVE.
ONE THAT TELLS YOU IT'S TIME TO LET GO.
NEVER.
NOT FOR A SECOND.
AS LONG AS I STILL BREATHE, MY ONLY THOUGHT WILL BE BREAKING YOUR NECK AND LICKING THE BLOOD AND BILE THAT OOZES FROM YOUR LIFELESS BODY.
I WON'T STOP.
EVER.
I RESPECT YOUR DECISION.
BANG.

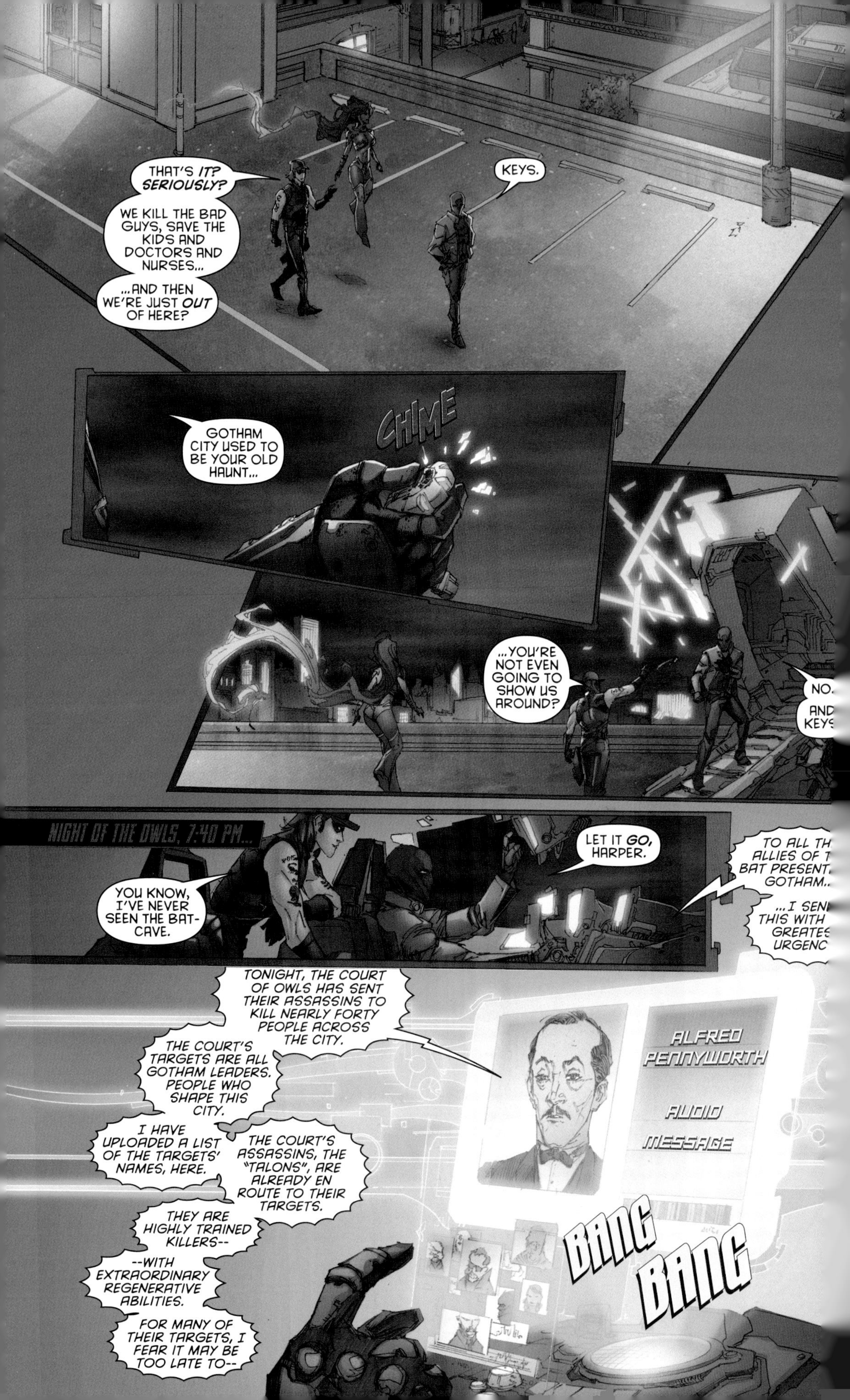

THAT'S IT? SERIOUSLY?
WE KILL THE BAD GUYS, SAVE THE KIDS AND DOCTORS AND NURSES...
...AND THEN WE'RE JUST OUT OF HERE?
KEYS.
CHIME
GOTHAM CITY USED TO BE YOUR OLD HAUNT...
...YOU'RE NOT EVEN GOING TO SHOW US AROUND?
NO.
AND KEYS
NIGHT OF THE OWLS, 7:40 PM...
YOU KNOW, I'VE NEVER SEEN THE BAT-CAVE.
LET IT GO, HARPER.
TO ALL TH ALLIES OF T BAT PRESENT GOTHAM...
...I SEN THIS WITH GREATES URGENC
TONIGHT, THE COURT OF OWLS HAS SENT THEIR ASSASSINS TO KILL NEARLY FORTY PEOPLE ACROSS THE CITY.
THE COURT'S TARGETS ARE ALL GOTHAM LEADERS. PEOPLE WHO SHAPE THIS CITY.
I HAVE UPLOADED A LIST OF THE TARGETS' NAMES, HERE.
THE COURT'S ASSASSINS, THE "TALONS", ARE ALREADY EN ROUTE TO THEIR TARGETS.
THEY ARE HIGHLY TRAINED KILLERS--
--WITH EXTRAORDINARY REGENERATIVE ABILITIES.
FOR MANY OF THEIR TARGETS, I FEAR IT MAY BE TOO LATE TO--
ALFRED PENNYWORTH
AUDIO MESSAGE
BANG
BANG

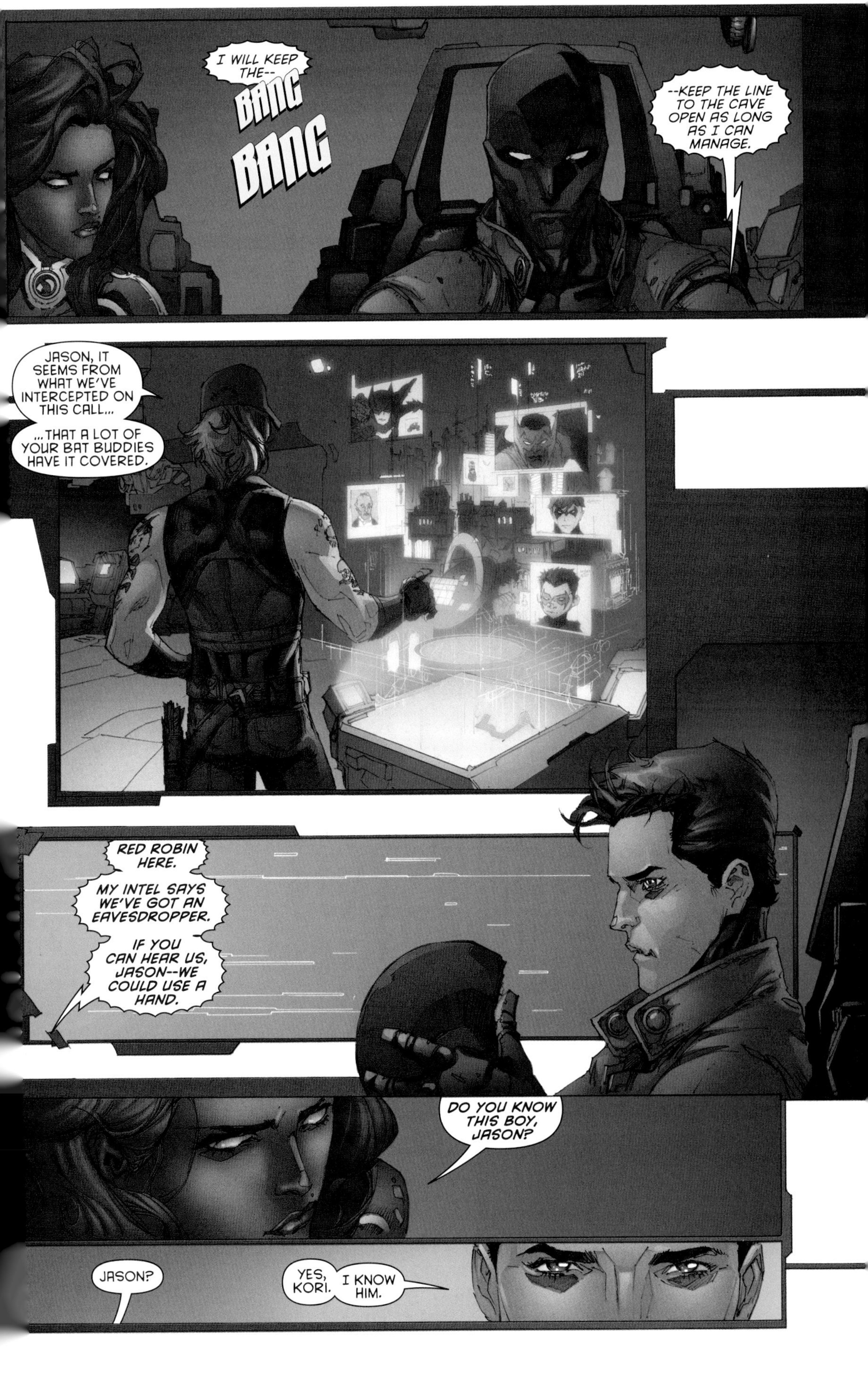
I WILL KEEP THE--
BANG
BANG
--KEEP THE LINE TO THE CAVE OPEN AS LONG AS I CAN MANAGE.
JASON, IT SEEMS FROM WHAT WE'VE INTERCEPTED ON THIS CALL...
...THAT A LOT OF YOUR BAT BUDDIES HAVE IT COVERED.
RED ROBIN HERE.
MY INTEL SAYS WE'VE GOT AN EAVESDROPPER.
IF YOU CAN HEAR US, JASON--WE COULD USE A HAND.
DO YOU KNOW THIS BOY, JASON?
JASON?
YES, KORI.
I KNOW HIM.

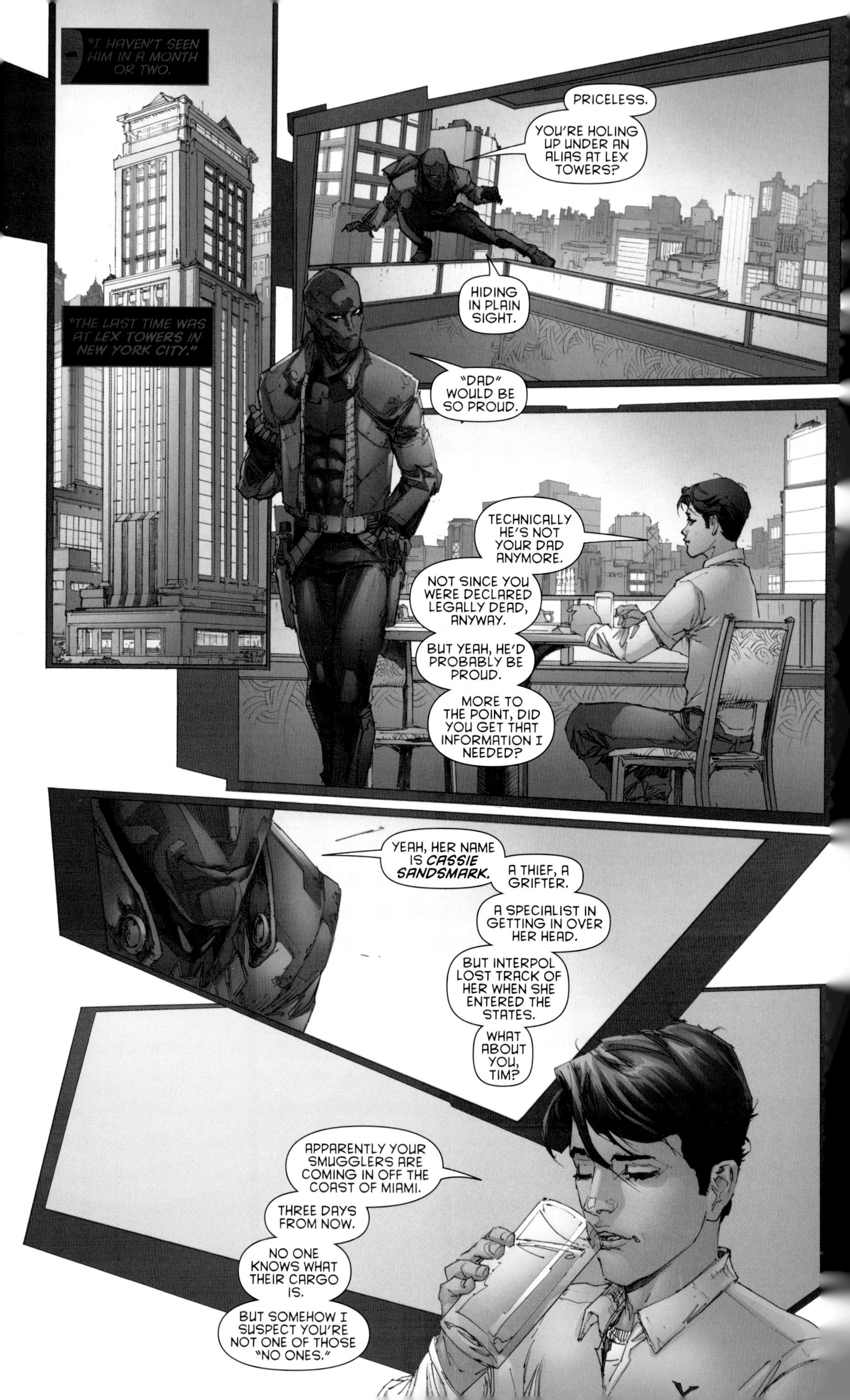
"I HAVEN'T SEEN HIM IN A MONTH OR TWO.
"THE LAST TIME WAS AT LEX TOWERS IN NEW YORK CITY."
PRICELESS.
YOU'RE HOLING UP UNDER AN ALIAS AT LEX TOWERS?
HIDING IN PLAIN SIGHT.
"DAD" WOULD BE SO PROUD.
TECHNICALLY HE'S NOT YOUR DAD ANYMORE.
NOT SINCE YOU WERE DECLARED LEGALLY DEAD, ANYWAY.
BUT YEAH, HE'D PROBABLY BE PROUD.
MORE TO THE POINT, DID YOU GET THAT INFORMATION I NEEDED?
YEAH, HER NAME IS CASSIE SANDSMARK.
A THIEF, A GRIFTER.
A SPECIALIST IN GETTING IN OVER HER HEAD.
BUT INTERPOL LOST TRACK OF HER WHEN SHE ENTERED THE STATES.
WHAT ABOUT YOU, TIM?
APPARENTLY YOUR SMUGGLERS ARE COMING IN OFF THE COAST OF MIAMI.
THREE DAYS FROM NOW.
NO ONE KNOWS WHAT THEIR CARGO IS.
BUT SOMEHOW I SUSPECT YOU'RE NOT ONE OF THOSE "NO ONES."

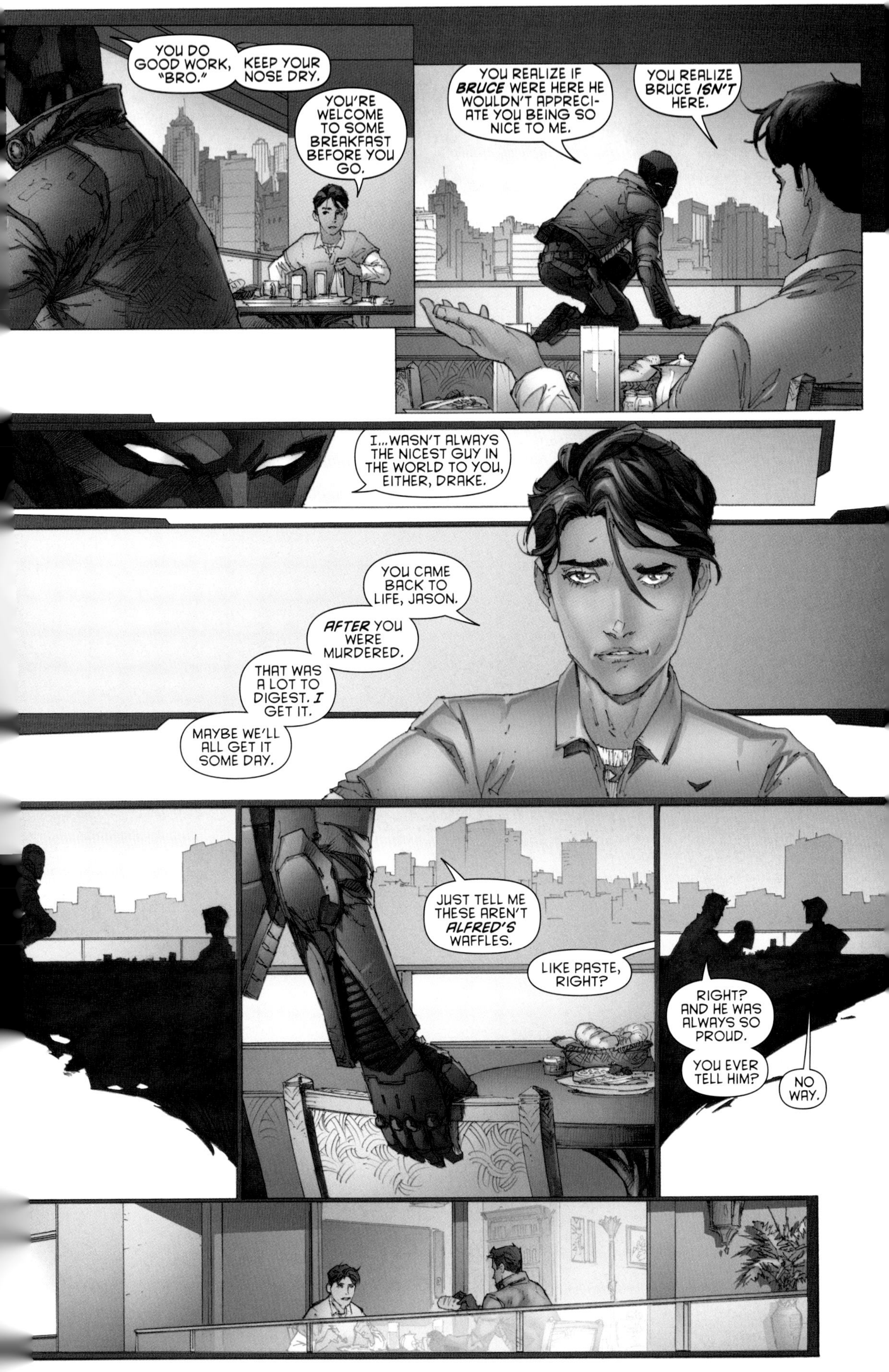
YOU DO GOOD WORK, "BRO."
KEEP YOUR NOSE DRY.
YOU'RE WELCOME TO SOME BREAKFAST BEFORE YOU GO.
YOU REALIZE IF BRUCE WERE HERE HE WOULDN'T APPRECIATE YOU BEING SO NICE TO ME.
YOU REALIZE BRUCE ISN'T HERE.
I...WASN'T ALWAYS THE NICEST GUY IN THE WORLD TO YOU, EITHER, DRAKE.
YOU CAME BACK TO LIFE, JASON.
AFTER YOU WERE MURDERED.
THAT WAS A LOT TO DIGEST. I GET IT.
MAYBE WE'LL ALL GET IT SOME DAY.
JUST TELL ME THESE AREN'T ALFRED'S WAFFLES.
LIKE PASTE, RIGHT?
RIGHT? AND HE WAS ALWAYS SO PROUD.
YOU EVER TELL HIM?
NO WAY.

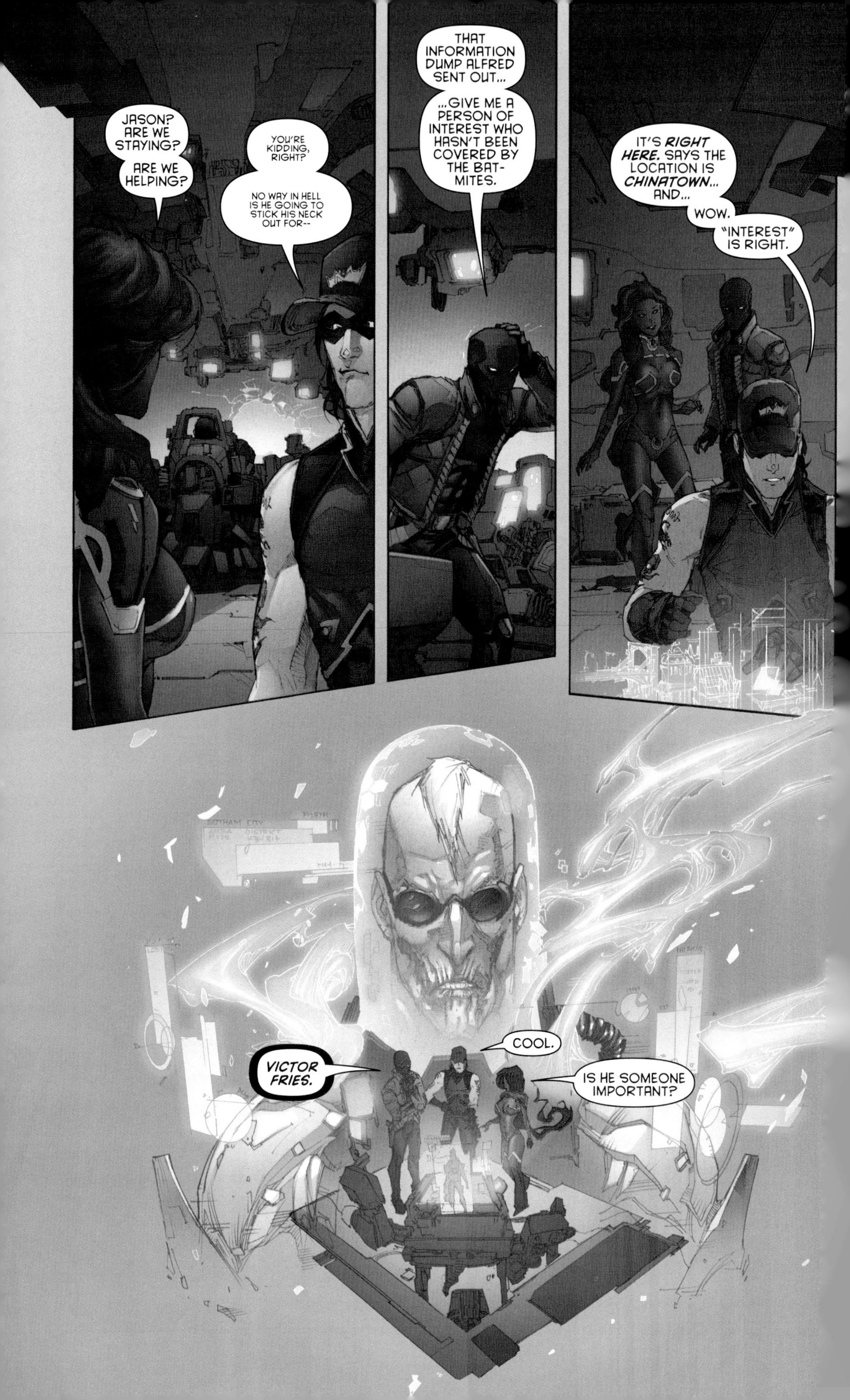
JASON? ARE WE STAYING?
ARE WE HELPING?
YOU'RE KIDDING, RIGHT?
NO WAY IN HELL IS HE GOING TO STICK HIS NECK OUT FOR--
THAT INFORMATION DUMP ALFRED SENT OUT...
...GIVE ME A PERSON OF INTEREST WHO HASN'T BEEN COVERED BY THE BAT-MITES.
IT'S RIGHT HERE. SAYS THE LOCATION IS CHINATOWN... AND...
WOW.
"INTEREST" IS RIGHT.
VICTOR FRIES.
COOL.
IS HE SOMEONE IMPORTANT?

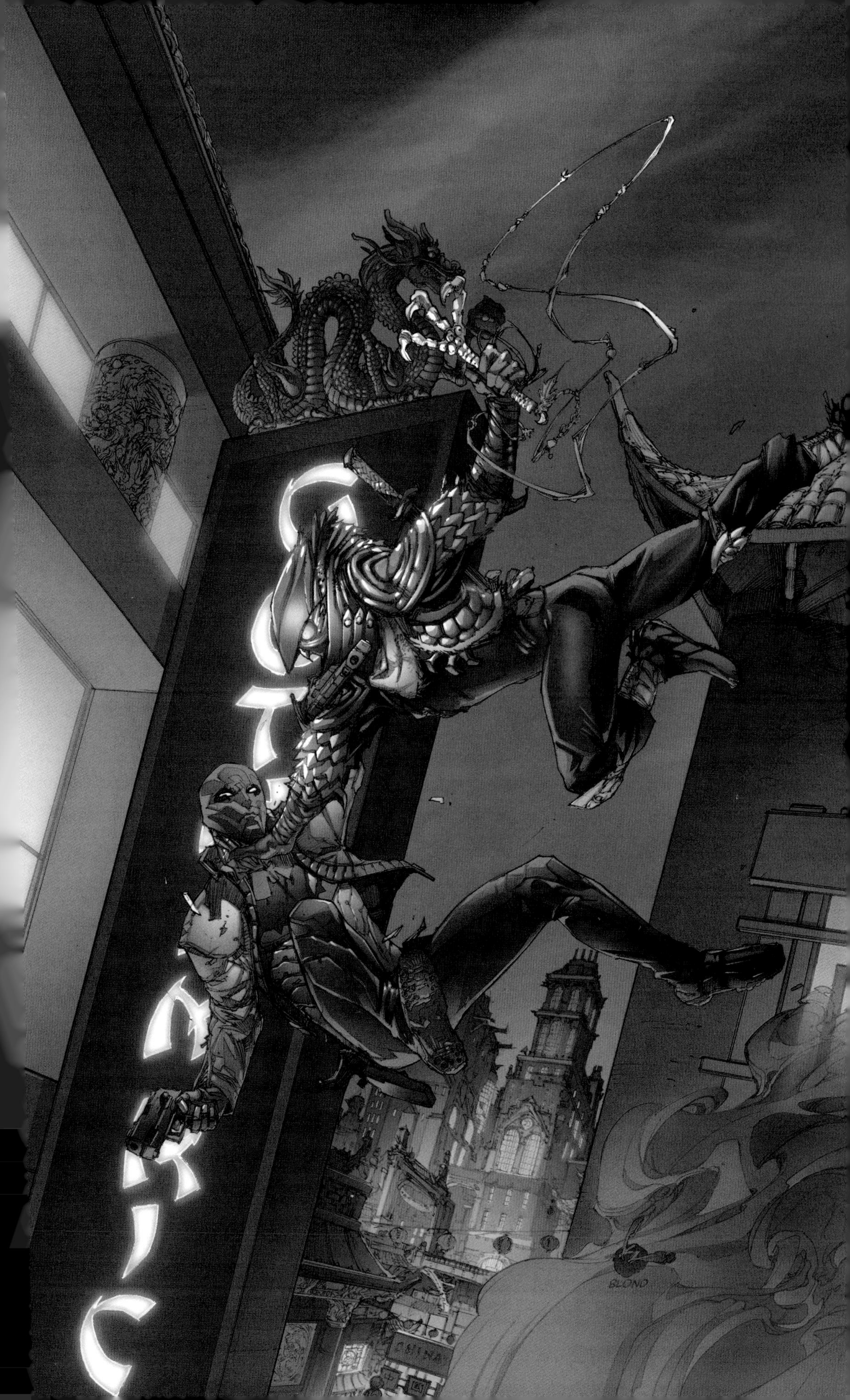
BLOND

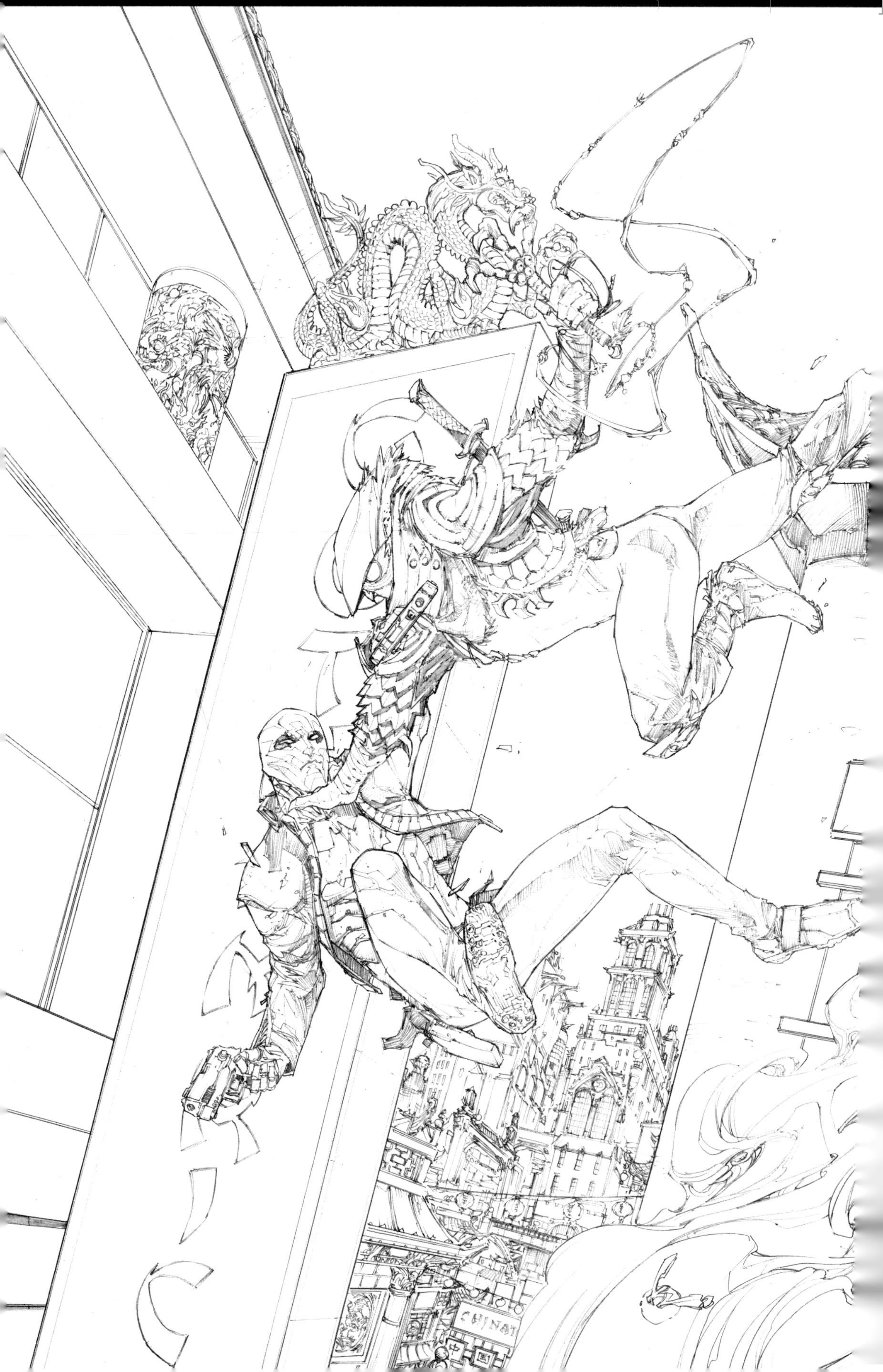

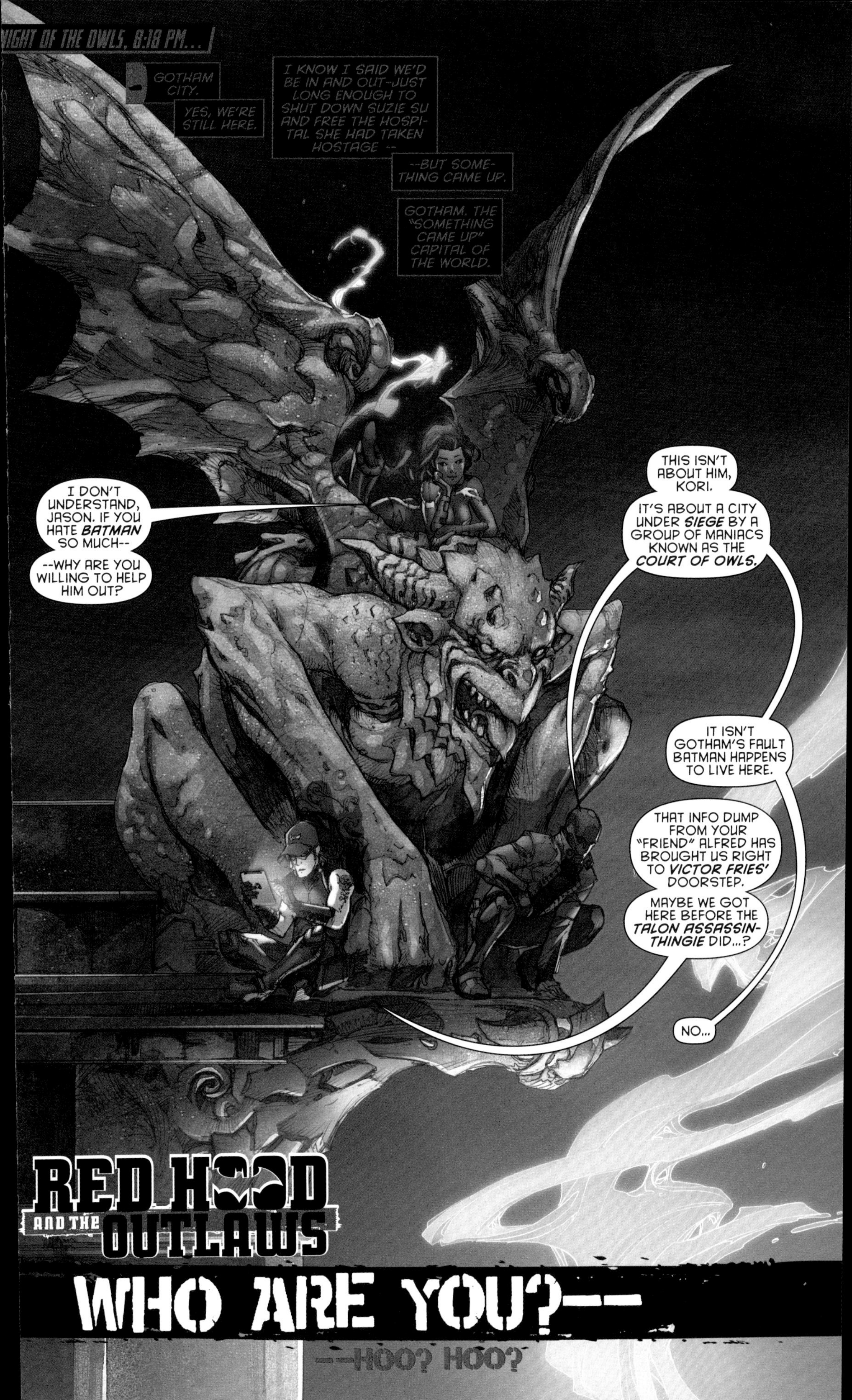
NIGHT OF THE OWLS, 8:18 PM...
GOTHAM CITY.
YES, WE'RE STILL HERE.
I KNOW I SAID WE'D BE IN AND OUT--JUST LONG ENOUGH TO SHUT DOWN SUZIE SU AND FREE THE HOSPITAL SHE HAD TAKEN HOSTAGE --
--BUT SOMETHING CAME UP.
GOTHAM. THE "SOMETHING CAME UP" CAPITAL OF THE WORLD.
I DON'T UNDERSTAND, JASON. IF YOU HATE BATMAN SO MUCH--
--WHY ARE YOU WILLING TO HELP HIM OUT?
THIS ISN'T ABOUT HIM, KORI.
IT'S ABOUT A CITY UNDER SIEGE BY A GROUP OF MANIACS KNOWN AS THE COURT OF OWLS.
IT ISN'T GOTHAM'S FAULT BATMAN HAPPENS TO LIVE HERE.
THAT INFO DUMP FROM YOUR "FRIEND" ALFRED HAS BROUGHT US RIGHT TO VICTOR FRIES' DOORSTEP.
MAYBE WE GOT HERE BEFORE THE TALON ASSASSIN-THINGIE DID...?
NO...
RED HOOD AND THE OUTLAWS
WHO ARE YOU?--
--HOO? HOO?

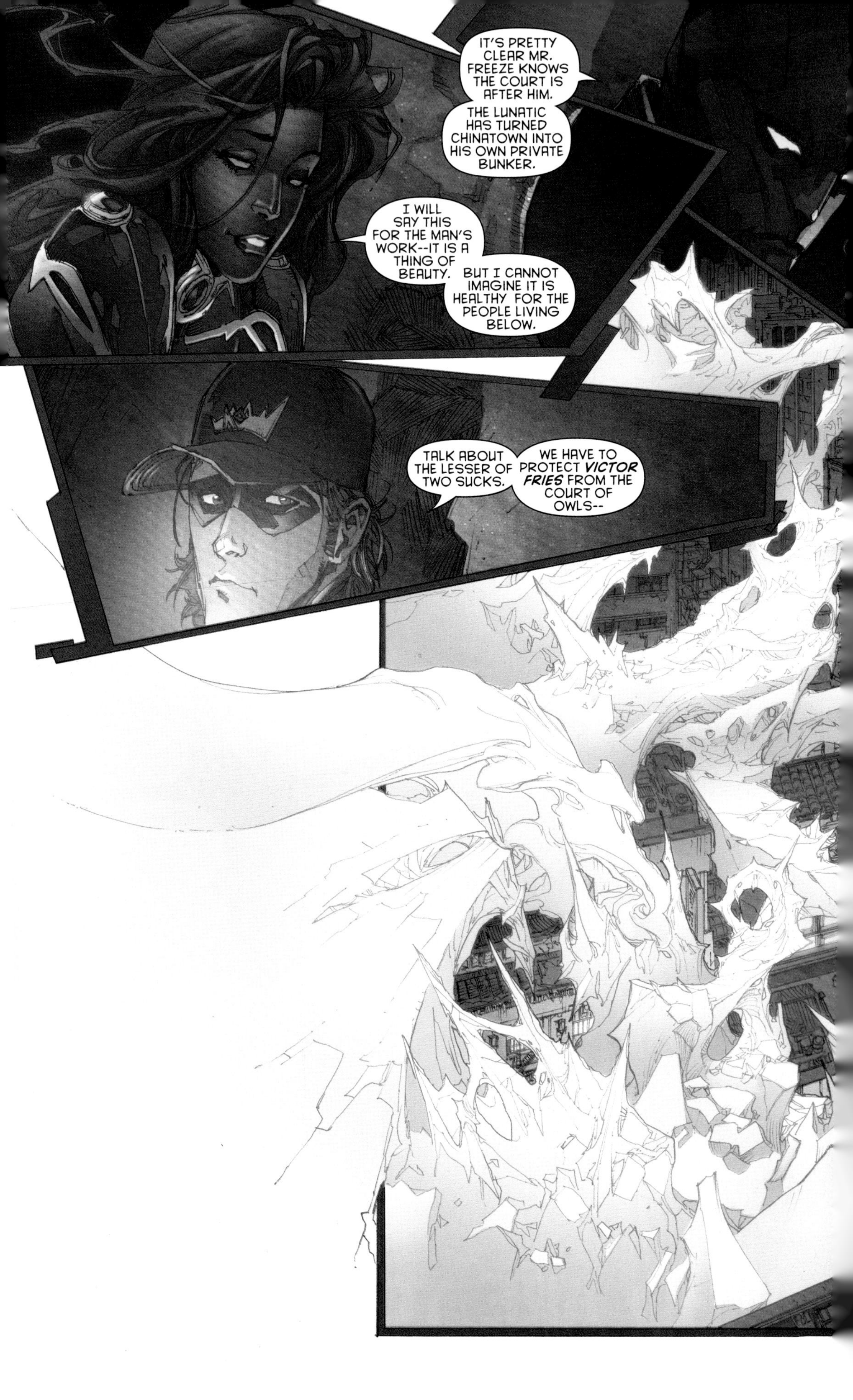
IT'S PRETTY CLEAR MR. FREEZE KNOWS THE COURT IS AFTER HIM.
THE LUNATIC HAS TURNED CHINATOWN INTO HIS OWN PRIVATE BUNKER.
I WILL SAY THIS FOR THE MAN'S WORK--IT IS A THING OF BEAUTY.
BUT I CANNOT IMAGINE IT IS HEALTHY FOR THE PEOPLE LIVING BELOW.
TALK ABOUT THE LESSER OF TWO SUCKS.
WE HAVE TO PROTECT VICTOR FRIES FROM THE COURT OF OWLS--

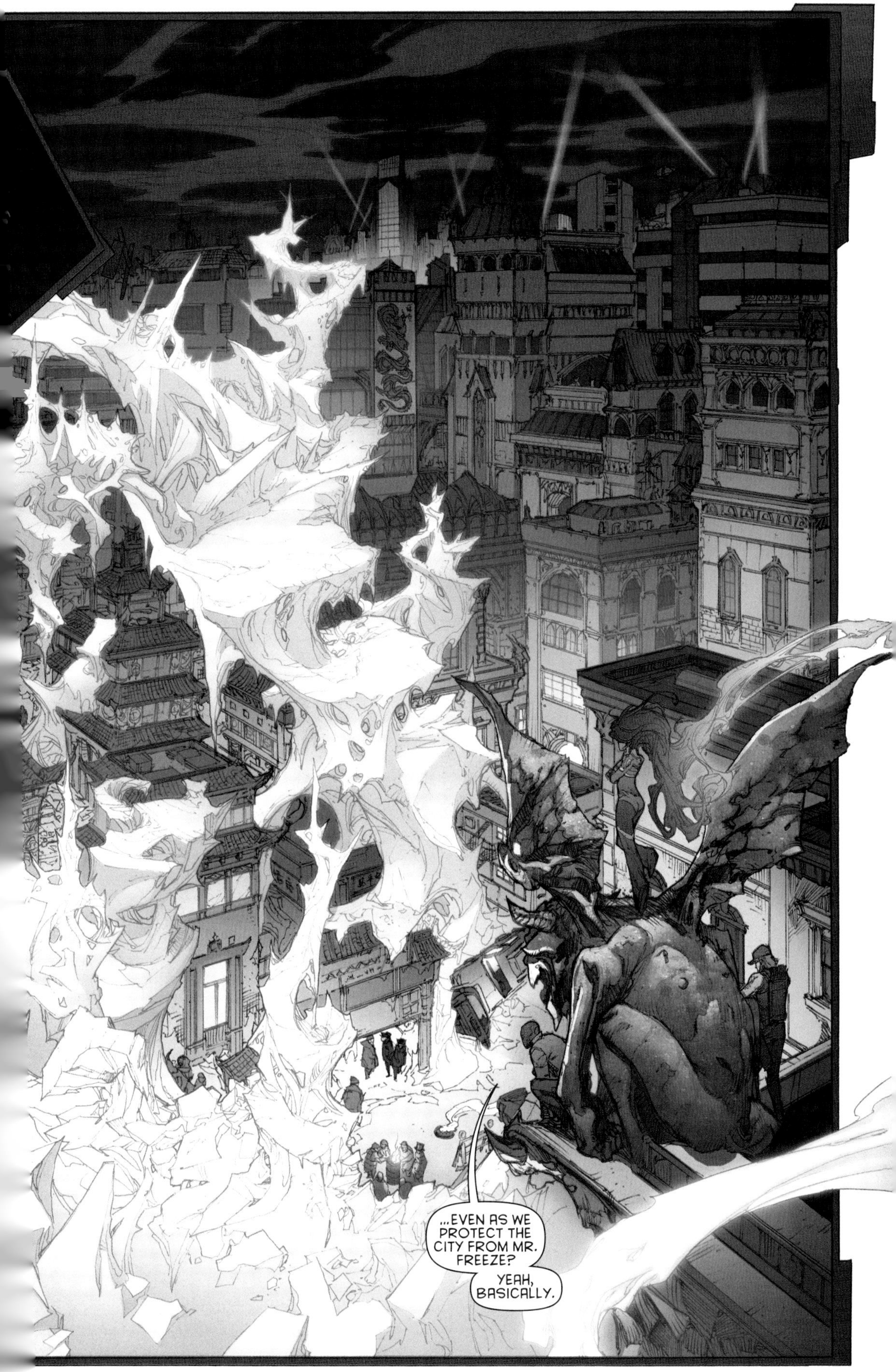
...EVEN AS WE PROTECT THE CITY FROM MR. FREEZE?
YEAH, BASICALLY.

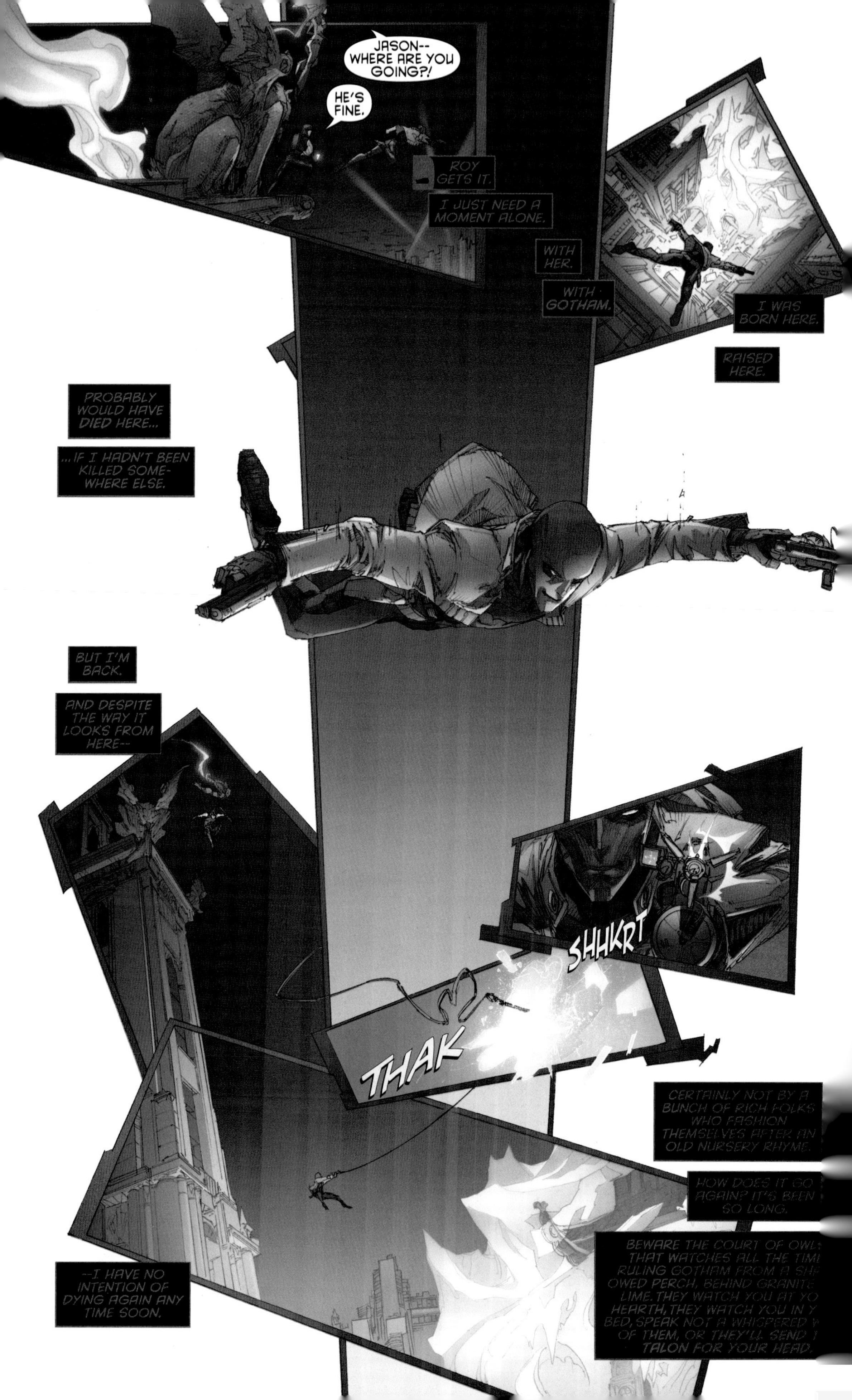
JASON-- WHERE ARE YOU GOING?!
HE'S FINE.
ROY GETS IT.
I JUST NEED A MOMENT ALONE.
WITH HER.
WITH GOTHAM.
I WAS BORN HERE.
RAISED HERE.
PROBABLY WOULD HAVE DIED HERE...
...IF I HADN'T BEEN KILLED SOME-WHERE ELSE.
BUT I'M BACK.
AND DESPITE THE WAY IT LOOKS FROM HERE--
SHHKRT
THAK
--I HAVE NO INTENTION OF DYING AGAIN ANY TIME SOON.
CERTAINLY NOT BY A BUNCH OF RICH FOLKS WHO FASHION THEMSELVES AFTER AN OLD NURSERY RHYME.
HOW DOES IT GO AGAIN? IT'S BEEN SO LONG.
BEWARE THE COURT OF OWL
THAT WATCHES ALL THE TIM
RULING GOTHAM FROM A SH
OWED PERCH, BEHIND GRANITE
LIME. THEY WATCH YOU AT YO
HEARTH, THEY WATCH YOU IN Y
BED, SPEAK NOT A WHISPERED
OF THEM, OR THEY'LL SEND
TALON FOR YOUR HEAD.

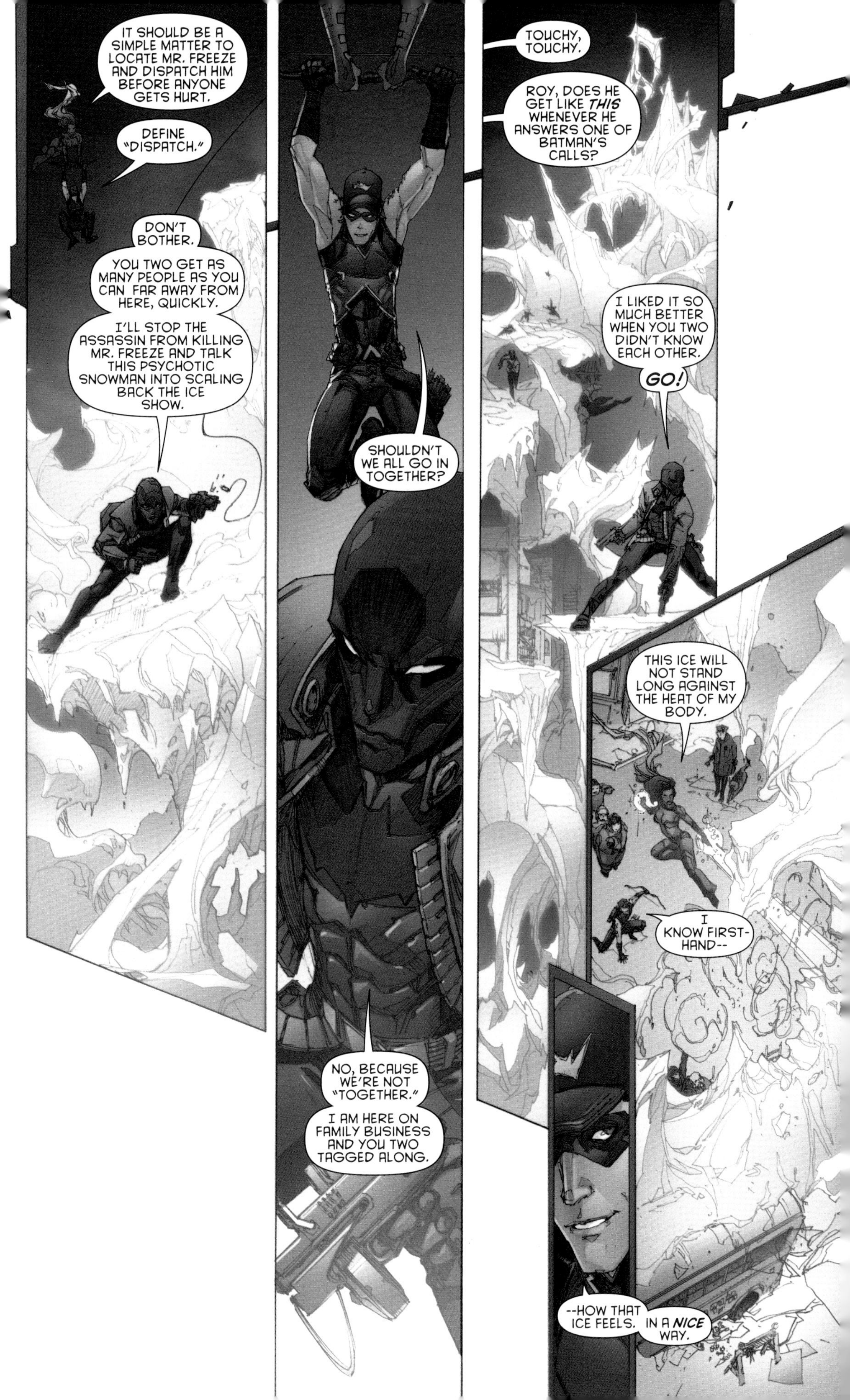
IT SHOULD BE A SIMPLE MATTER TO LOCATE MR. FREEZE AND DISPATCH HIM BEFORE ANYONE GETS HURT.
DEFINE "DISPATCH."
DON'T BOTHER.
YOU TWO GET AS MANY PEOPLE AS YOU CAN FAR AWAY FROM HERE, QUICKLY.
I'LL STOP THE ASSASSIN FROM KILLING MR. FREEZE AND TALK THIS PSYCHOTIC SNOWMAN INTO SCALING BACK THE ICE SHOW.
SHOULDN'T WE ALL GO IN TOGETHER?
NO, BECAUSE WE'RE NOT "TOGETHER."
I AM HERE ON FAMILY BUSINESS AND YOU TWO TAGGED ALONG.
TOUCHY, TOUCHY.
ROY, DOES HE GET LIKE *THIS* WHENEVER HE ANSWERS ONE OF BATMAN'S CALLS?
I LIKED IT SO MUCH BETTER WHEN YOU TWO DIDN'T KNOW EACH OTHER.
GO!
THIS ICE WILL NOT STAND LONG AGAINST THE HEAT OF MY BODY.
I KNOW FIRST-HAND--
--HOW THAT ICE FEELS.
IN A *NICE* WAY.

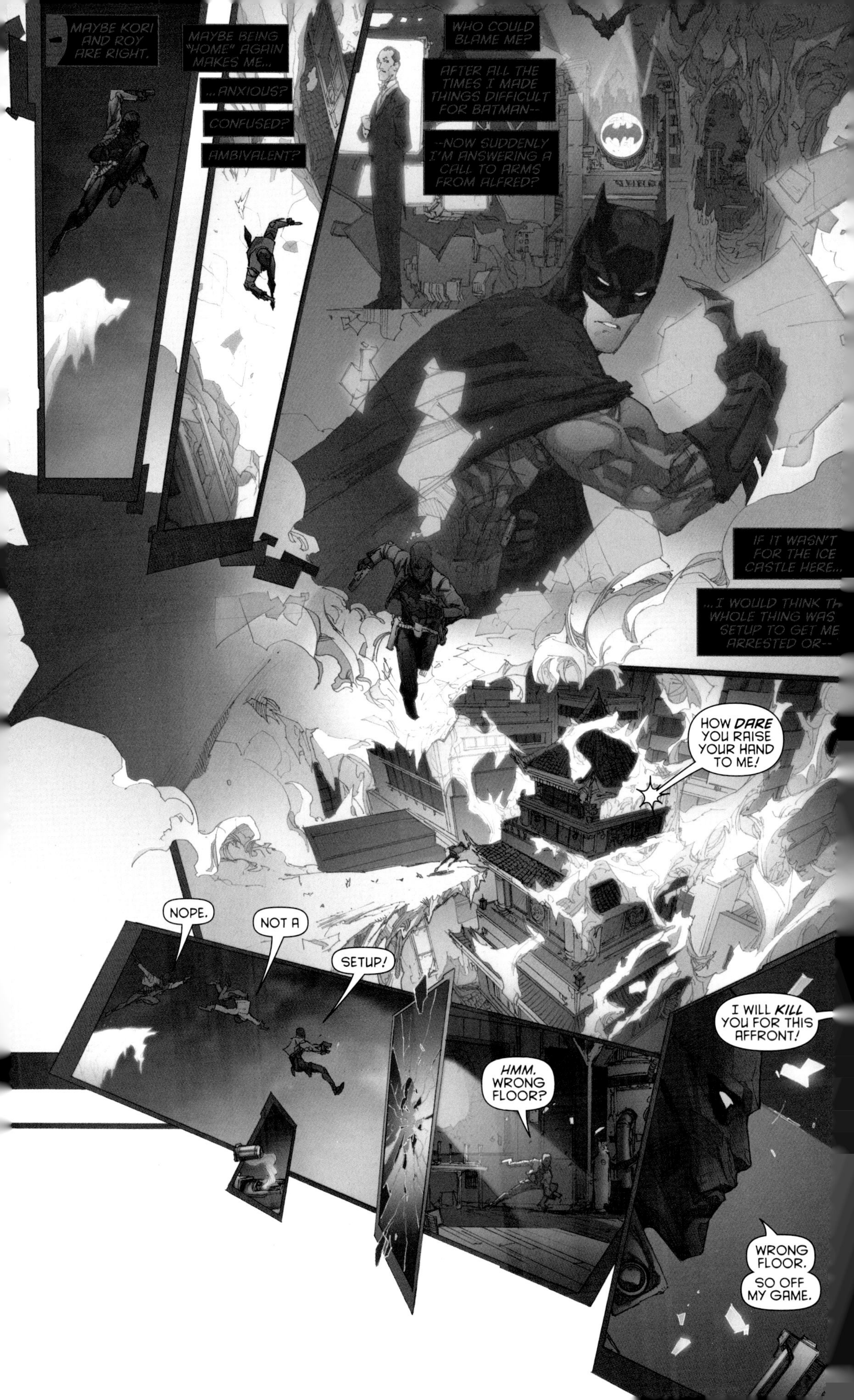

MAYBE KORI AND ROY ARE RIGHT.
MAYBE BEING "HOME" AGAIN MAKES ME...
...ANXIOUS?
CONFUSED?
AMBIVALENT?
WHO COULD BLAME ME?
AFTER ALL THE TIMES I MADE THINGS DIFFICULT FOR BATMAN--
--NOW SUDDENLY I'M ANSWERING A CALL TO ARMS FROM ALFRED?
IF IT WASN'T FOR THE ICE CASTLE HERE...
...I WOULD THINK TH WHOLE THING WAS SETUP TO GET ME ARRESTED OR--
HOW DARE YOU RAISE YOUR HAND TO ME!
NOPE.
NOT A
SETUP!
I WILL KILL YOU FOR THIS AFFRONT!
HMM. WRONG FLOOR?
WRONG FLOOR.
SO OFF MY GAME.

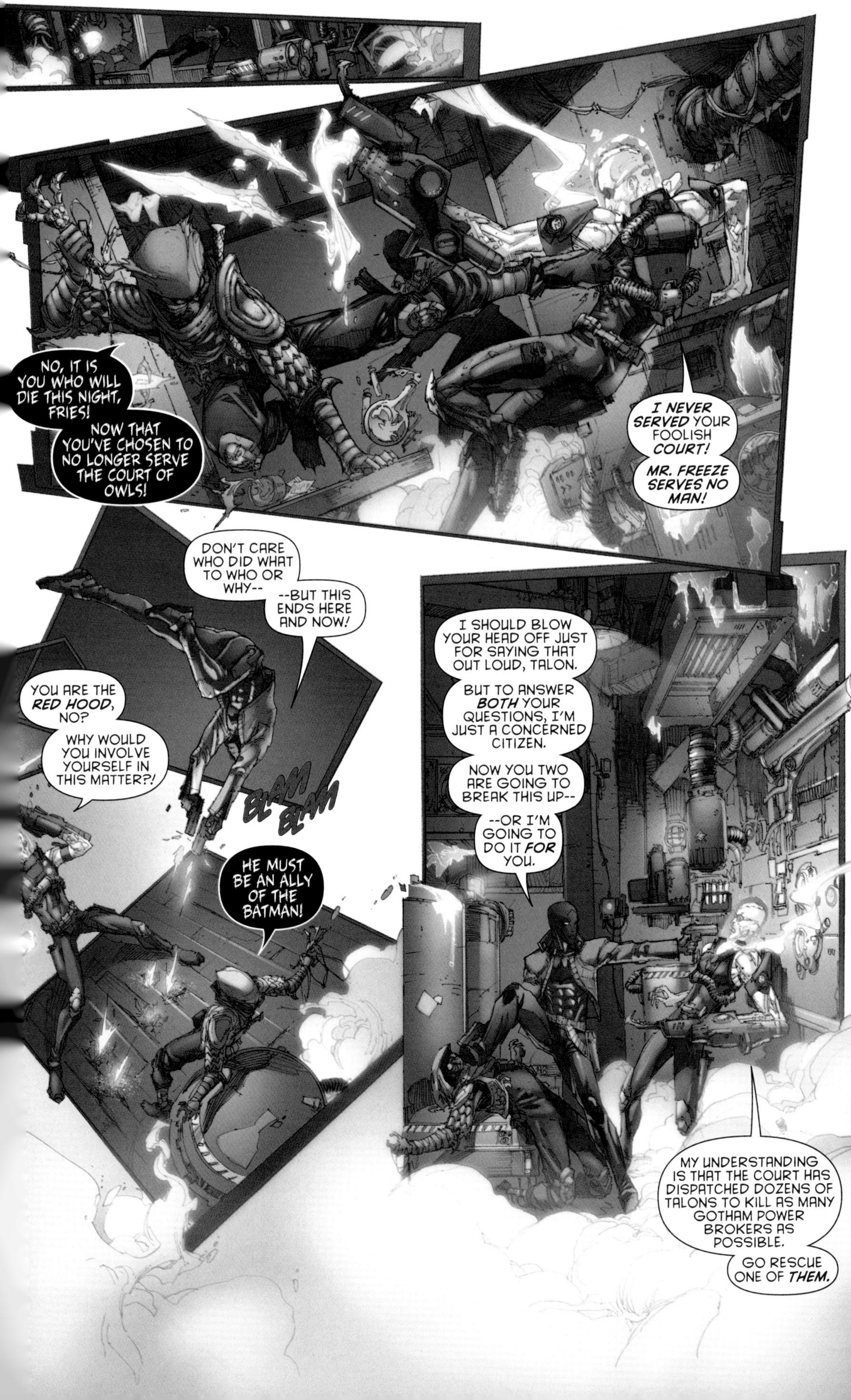
NO, IT IS YOU WHO WILL DIE THIS NIGHT, FRIES!
NOW THAT YOU'VE CHOSEN TO NO LONGER SERVE THE COURT OF OWLS!
I NEVER SERVED YOUR FOOLISH COURT!
MR. FREEZE SERVES NO MAN!
DON'T CARE WHO DID WHAT TO WHO OR WHY--
--BUT THIS ENDS HERE AND NOW!
YOU ARE THE RED HOOD, NO?
WHY WOULD YOU INVOLVE YOURSELF IN THIS MATTER?!
BLAM BLAM
HE MUST BE AN ALLY OF THE BATMAN!
I SHOULD BLOW YOUR HEAD OFF JUST FOR SAYING THAT OUT LOUD, TALON.
BUT TO ANSWER BOTH YOUR QUESTIONS, I'M JUST A CONCERNED CITIZEN.
NOW YOU TWO ARE GOING TO BREAK THIS UP--
--OR I'M GOING TO DO IT FOR YOU.
MY UNDERSTANDING IS THAT THE COURT HAS DISPATCHED DOZENS OF TALONS TO KILL AS MANY GOTHAM POWER BROKERS AS POSSIBLE.
GO RESCUE ONE OF THEM.

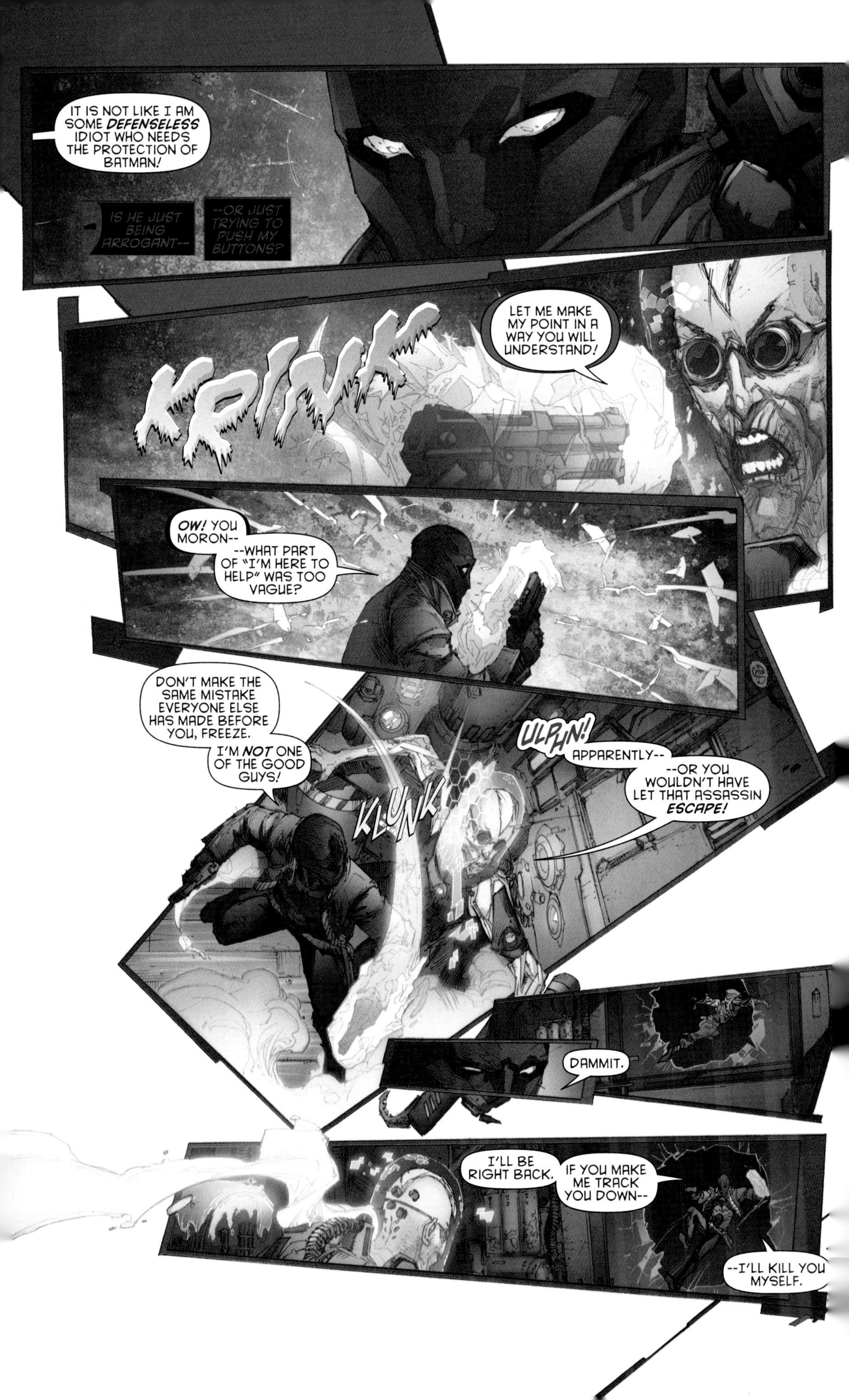
IT IS NOT LIKE I AM SOME DEFENSELESS IDIOT WHO NEEDS THE PROTECTION OF BATMAN!
IS HE JUST BEING ARROGANT--
--OR JUST TRYING TO PUSH MY BUTTONS?
KRINK
LET ME MAKE MY POINT IN A WAY YOU WILL UNDERSTAND!
OW! YOU MORON--
--WHAT PART OF "I'M HERE TO HELP" WAS TOO VAGUE?
DON'T MAKE THE SAME MISTAKE EVERYONE ELSE HAS MADE BEFORE YOU, FREEZE.
I'M NOT ONE OF THE GOOD GUYS!
KLUNK
ULPHN!
APPARENTLY--
--OR YOU WOULDN'T HAVE LET THAT ASSASSIN ESCAPE!
DAMMIT.
I'LL BE RIGHT BACK.
IF YOU MAKE ME TRACK YOU DOWN--
--I'LL KILL YOU MYSELF.

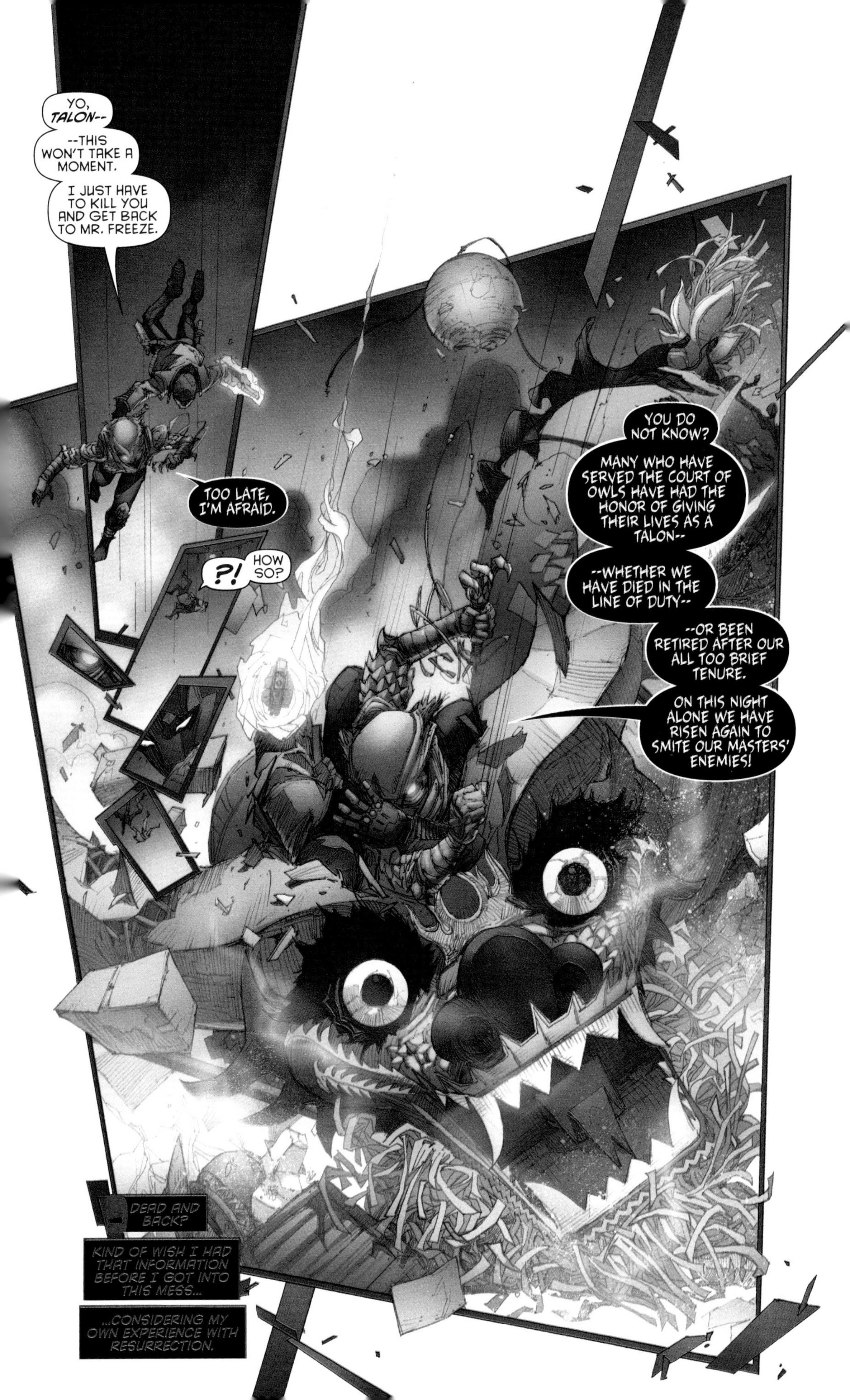
YO, TALON--
--THIS WON'T TAKE A MOMENT.
I JUST HAVE TO KILL YOU AND GET BACK TO MR. FREEZE.
TOO LATE, I'M AFRAID.
?!
HOW SO?
YOU DO NOT KNOW?
MANY WHO HAVE SERVED THE COURT OF OWLS HAVE HAD THE HONOR OF GIVING THEIR LIVES AS A TALON--
--WHETHER WE HAVE DIED IN THE LINE OF DUTY--
--OR BEEN RETIRED AFTER OUR ALL TOO BRIEF TENURE.
ON THIS NIGHT ALONE WE HAVE RISEN AGAIN TO SMITE OUR MASTERS' ENEMIES!
DEAD AND BACK?
KIND OF WISH I HAD THAT INFORMATION BEFORE I GOT INTO THIS MESS...
...CONSIDERING MY OWN EXPERIENCE WITH RESURRECTION.

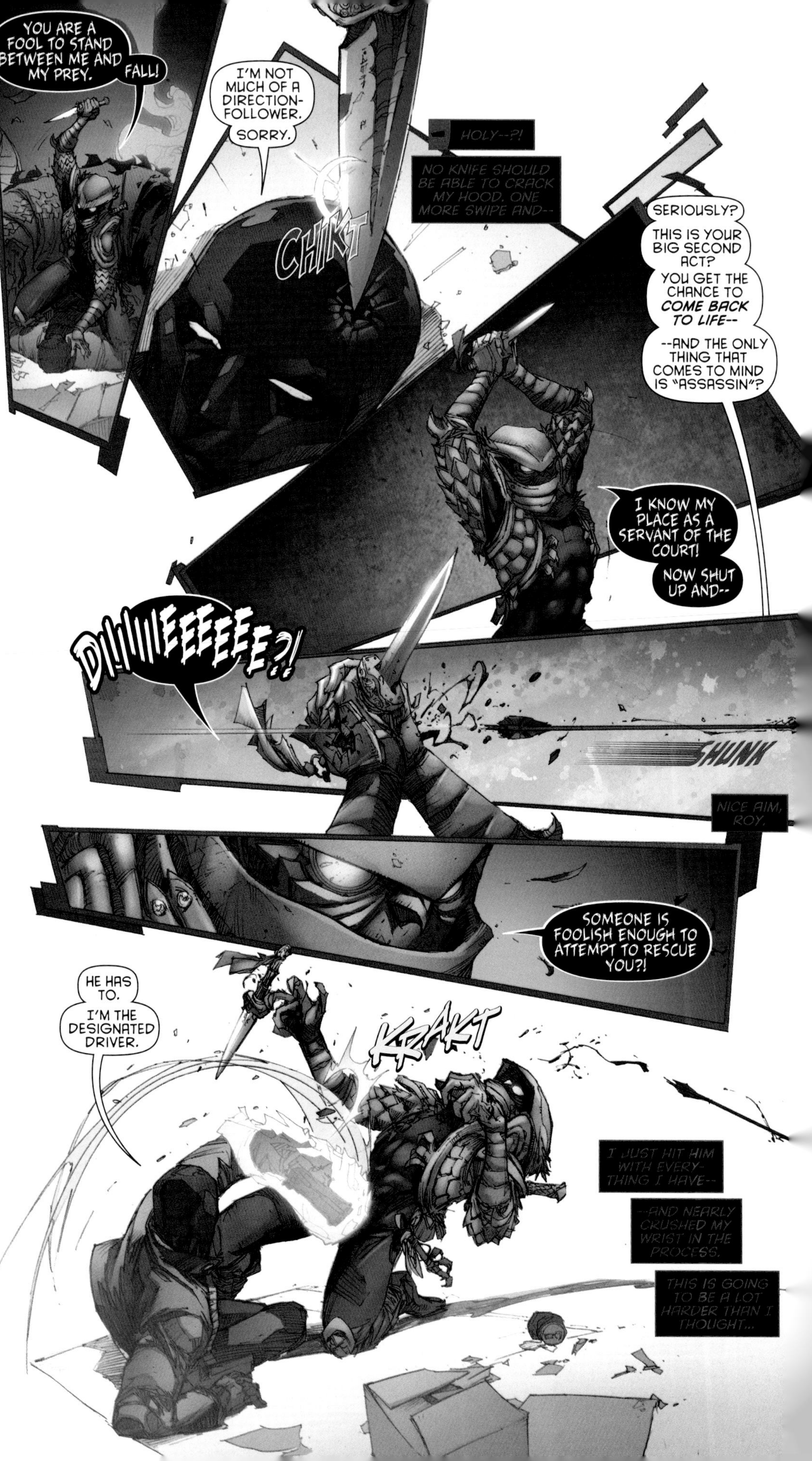
YOU ARE A FOOL TO STAND BETWEEN ME AND MY PREY.
FALL!
I'M NOT MUCH OF A DIRECTION-FOLLOWER.
SORRY.
CHIKT
HOLY--?!
NO KNIFE SHOULD BE ABLE TO CRACK MY HOOD. ONE MORE SWIPE AND--
SERIOUSLY?
THIS IS YOUR BIG SECOND ACT?
YOU GET THE CHANCE TO COME BACK TO LIFE--
--AND THE ONLY THING THAT COMES TO MIND IS "ASSASSIN"?
I KNOW MY PLACE AS A SERVANT OF THE COURT!
NOW SHUT UP AND--
DIIIIIEEEEEE?!
SHUNK
NICE AIM, ROY.
SOMEONE IS FOOLISH ENOUGH TO ATTEMPT TO RESCUE YOU?!
HE HAS TO.
I'M THE DESIGNATED DRIVER.
KRAKT
I JUST HIT HIM WITH EVERY-THING I HAVE--
--AND NEARLY CRUSHED MY WRIST IN THE PROCESS.
THIS IS GOING TO BE A LOT HARDER THAN I THOUGHT...

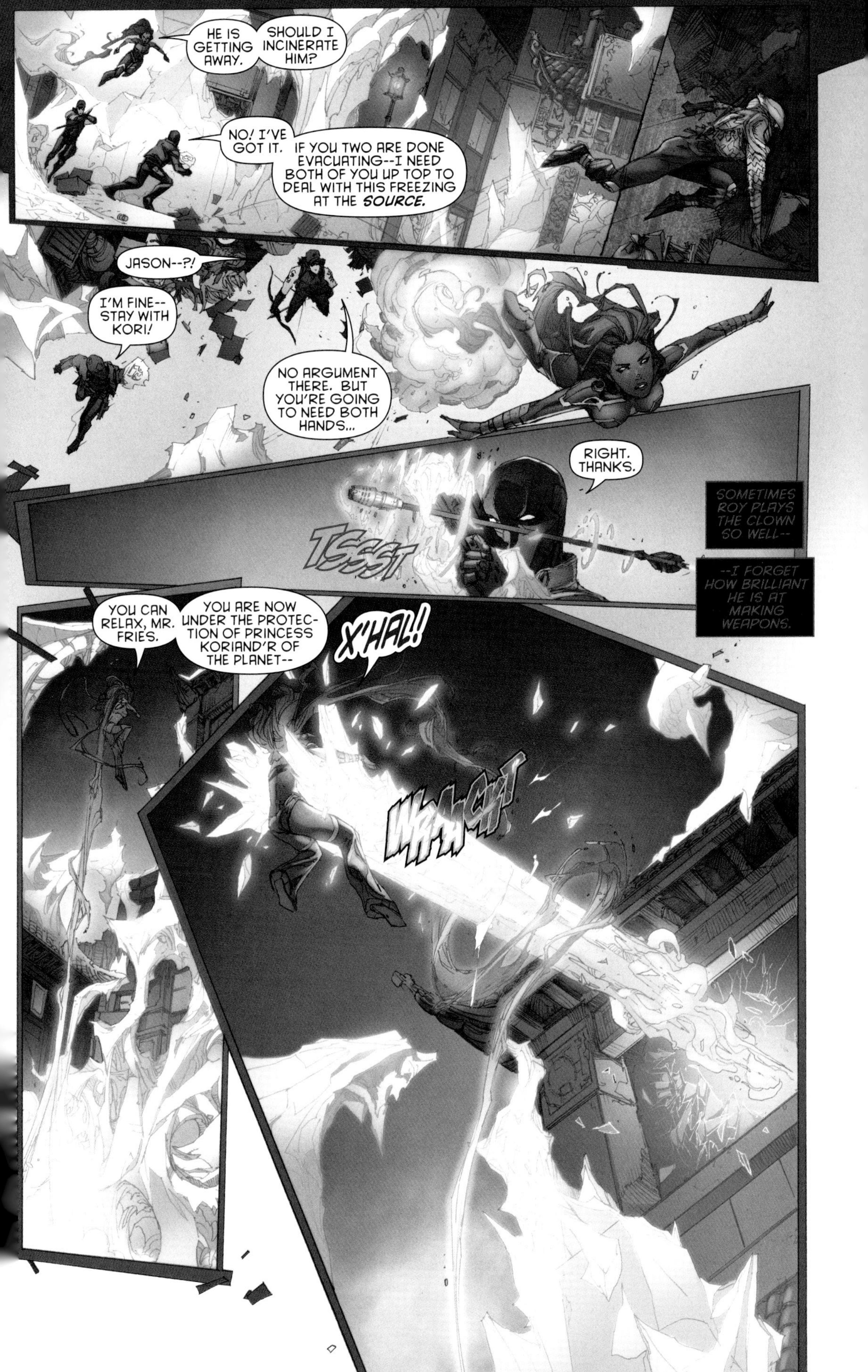

HE IS GETTING AWAY.
SHOULD I INCINERATE HIM?
NO! I'VE GOT IT.
IF YOU TWO ARE DONE EVACUATING--I NEED BOTH OF YOU UP TOP TO DEAL WITH THIS FREEZING AT THE SOURCE.
JASON--?!
I'M FINE--STAY WITH KORI!
NO ARGUMENT THERE. BUT YOU'RE GOING TO NEED BOTH HANDS...
RIGHT. THANKS.
SOMETIMES ROY PLAYS THE CLOWN SO WELL--
TSSST
--I FORGET HOW BRILLIANT HE IS AT MAKING WEAPONS.
YOU CAN RELAX, MR. FRIES.
YOU ARE NOW UNDER THE PROTECTION OF PRINCESS KORIAND'R OF THE PLANET--
X'HAL!
WRAACKT

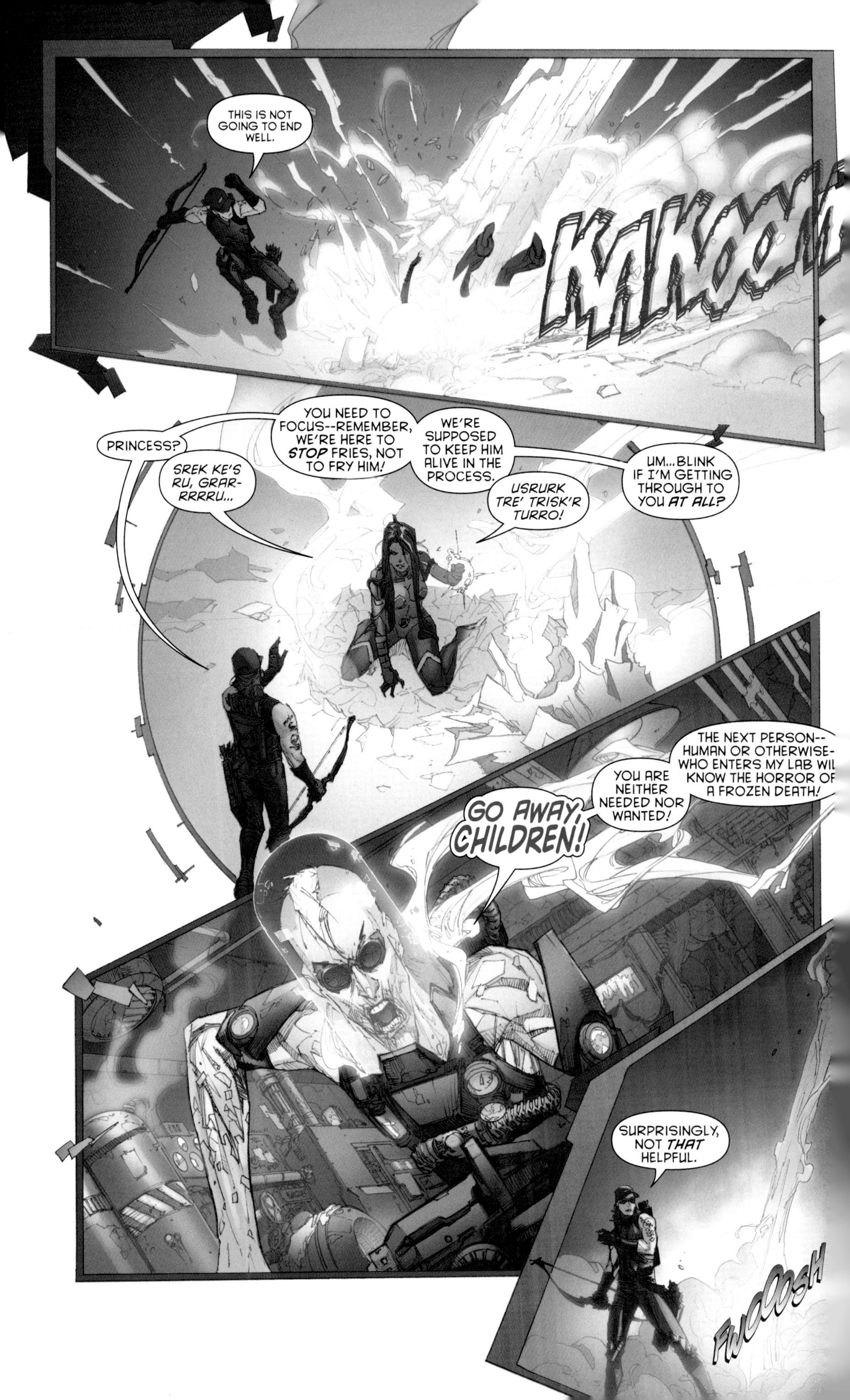
THIS IS NOT GOING TO END WELL.
PRINCESS?
YOU NEED TO FOCUS--REMEMBER, WE'RE HERE TO *STOP* FRIES, NOT TO FRY HIM!
SREK KE'S RU, GRAR-RRRRU...
WE'RE SUPPOSED TO KEEP HIM ALIVE IN THE PROCESS.
USRURK TRE' TRISK'R TURRO!
UM...BLINK IF I'M GETTING THROUGH TO YOU *AT ALL?*
GO AWAY, CHILDREN!
YOU ARE NEITHER NEEDED NOR WANTED!
THE NEXT PERSON--HUMAN OR OTHERWISE-WHO ENTERS MY LAB WIL KNOW THE HORROR OF A FROZEN DEATH!
SURPRISINGLY, NOT *THAT* HELPFUL.
FWOOOSH

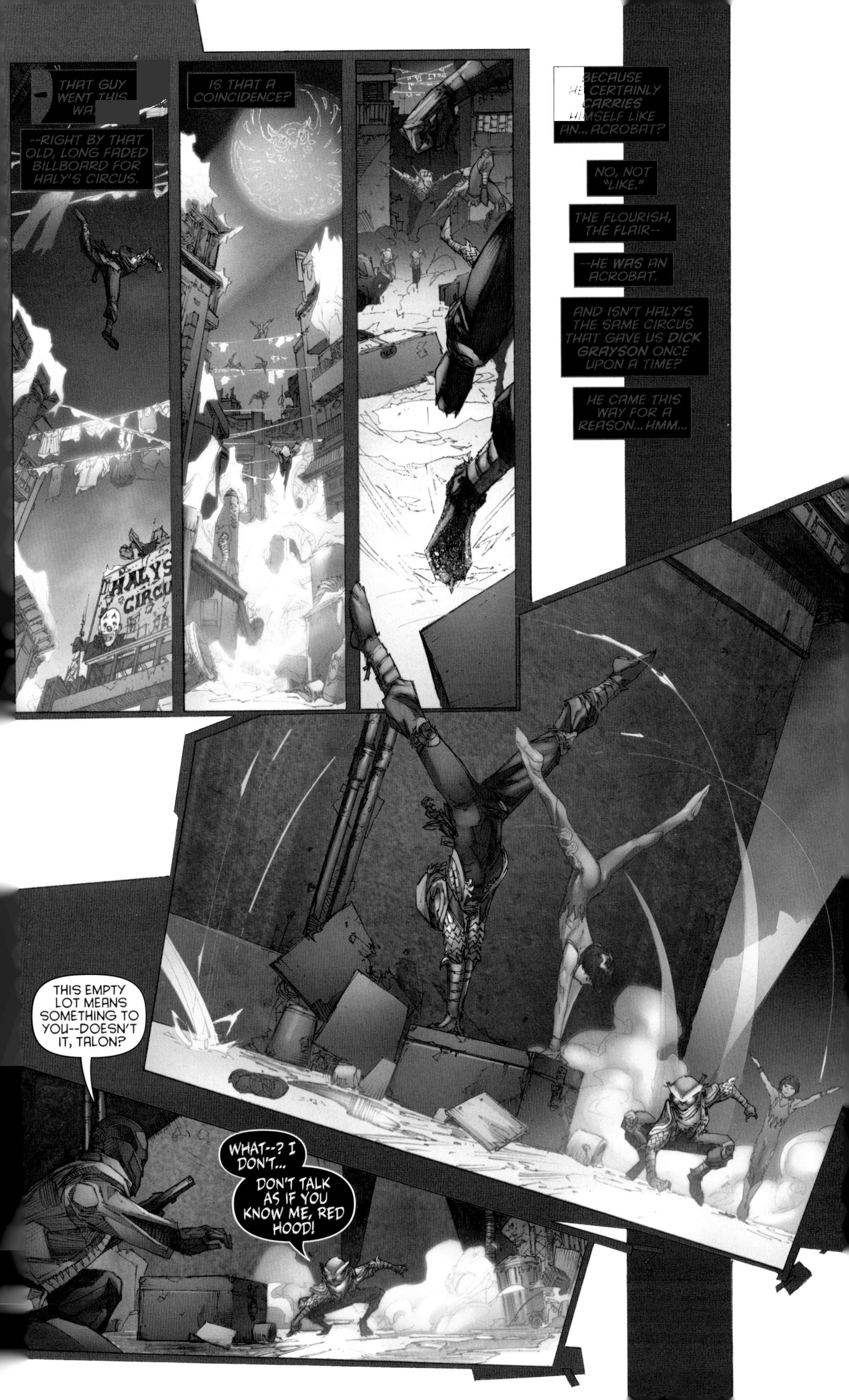
THAT GUY WENT THIS WA[redacted]
--RIGHT BY THAT OLD, LONG FADED BILLBOARD FOR HALY'S CIRCUS.
HALY'S CIRCUS
IS THAT A COINCIDENCE?
BECAUSE HE CERTAINLY CARRIES HIMSELF LIKE AN...ACROBAT?
NO, NOT "LIKE."
THE FLOURISH, THE FLAIR--
--HE WAS AN ACROBAT.
AND ISN'T HALY'S THE SAME CIRCUS THAT GAVE US DICK GRAYSON ONCE UPON A TIME?
HE CAME THIS WAY FOR A REASON...HMM...
THIS EMPTY LOT MEANS SOMETHING TO YOU--DOESN'T IT, TALON?
WHAT--? I DON'T...
DON'T TALK AS IF YOU KNOW ME, RED HOOD!

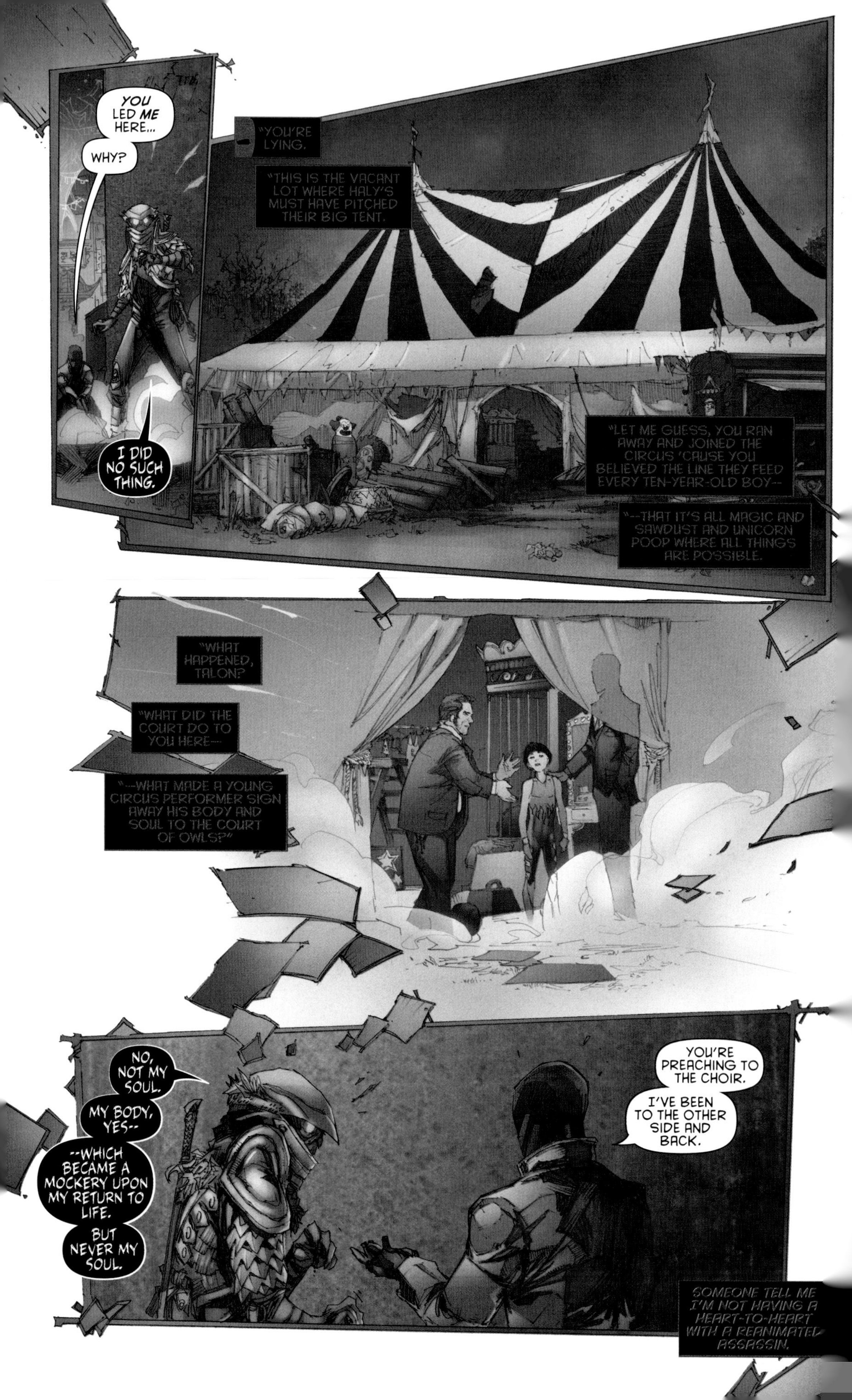

YOU LED ME HERE...
WHY?
"YOU'RE LYING.
"THIS IS THE VACANT LOT WHERE HALY'S MUST HAVE PITCHED THEIR BIG TENT.
I DID NO SUCH THING.
"LET ME GUESS, YOU RAN AWAY AND JOINED THE CIRCUS 'CAUSE YOU BELIEVED THE LINE THEY FEED EVERY TEN-YEAR-OLD BOY--
"--THAT IT'S ALL MAGIC AND SAWDUST AND UNICORN POOP WHERE ALL THINGS ARE POSSIBLE.
"WHAT HAPPENED, TALON?
"WHAT DID THE COURT DO TO YOU HERE--
"--WHAT MADE A YOUNG CIRCUS PERFORMER SIGN AWAY HIS BODY AND SOUL TO THE COURT OF OWLS?"
NO, NOT MY SOUL.
MY BODY, YES--
--WHICH BECAME A MOCKERY UPON MY RETURN TO LIFE.
BUT NEVER MY SOUL.
YOU'RE PREACHING TO THE CHOIR.
I'VE BEEN TO THE OTHER SIDE AND BACK.
SOMEONE TELL ME I'M NOT HAVING A HEART-TO-HEART WITH A REANIMATED ASSASSIN.

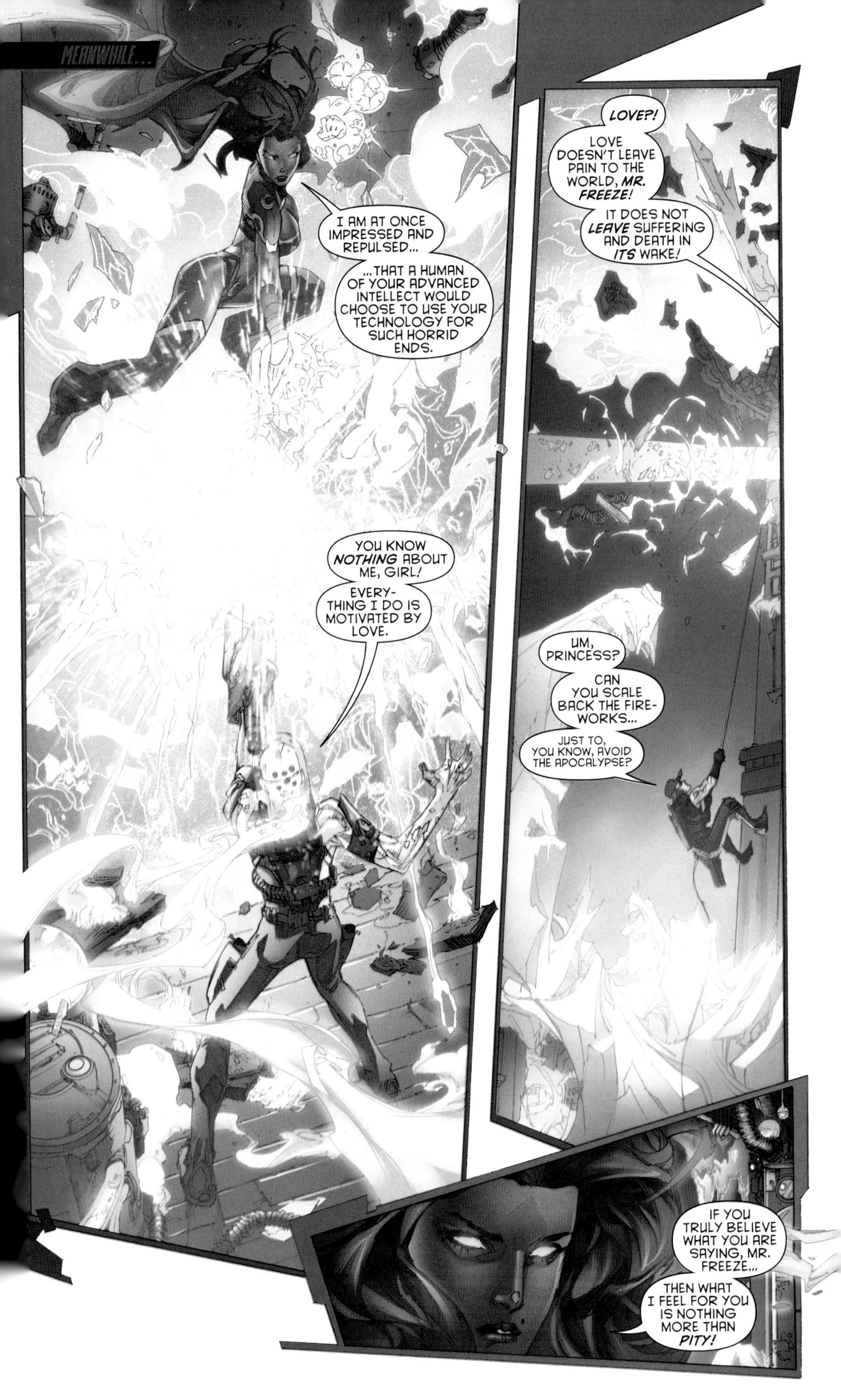
MEANWHILE...
I AM AT ONCE IMPRESSED AND REPULSED...
...THAT A HUMAN OF YOUR ADVANCED INTELLECT WOULD CHOOSE TO USE YOUR TECHNOLOGY FOR SUCH HORRID ENDS.
YOU KNOW NOTHING ABOUT ME, GIRL!
EVERY-THING I DO IS MOTIVATED BY LOVE.
LOVE?!
LOVE DOESN'T LEAVE PAIN TO THE WORLD, MR. FREEZE!
IT DOES NOT LEAVE SUFFERING AND DEATH IN ITS WAKE!
UM, PRINCESS?
CAN YOU SCALE BACK THE FIRE-WORKS...
JUST TO, YOU KNOW, AVOID THE APOCALYPSE?
IF YOU TRULY BELIEVE WHAT YOU ARE SAYING, MR. FREEZE...
THEN WHAT I FEEL FOR YOU IS NOTHING MORE THAN PITY!

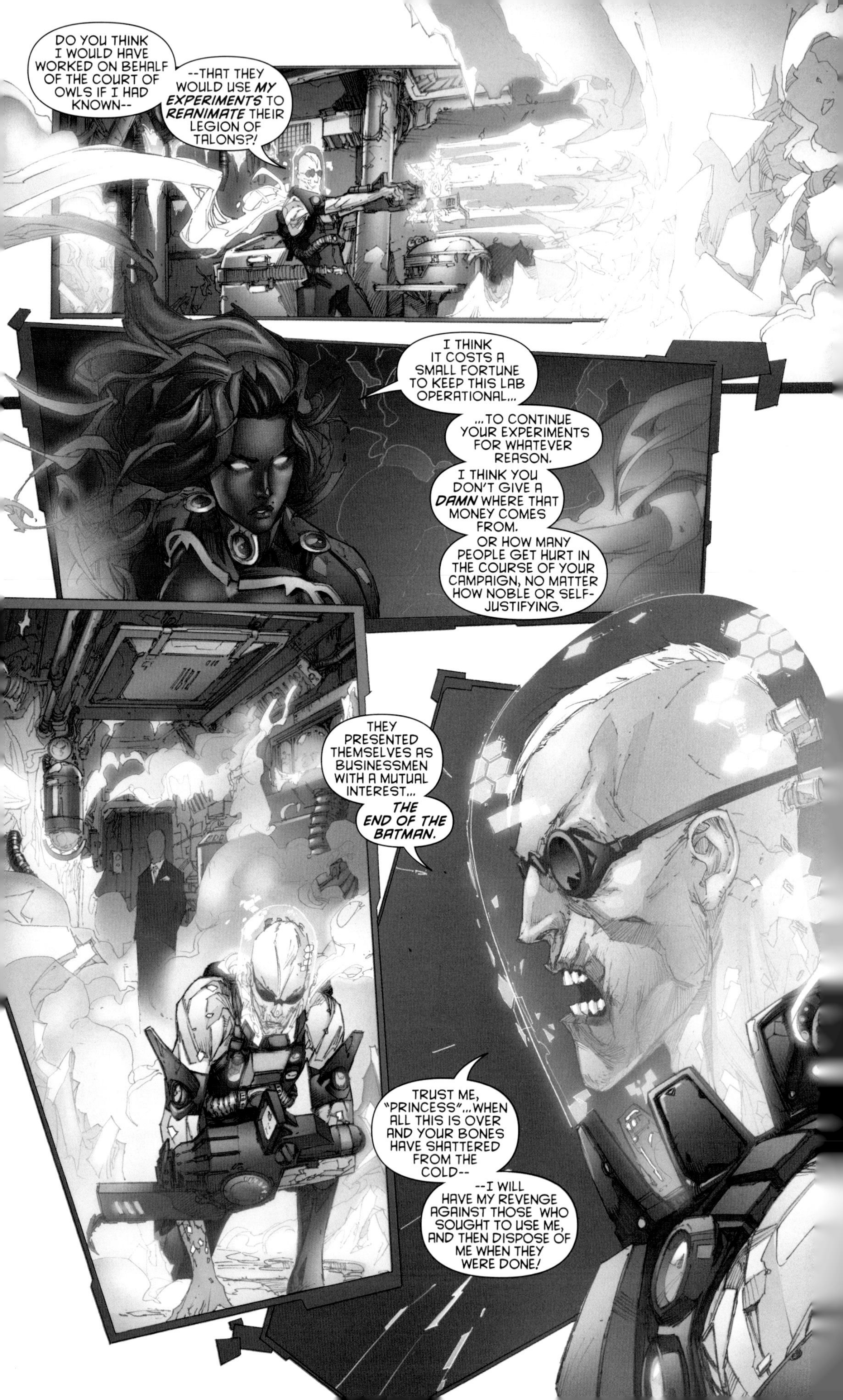
DO YOU THINK I WOULD HAVE WORKED ON BEHALF OF THE COURT OF OWLS IF I HAD KNOWN--
--THAT THEY WOULD USE MY EXPERIMENTS TO REANIMATE THEIR LEGION OF TALONS?!
I THINK IT COSTS A SMALL FORTUNE TO KEEP THIS LAB OPERATIONAL...
...TO CONTINUE YOUR EXPERIMENTS FOR WHATEVER REASON.
I THINK YOU DON'T GIVE A DAMN WHERE THAT MONEY COMES FROM.
OR HOW MANY PEOPLE GET HURT IN THE COURSE OF YOUR CAMPAIGN, NO MATTER HOW NOBLE OR SELF-JUSTIFYING.
THEY PRESENTED THEMSELVES AS BUSINESSMEN WITH A MUTUAL INTEREST...
THE END OF THE BATMAN.
TRUST ME, "PRINCESS"...WHEN ALL THIS IS OVER AND YOUR BONES HAVE SHATTERED FROM THE COLD--
--I WILL HAVE MY REVENGE AGAINST THOSE WHO SOUGHT TO USE ME, AND THEN DISPOSE OF ME WHEN THEY WERE DONE!

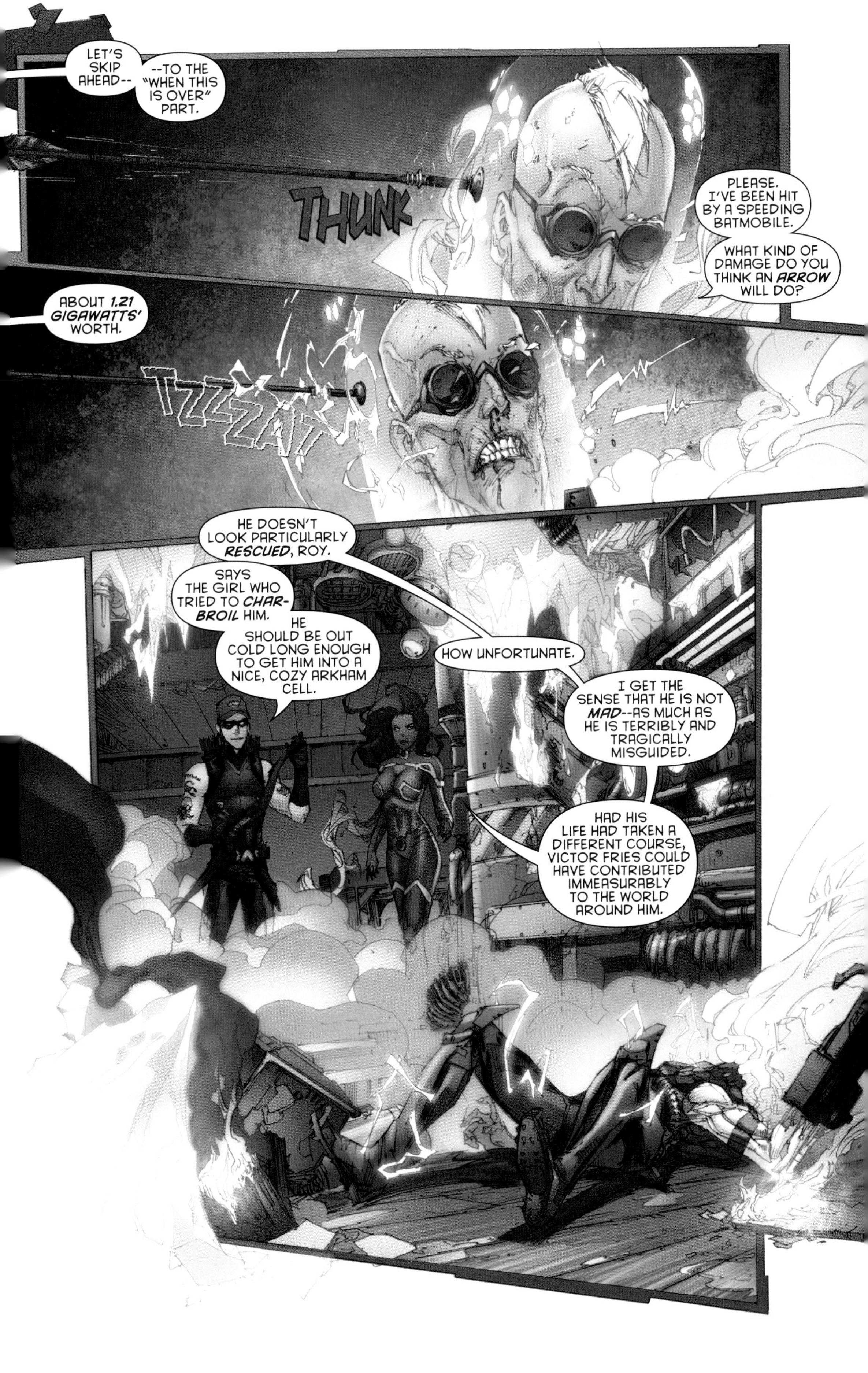
LET'S SKIP AHEAD--
--TO THE "WHEN THIS IS OVER" PART.
THUNK
PLEASE. I'VE BEEN HIT BY A SPEEDING BATMOBILE.
WHAT KIND OF DAMAGE DO YOU THINK AN ARROW WILL DO?
ABOUT 1.21 GIGAWATTS' WORTH.
TZZZAT
HE DOESN'T LOOK PARTICULARLY RESCUED, ROY.
SAYS THE GIRL WHO TRIED TO CHAR-BROIL HIM.
HE SHOULD BE OUT COLD LONG ENOUGH TO GET HIM INTO A NICE, COZY ARKHAM CELL.
HOW UNFORTUNATE.
I GET THE SENSE THAT HE IS NOT MAD--AS MUCH AS HE IS TERRIBLY AND TRAGICALLY MISGUIDED.
HAD HIS LIFE HAD TAKEN A DIFFERENT COURSE, VICTOR FRIES COULD HAVE CONTRIBUTED IMMEASURABLY TO THE WORLD AROUND HIM.

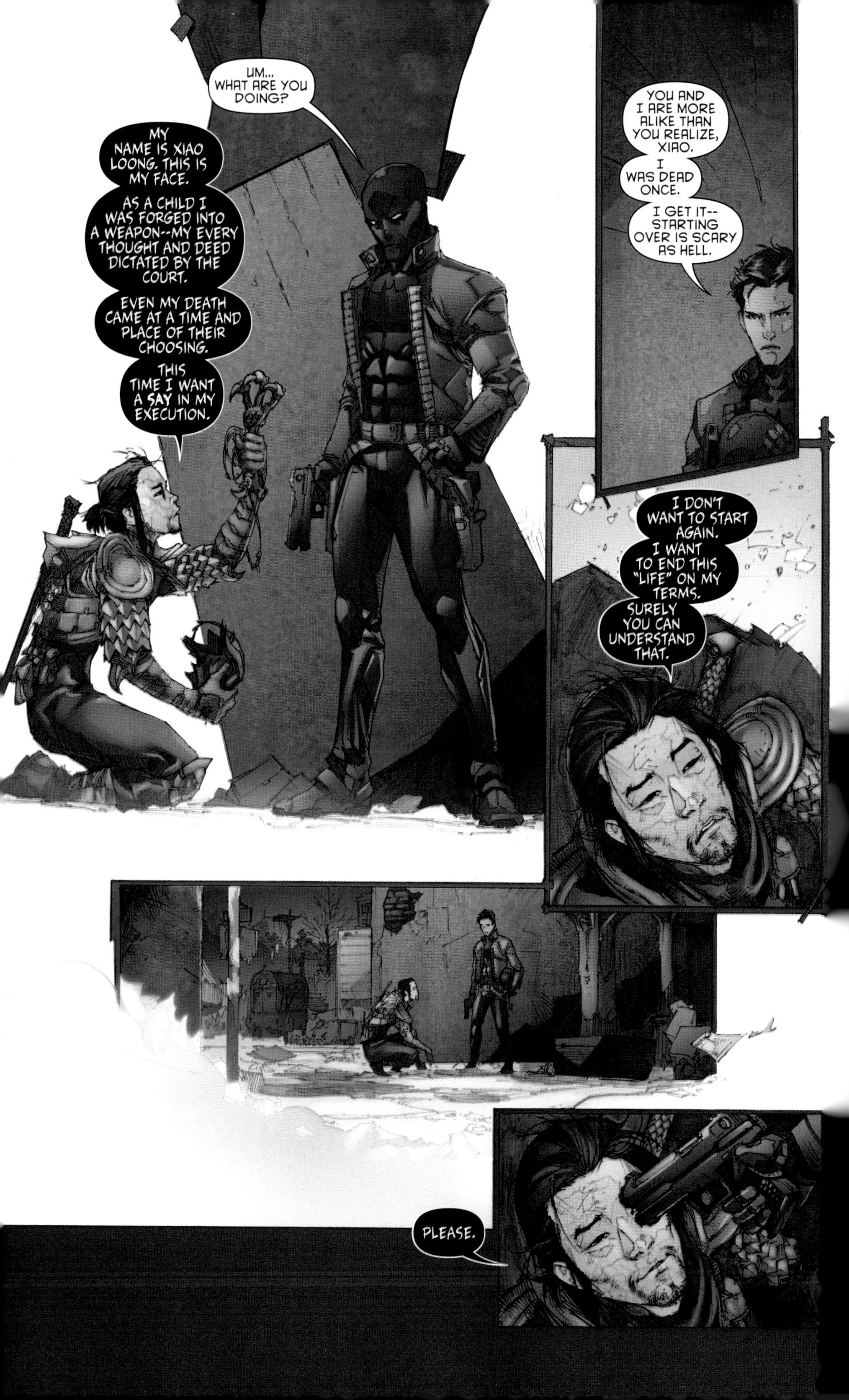
UM... WHAT ARE YOU DOING?
MY NAME IS XIAO LOONG. THIS IS MY FACE.
AS A CHILD I WAS FORGED INTO A WEAPON--MY EVERY THOUGHT AND DEED DICTATED BY THE COURT.
EVEN MY DEATH CAME AT A TIME AND PLACE OF THEIR CHOOSING.
THIS TIME I WANT A SAY IN MY EXECUTION.
YOU AND I ARE MORE ALIKE THAN YOU REALIZE, XIAO.
I WAS DEAD ONCE.
I GET IT--STARTING OVER IS SCARY AS HELL.
I DON'T WANT TO START AGAIN.
I WANT TO END THIS "LIFE" ON MY TERMS.
SURELY YOU CAN UNDERSTAND THAT.
PLEASE.

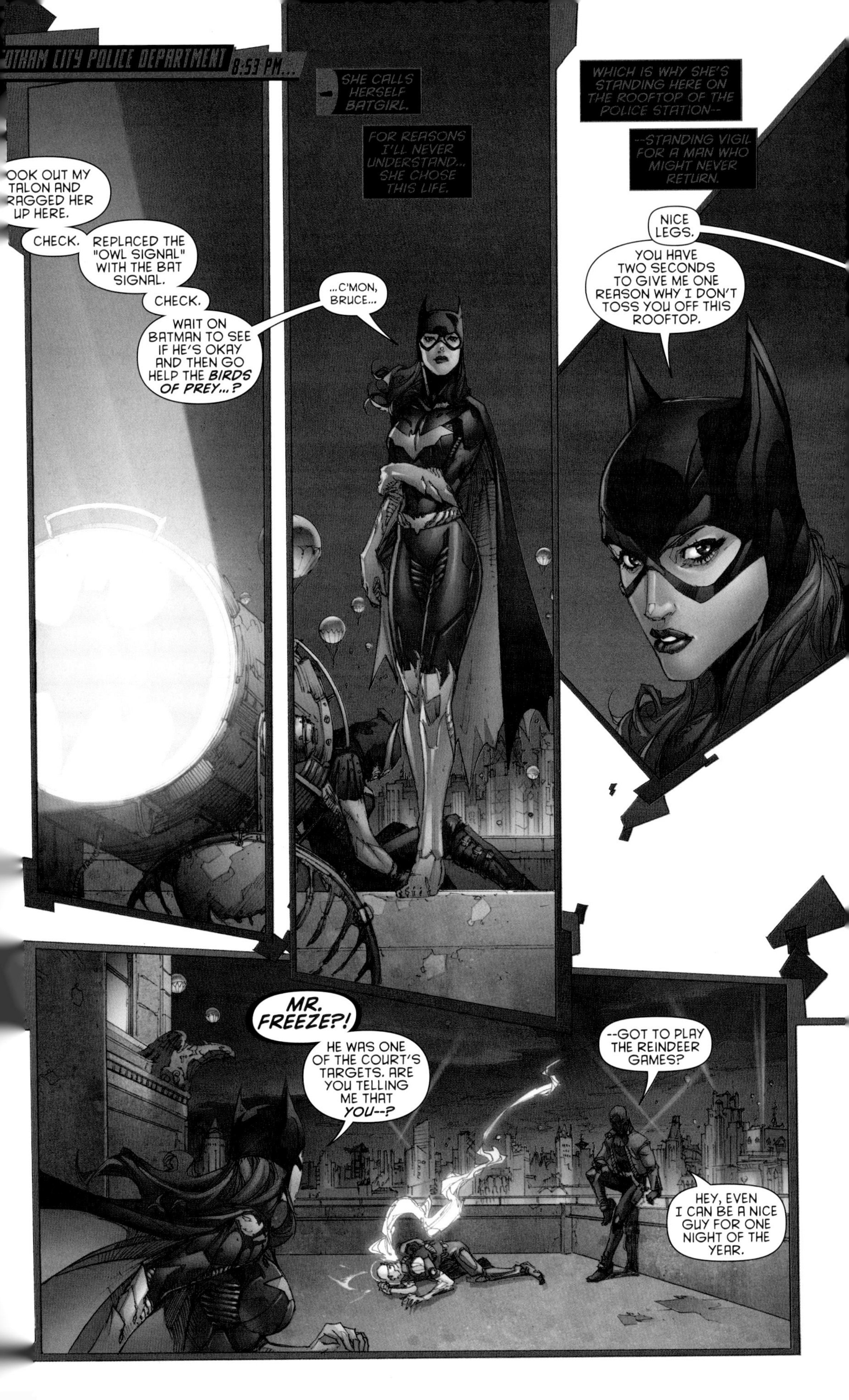

GOTHAM CITY POLICE DEPARTMENT 8:53 PM...
OOK OUT MY TALON AND RAGGED HER UP HERE.
CHECK.
REPLACED THE "OWL SIGNAL" WITH THE BAT SIGNAL.
CHECK.
WAIT ON BATMAN TO SEE IF HE'S OKAY AND THEN GO HELP THE BIRDS OF PREY...?
SHE CALLS HERSELF BATGIRL.
FOR REASONS I'LL NEVER UNDERSTAND... SHE CHOSE THIS LIFE.
...C'MON, BRUCE...
WHICH IS WHY SHE'S STANDING HERE ON THE ROOFTOP OF THE POLICE STATION--
--STANDING VIGIL FOR A MAN WHO MIGHT NEVER RETURN.
NICE LEGS.
YOU HAVE TWO SECONDS TO GIVE ME ONE REASON WHY I DON'T TOSS YOU OFF THIS ROOFTOP.
MR. FREEZE?!
HE WAS ONE OF THE COURT'S TARGETS. ARE YOU TELLING ME THAT YOU--?
--GOT TO PLAY THE REINDEER GAMES?
HEY, EVEN I CAN BE A NICE GUY FOR ONE NIGHT OF THE YEAR.

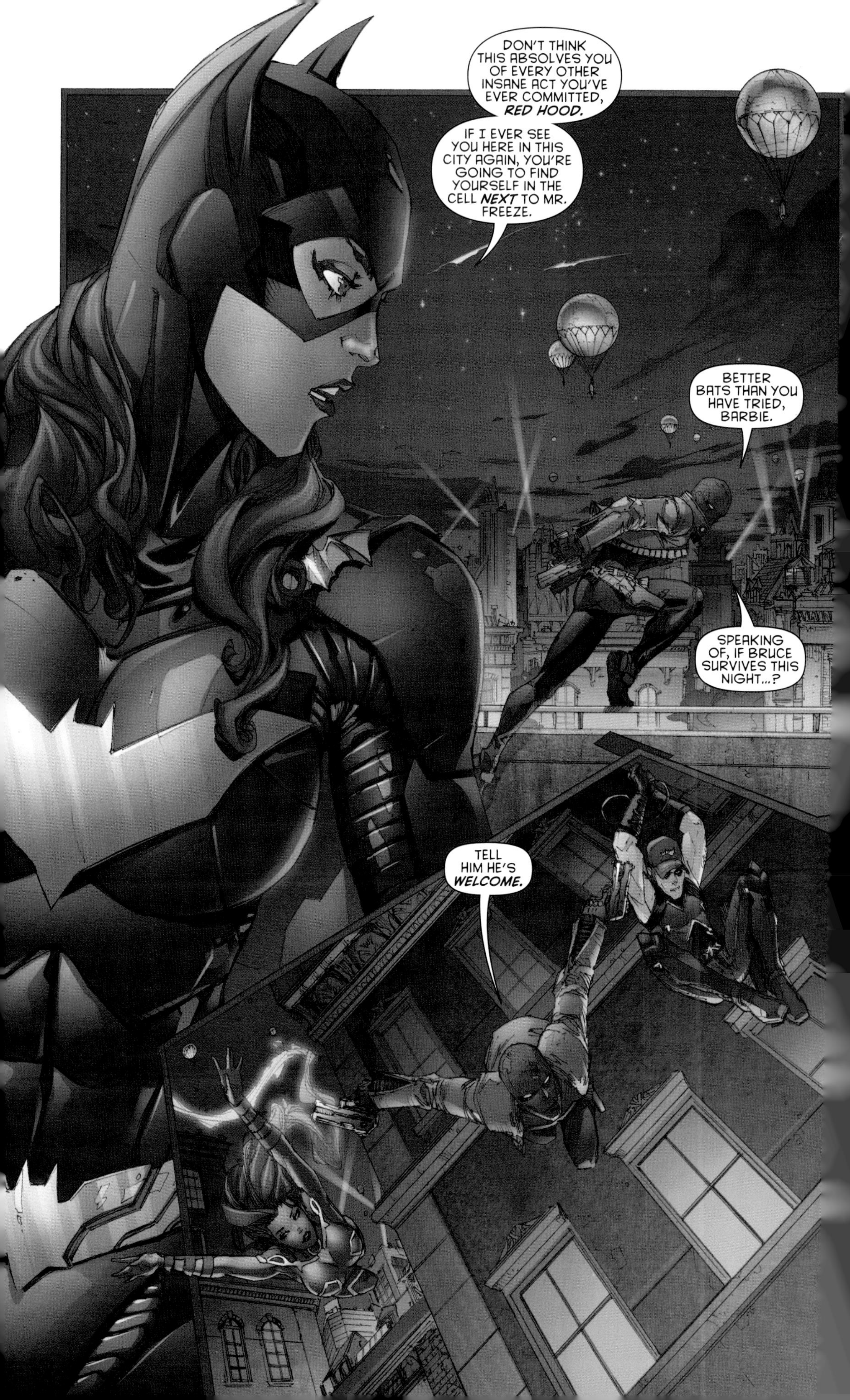
DON'T THINK THIS ABSOLVES YOU OF EVERY OTHER INSANE ACT YOU'VE EVER COMMITTED, RED HOOD.
IF I EVER SEE YOU HERE IN THIS CITY AGAIN, YOU'RE GOING TO FIND YOURSELF IN THE CELL NEXT TO MR. FREEZE.
BETTER BATS THAN YOU HAVE TRIED, BARBIE.
SPEAKING OF, IF BRUCE SURVIVES THIS NIGHT...?
TELL HIM HE'S WELCOME.

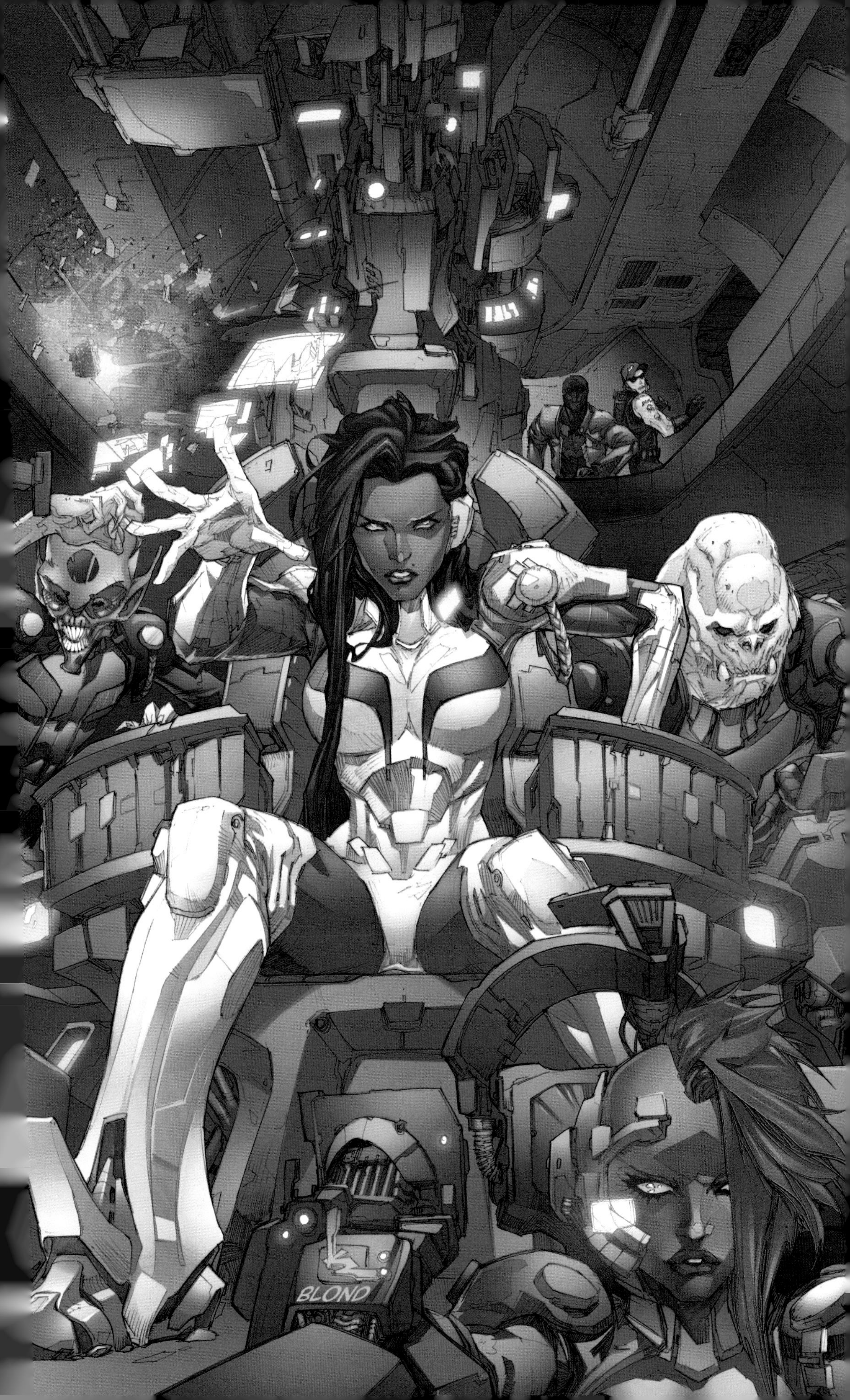
BLOND

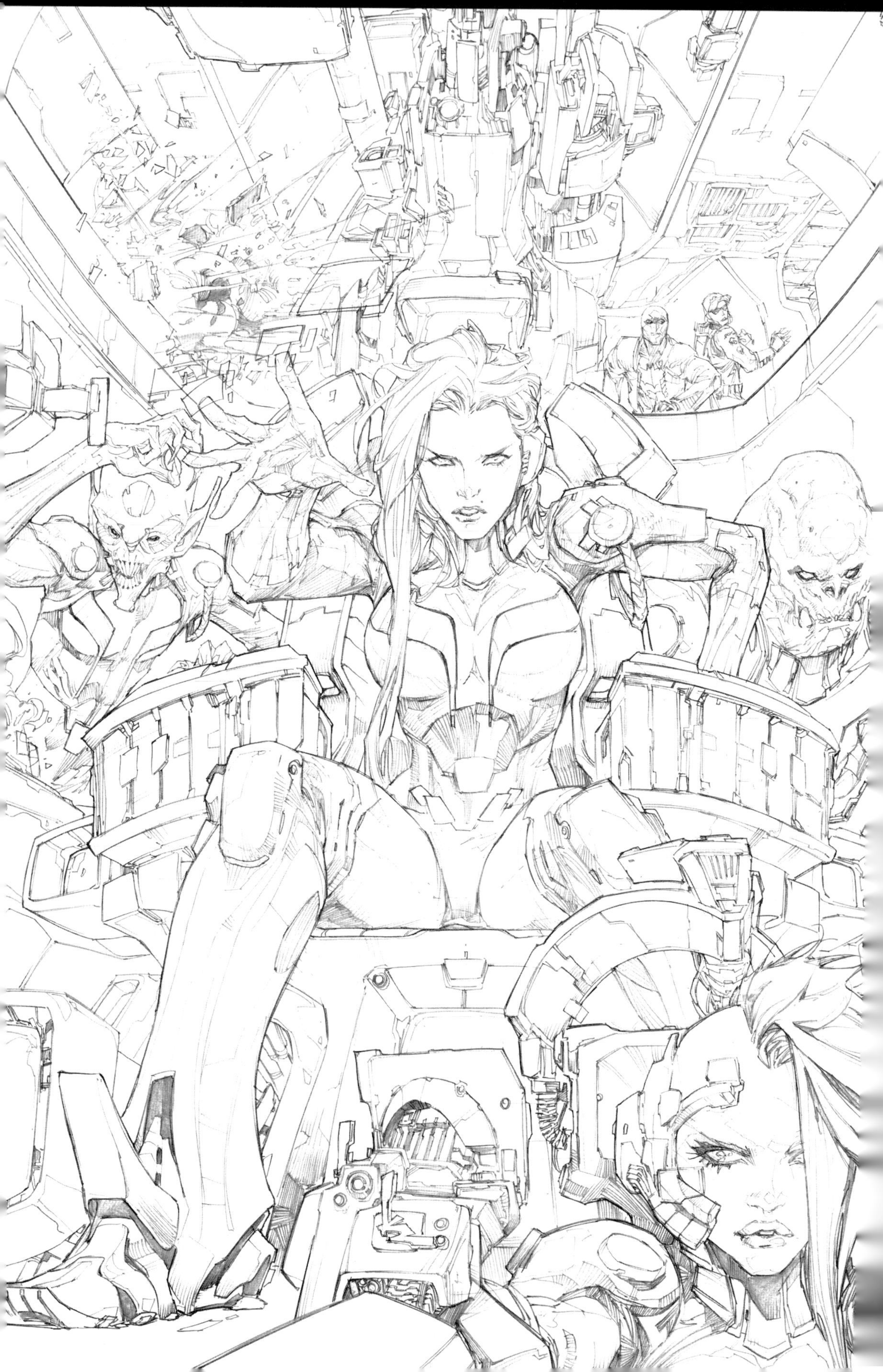

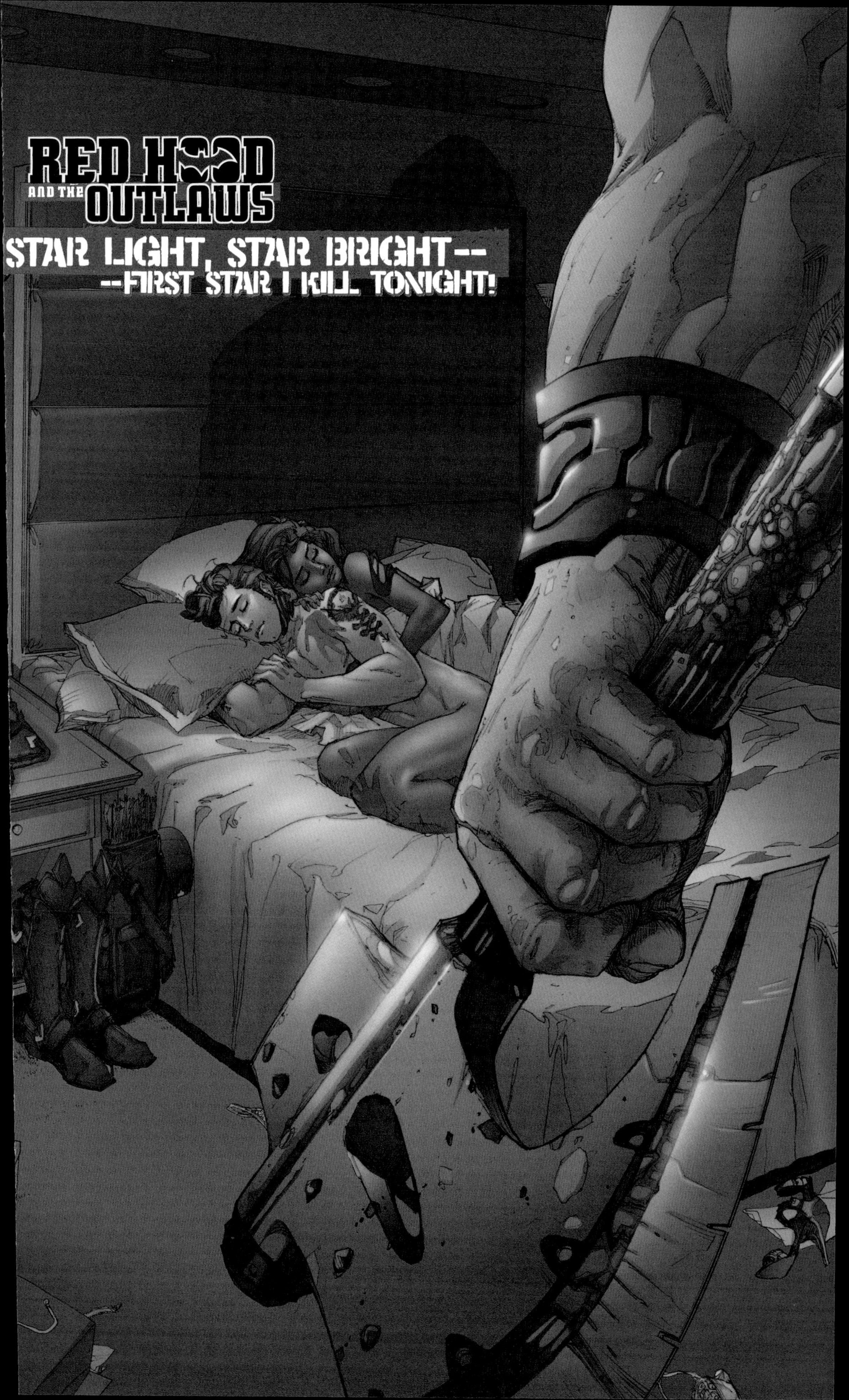
RED HOOD AND THE OUTLAWS
STAR LIGHT, STAR BRIGHT--
--FIRST STAR I KILL TONIGHT!

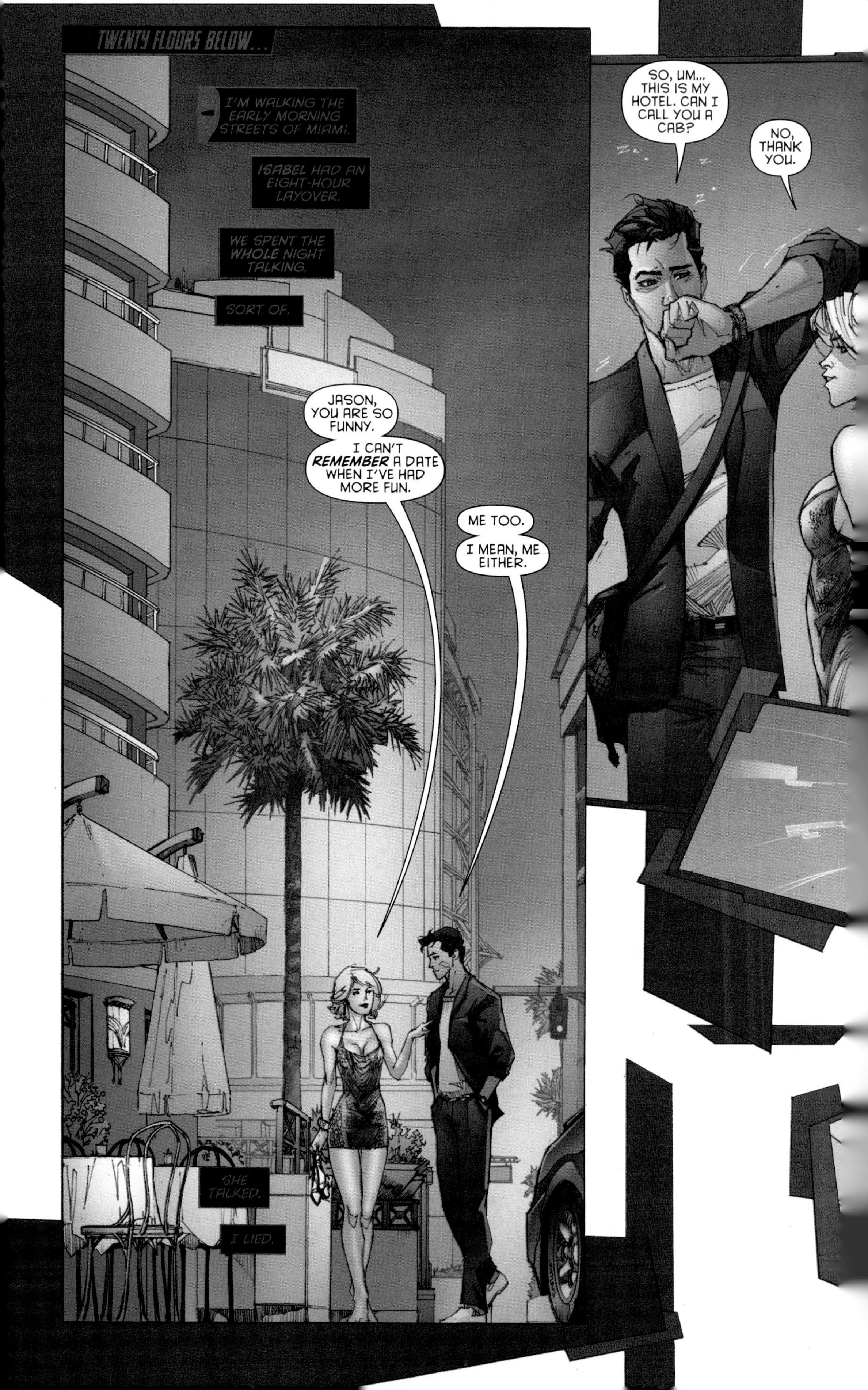
TWENTY FLOORS BELOW...
I'M WALKING THE EARLY MORNING STREETS OF MIAMI.
ISABEL HAD AN EIGHT-HOUR LAYOVER.
WE SPENT THE WHOLE NIGHT TALKING.
SORT OF.
JASON, YOU ARE SO FUNNY.
I CAN'T REMEMBER A DATE WHEN I'VE HAD MORE FUN.
ME TOO.
I MEAN, ME EITHER.
SHE TALKED.
I LIED.
SO, UM... THIS IS MY HOTEL. CAN I CALL YOU A CAB?
NO, THANK YOU.

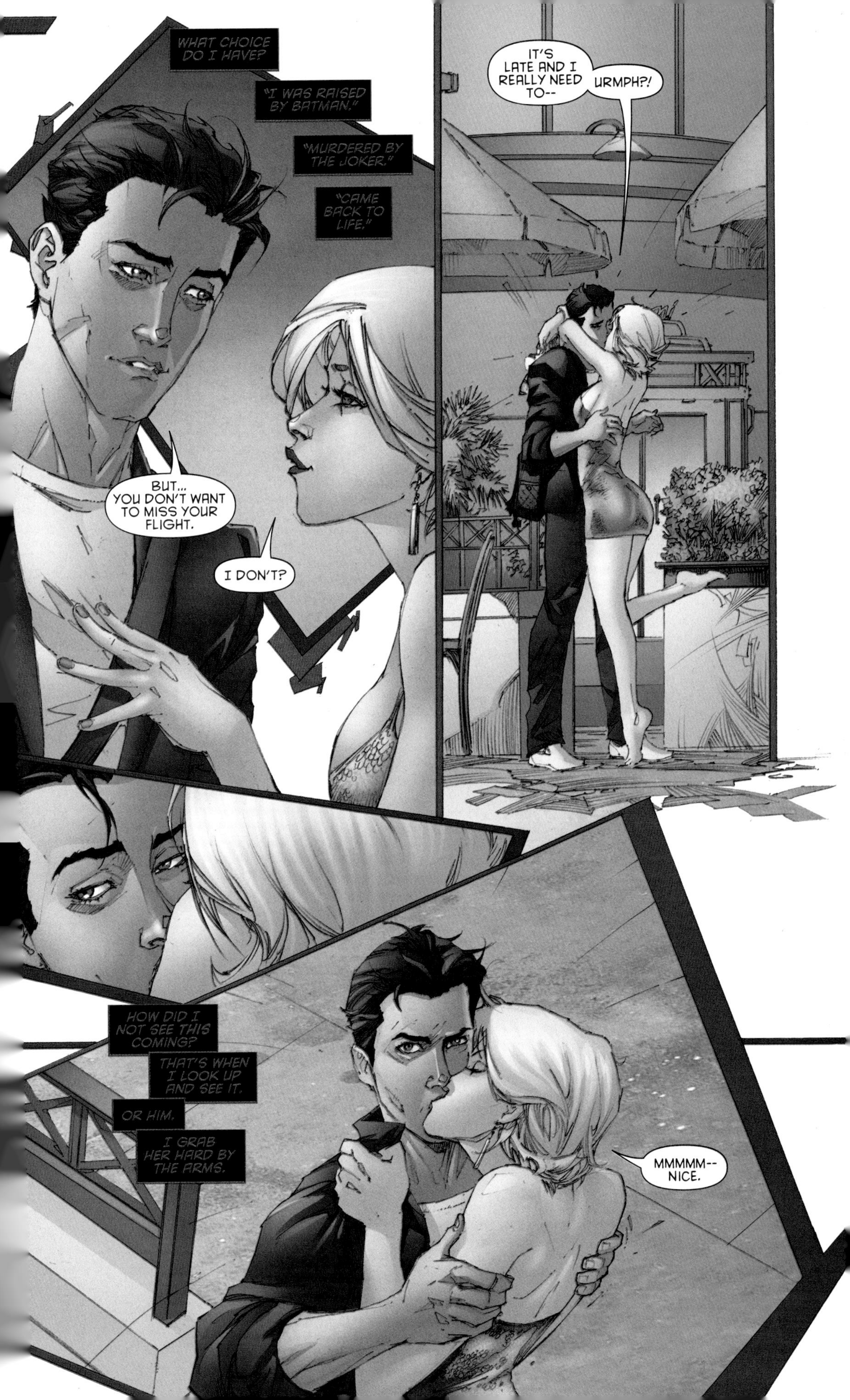
WHAT CHOICE DO I HAVE?
"I WAS RAISED BY BATMAN."
"MURDERED BY THE JOKER."
"CAME BACK TO LIFE."
BUT... YOU DON'T WANT TO MISS YOUR FLIGHT.
I DON'T?
IT'S LATE AND I REALLY NEED TO--
URMPH?!
HOW DID I NOT SEE THIS COMING?
THAT'S WHEN I LOOK UP AND SEE IT.
OR HIM.
I GRAB HER HARD BY THE ARMS.
MMMMM--NICE.

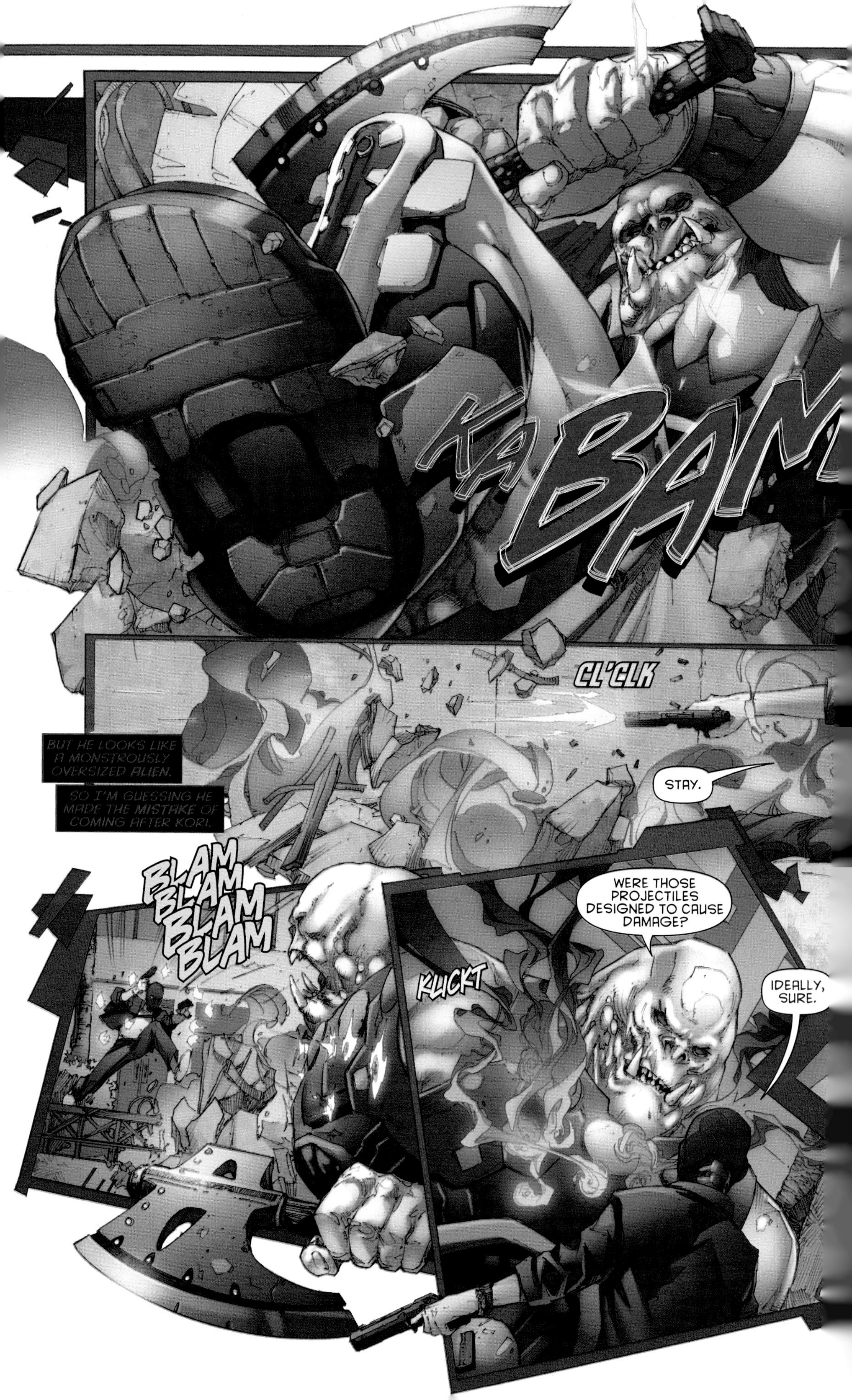
KA BAM
CL'CLK
BUT HE LOOKS LIKE A MONSTROUSLY OVERSIZED ALIEN.
SO I'M GUESSING HE MADE THE MISTAKE OF COMING AFTER KORI.
STAY.
BLAM BLAM BLAM BLAM
KLICKT
WERE THOSE PROJECTILES DESIGNED TO CAUSE DAMAGE?
IDEALLY, SURE.

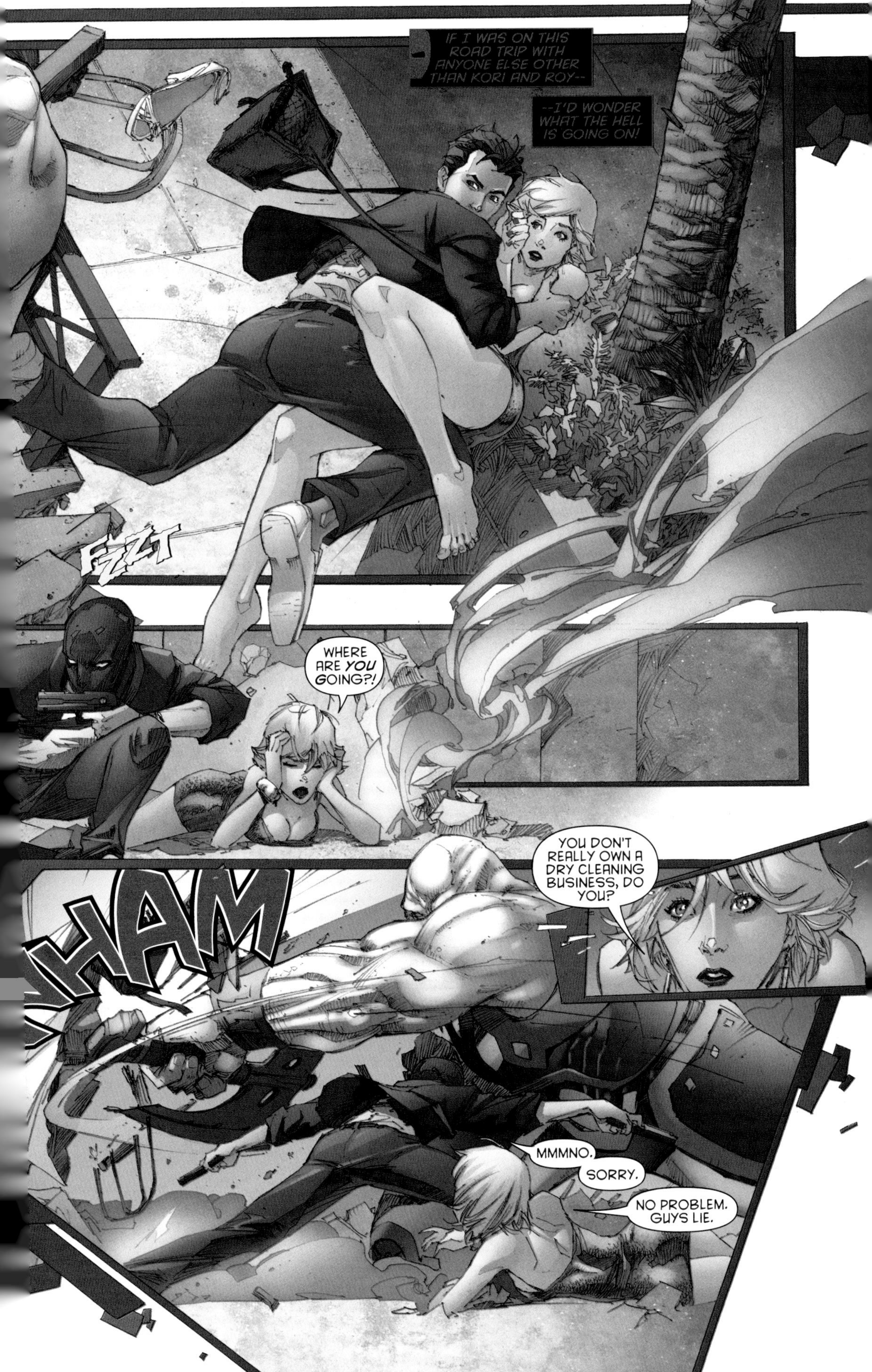
IF I WAS ON THIS ROAD TRIP WITH ANYONE ELSE OTHER THAN KORI AND ROY--
--I'D WONDER WHAT THE HELL IS GOING ON!
FZZZT
WHERE ARE YOU GOING?!
WHAM
YOU DON'T REALLY OWN A DRY CLEANING BUSINESS, DO YOU?
MMMNO.
SORRY.
NO PROBLEM. GUYS LIE.

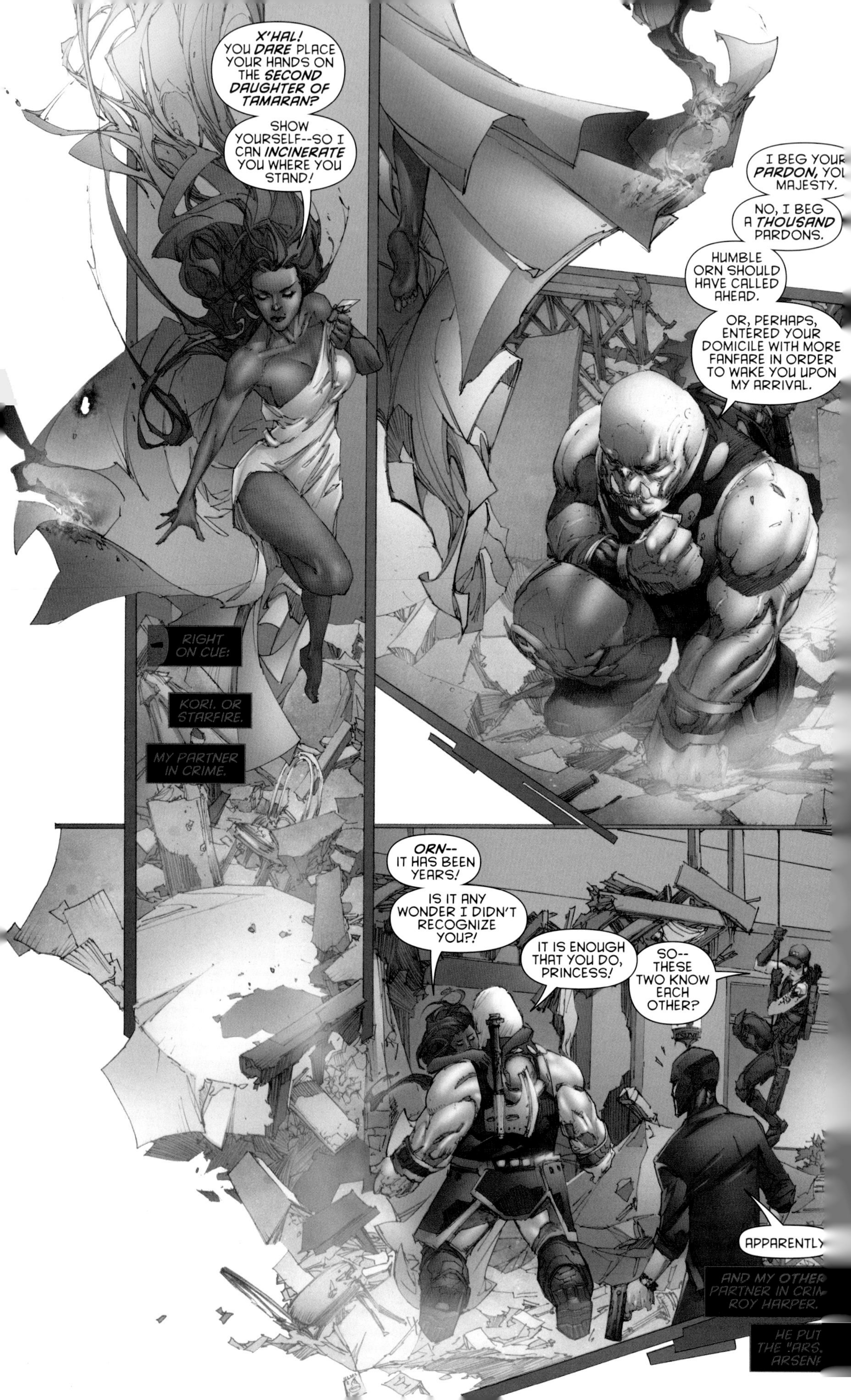
X'HAL! YOU DARE PLACE YOUR HANDS ON THE SECOND DAUGHTER OF TAMARAN?
SHOW YOURSELF--SO I CAN INCINERATE YOU WHERE YOU STAND!
RIGHT ON CUE:
KORI. OR STARFIRE.
MY PARTNER IN CRIME.
I BEG YOUR PARDON, YOU MAJESTY.
NO, I BEG A THOUSAND PARDONS.
HUMBLE ORN SHOULD HAVE CALLED AHEAD.
OR, PERHAPS, ENTERED YOUR DOMICILE WITH MORE FANFARE IN ORDER TO WAKE YOU UPON MY ARRIVAL.
ORN-- IT HAS BEEN YEARS!
IS IT ANY WONDER I DIDN'T RECOGNIZE YOU?!
IT IS ENOUGH THAT YOU DO, PRINCESS!
SO-- THESE TWO KNOW EACH OTHER?
APPARENTLY
AND MY OTHE PARTNER IN CRI ROY HARPER.
HE PUT THE "ARS. ARSEN

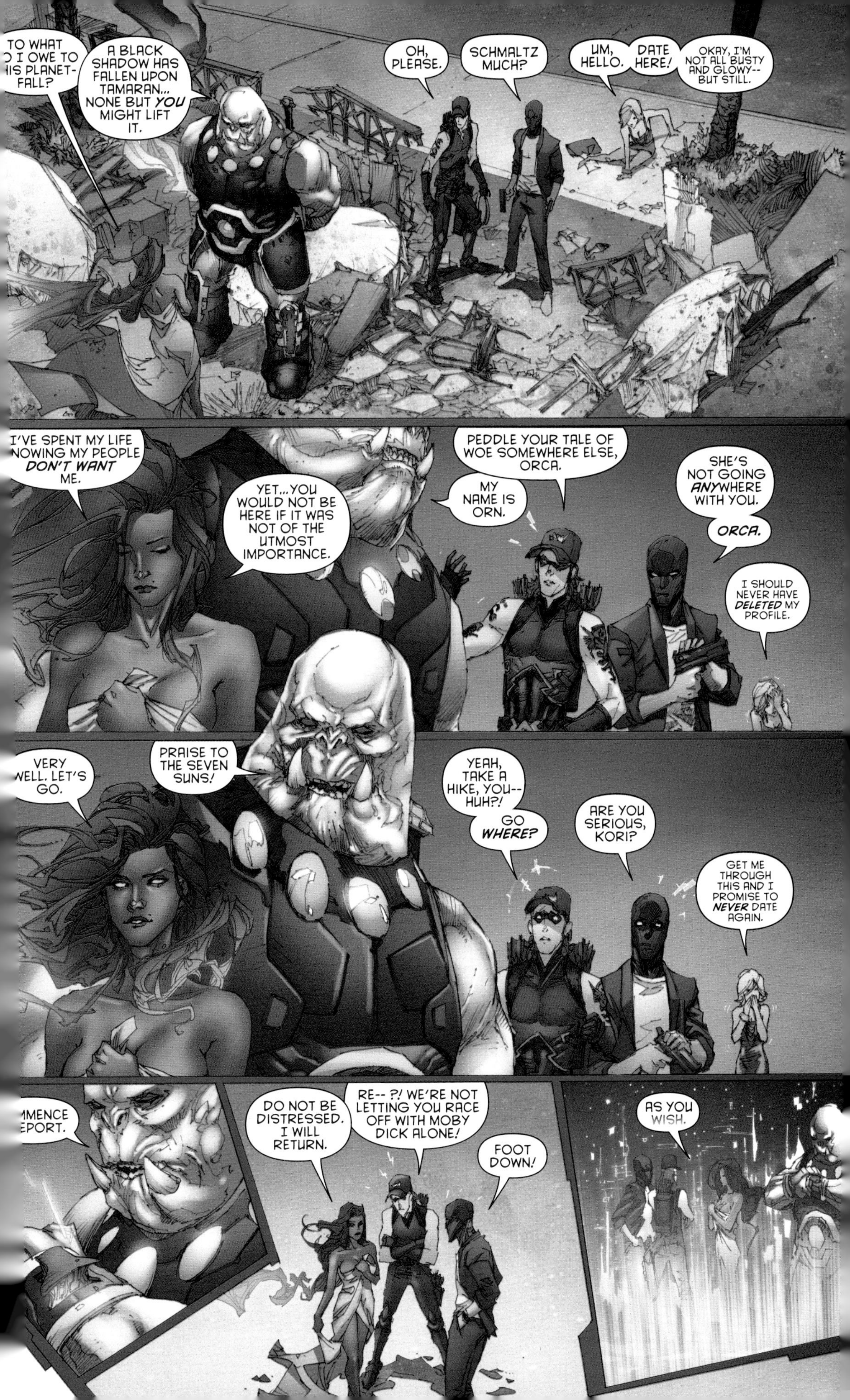
TO WHAT
I OWE TO
IS PLANET-
FALL?
A BLACK SHADOW HAS FALLEN UPON TAMARAN... NONE BUT *YOU* MIGHT LIFT IT.
OH, PLEASE.
SCHMALTZ MUCH?
UM, HELLO.
DATE HERE!
OKAY, I'M NOT ALL BUSTY AND GLOWY-- BUT STILL.
I'VE SPENT MY LIFE
NOWING MY PEOPLE *DON'T WANT* ME.
YET...YOU WOULD NOT BE HERE IF IT WAS NOT OF THE UTMOST IMPORTANCE.
PEDDLE YOUR TALE OF WOE SOMEWHERE ELSE, ORCA.
MY NAME IS ORN.
SHE'S NOT GOING *ANY*WHERE WITH YOU.
ORCA.
I SHOULD NEVER HAVE *DELETED* MY PROFILE.
VERY
ELL. LET'S GO.
PRAISE TO THE SEVEN SUNS!
YEAH, TAKE A HIKE, YOU-- HUH?!
GO *WHERE?*
ARE YOU SERIOUS, KORI?
GET ME THROUGH THIS AND I PROMISE TO *NEVER* DATE AGAIN.
MMENCE
EPORT.
DO NOT BE DISTRESSED. I WILL RETURN.
RE-- ?! WE'RE NOT LETTING YOU RACE OFF WITH MOBY DICK ALONE!
FOOT DOWN!
AS YOU WISH.

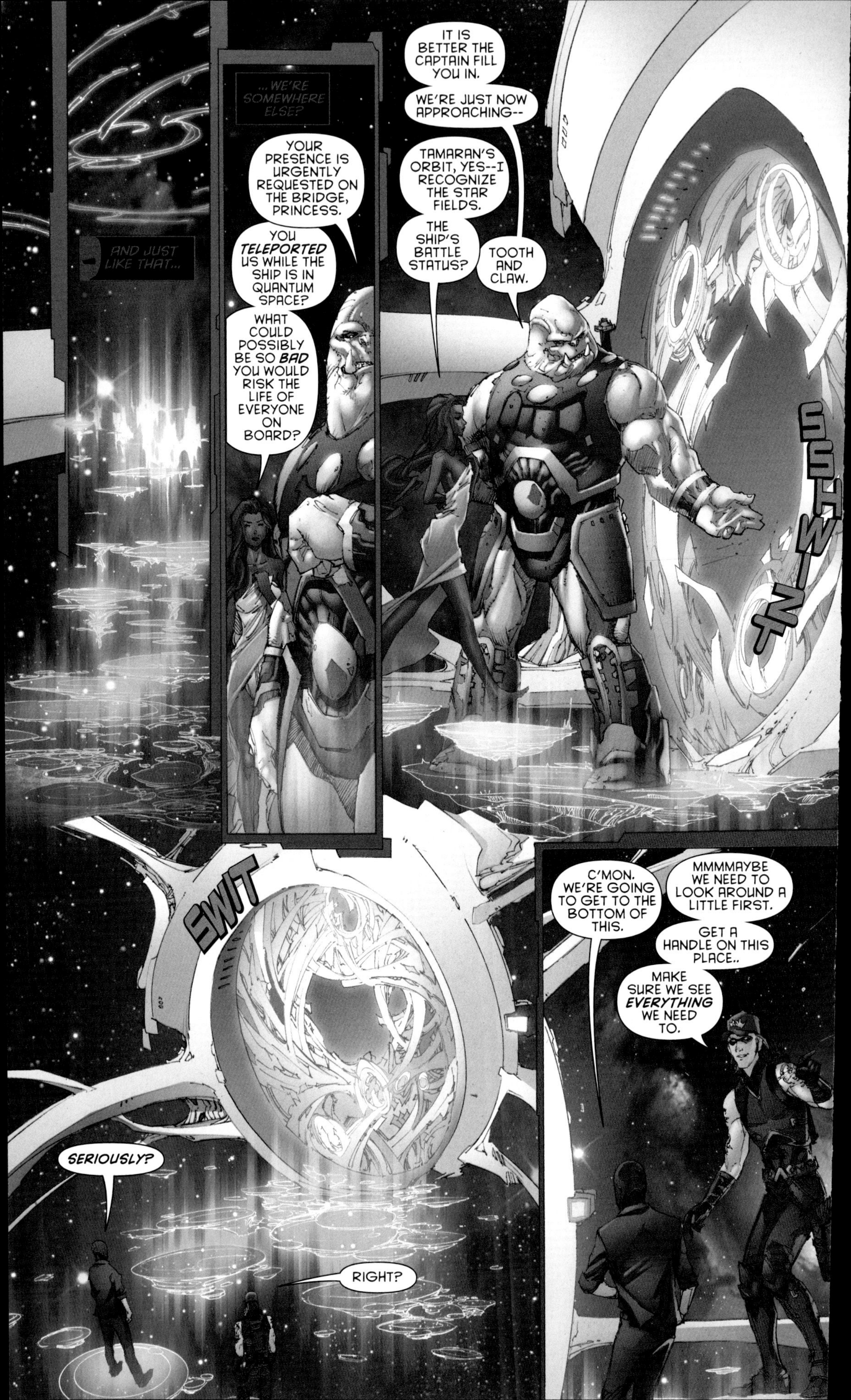
AND JUST LIKE THAT...
...WE'RE SOMEWHERE ELSE?
YOUR PRESENCE IS URGENTLY REQUESTED ON THE BRIDGE, PRINCESS.
YOU TELEPORTED US WHILE THE SHIP IS IN QUANTUM SPACE?
WHAT COULD POSSIBLY BE SO BAD YOU WOULD RISK THE LIFE OF EVERYONE ON BOARD?
IT IS BETTER THE CAPTAIN FILL YOU IN.
WE'RE JUST NOW APPROACHING--
TAMARAN'S ORBIT, YES--I RECOGNIZE THE STAR FIELDS.
THE SHIP'S BATTLE STATUS?
TOOTH AND CLAW.
SSHWINT
SWIT
SERIOUSLY?
RIGHT?
C'MON. WE'RE GOING TO GET TO THE BOTTOM OF THIS.
MMMMAYBE WE NEED TO LOOK AROUND A LITTLE FIRST.
GET A HANDLE ON THIS PLACE..
MAKE SURE WE SEE EVERYTHING WE NEED TO.

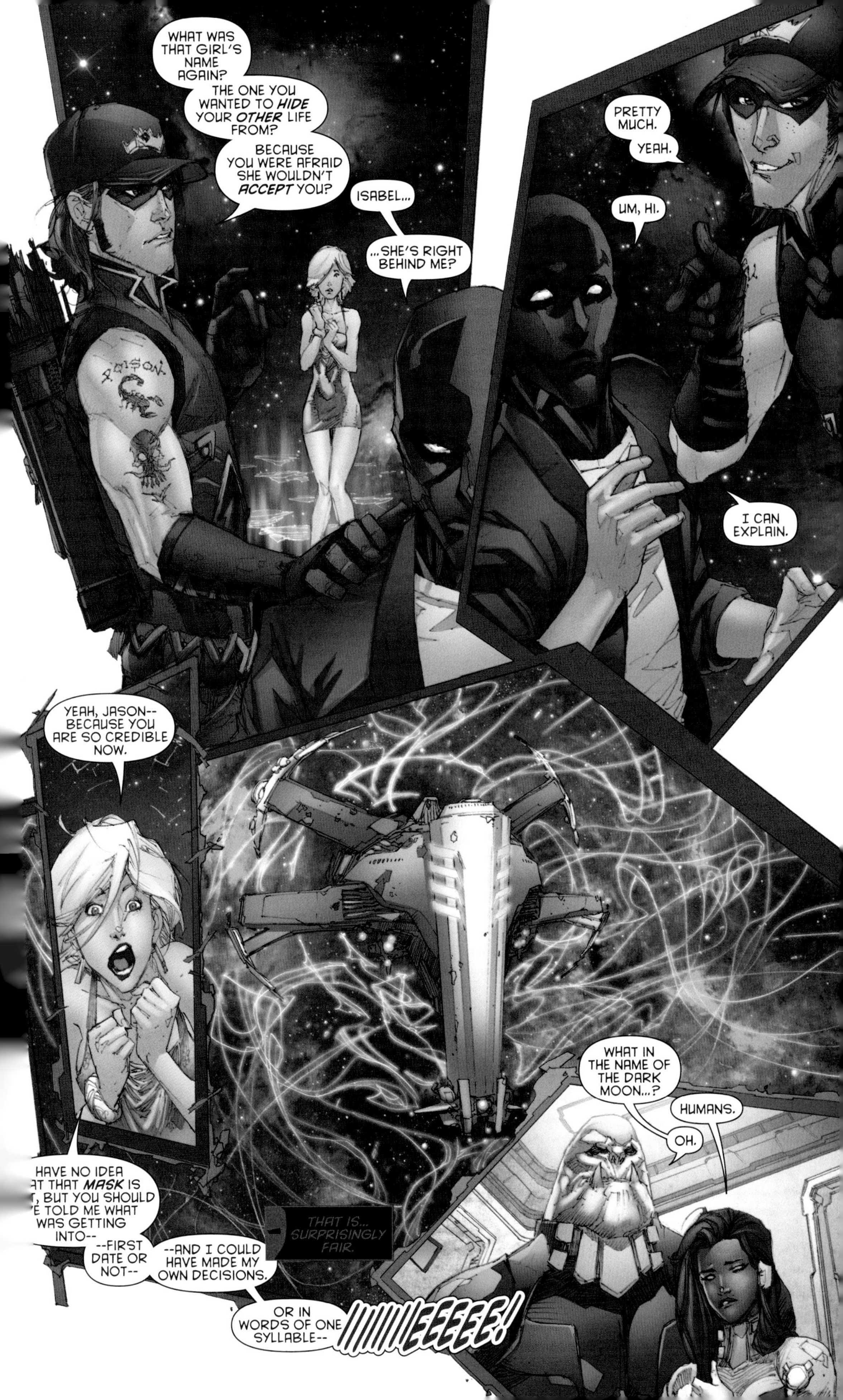
WHAT WAS THAT GIRL'S NAME AGAIN?
THE ONE YOU WANTED TO *HIDE* YOUR *OTHER* LIFE FROM?
BECAUSE YOU WERE AFRAID SHE WOULDN'T *ACCEPT* YOU?
ISABEL...
...SHE'S RIGHT BEHIND ME?
PRETTY MUCH.
YEAH.
UM, HI.
I CAN EXPLAIN.
YEAH, JASON-- BECAUSE YOU ARE SO CREDIBLE NOW.
HAVE NO IDEA AT THAT *MASK* IS T, BUT YOU SHOULD E TOLD ME WHAT WAS GETTING INTO--
--FIRST DATE OR NOT--
--AND I COULD HAVE MADE MY OWN DECISIONS.
THAT IS... SURPRISINGLY FAIR.
WHAT IN THE NAME OF THE DARK MOON...?
HUMANS.
OH.
OR IN WORDS OF ONE SYLLABLE--
IIIIIIIEEEEEE!

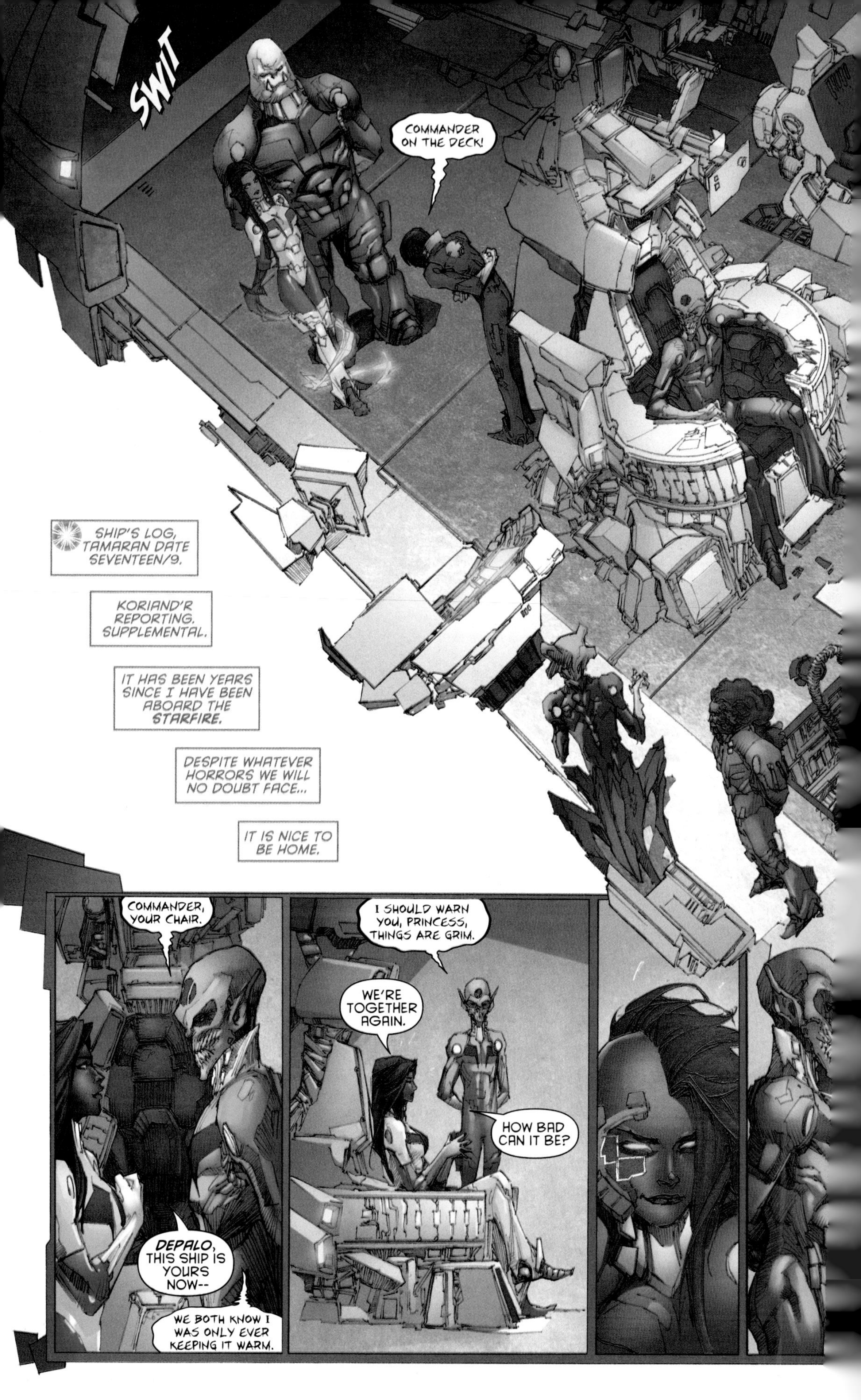
SWIT
COMMANDER ON THE DECK!
SHIP'S LOG, TAMARAN DATE SEVENTEEN/9.
KORIAND'R REPORTING. SUPPLEMENTAL.
IT HAS BEEN YEARS SINCE I HAVE BEEN ABOARD THE STARFIRE.
DESPITE WHATEVER HORRORS WE WILL NO DOUBT FACE...
IT IS NICE TO BE HOME.
COMMANDER, YOUR CHAIR.
DEPALO, THIS SHIP IS YOURS NOW--
WE BOTH KNOW I WAS ONLY EVER KEEPING IT WARM.
I SHOULD WARN YOU, PRINCESS, THINGS ARE GRIM.
WE'RE TOGETHER AGAIN.
HOW BAD CAN IT BE?

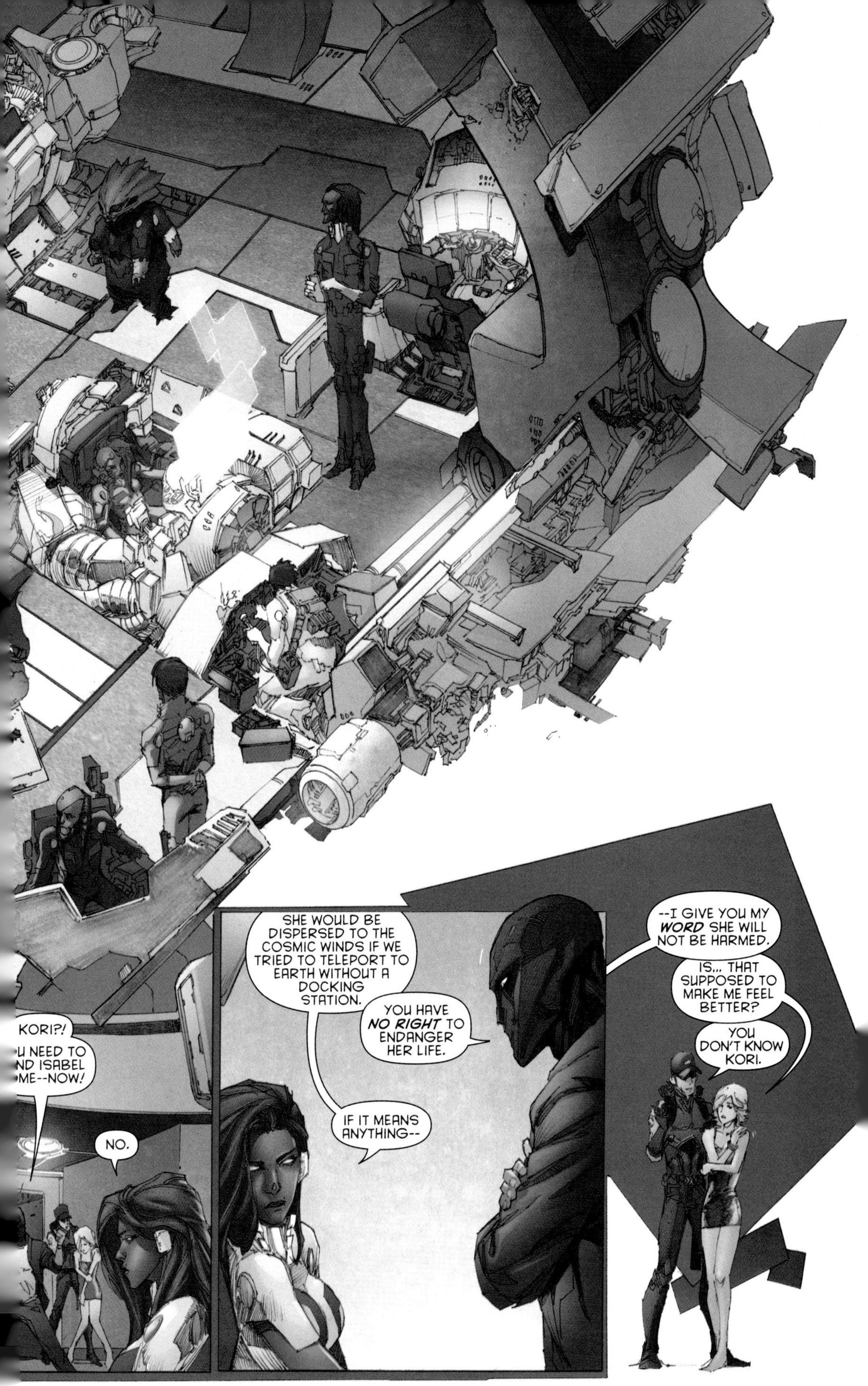
KORI?!
U NEED TO
ND ISABEL
OME--NOW!
NO.
SHE WOULD BE DISPERSED TO THE COSMIC WINDS IF WE TRIED TO TELEPORT TO EARTH WITHOUT A DOCKING STATION.
YOU HAVE NO RIGHT TO ENDANGER HER LIFE.
IF IT MEANS ANYTHING--
--I GIVE YOU MY WORD SHE WILL NOT BE HARMED.
IS... THAT SUPPOSED TO MAKE ME FEEL BETTER?
YOU DON'T KNOW KORI.

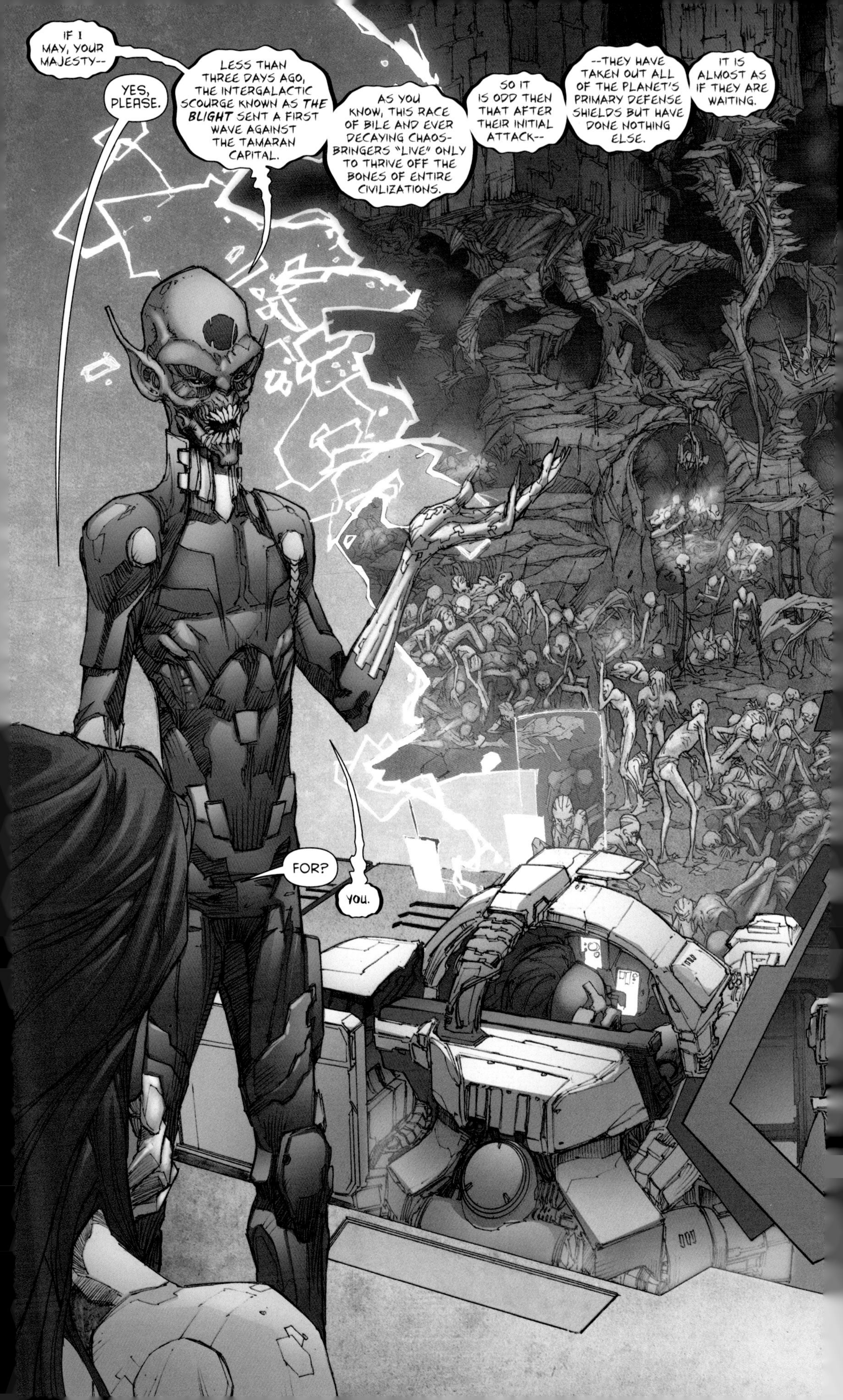
IF I MAY, YOUR MAJESTY--
YES, PLEASE.
LESS THAN THREE DAYS AGO, THE INTERGALACTIC SCOURGE KNOWN AS *THE BLIGHT* SENT A FIRST WAVE AGAINST THE TAMARAN CAPITAL.
AS YOU KNOW, THIS RACE OF BILE AND EVER DECAYING CHAOS-BRINGERS "LIVE" ONLY TO THRIVE OFF THE BONES OF ENTIRE CIVILIZATIONS.
SO IT IS ODD THEN THAT AFTER THEIR INITIAL ATTACK--
--THEY HAVE TAKEN OUT ALL OF THE PLANET'S PRIMARY DEFENSE SHIELDS BUT HAVE DONE NOTHING ELSE.
IT IS ALMOST AS IF THEY ARE WAITING.
FOR?
YOU.

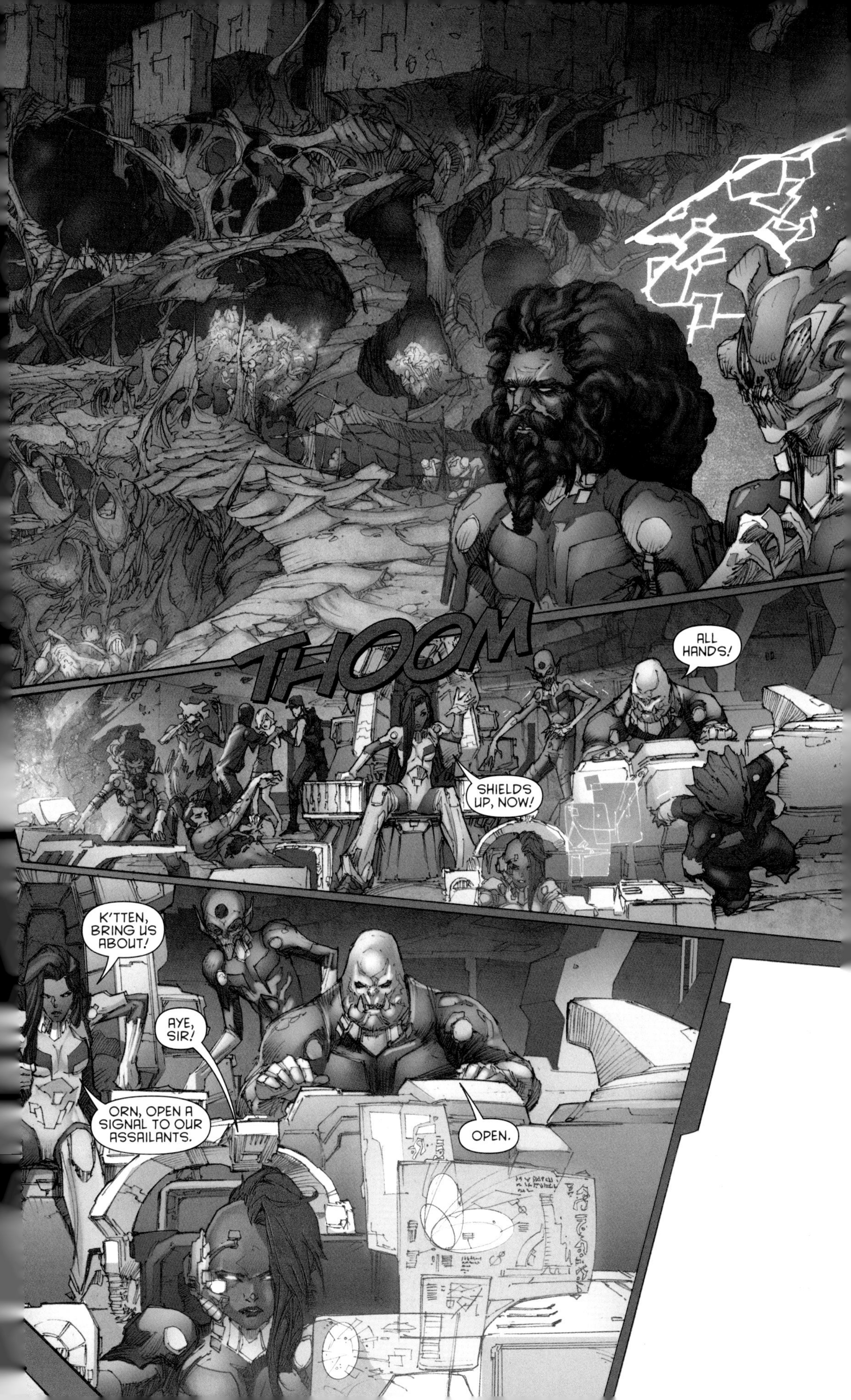
THOOM
ALL HANDS!
SHIELDS UP, NOW!
K'TTEN, BRING US ABOUT!
AYE, SIR!
ORN, OPEN A SIGNAL TO OUR ASSAILANTS.
OPEN.

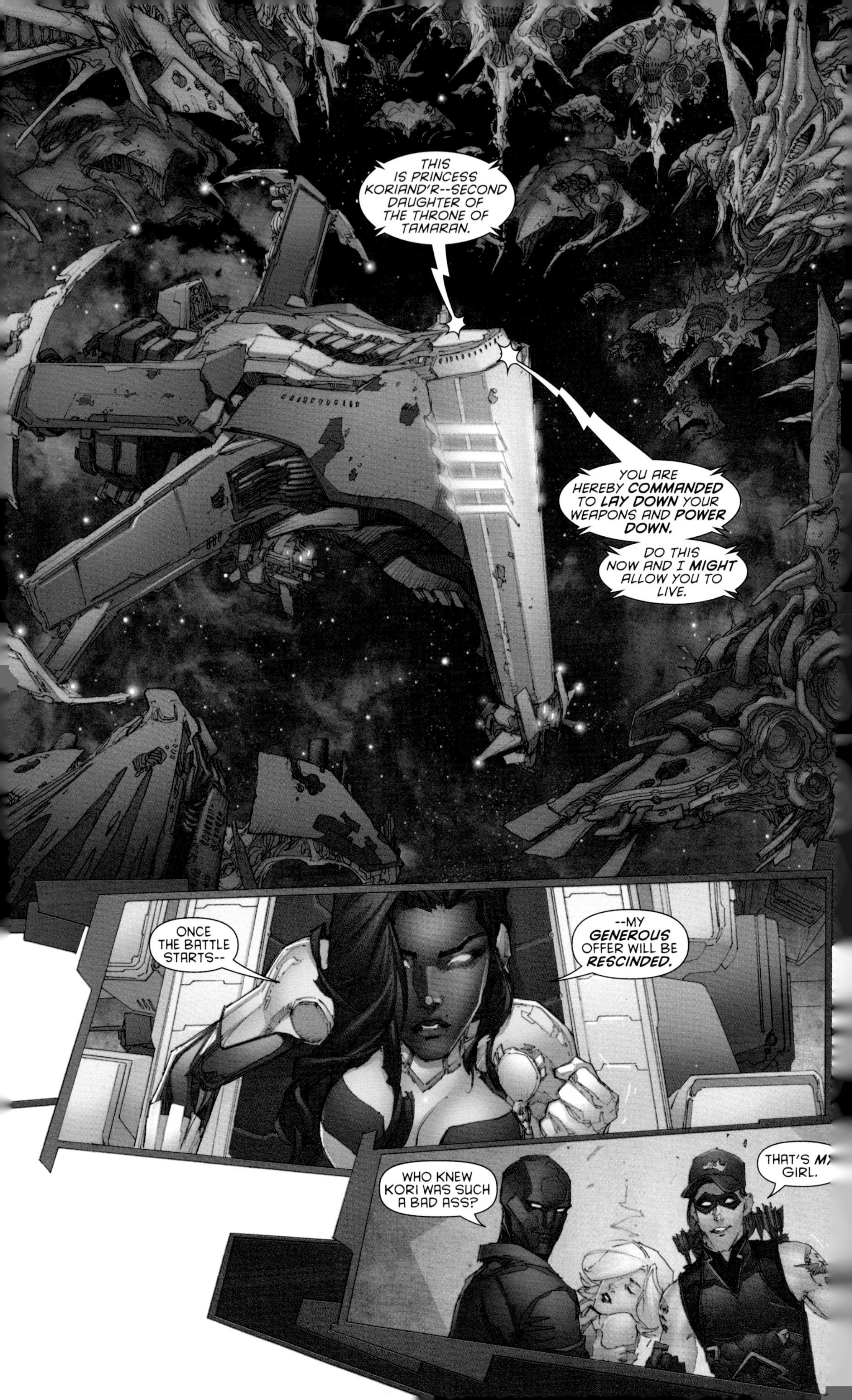
THIS IS PRINCESS KORIAND'R--SECOND DAUGHTER OF THE THRONE OF TAMARAN.
YOU ARE HEREBY COMMANDED TO LAY DOWN YOUR WEAPONS AND POWER DOWN.
DO THIS NOW AND I MIGHT ALLOW YOU TO LIVE.
ONCE THE BATTLE STARTS--
--MY GENEROUS OFFER WILL BE RESCINDED.
WHO KNEW KORI WAS SUCH A BAD ASS?
THAT'S MY GIRL.

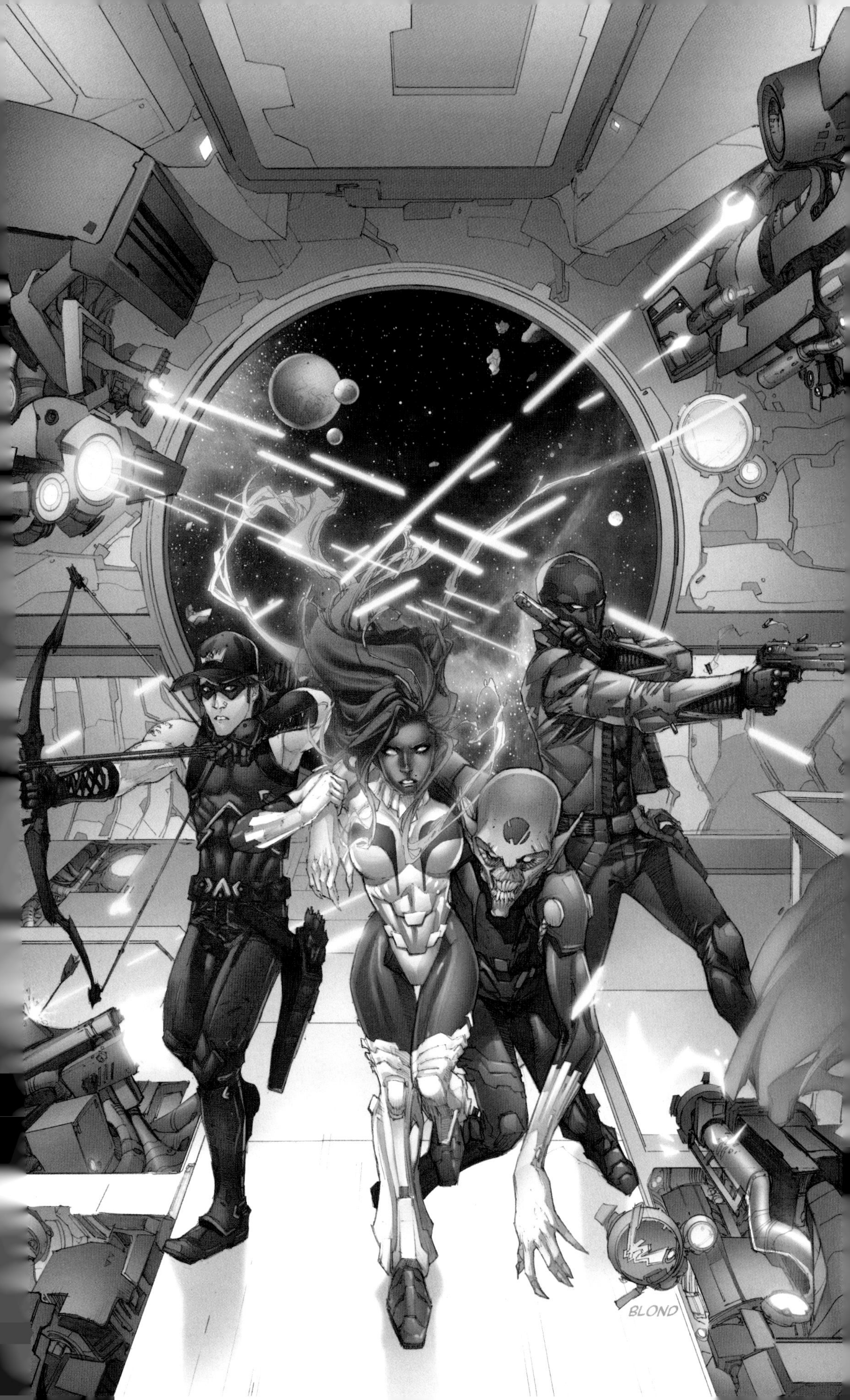
BLOND

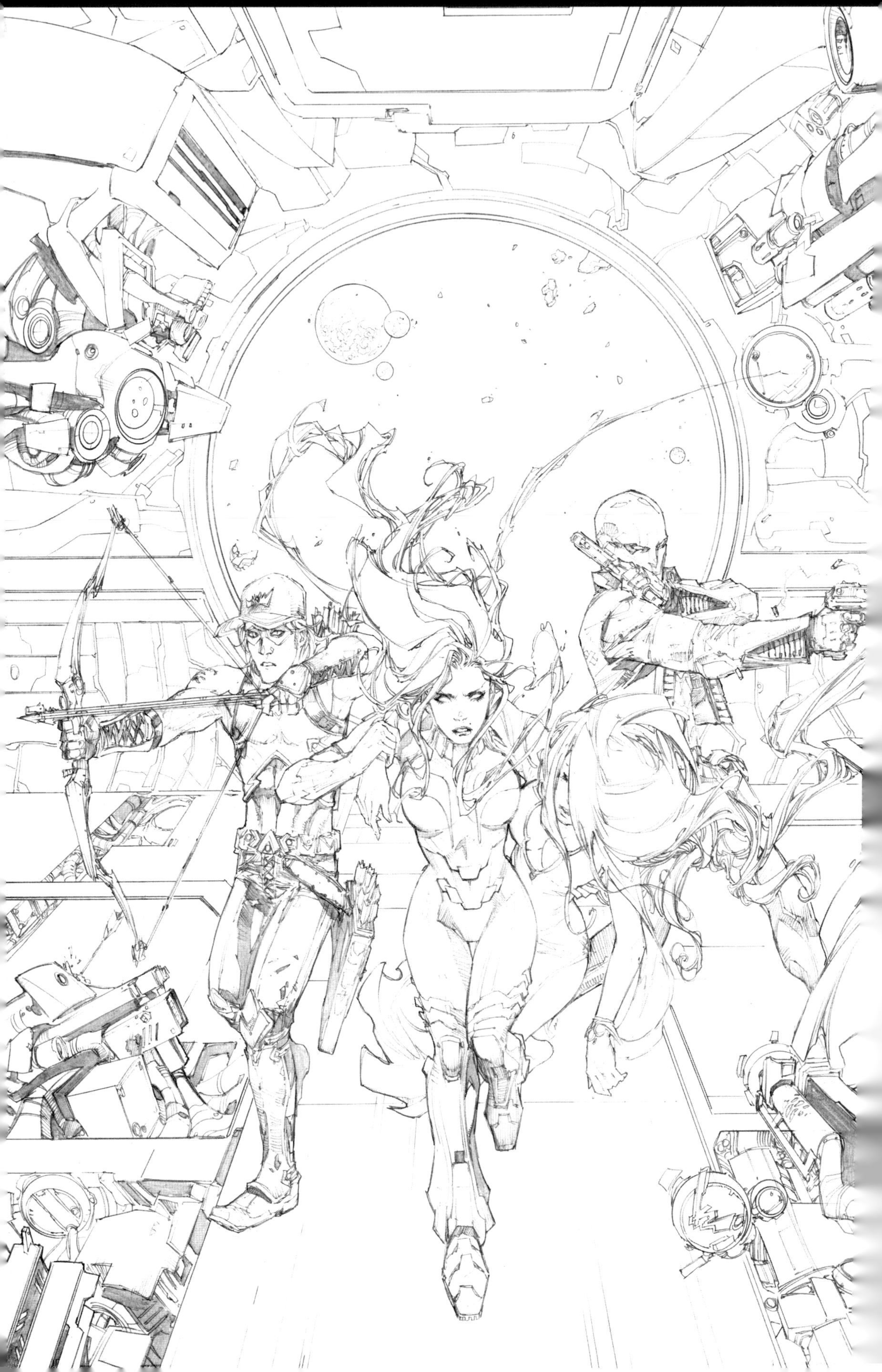

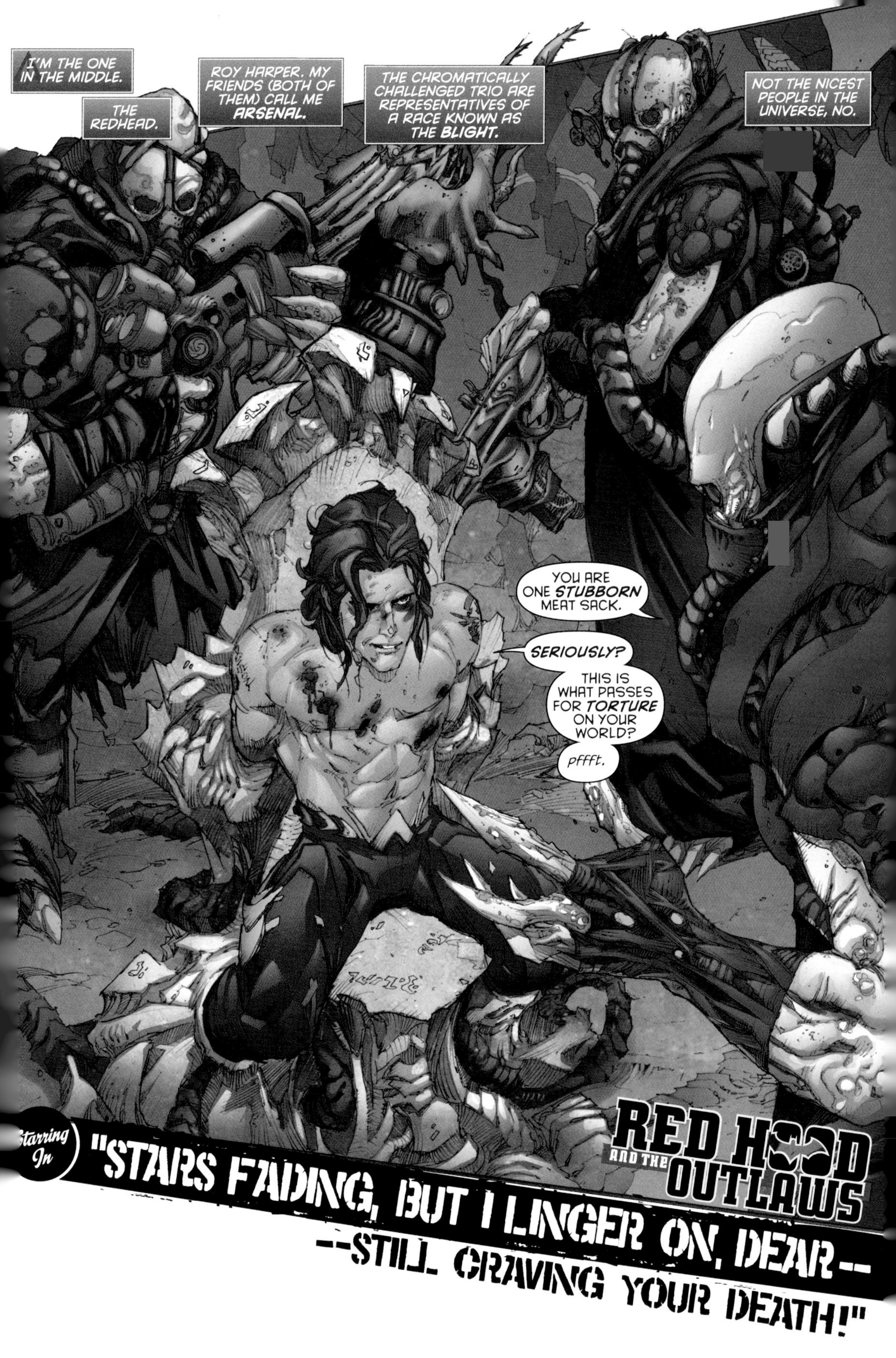
I'M THE ONE IN THE MIDDLE.
THE REDHEAD.
ROY HARPER. MY FRIENDS (BOTH OF THEM) CALL ME ARSENAL.
THE CHROMATICALLY CHALLENGED TRIO ARE REPRESENTATIVES OF A RACE KNOWN AS THE BLIGHT.
NOT THE NICEST PEOPLE IN THE UNIVERSE, NO.
YOU ARE ONE STUBBORN MEAT SACK.
SERIOUSLY?
THIS IS WHAT PASSES FOR TORTURE ON YOUR WORLD?
pffft.
Starring In
RED HOOD AND THE OUTLAWS
"STARS FADING, BUT I LINGER ON, DEAR--
--STILL CRAVING YOUR DEATH!"

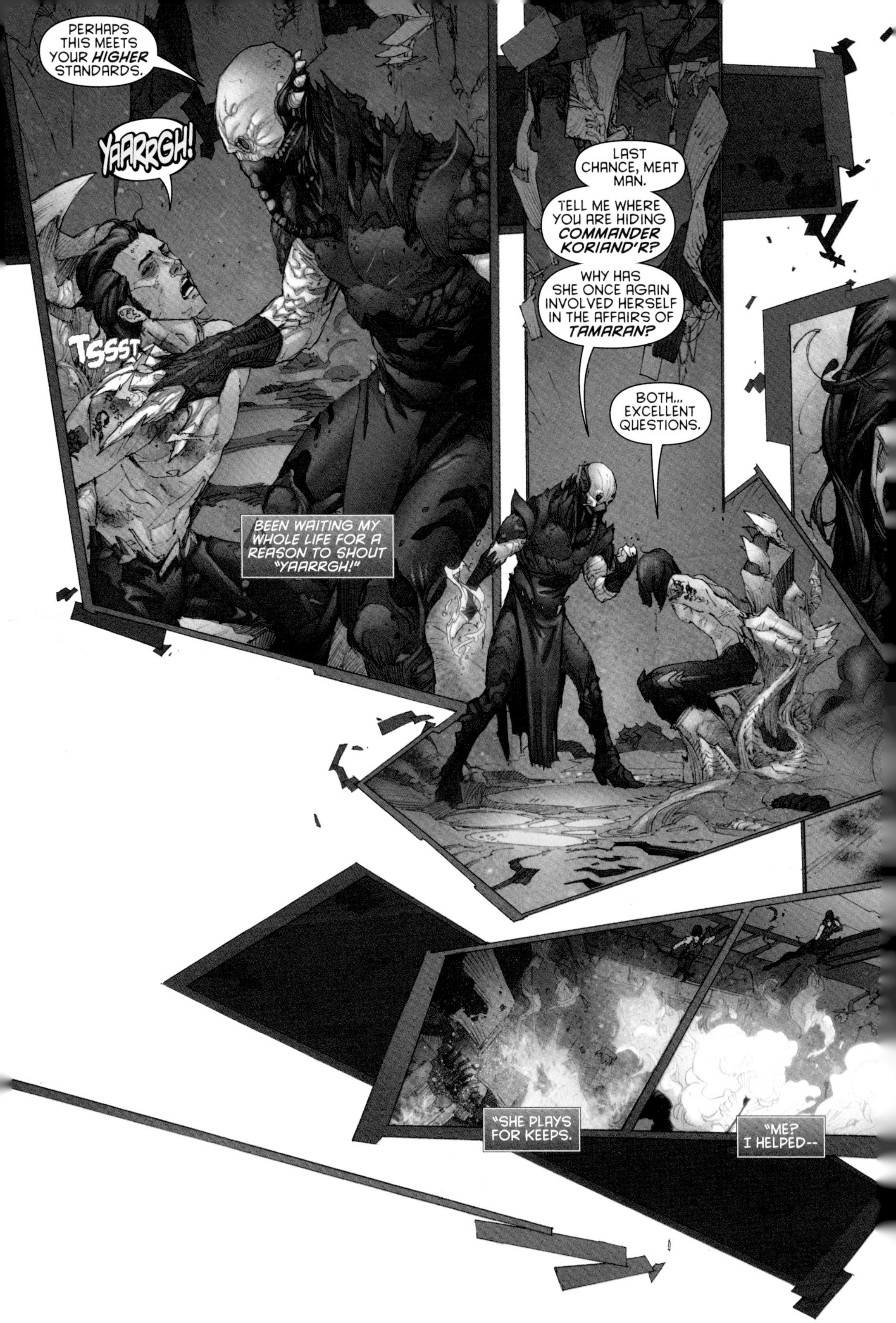
PERHAPS THIS MEETS YOUR *HIGHER* STANDARDS.
YAARRGH!
TSSST
BEEN WAITING MY WHOLE LIFE FOR A REASON TO SHOUT "YAARRGH!"
LAST CHANCE, MEAT MAN.
TELL ME WHERE YOU ARE HIDING *COMMANDER KORIAND'R?*
WHY HAS SHE ONCE AGAIN INVOLVED HERSELF IN THE AFFAIRS OF *TAMARAN?*
BOTH... EXCELLENT QUESTIONS.
"SHE PLAYS FOR KEEPS.
"ME? I HELPED--

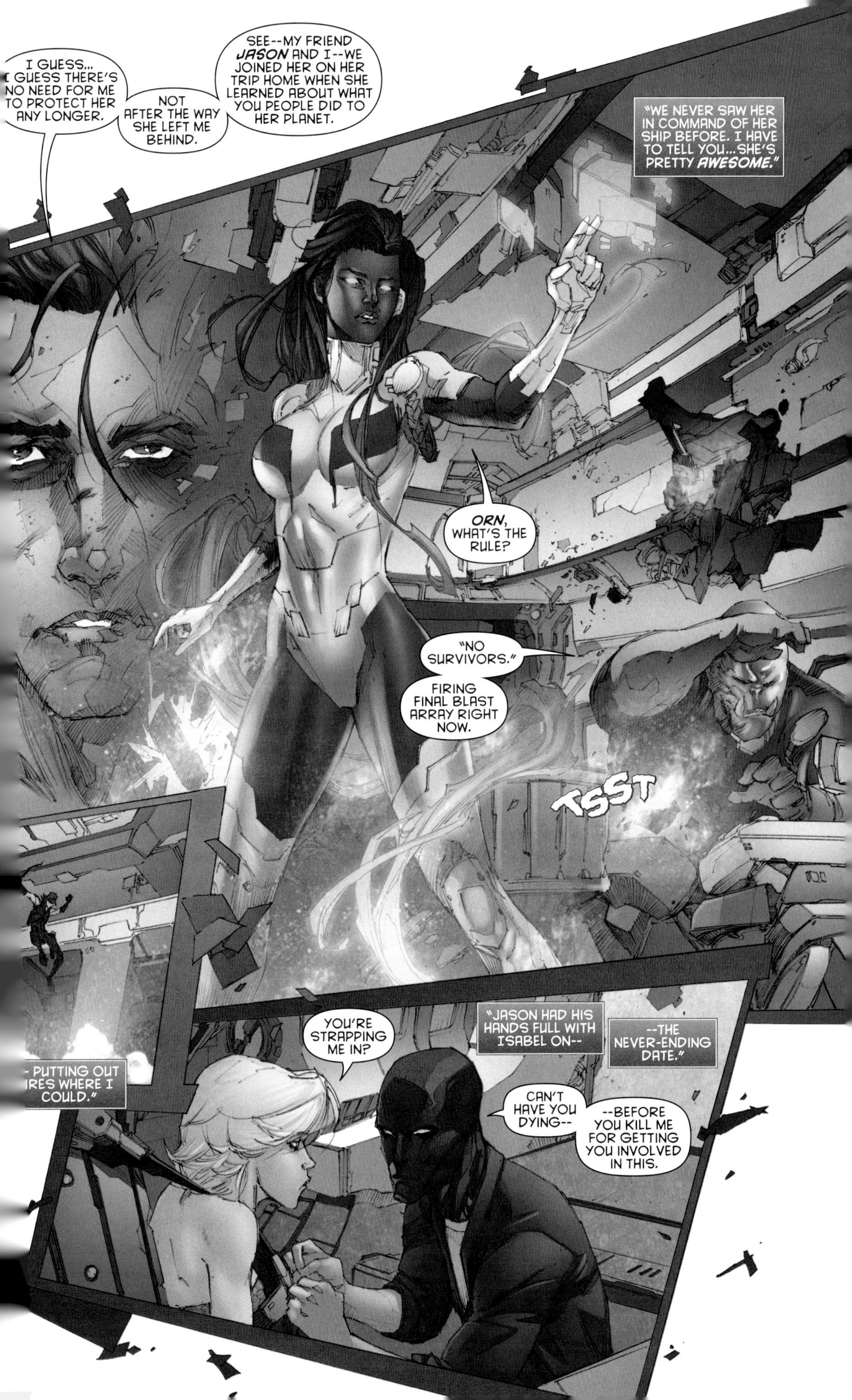
I GUESS...
I GUESS THERE'S NO NEED FOR ME TO PROTECT HER ANY LONGER.
NOT AFTER THE WAY SHE LEFT ME BEHIND.
SEE--MY FRIEND JASON AND I--WE JOINED HER ON HER TRIP HOME WHEN SHE LEARNED ABOUT WHAT YOU PEOPLE DID TO HER PLANET.
"WE NEVER SAW HER IN COMMAND OF HER SHIP BEFORE. I HAVE TO TELL YOU...SHE'S PRETTY AWESOME."
ORN, WHAT'S THE RULE?
"NO SURVIVORS."
FIRING FINAL BLAST ARRAY RIGHT NOW.
TSST
- PUTTING OUT IRES WHERE I COULD."
YOU'RE STRAPPING ME IN?
"JASON HAD HIS HANDS FULL WITH ISABEL ON--
--THE NEVER-ENDING DATE."
CAN'T HAVE YOU DYING--
--BEFORE YOU KILL ME FOR GETTING YOU INVOLVED IN THIS.

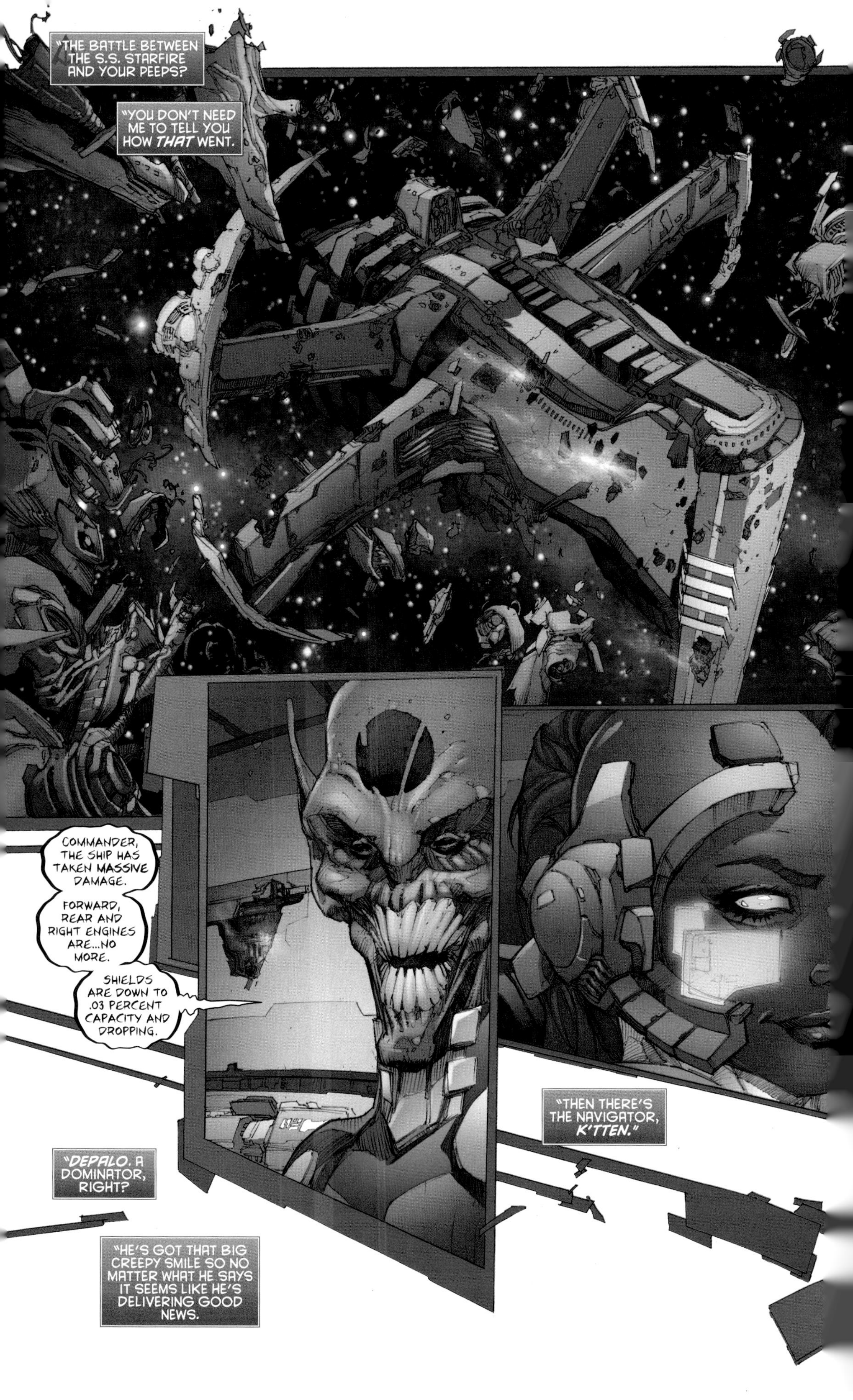
"THE BATTLE BETWEEN THE S.S. STARFIRE AND YOUR PEEPS?
"YOU DON'T NEED ME TO TELL YOU HOW *THAT* WENT.
COMMANDER, THE SHIP HAS TAKEN MASSIVE DAMAGE.
FORWARD, REAR AND RIGHT ENGINES ARE...NO MORE.
SHIELDS ARE DOWN TO .03 PERCENT CAPACITY AND DROPPING.
"THEN THERE'S THE NAVIGATOR, *K'TTEN.*"
"*DEPALO.* A DOMINATOR, RIGHT?
"HE'S GOT THAT BIG CREEPY SMILE SO NO MATTER WHAT HE SAYS IT SEEMS LIKE HE'S DELIVERING GOOD NEWS.

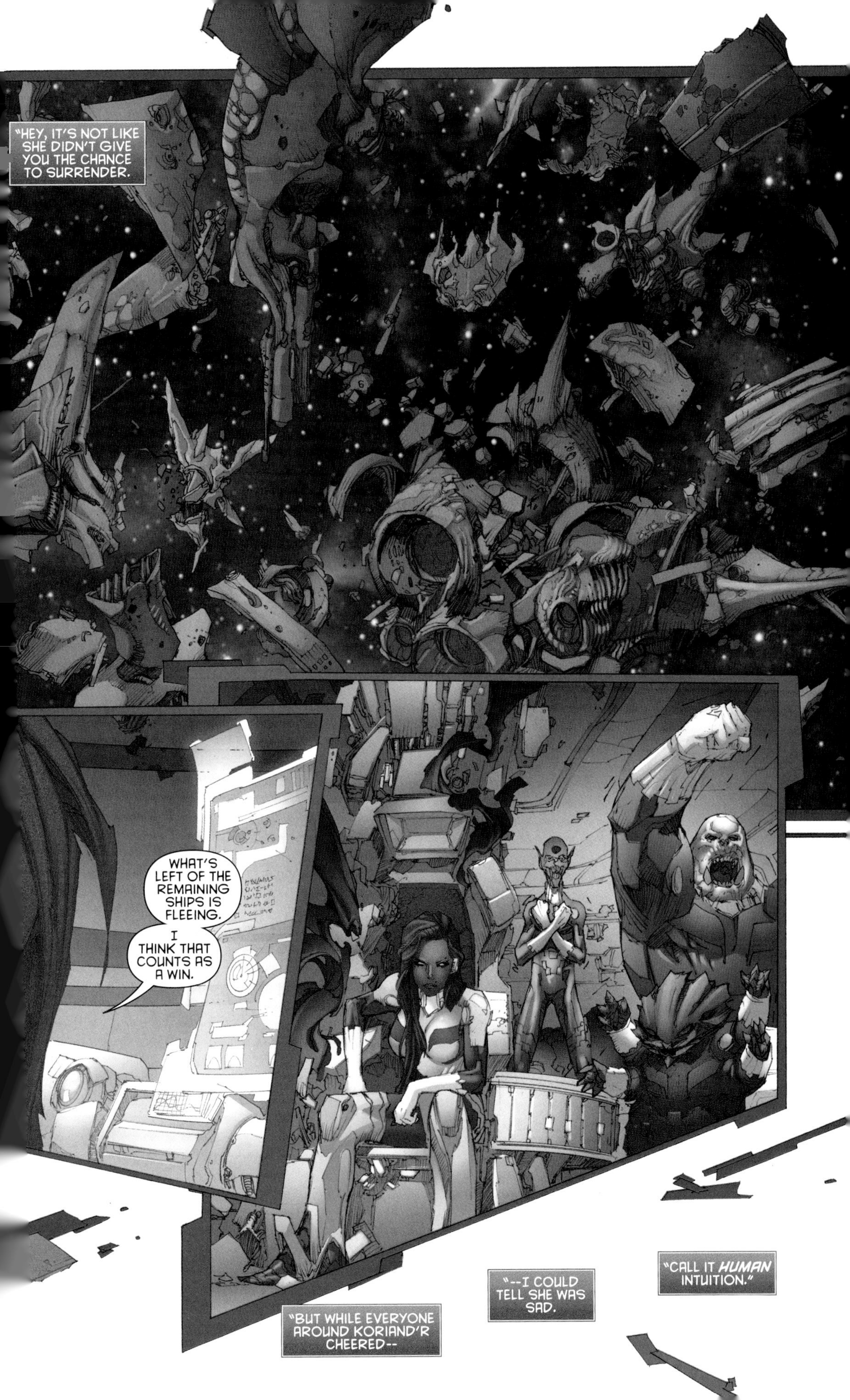
"HEY, IT'S NOT LIKE SHE DIDN'T GIVE YOU THE CHANCE TO SURRENDER.
WHAT'S LEFT OF THE REMAINING SHIPS IS FLEEING.
I THINK THAT COUNTS AS A WIN.
"BUT WHILE EVERYONE AROUND KORIAND'R CHEERED--
"--I COULD TELL SHE WAS SAD.
"CALL IT *HUMAN* INTUITION."

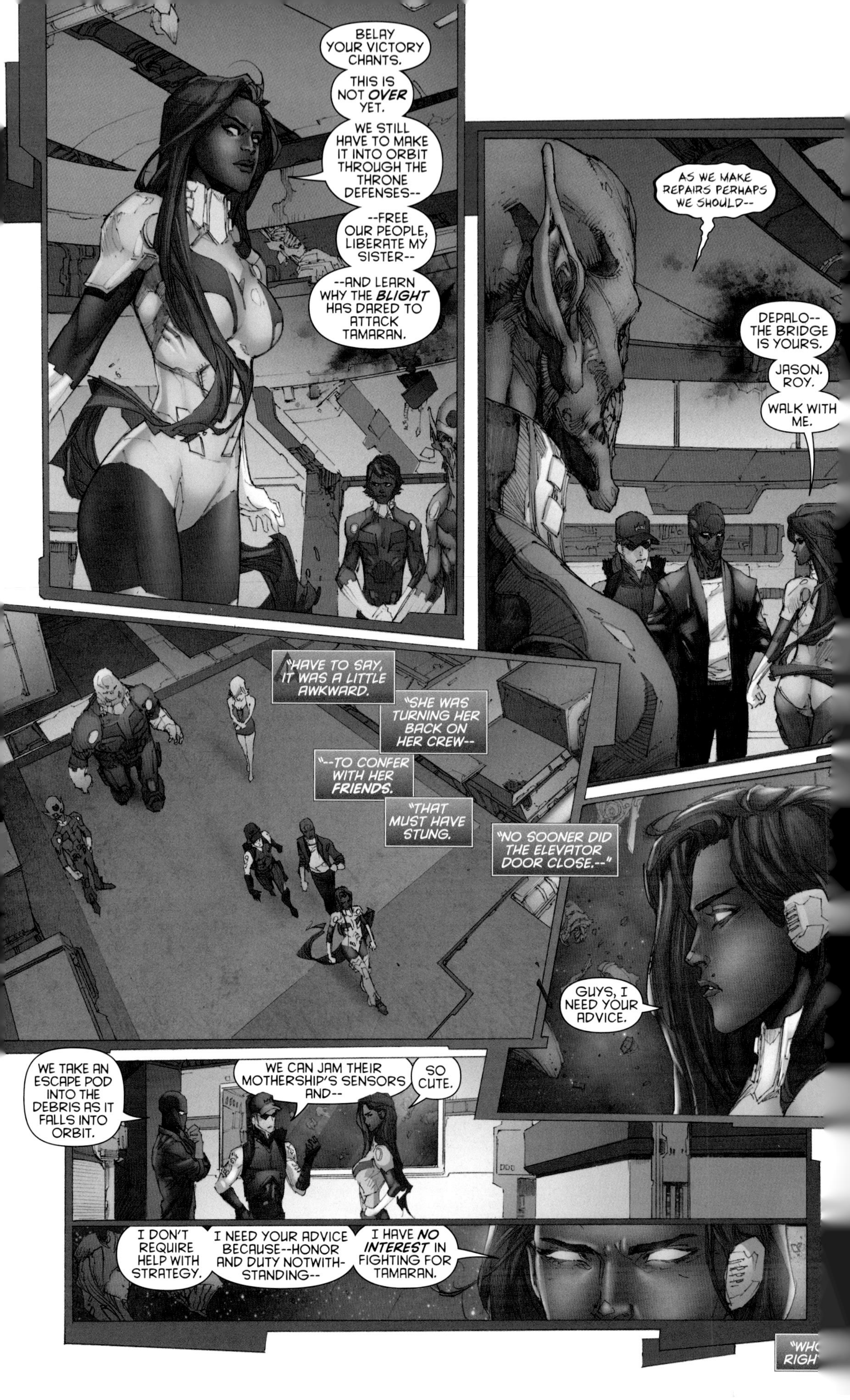
BELAY YOUR VICTORY CHANTS.
THIS IS NOT *OVER* YET.
WE STILL HAVE TO MAKE IT INTO ORBIT THROUGH THE THRONE DEFENSES--
--FREE OUR PEOPLE, LIBERATE MY SISTER--
--AND LEARN WHY THE *BLIGHT* HAS DARED TO ATTACK TAMARAN.
AS WE MAKE REPAIRS PERHAPS WE SHOULD--
DEPALO--THE BRIDGE IS YOURS.
JASON. ROY.
WALK WITH ME.
"HAVE TO SAY, IT WAS A LITTLE AWKWARD.
"SHE WAS TURNING HER BACK ON HER CREW--
"--TO CONFER WITH HER *FRIENDS*.
"THAT MUST HAVE STUNG.
"NO SOONER DID THE ELEVATOR DOOR CLOSE.--"
GUYS, I NEED YOUR ADVICE.
WE TAKE AN ESCAPE POD INTO THE DEBRIS AS IT FALLS INTO ORBIT.
WE CAN JAM THEIR MOTHERSHIP'S SENSORS AND--
SO CUTE.
I DON'T REQUIRE HELP WITH STRATEGY.
I NEED YOUR ADVICE BECAUSE--HONOR AND DUTY NOTWITH-STANDING--
I HAVE *NO INTEREST* IN FIGHTING FOR TAMARAN.

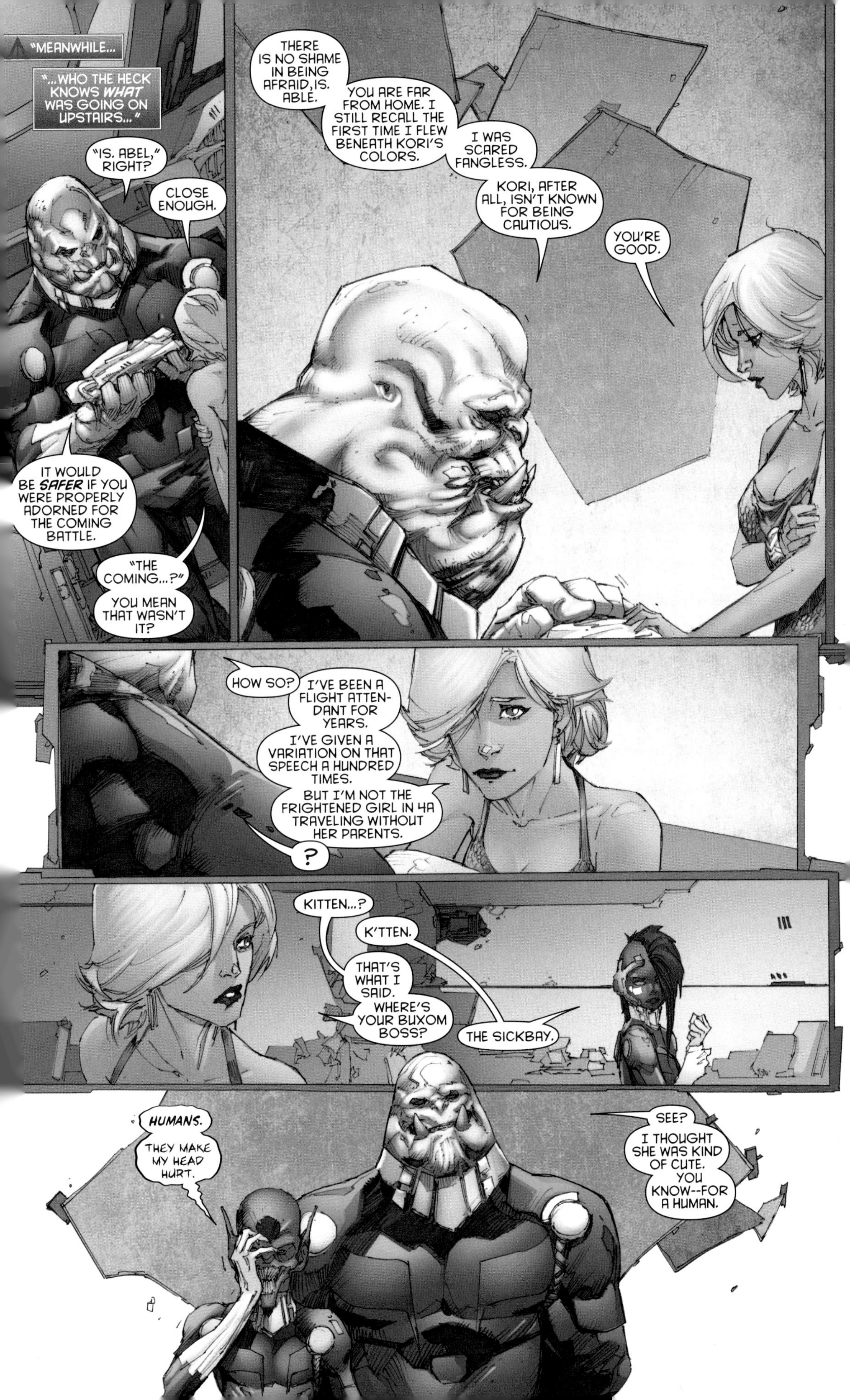
"MEANWHILE...
"...WHO THE HECK KNOWS *WHAT* WAS GOING ON UPSTAIRS..."
"IS. ABEL," RIGHT?
CLOSE ENOUGH.
IT WOULD BE *SAFER* IF YOU WERE PROPERLY ADORNED FOR THE COMING BATTLE.
"THE COMING...?"
YOU MEAN THAT WASN'T IT?
THERE IS NO SHAME IN BEING AFRAID, IS. ABLE.
YOU ARE FAR FROM HOME. I STILL RECALL THE FIRST TIME I FLEW BENEATH KORI'S COLORS.
I WAS SCARED FANGLESS.
KORI, AFTER ALL, ISN'T KNOWN FOR BEING CAUTIOUS.
YOU'RE GOOD.
HOW SO?
I'VE BEEN A FLIGHT ATTEN-DANT FOR YEARS.
I'VE GIVEN A VARIATION ON THAT SPEECH A HUNDRED TIMES.
BUT I'M NOT THE FRIGHTENED GIRL IN 4A TRAVELING WITHOUT HER PARENTS.
?
KITTEN...?
K'TTEN.
THAT'S WHAT I SAID. WHERE'S YOUR BUXOM BOSS?
THE SICKBAY.
HUMANS.
THEY MAKE MY HEAD HURT.
SEE?
I THOUGHT SHE WAS KIND OF CUTE. YOU KNOW--FOR A HUMAN.

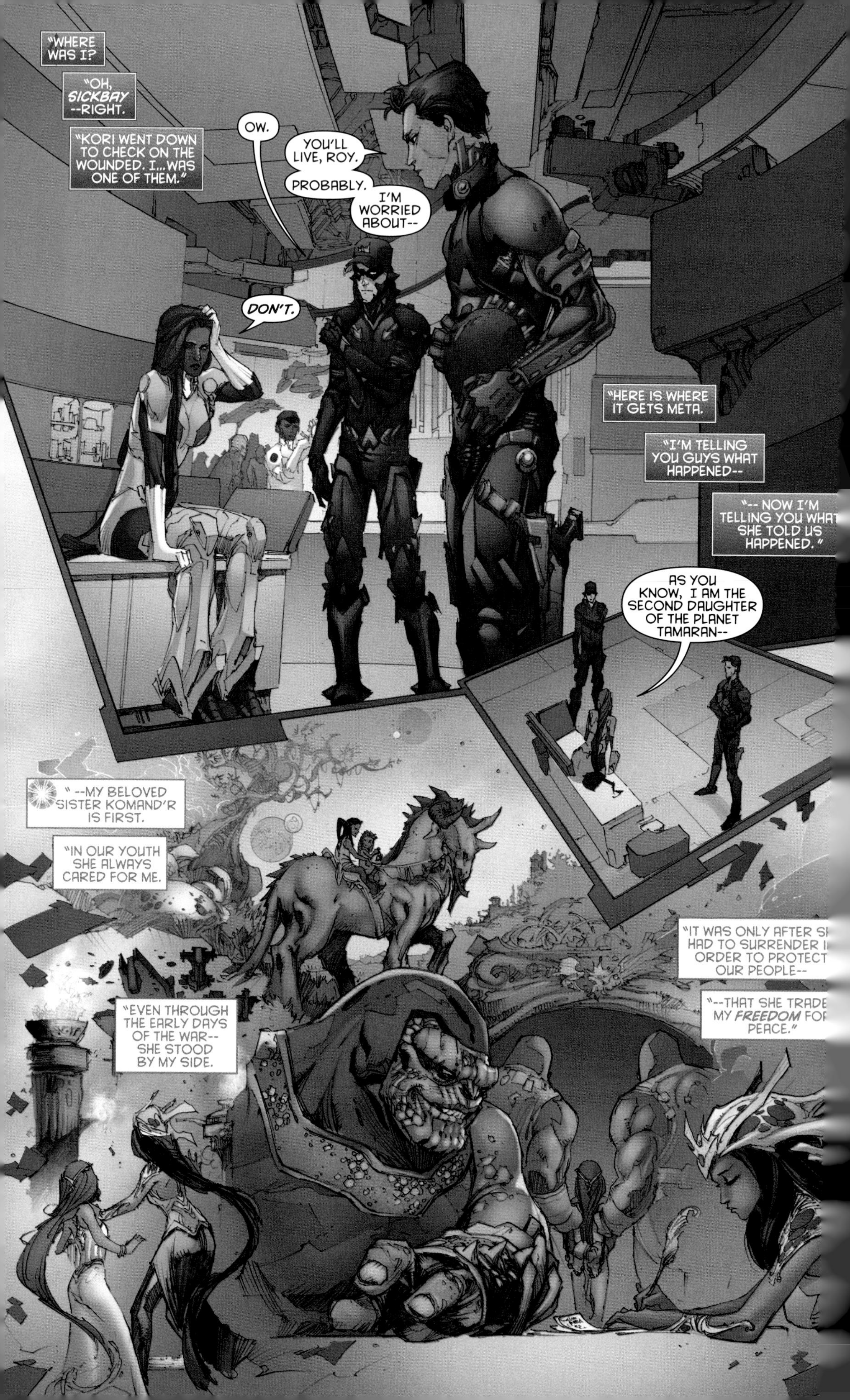
"WHERE WAS I?
"OH, SICKBAY --RIGHT.
"KORI WENT DOWN TO CHECK ON THE WOUNDED. I...WAS ONE OF THEM."
OW.
YOU'LL LIVE, ROY.
PROBABLY.
I'M WORRIED ABOUT--
DON'T.
"HERE IS WHERE IT GETS META.
"I'M TELLING YOU GUYS WHAT HAPPENED--
"-- NOW I'M TELLING YOU WHAT SHE TOLD US HAPPENED."
AS YOU KNOW, I AM THE SECOND DAUGHTER OF THE PLANET TAMARAN--
"--MY BELOVED SISTER KOMAND'R IS FIRST.
"IN OUR YOUTH SHE ALWAYS CARED FOR ME.
"EVEN THROUGH THE EARLY DAYS OF THE WAR-- SHE STOOD BY MY SIDE.
"IT WAS ONLY AFTER SH HAD TO SURRENDER I ORDER TO PROTECT OUR PEOPLE--
"--THAT SHE TRADE MY FREEDOM FOR PEACE."

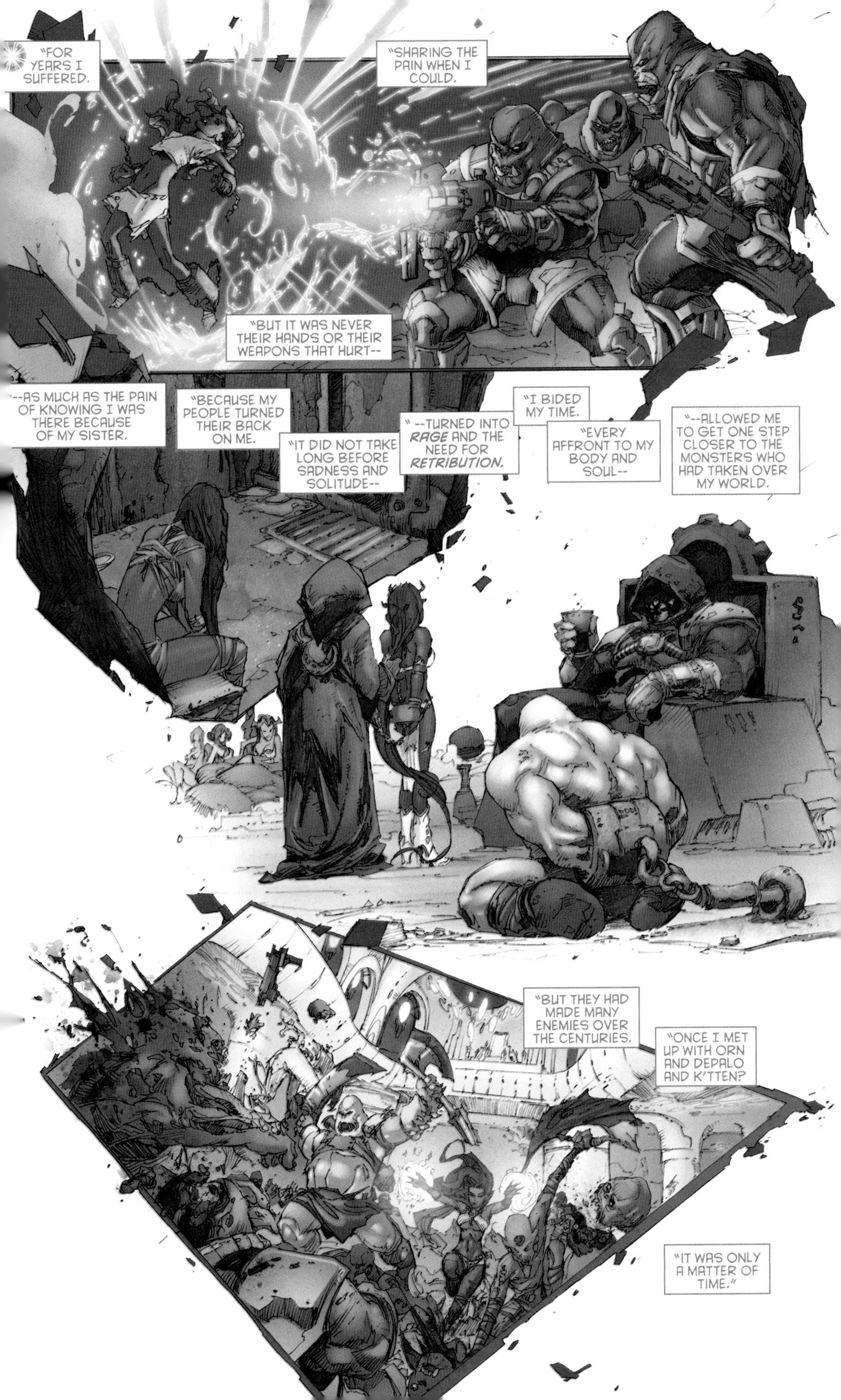
"FOR YEARS I SUFFERED.
"SHARING THE PAIN WHEN I COULD.
"BUT IT WAS NEVER THEIR HANDS OR THEIR WEAPONS THAT HURT--
--AS MUCH AS THE PAIN OF KNOWING I WAS THERE BECAUSE OF MY SISTER.
"BECAUSE MY PEOPLE TURNED THEIR BACK ON ME.
"IT DID NOT TAKE LONG BEFORE SADNESS AND SOLITUDE--
" --TURNED INTO RAGE AND THE NEED FOR RETRIBUTION.
"I BIDED MY TIME.
"EVERY AFFRONT TO MY BODY AND SOUL--
"--ALLOWED ME TO GET ONE STEP CLOSER TO THE MONSTERS WHO HAD TAKEN OVER MY WORLD.
"BUT THEY HAD MADE MANY ENEMIES OVER THE CENTURIES.
"ONCE I MET UP WITH ORN AND DEPALO AND K'TTEN?
"IT WAS ONLY A MATTER OF TIME."

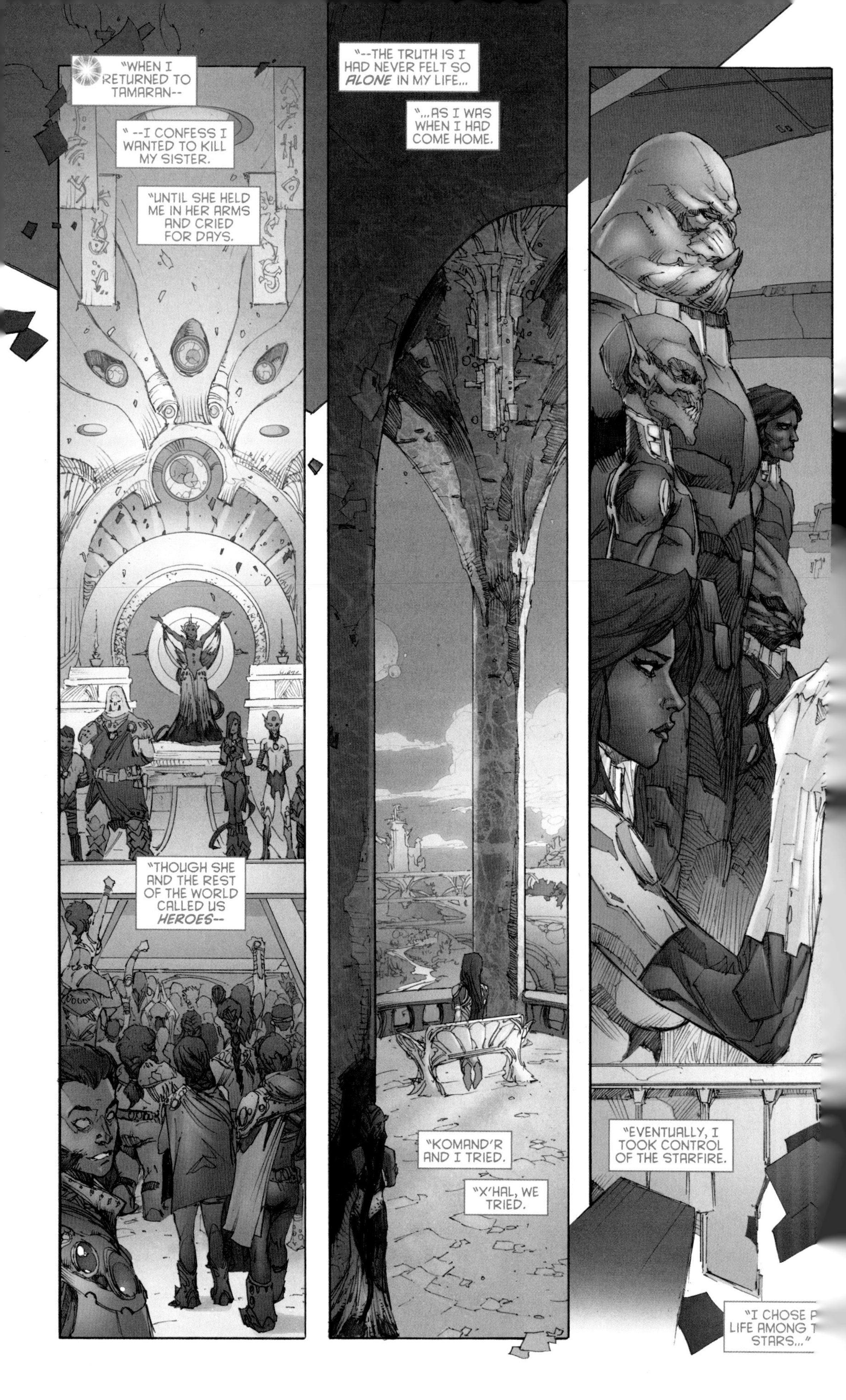
"WHEN I RETURNED TO TAMARAN--
"--I CONFESS I WANTED TO KILL MY SISTER.
"UNTIL SHE HELD ME IN HER ARMS AND CRIED FOR DAYS.
"THOUGH SHE AND THE REST OF THE WORLD CALLED US *HEROES*--
"--THE TRUTH IS I HAD NEVER FELT SO *ALONE* IN MY LIFE...
"...AS I WAS WHEN I HAD COME HOME.
"KOMAND'R AND I TRIED.
"X'HAL, WE TRIED.
"EVENTUALLY, I TOOK CONTROL OF THE STARFIRE.
"I CHOSE LIFE AMONG STARS..."

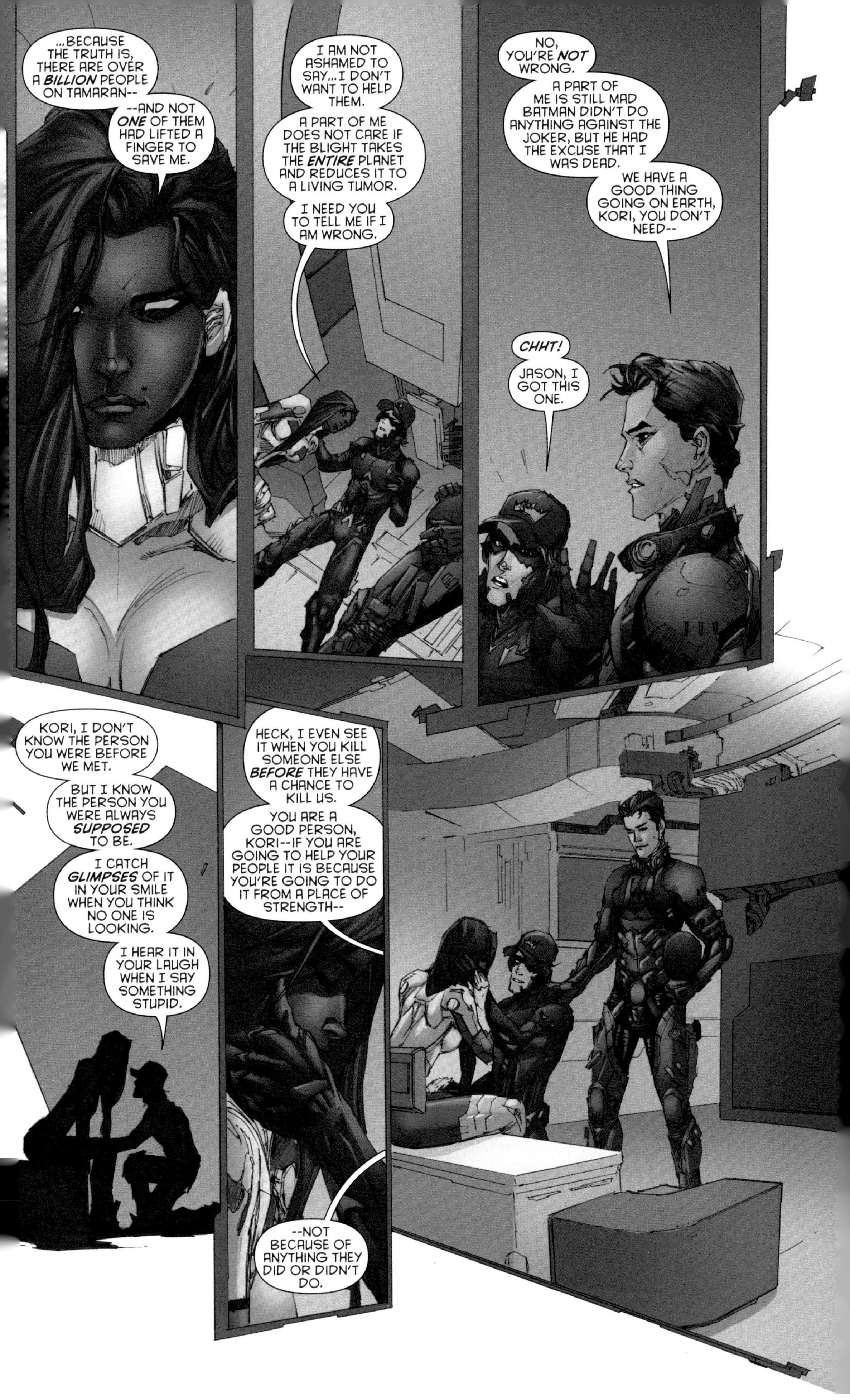
...BECAUSE THE TRUTH IS, THERE ARE OVER A BILLION PEOPLE ON TAMARAN--
--AND NOT ONE OF THEM HAD LIFTED A FINGER TO SAVE ME.
I AM NOT ASHAMED TO SAY...I DON'T WANT TO HELP THEM.
A PART OF ME DOES NOT CARE IF THE BLIGHT TAKES THE ENTIRE PLANET AND REDUCES IT TO A LIVING TUMOR.
I NEED YOU TO TELL ME IF I AM WRONG.
NO, YOU'RE NOT WRONG.
A PART OF ME IS STILL MAD BATMAN DIDN'T DO ANYTHING AGAINST THE JOKER, BUT HE HAD THE EXCUSE THAT I WAS DEAD.
WE HAVE A GOOD THING GOING ON EARTH, KORI, YOU DON'T NEED--
CHHT!
JASON, I GOT THIS ONE.
KORI, I DON'T KNOW THE PERSON YOU WERE BEFORE WE MET.
BUT I KNOW THE PERSON YOU WERE ALWAYS SUPPOSED TO BE.
I CATCH GLIMPSES OF IT IN YOUR SMILE WHEN YOU THINK NO ONE IS LOOKING.
I HEAR IT IN YOUR LAUGH WHEN I SAY SOMETHING STUPID.
HECK, I EVEN SEE IT WHEN YOU KILL SOMEONE ELSE BEFORE THEY HAVE A CHANCE TO KILL US.
YOU ARE A GOOD PERSON, KORI--IF YOU ARE GOING TO HELP YOUR PEOPLE IT IS BECAUSE YOU'RE GOING TO DO IT FROM A PLACE OF STRENGTH--
--NOT BECAUSE OF ANYTHING THEY DID OR DIDN'T DO.

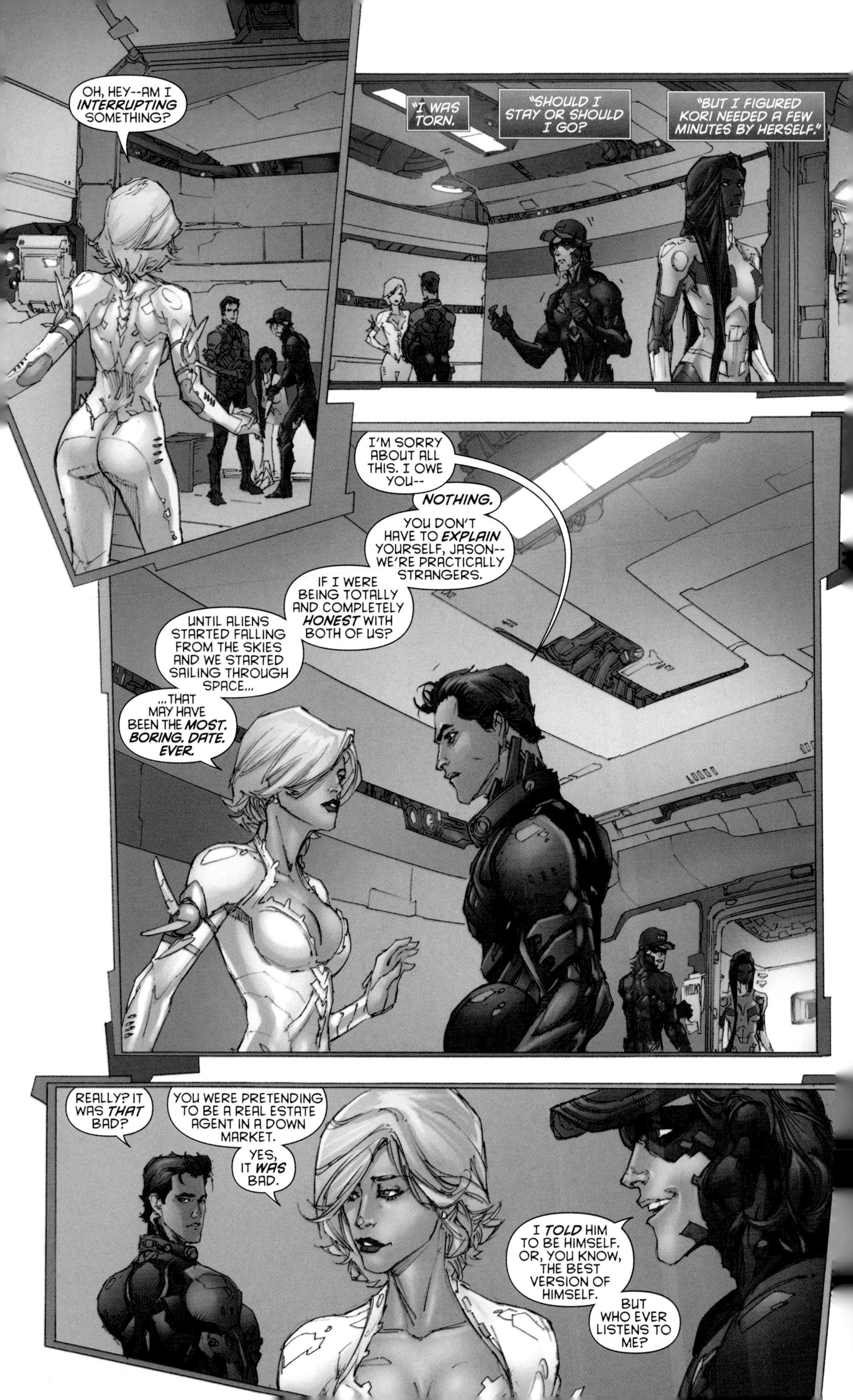
OH, HEY--AM I INTERRUPTING SOMETHING?
"I WAS TORN.
"SHOULD I STAY OR SHOULD I GO?
"BUT I FIGURED KORI NEEDED A FEW MINUTES BY HERSELF."
I'M SORRY ABOUT ALL THIS. I OWE YOU--
NOTHING.
YOU DON'T HAVE TO EXPLAIN YOURSELF, JASON-- WE'RE PRACTICALLY STRANGERS.
IF I WERE BEING TOTALLY AND COMPLETELY HONEST WITH BOTH OF US?
UNTIL ALIENS STARTED FALLING FROM THE SKIES AND WE STARTED SAILING THROUGH SPACE...
...THAT MAY HAVE BEEN THE MOST. BORING. DATE. EVER.
REALLY? IT WAS THAT BAD?
YOU WERE PRETENDING TO BE A REAL ESTATE AGENT IN A DOWN MARKET.
YES, IT WAS BAD.
I TOLD HIM TO BE HIMSELF. OR, YOU KNOW, THE BEST VERSION OF HIMSELF.
BUT WHO EVER LISTENS TO ME?

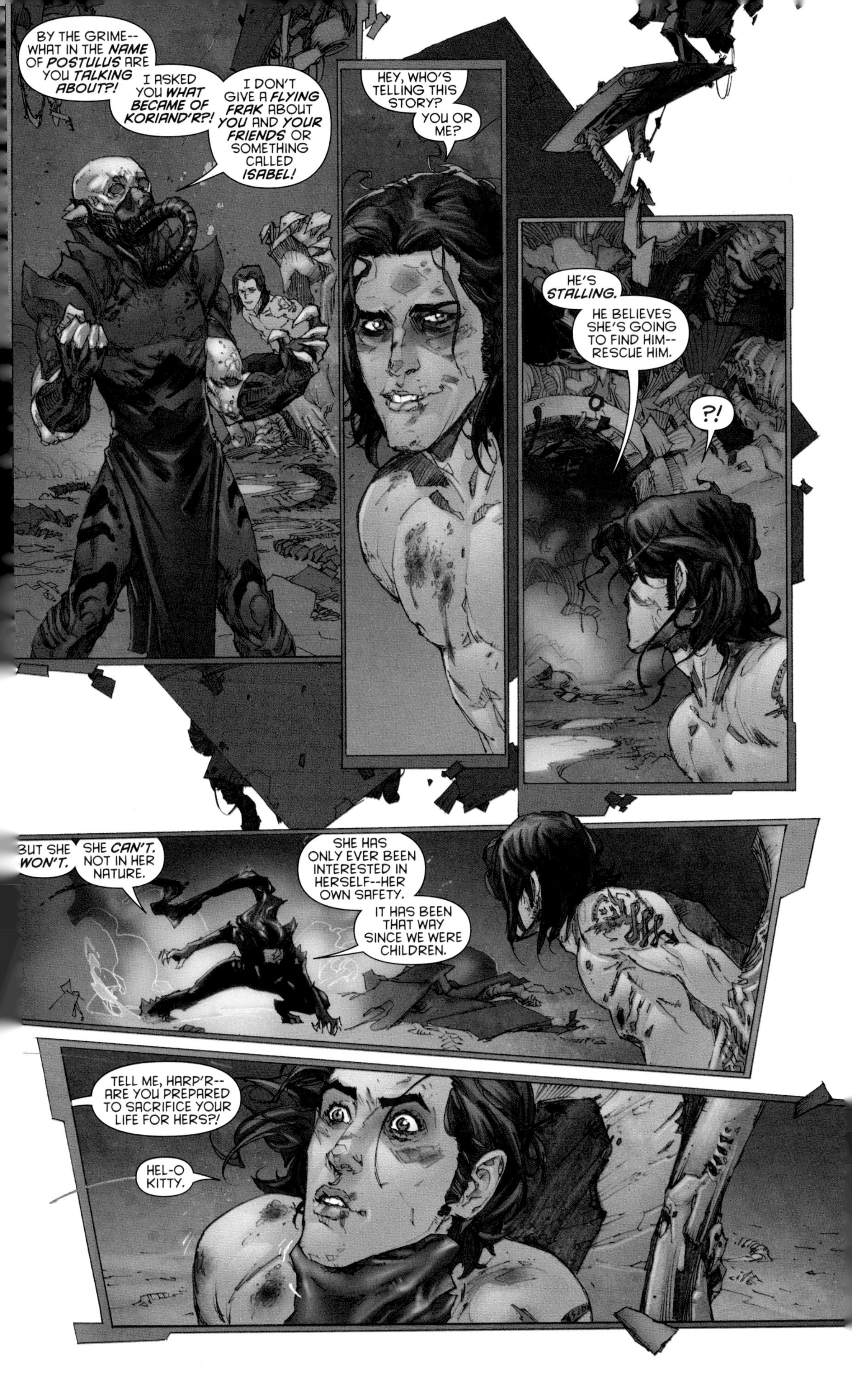

BY THE GRIME--WHAT IN THE NAME OF POSTULUS ARE YOU TALKING ABOUT?!
I ASKED YOU WHAT BECAME OF KORIAND'R?!
I DON'T GIVE A FLYING FRAK ABOUT YOU AND YOUR FRIENDS OR SOMETHING CALLED ISABEL!
HEY, WHO'S TELLING THIS STORY?
YOU OR ME?
HE'S STALLING.
HE BELIEVES SHE'S GOING TO FIND HIM--RESCUE HIM.
?!
BUT SHE WON'T.
SHE CAN'T. NOT IN HER NATURE.
SHE HAS ONLY EVER BEEN INTERESTED IN HERSELF--HER OWN SAFETY.
IT HAS BEEN THAT WAY SINCE WE WERE CHILDREN.
TELL ME, HARP'R--ARE YOU PREPARED TO SACRIFICE YOUR LIFE FOR HERS?!
HEL-O KITTY.

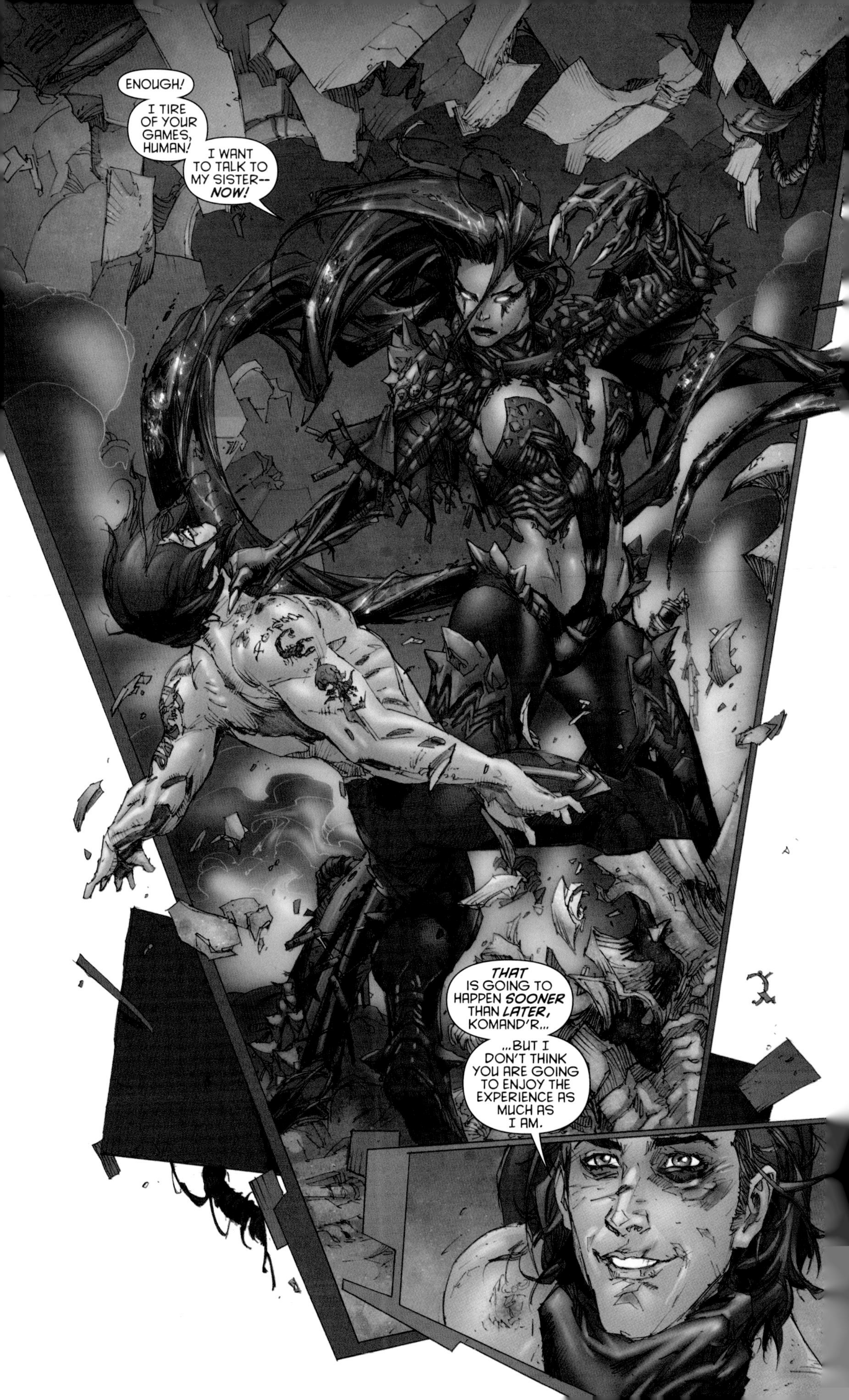
ENOUGH!
I TIRE OF YOUR GAMES, HUMAN!
I WANT TO TALK TO MY SISTER-- NOW!
THAT IS GOING TO HAPPEN SOONER THAN LATER, KOMAND'R...
...BUT I DON'T THINK YOU ARE GOING TO ENJOY THE EXPERIENCE AS MUCH AS I AM.

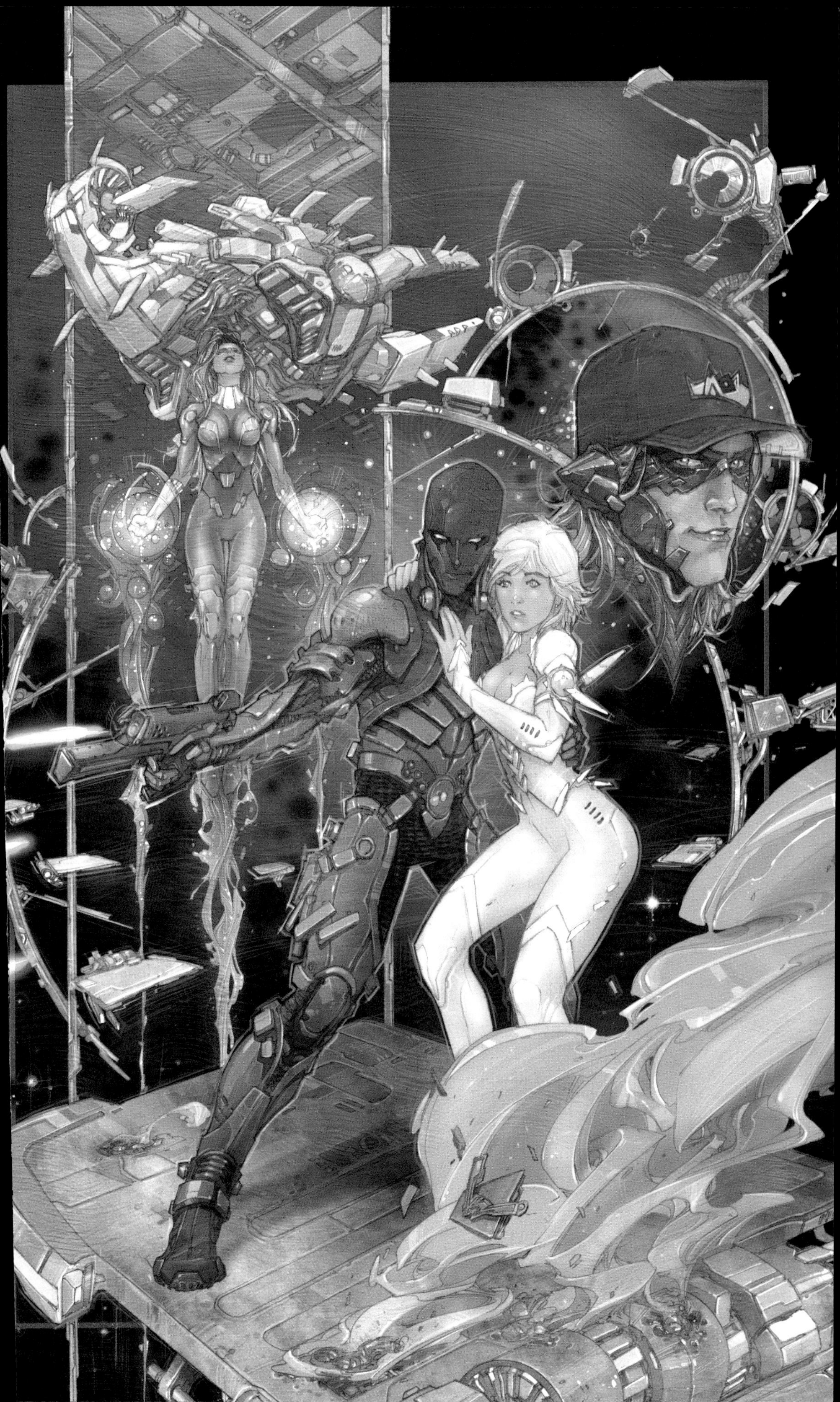

SCOTT LOBDELL writer TIMOTHY GREEN II artist cover art by KENNETH ROCAFORT & BLOND

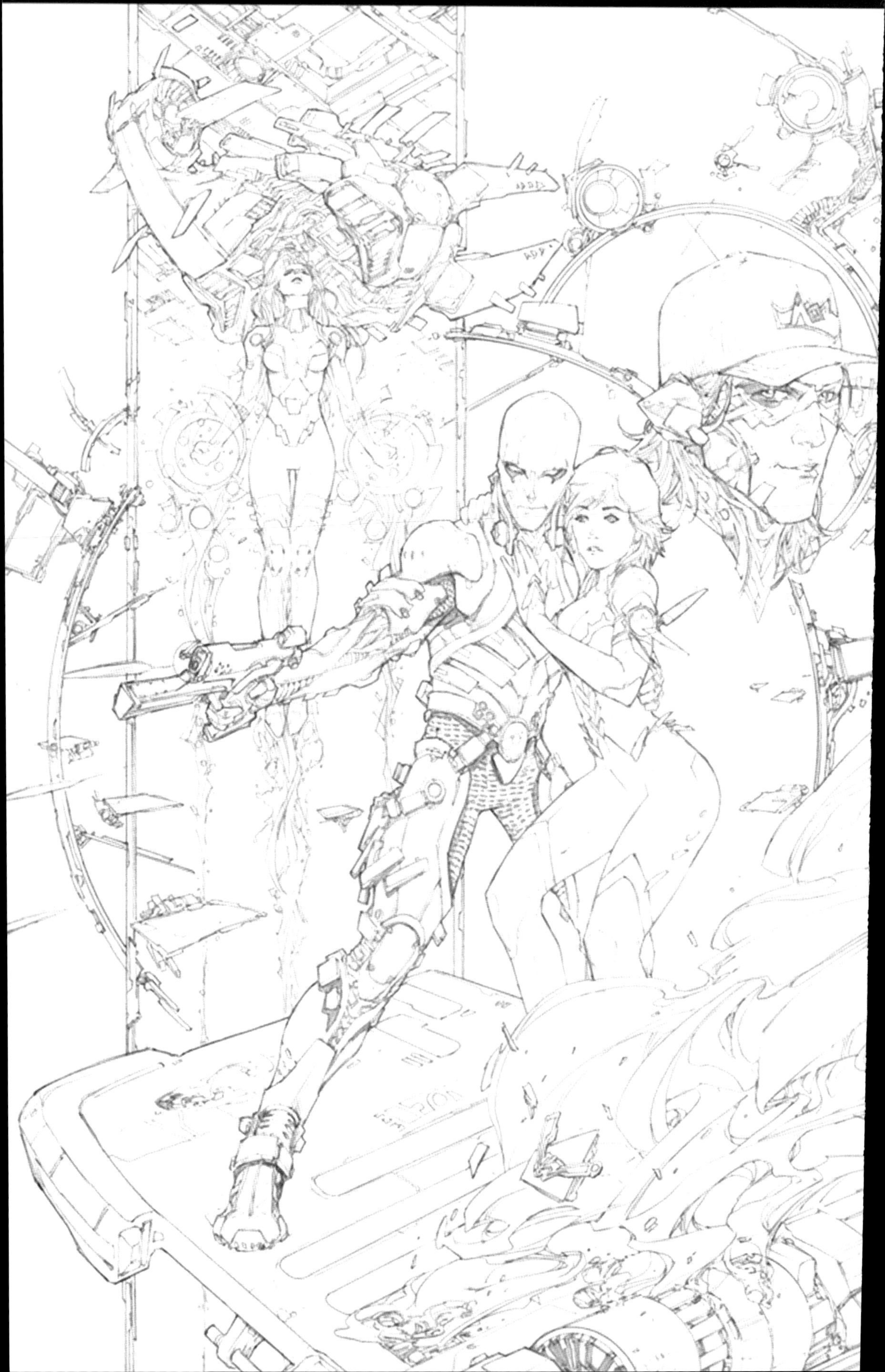

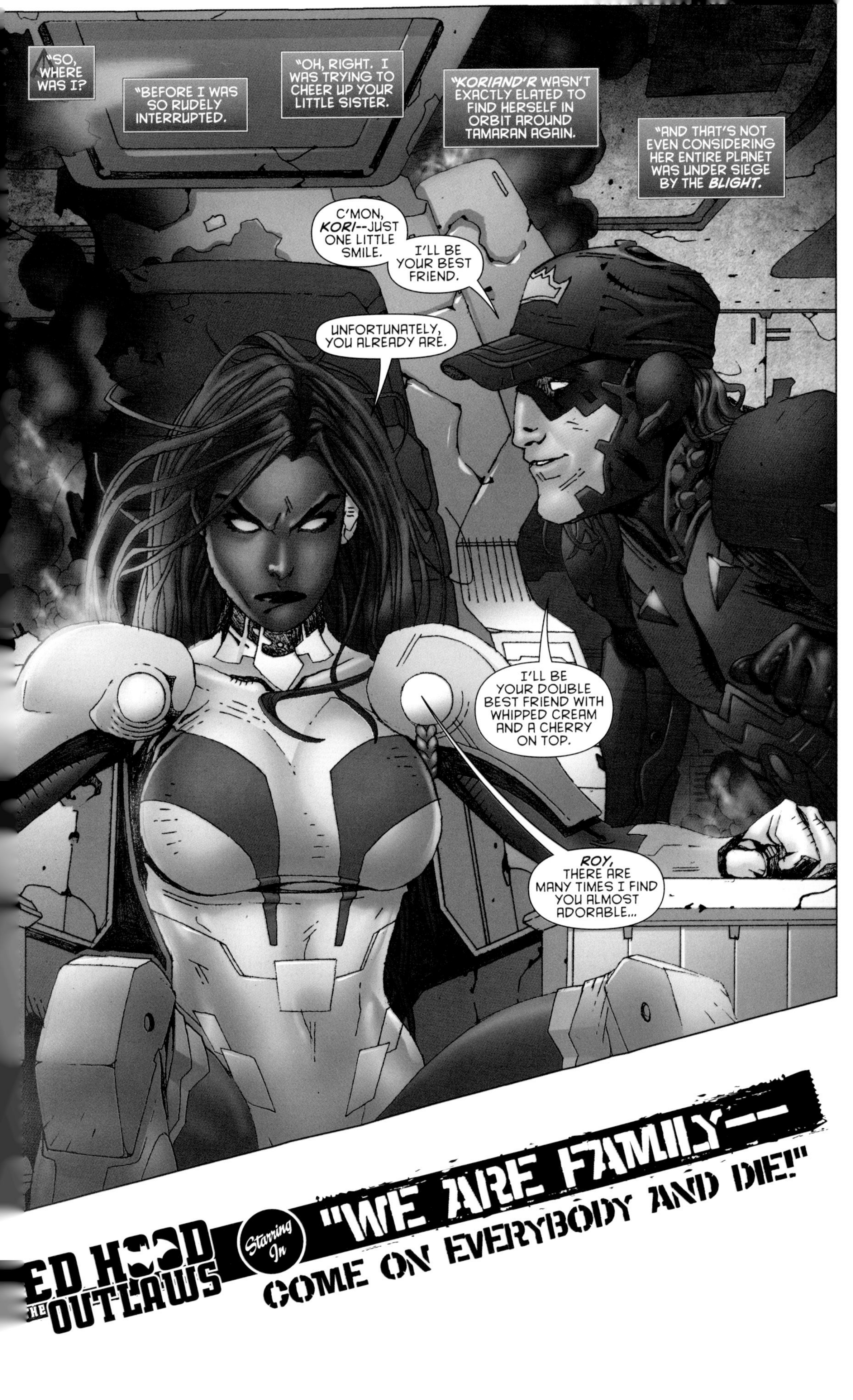

"SO, WHERE WAS I?
"BEFORE I WAS SO RUDELY INTERRUPTED.
"OH, RIGHT. I WAS TRYING TO CHEER UP YOUR LITTLE SISTER.
"KORIAND'R WASN'T EXACTLY ELATED TO FIND HERSELF IN ORBIT AROUND TAMARAN AGAIN.
"AND THAT'S NOT EVEN CONSIDERING HER ENTIRE PLANET WAS UNDER SIEGE BY THE BLIGHT.
C'MON, KORI--JUST ONE LITTLE SMILE.
I'LL BE YOUR BEST FRIEND.
UNFORTUNATELY, YOU ALREADY ARE.
I'LL BE YOUR DOUBLE BEST FRIEND WITH WHIPPED CREAM AND A CHERRY ON TOP.
ROY, THERE ARE MANY TIMES I FIND YOU ALMOST ADORABLE...
ED HOOD THE OUTLAWS
Starring In
"WE ARE FAMILY--
COME ON EVERYBODY AND DIE!"

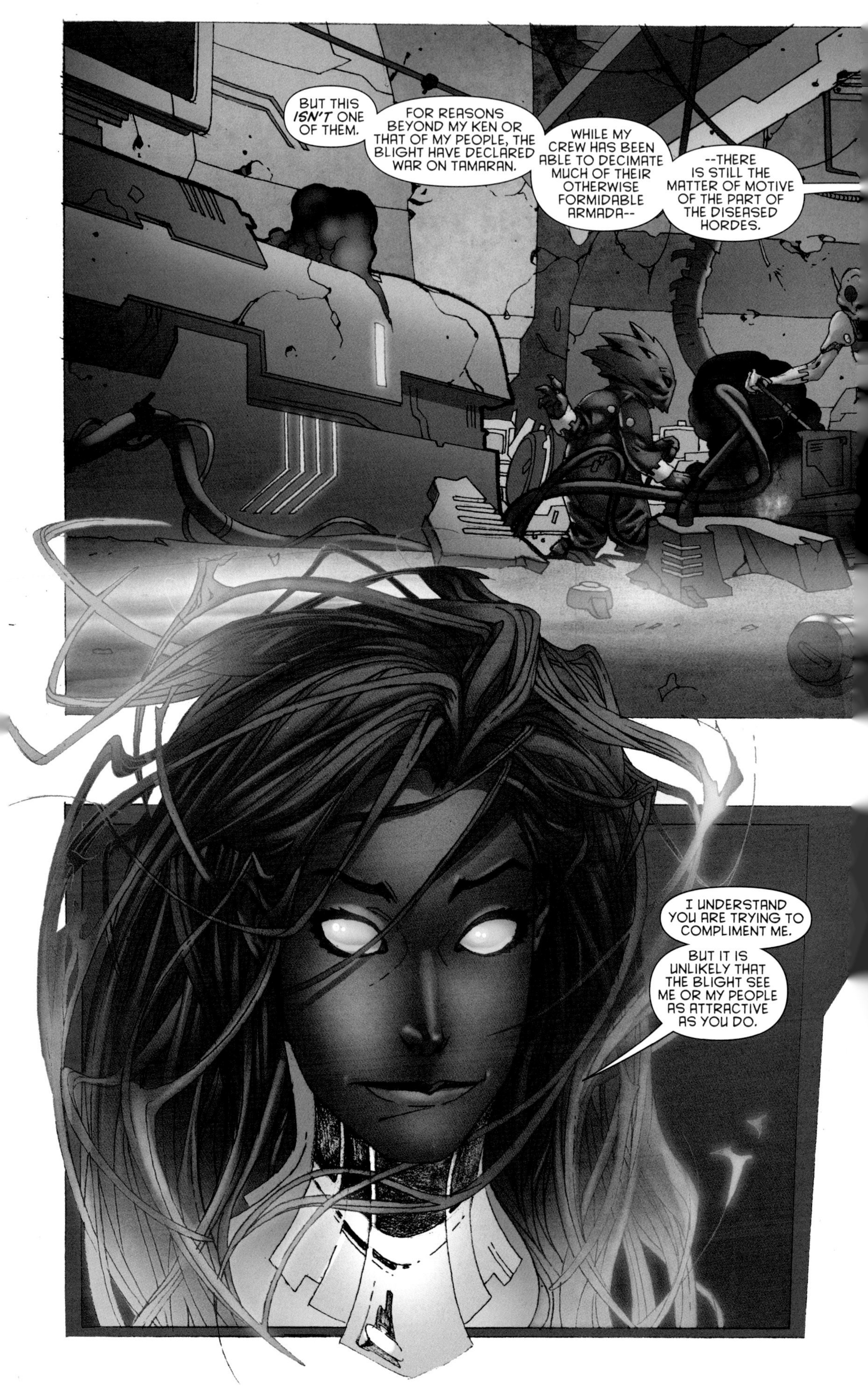
BUT THIS ISN'T ONE OF THEM.
FOR REASONS BEYOND MY KEN OR THAT OF MY PEOPLE, THE BLIGHT HAVE DECLARED WAR ON TAMARAN.
WHILE MY CREW HAS BEEN ABLE TO DECIMATE MUCH OF THEIR OTHERWISE FORMIDABLE ARMADA--
--THERE IS STILL THE MATTER OF MOTIVE OF THE PART OF THE DISEASED HORDES.
I UNDERSTAND YOU ARE TRYING TO COMPLIMENT ME.
BUT IT IS UNLIKELY THAT THE BLIGHT SEE ME OR MY PEOPLE AS ATTRACTIVE AS YOU DO.

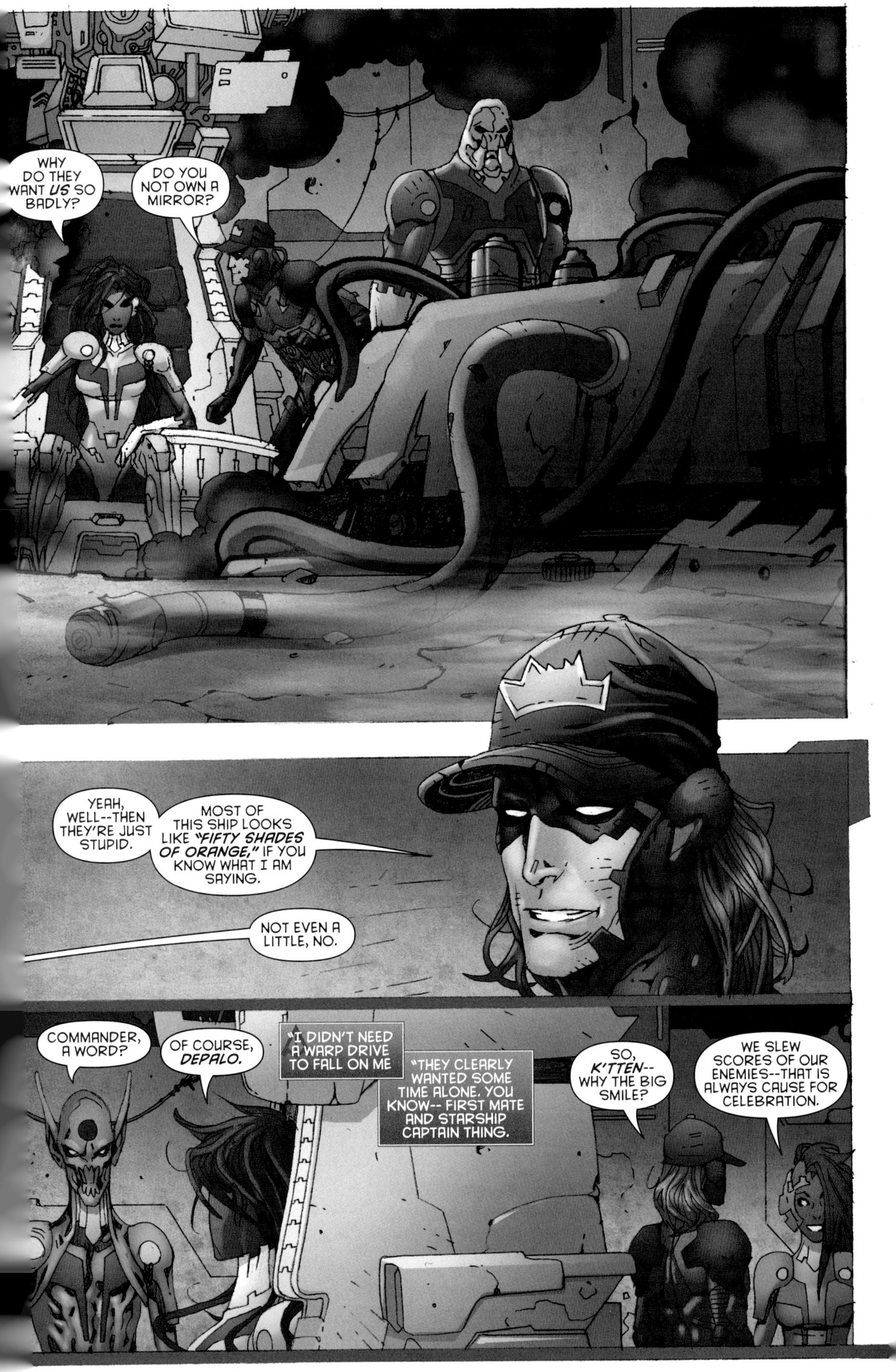
WHY DO THEY WANT *US* SO BADLY?
DO YOU NOT OWN A MIRROR?
YEAH, WELL--THEN THEY'RE JUST STUPID.
MOST OF THIS SHIP LOOKS LIKE *"FIFTY SHADES OF ORANGE,"* IF YOU KNOW WHAT I AM SAYING.
NOT EVEN A LITTLE, NO.
COMMANDER, A WORD?
OF COURSE, *DEPALO.*
"I DIDN'T NEED A WARP DRIVE TO FALL ON ME
"THEY CLEARLY WANTED SOME TIME ALONE. YOU KNOW-- FIRST MATE AND STARSHIP CAPTAIN THING.
SO, *K'TTEN*-- WHY THE BIG SMILE?
WE SLEW SCORES OF OUR ENEMIES--THAT IS ALWAYS CAUSE FOR CELEBRATION.

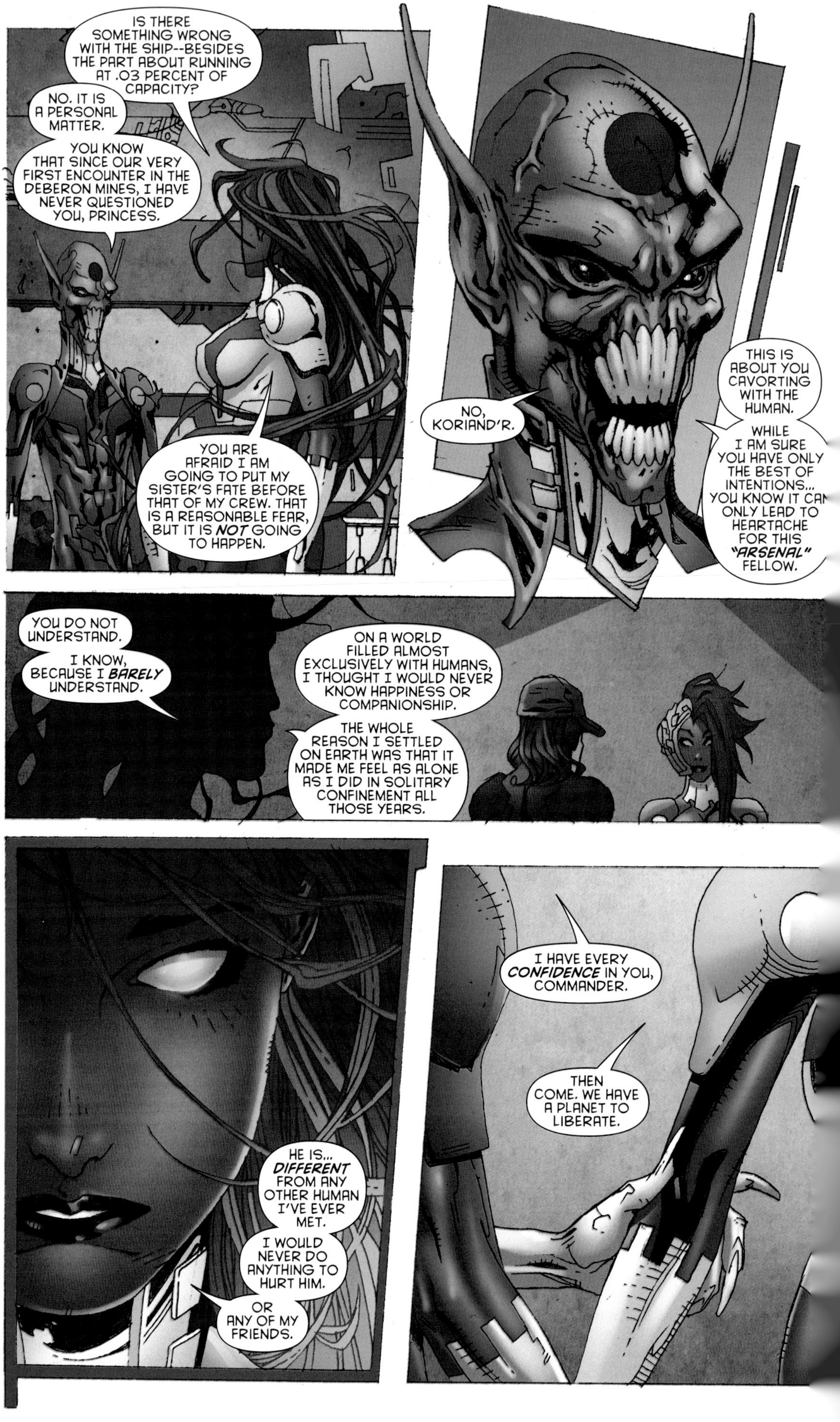

IS THERE SOMETHING WRONG WITH THE SHIP--BESIDES THE PART ABOUT RUNNING AT .03 PERCENT OF CAPACITY?
NO. IT IS A PERSONAL MATTER.
YOU KNOW THAT SINCE OUR VERY FIRST ENCOUNTER IN THE DEBERON MINES, I HAVE NEVER QUESTIONED YOU, PRINCESS.
YOU ARE AFRAID I AM GOING TO PUT MY SISTER'S FATE BEFORE THAT OF MY CREW. THAT IS A REASONABLE FEAR, BUT IT IS *NOT* GOING TO HAPPEN.
NO, KORIAND'R.
THIS IS ABOUT YOU CAVORTING WITH THE HUMAN.
WHILE I AM SURE YOU HAVE ONLY THE BEST OF INTENTIONS... YOU KNOW IT CAN ONLY LEAD TO HEARTACHE FOR THIS *"ARSENAL"* FELLOW.
YOU DO NOT UNDERSTAND.
I KNOW, BECAUSE I *BARELY* UNDERSTAND.
ON A WORLD FILLED ALMOST EXCLUSIVELY WITH HUMANS, I THOUGHT I WOULD NEVER KNOW HAPPINESS OR COMPANIONSHIP.
THE WHOLE REASON I SETTLED ON EARTH WAS THAT IT MADE ME FEEL AS ALONE AS I DID IN SOLITARY CONFINEMENT ALL THOSE YEARS.
HE IS... *DIFFERENT* FROM ANY OTHER HUMAN I'VE EVER MET.
I WOULD NEVER DO ANYTHING TO HURT HIM.
OR ANY OF MY FRIENDS.
I HAVE EVERY *CONFIDENCE* IN YOU, COMMANDER.
THEN COME. WE HAVE A PLANET TO LIBERATE.

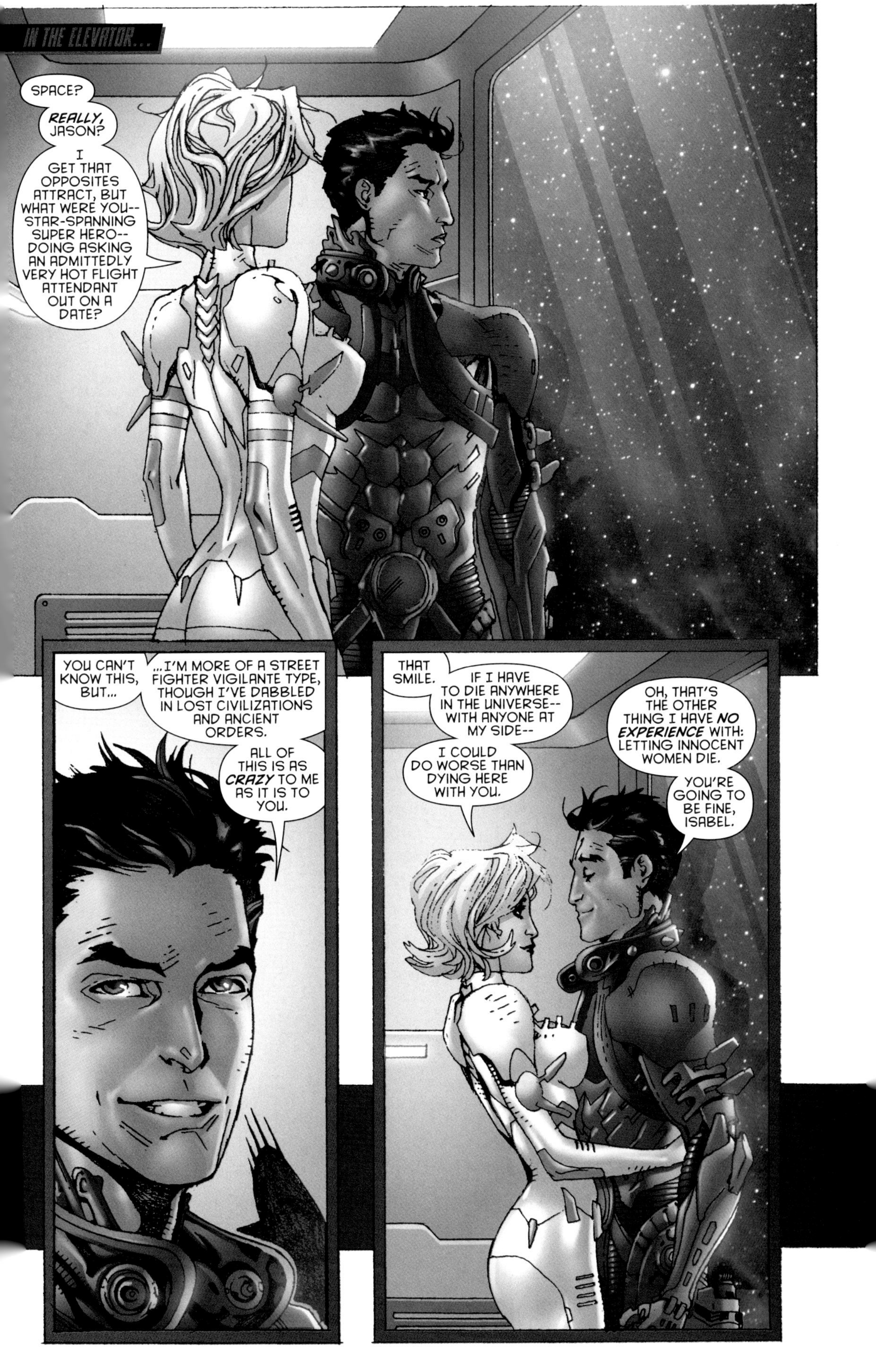
IN THE ELEVATOR...
SPACE?
REALLY, JASON?
I GET THAT OPPOSITES ATTRACT, BUT WHAT WERE YOU--STAR-SPANNING SUPER HERO--DOING ASKING AN ADMITTEDLY VERY HOT FLIGHT ATTENDANT OUT ON A DATE?
YOU CAN'T KNOW THIS, BUT...
...I'M MORE OF A STREET FIGHTER VIGILANTE TYPE, THOUGH I'VE DABBLED IN LOST CIVILIZATIONS AND ANCIENT ORDERS.
ALL OF THIS IS AS CRAZY TO ME AS IT IS TO YOU.
THAT SMILE.
IF I HAVE TO DIE ANYWHERE IN THE UNIVERSE--WITH ANYONE AT MY SIDE--
I COULD DO WORSE THAN DYING HERE WITH YOU.
OH, THAT'S THE OTHER THING I HAVE NO EXPERIENCE WITH: LETTING INNOCENT WOMEN DIE.
YOU'RE GOING TO BE FINE, ISABEL.

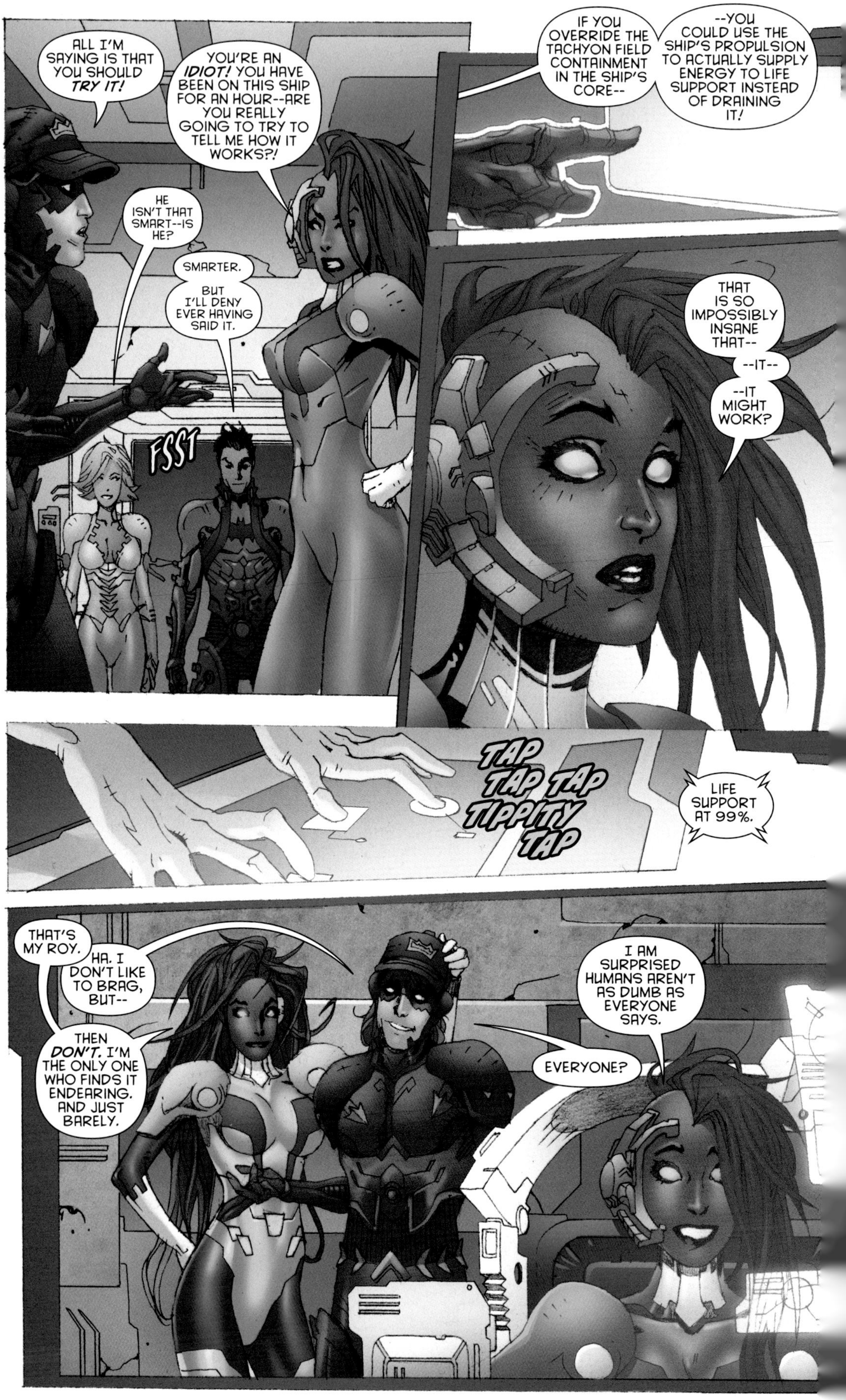
ALL I'M SAYING IS THAT YOU SHOULD TRY IT!
YOU'RE AN IDIOT! YOU HAVE BEEN ON THIS SHIP FOR AN HOUR--ARE YOU REALLY GOING TO TRY TO TELL ME HOW IT WORKS?!
HE ISN'T THAT SMART--IS HE?
SMARTER.
BUT I'LL DENY EVER HAVING SAID IT.
FSST
IF YOU OVERRIDE THE TACHYON FIELD CONTAINMENT IN THE SHIP'S CORE--
--YOU COULD USE THE SHIP'S PROPULSION TO ACTUALLY SUPPLY ENERGY TO LIFE SUPPORT INSTEAD OF DRAINING IT!
THAT IS SO IMPOSSIBLY INSANE THAT--
--IT--
--IT MIGHT WORK?
TAP TAP TAP TIPPITY TAP
LIFE SUPPORT AT 99%.
THAT'S MY ROY.
HA. I DON'T LIKE TO BRAG, BUT--
THEN DON'T. I'M THE ONLY ONE WHO FINDS IT ENDEARING. AND JUST BARELY.
I AM SURPRISED HUMANS AREN'T AS DUMB AS EVERYONE SAYS.
EVERYONE?

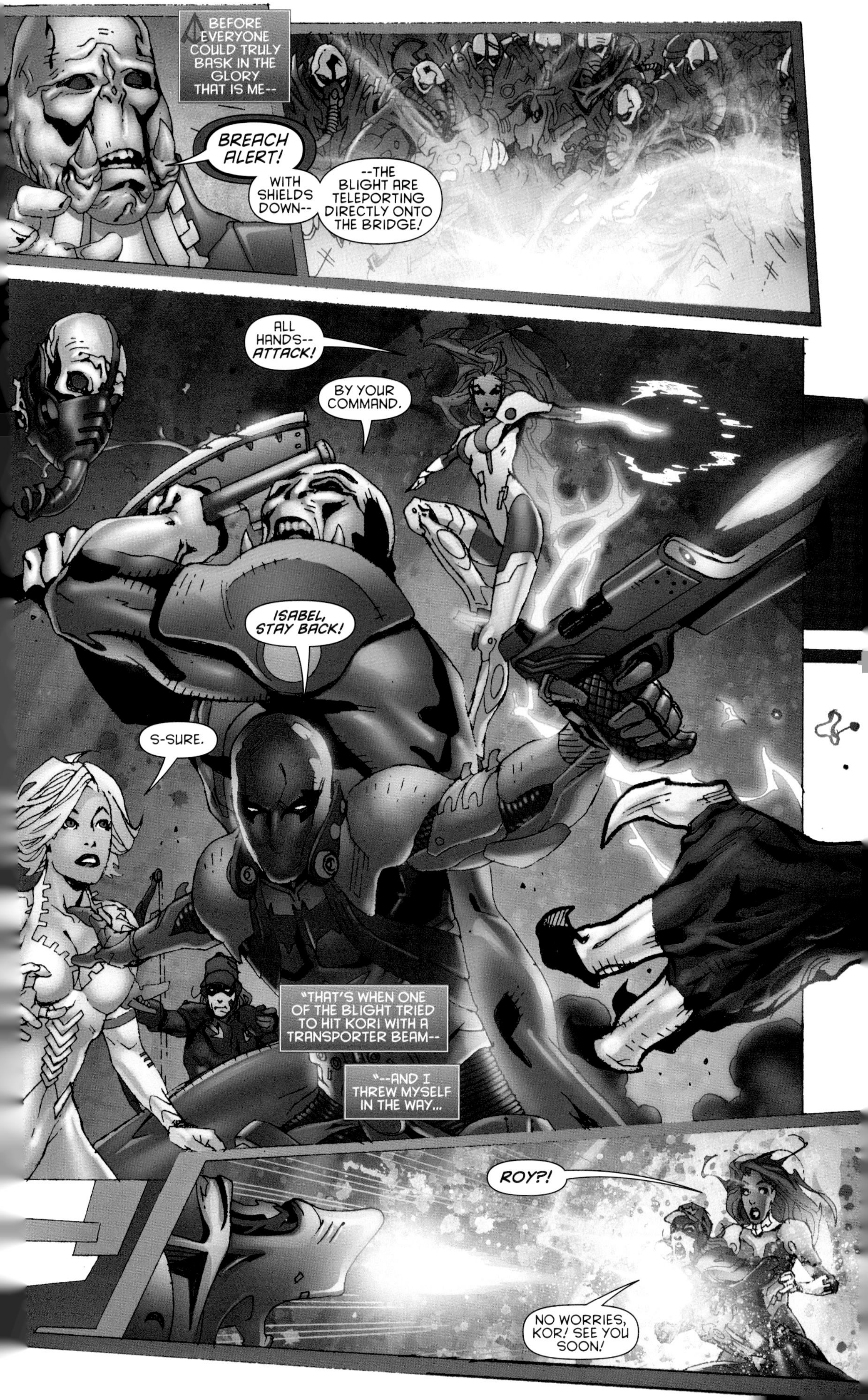
BEFORE EVERYONE COULD TRULY BASK IN THE GLORY THAT IS ME--
BREACH ALERT!
WITH SHIELDS DOWN--
--THE BLIGHT ARE TELEPORTING DIRECTLY ONTO THE BRIDGE!
ALL HANDS-- ATTACK!
BY YOUR COMMAND.
ISABEL, STAY BACK!
S-SURE.
"THAT'S WHEN ONE OF THE BLIGHT TRIED TO HIT KORI WITH A TRANSPORTER BEAM--
"--AND I THREW MYSELF IN THE WAY...
ROY?!
NO WORRIES, KOR! SEE YOU SOON!

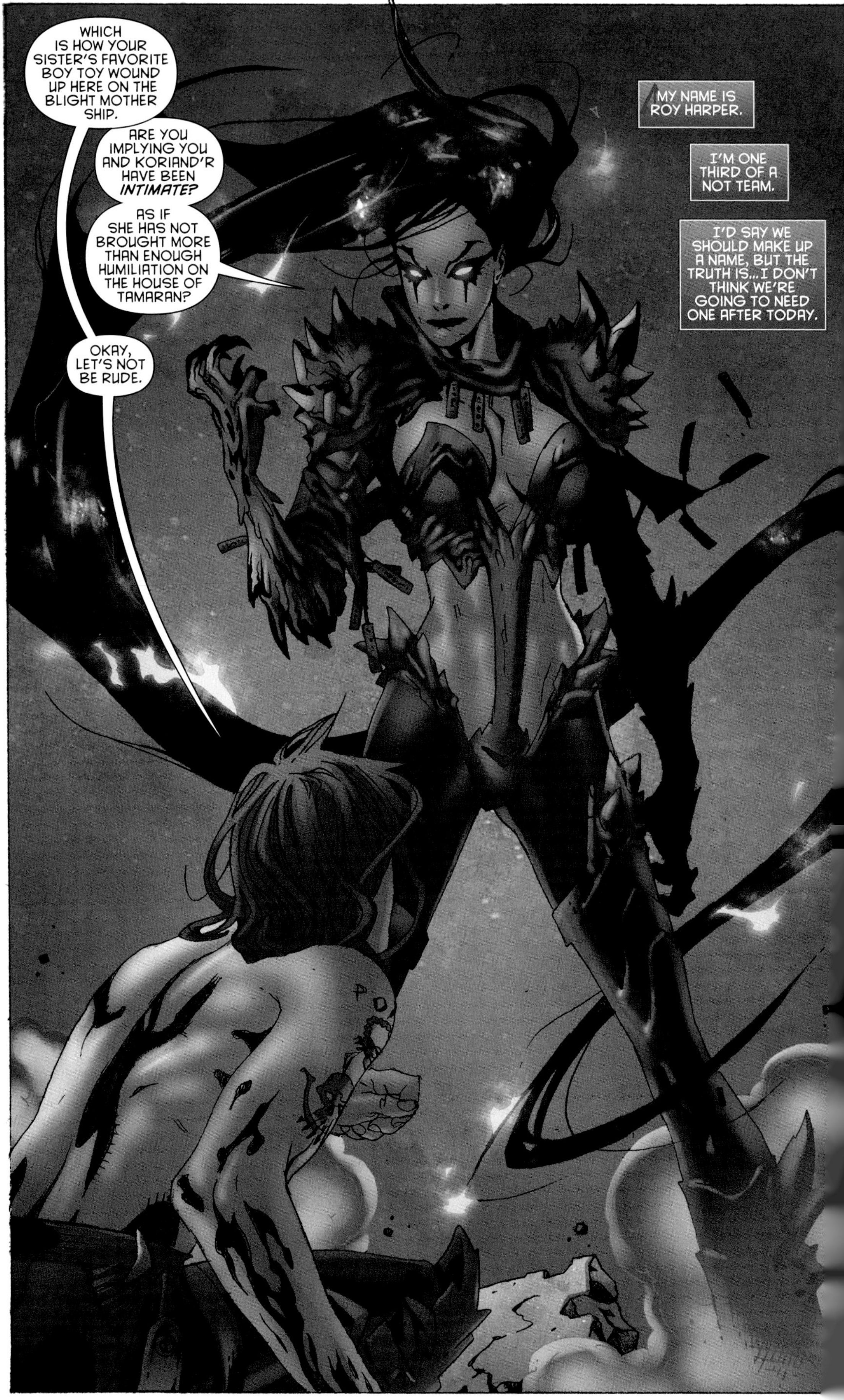
WHICH IS HOW YOUR SISTER'S FAVORITE BOY TOY WOUND UP HERE ON THE BLIGHT MOTHER SHIP.
ARE YOU IMPLYING YOU AND KORIAND'R HAVE BEEN *INTIMATE?*
AS IF SHE HAS NOT BROUGHT MORE THAN ENOUGH HUMILIATION ON THE HOUSE OF TAMARAN?
OKAY, LET'S NOT BE RUDE.
MY NAME IS ROY HARPER.
I'M ONE THIRD OF A NOT TEAM.
I'D SAY WE SHOULD MAKE UP A NAME, BUT THE TRUTH IS...I DON'T THINK WE'RE GOING TO NEED ONE AFTER TODAY.

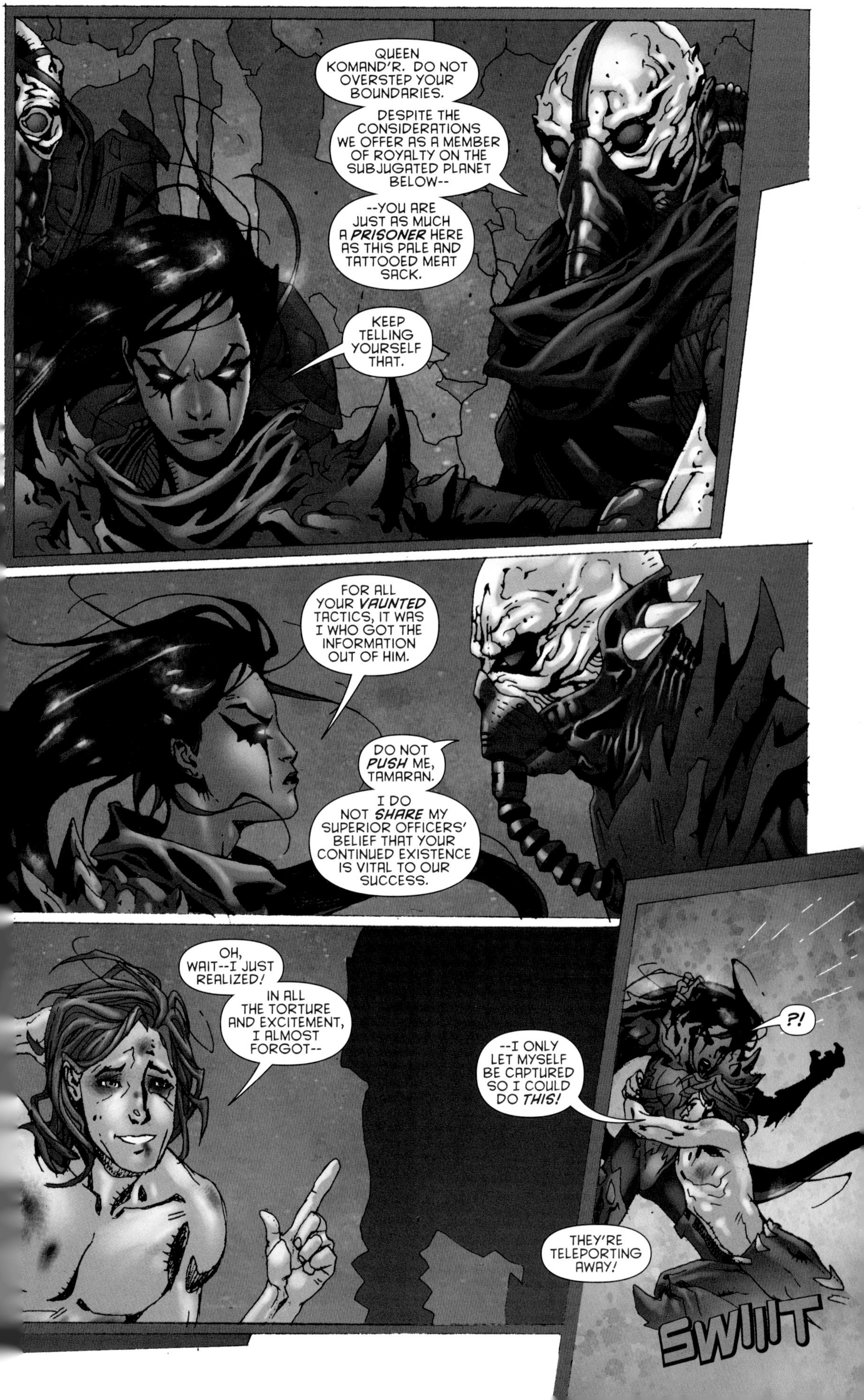
QUEEN KOMAND'R. DO NOT OVERSTEP YOUR BOUNDARIES.
DESPITE THE CONSIDERATIONS WE OFFER AS A MEMBER OF ROYALTY ON THE SUBJUGATED PLANET BELOW--
--YOU ARE JUST AS MUCH A *PRISONER* HERE AS THIS PALE AND TATTOOED MEAT SACK.
KEEP TELLING YOURSELF THAT.
FOR ALL YOUR *VAUNTED* TACTICS, IT WAS I WHO GOT THE INFORMATION OUT OF HIM.
DO NOT *PUSH* ME, TAMARAN.
I DO NOT *SHARE* MY SUPERIOR OFFICERS' BELIEF THAT YOUR CONTINUED EXISTENCE IS VITAL TO OUR SUCCESS.
OH, WAIT--I JUST REALIZED!
IN ALL THE TORTURE AND EXCITEMENT, I ALMOST FORGOT--
--I ONLY LET MYSELF BE CAPTURED SO I COULD DO *THIS!*
?!
THEY'RE TELEPORTING AWAY!
SWIIIT

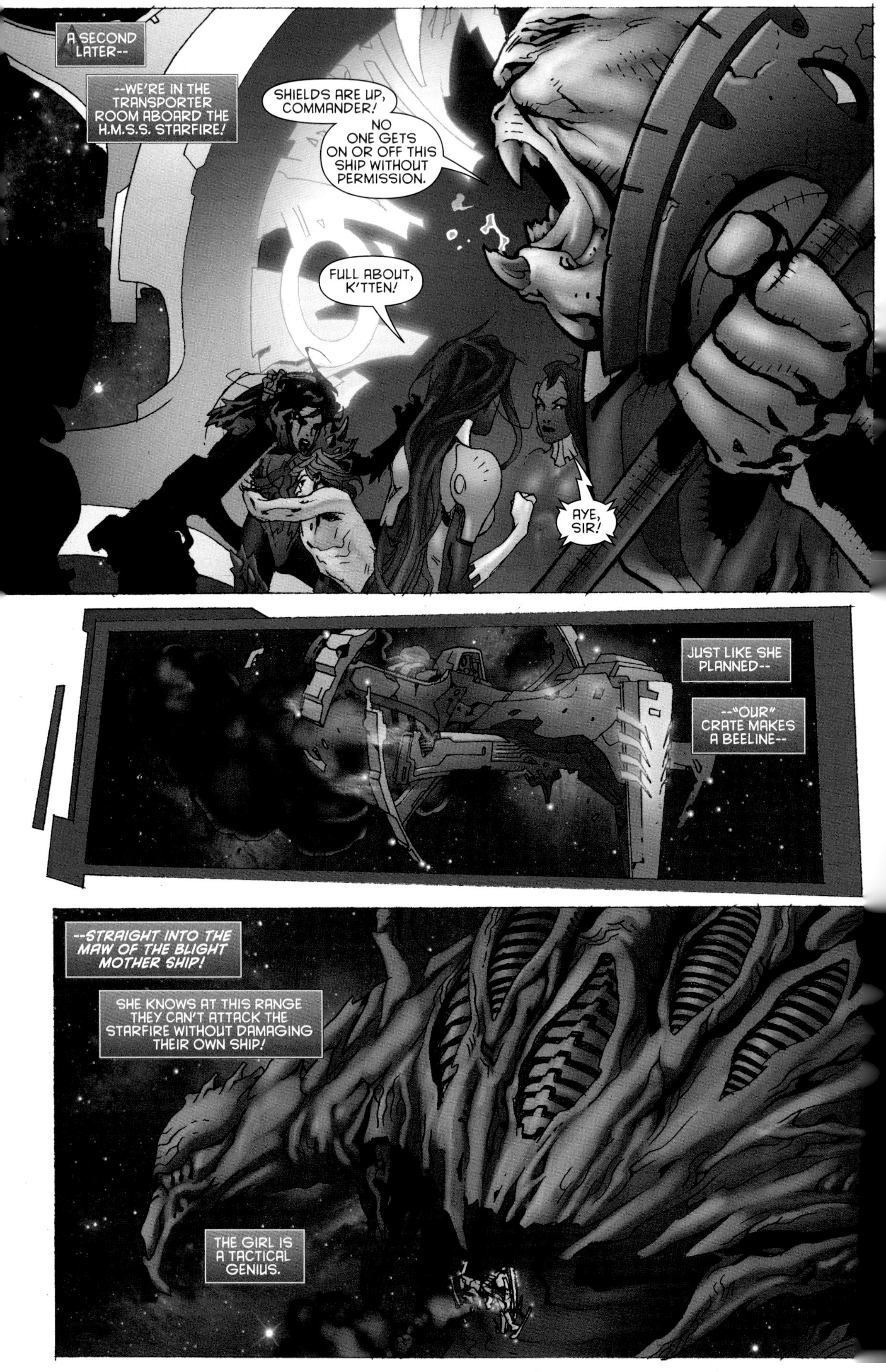
A SECOND LATER--
--WE'RE IN THE TRANSPORTER ROOM ABOARD THE H.M.S.S. STARFIRE!
SHIELDS ARE UP, COMMANDER!
NO ONE GETS ON OR OFF THIS SHIP WITHOUT PERMISSION.
FULL ABOUT, K'TTEN!
AYE, SIR!
JUST LIKE SHE PLANNED--
--"OUR" CRATE MAKES A BEELINE--
--STRAIGHT INTO THE MAW OF THE BLIGHT MOTHER SHIP!
SHE KNOWS AT THIS RANGE THEY CAN'T ATTACK THE STARFIRE WITHOUT DAMAGING THEIR OWN SHIP!
THE GIRL IS A TACTICAL GENIUS.

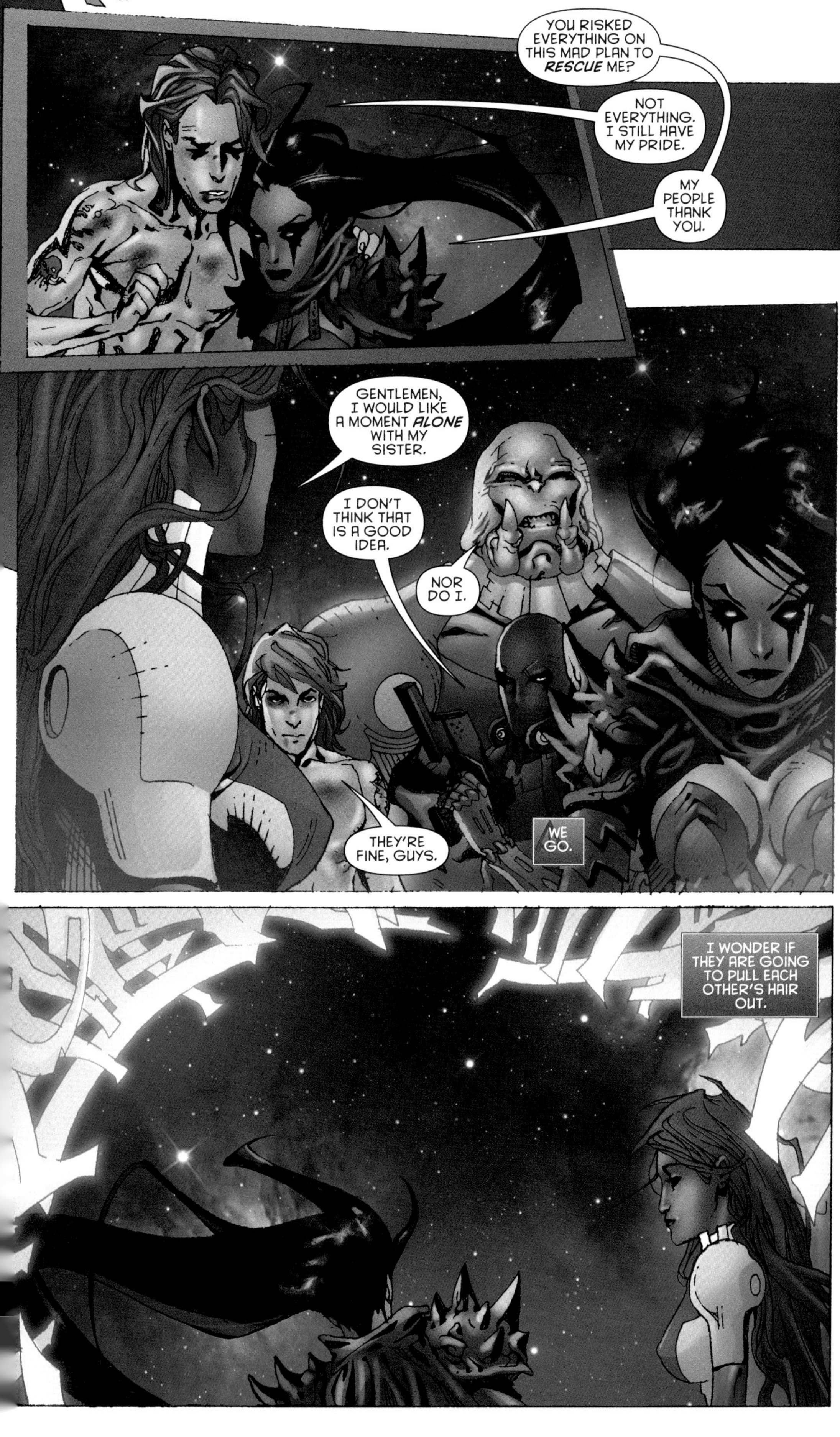
YOU RISKED EVERYTHING ON THIS MAD PLAN TO *RESCUE* ME?
NOT EVERYTHING. I STILL HAVE MY PRIDE.
MY PEOPLE THANK YOU.
GENTLEMEN, I WOULD LIKE A MOMENT *ALONE* WITH MY SISTER.
I DON'T THINK THAT IS A GOOD IDEA.
NOR DO I.
THEY'RE FINE, GUYS.
WE GO.
I WONDER IF THEY ARE GOING TO PULL EACH OTHER'S HAIR OUT.

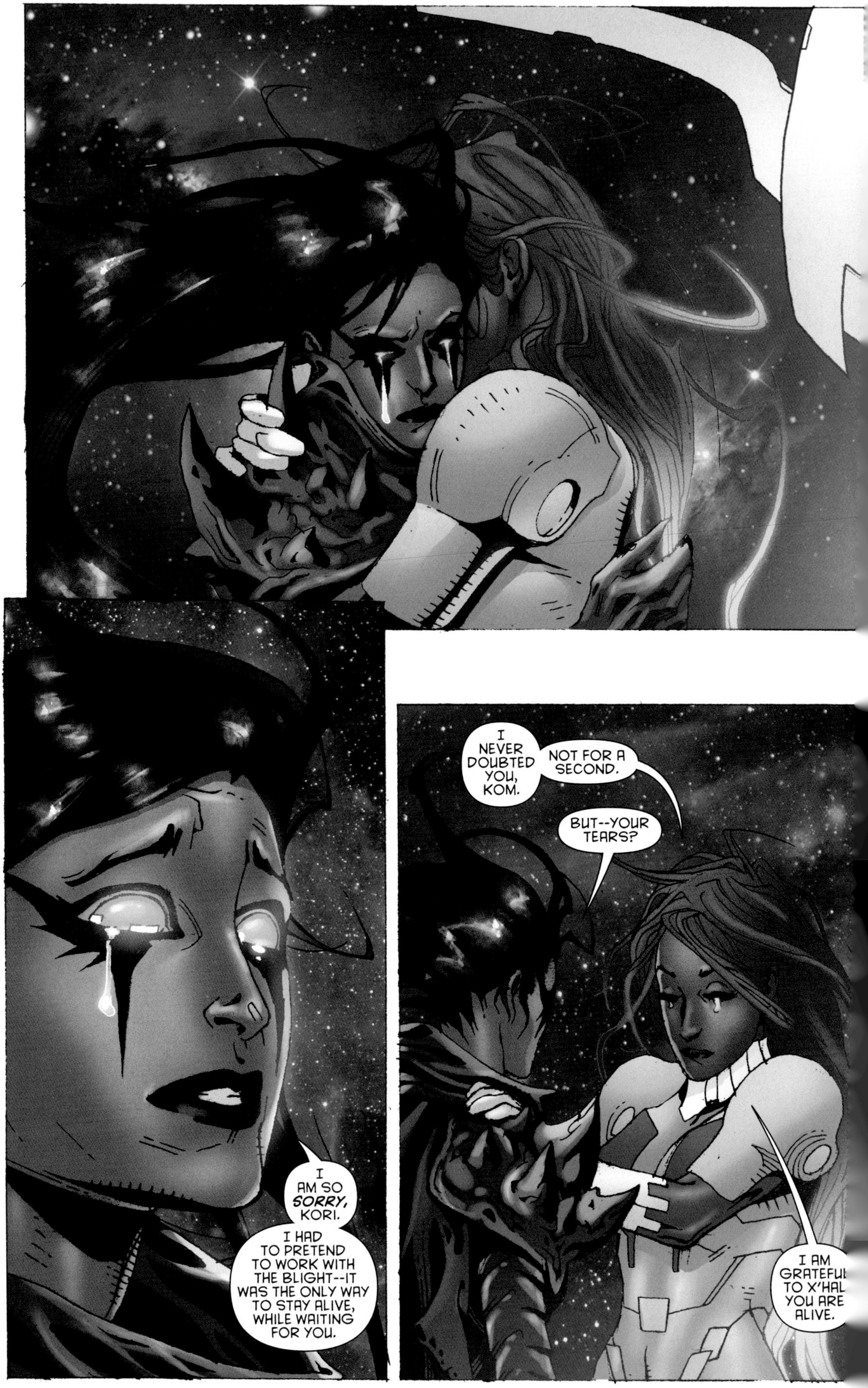
I AM SO *SORRY,* KORI.
I HAD TO PRETEND TO WORK WITH THE BLIGHT--IT WAS THE ONLY WAY TO STAY ALIVE, WHILE WAITING FOR YOU.
I NEVER DOUBTED YOU, KOM.
NOT FOR A SECOND.
BUT--YOUR TEARS?
I AM GRATEFU TO X'HAL YOU ARE ALIVE.

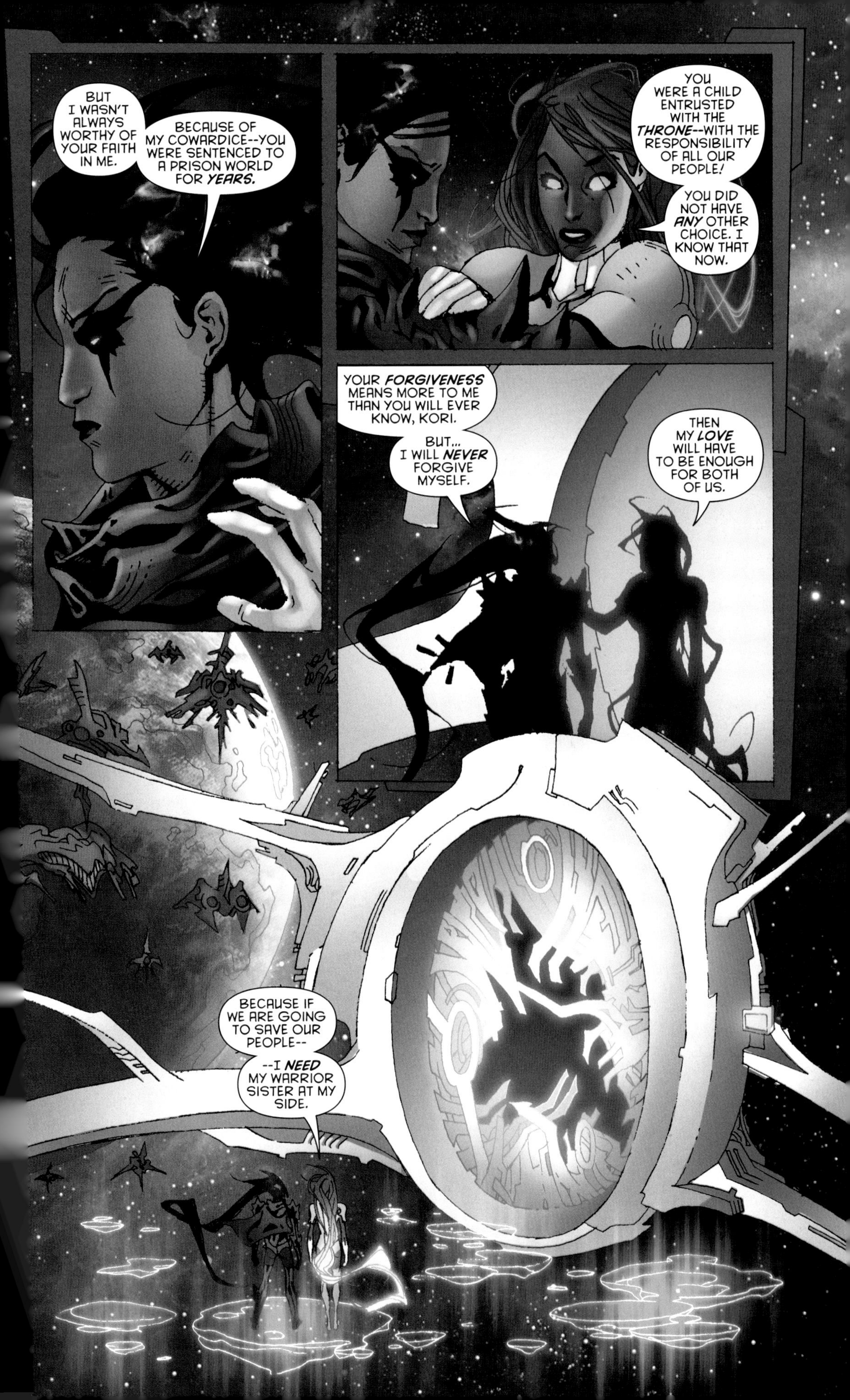

BUT I WASN'T ALWAYS WORTHY OF YOUR FAITH IN ME.
BECAUSE OF MY COWARDICE--YOU WERE SENTENCED TO A PRISON WORLD FOR *YEARS.*
YOU WERE A CHILD ENTRUSTED WITH THE *THRONE*--WITH THE RESPONSIBILITY OF ALL OUR PEOPLE!
YOU DID NOT HAVE *ANY* OTHER CHOICE. I KNOW THAT NOW.
YOUR *FORGIVENESS* MEANS MORE TO ME THAN YOU WILL EVER KNOW, KORI.
BUT... I WILL *NEVER* FORGIVE MYSELF.
THEN MY *LOVE* WILL HAVE TO BE ENOUGH FOR BOTH OF US.
BECAUSE IF WE ARE GOING TO SAVE OUR PEOPLE--
--I *NEED* MY WARRIOR SISTER AT MY SIDE.

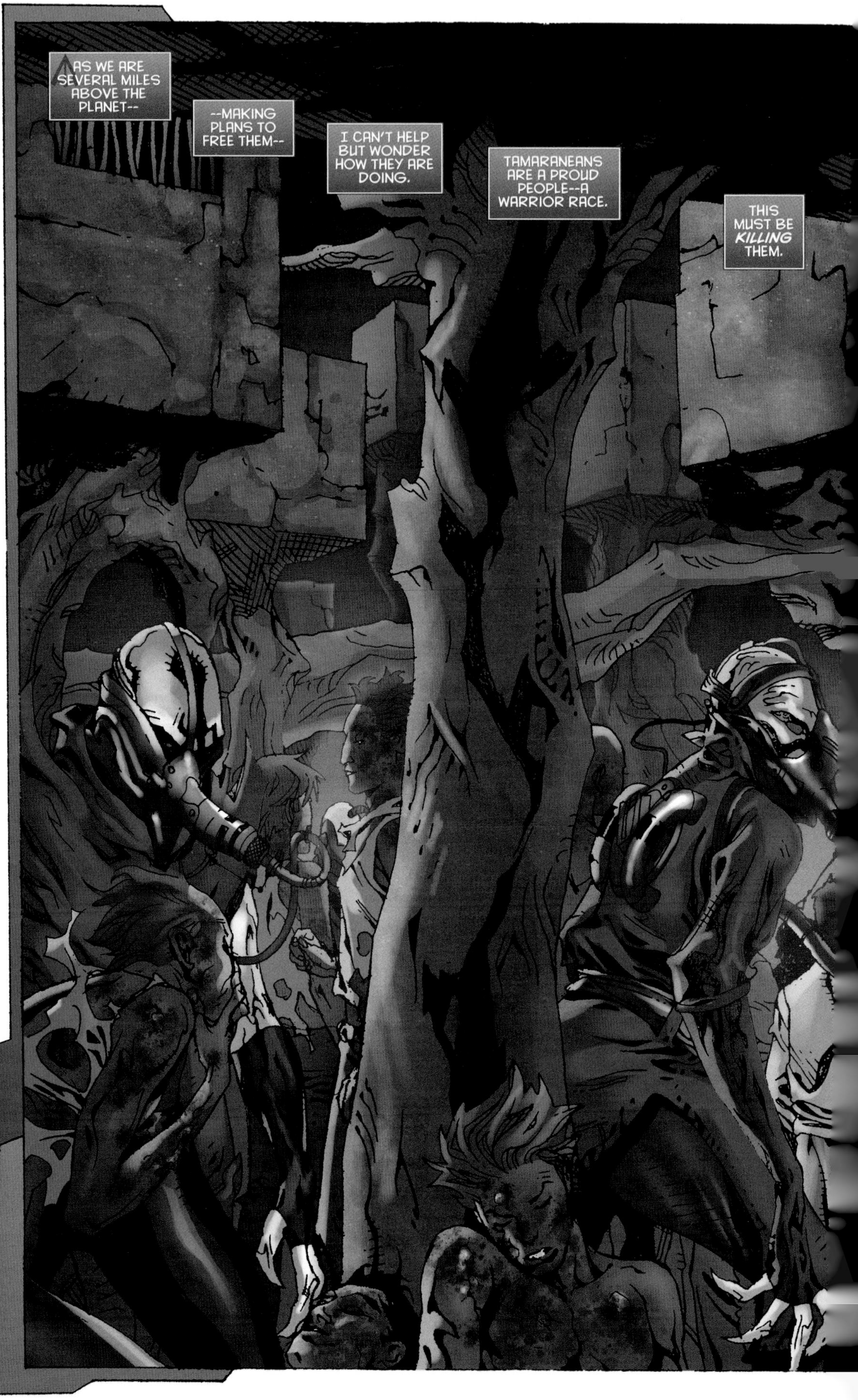
AS WE ARE SEVERAL MILES ABOVE THE PLANET--
--MAKING PLANS TO FREE THEM--
I CAN'T HELP BUT WONDER HOW THEY ARE DOING.
TAMARANEANS ARE A PROUD PEOPLE--A WARRIOR RACE.
THIS MUST BE *KILLING* THEM.

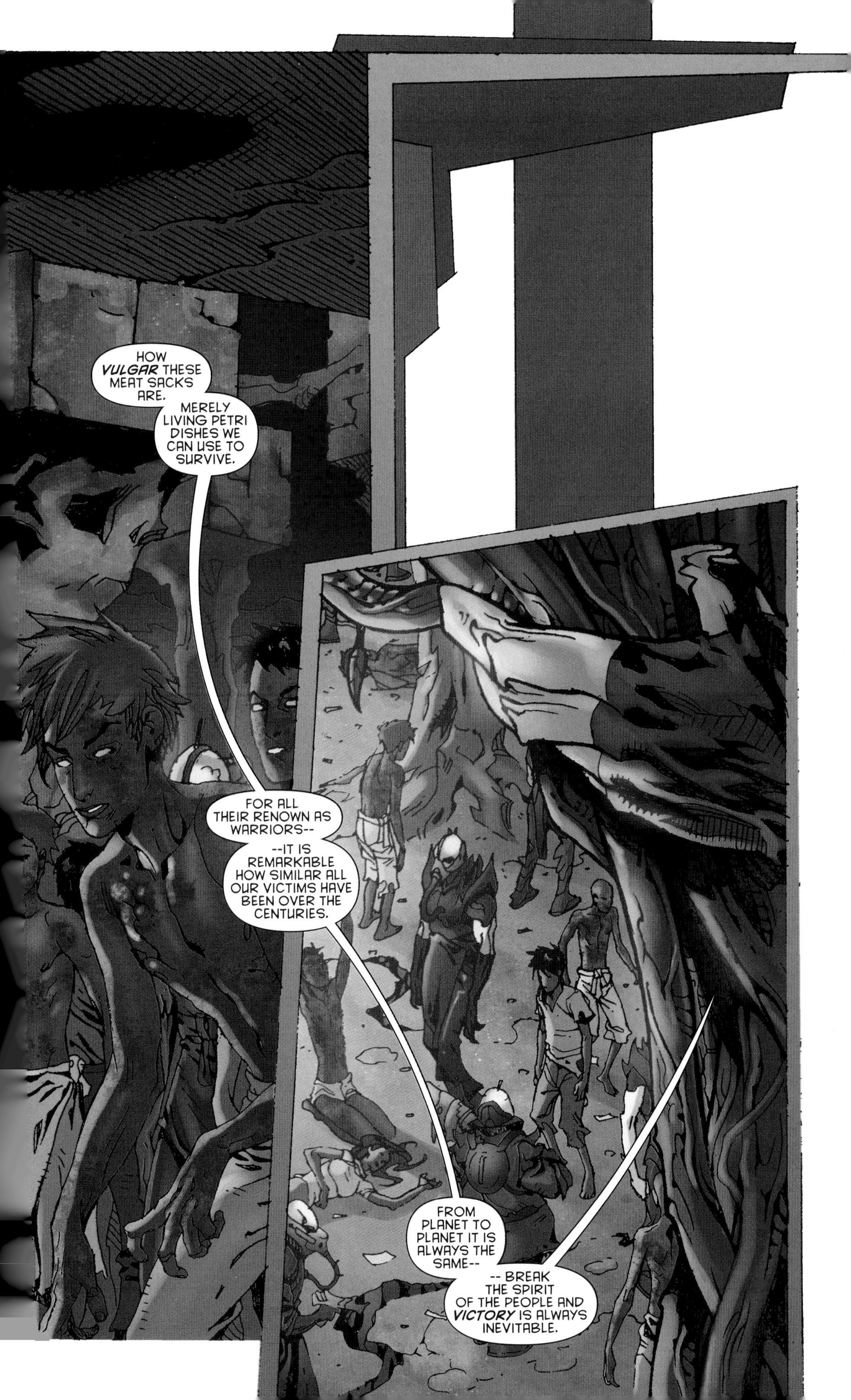
HOW VULGAR THESE MEAT SACKS ARE.
MERELY LIVING PETRI DISHES WE CAN USE TO SURVIVE.
FOR ALL THEIR RENOWN AS WARRIORS--
--IT IS REMARKABLE HOW SIMILAR ALL OUR VICTIMS HAVE BEEN OVER THE CENTURIES.
FROM PLANET TO PLANET IT IS ALWAYS THE SAME--
-- BREAK THE SPIRIT OF THE PEOPLE AND VICTORY IS ALWAYS INEVITABLE.

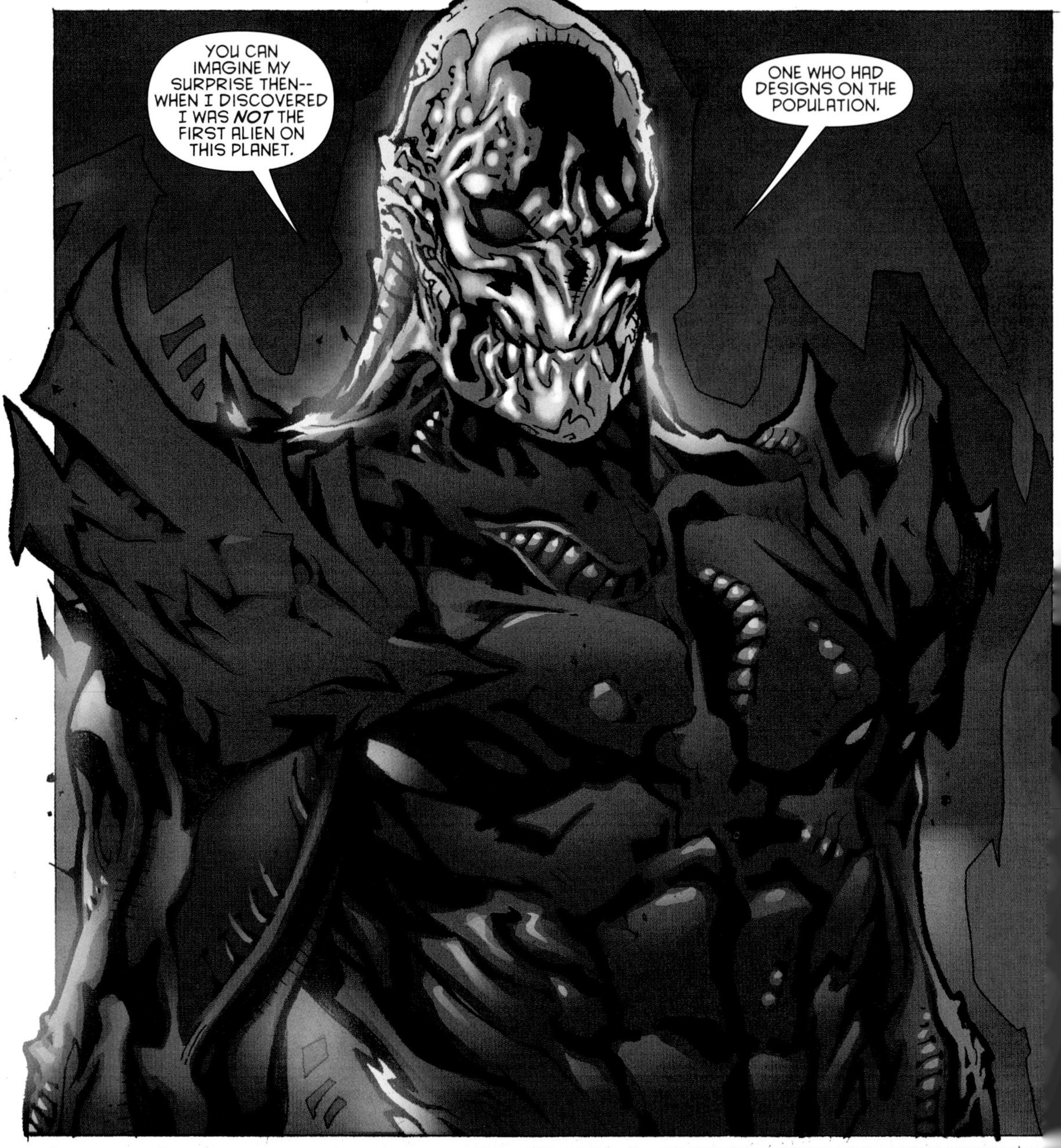
YOU CAN IMAGINE MY SURPRISE THEN-- WHEN I DISCOVERED I WAS *NOT* THE FIRST ALIEN ON THIS PLANET.
ONE WHO HAD DESIGNS ON THE POPULATION.

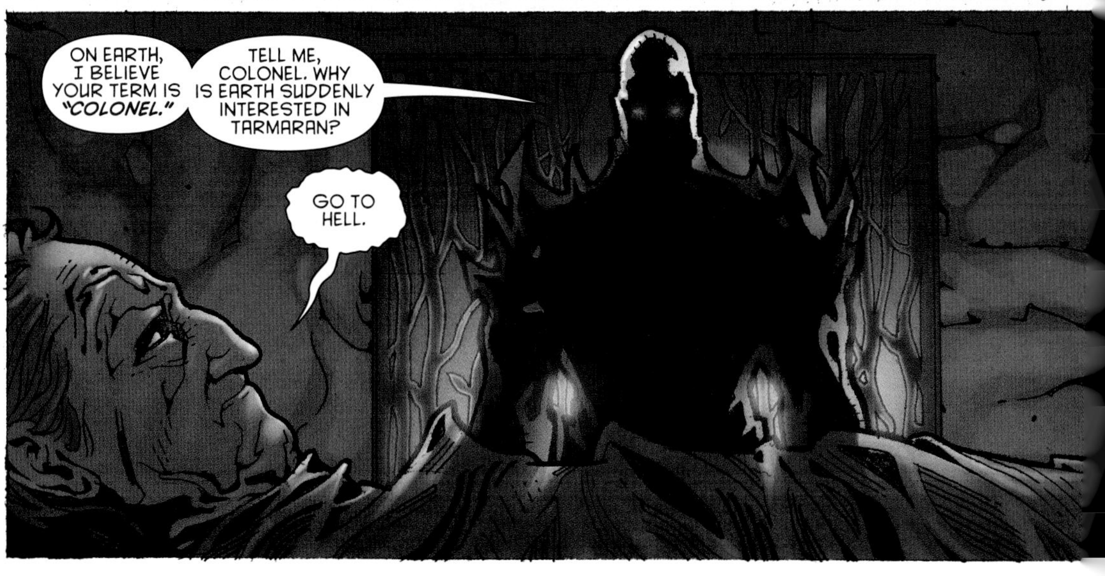
ON EARTH, I BELIEVE YOUR TERM IS *"COLONEL."*
TELL ME, COLONEL. WHY IS EARTH SUDDENLY INTERESTED IN TARMARAN?
GO TO HELL.

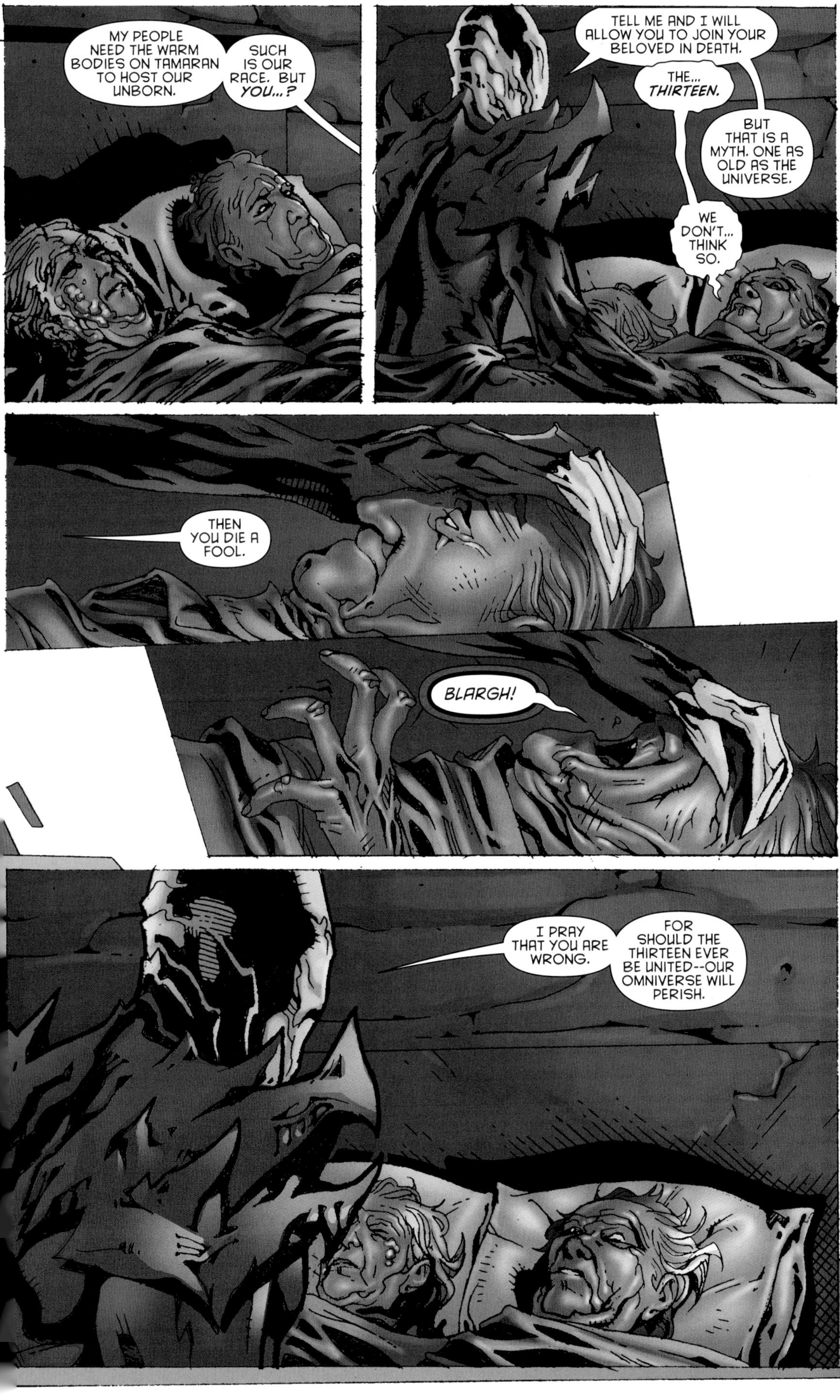
MY PEOPLE NEED THE WARM BODIES ON TAMARAN TO HOST OUR UNBORN.
SUCH IS OUR RACE. BUT *YOU...?*
TELL ME AND I WILL ALLOW YOU TO JOIN YOUR BELOVED IN DEATH.
THE... *THIRTEEN.*
BUT THAT IS A MYTH. ONE AS OLD AS THE UNIVERSE.
WE DON'T... THINK SO.
THEN YOU DIE A FOOL.
BLARGH!
I PRAY THAT YOU ARE WRONG.
FOR SHOULD THE THIRTEEN EVER BE UNITED--OUR OMNIVERSE WILL PERISH.

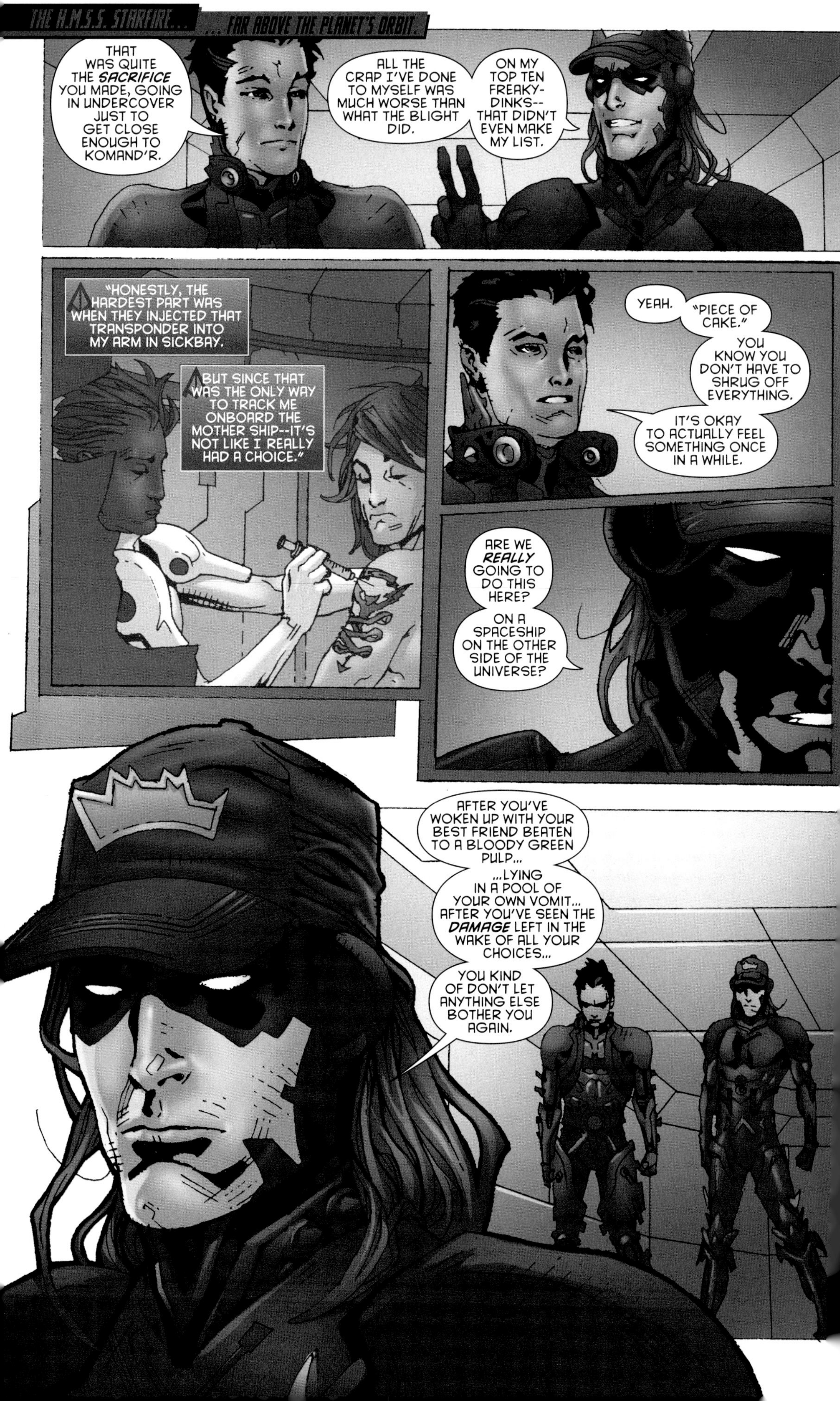
THE H.M.S.S. STARFIRE...
...FAR ABOVE THE PLANET'S ORBIT.
THAT WAS QUITE THE SACRIFICE YOU MADE, GOING IN UNDERCOVER JUST TO GET CLOSE ENOUGH TO KOMAND'R.
ALL THE CRAP I'VE DONE TO MYSELF WAS MUCH WORSE THAN WHAT THE BLIGHT DID.
ON MY TOP TEN FREAKY-DINKS--THAT DIDN'T EVEN MAKE MY LIST.
"HONESTLY, THE HARDEST PART WAS WHEN THEY INJECTED THAT TRANSPONDER INTO MY ARM IN SICKBAY.
BUT SINCE THAT WAS THE ONLY WAY TO TRACK ME ONBOARD THE MOTHER SHIP--IT'S NOT LIKE I REALLY HAD A CHOICE."
YEAH.
"PIECE OF CAKE."
YOU KNOW YOU DON'T HAVE TO SHRUG OFF EVERYTHING.
IT'S OKAY TO ACTUALLY FEEL SOMETHING ONCE IN A WHILE.
ARE WE REALLY GOING TO DO THIS HERE?
ON A SPACESHIP ON THE OTHER SIDE OF THE UNIVERSE?
AFTER YOU'VE WOKEN UP WITH YOUR BEST FRIEND BEATEN TO A BLOODY GREEN PULP...
...LYING IN A POOL OF YOUR OWN VOMIT... AFTER YOU'VE SEEN THE DAMAGE LEFT IN THE WAKE OF ALL YOUR CHOICES...
YOU KIND OF DON'T LET ANYTHING ELSE BOTHER YOU AGAIN.

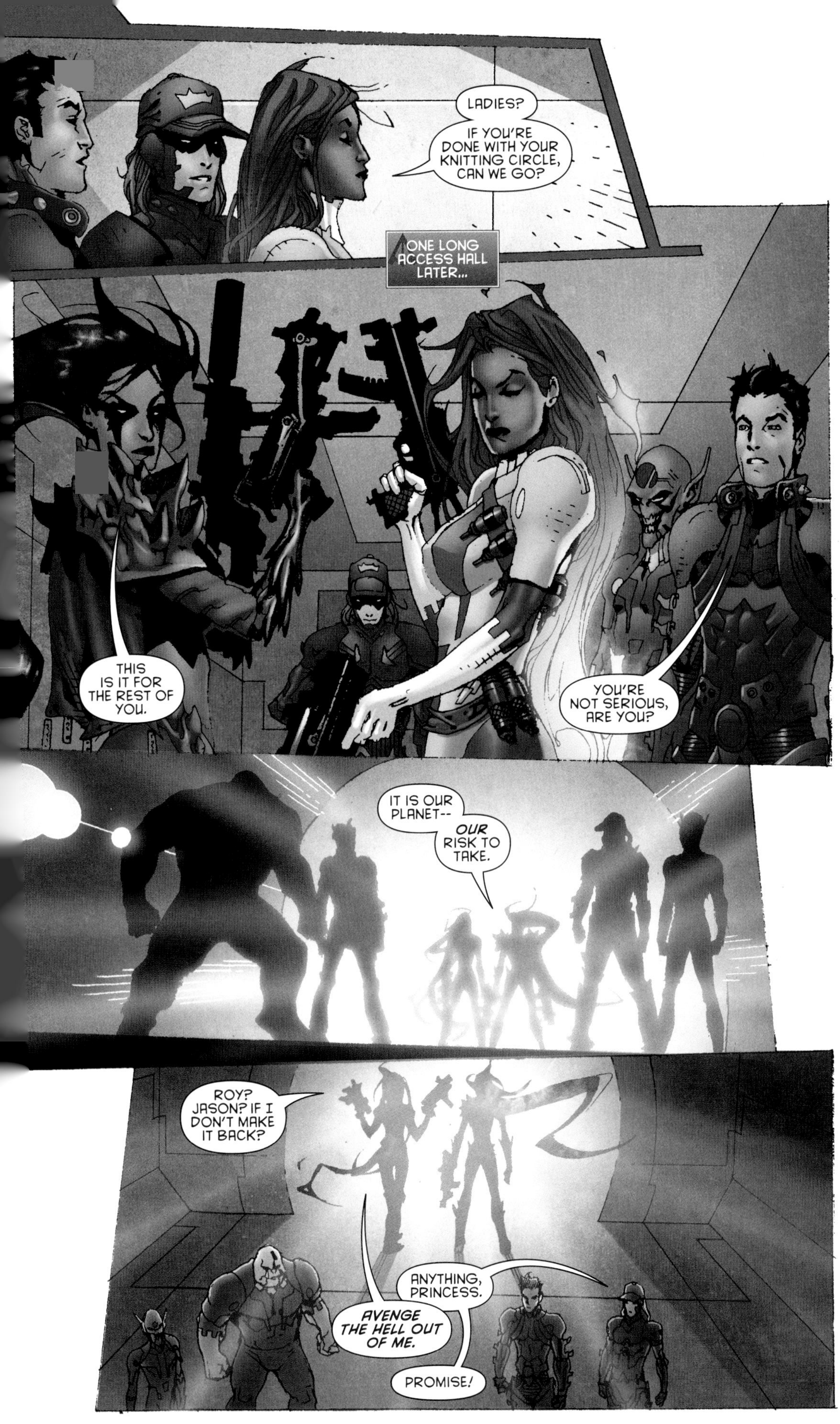
LADIES?
IF YOU'RE DONE WITH YOUR KNITTING CIRCLE, CAN WE GO?
ONE LONG ACCESS HALL LATER...
THIS IS IT FOR THE REST OF YOU.
YOU'RE NOT SERIOUS, ARE YOU?
IT IS OUR PLANET--
OUR RISK TO TAKE.
ROY? JASON? IF I DON'T MAKE IT BACK?
ANYTHING, PRINCESS.
AVENGE THE HELL OUT OF ME.
PROMISE!

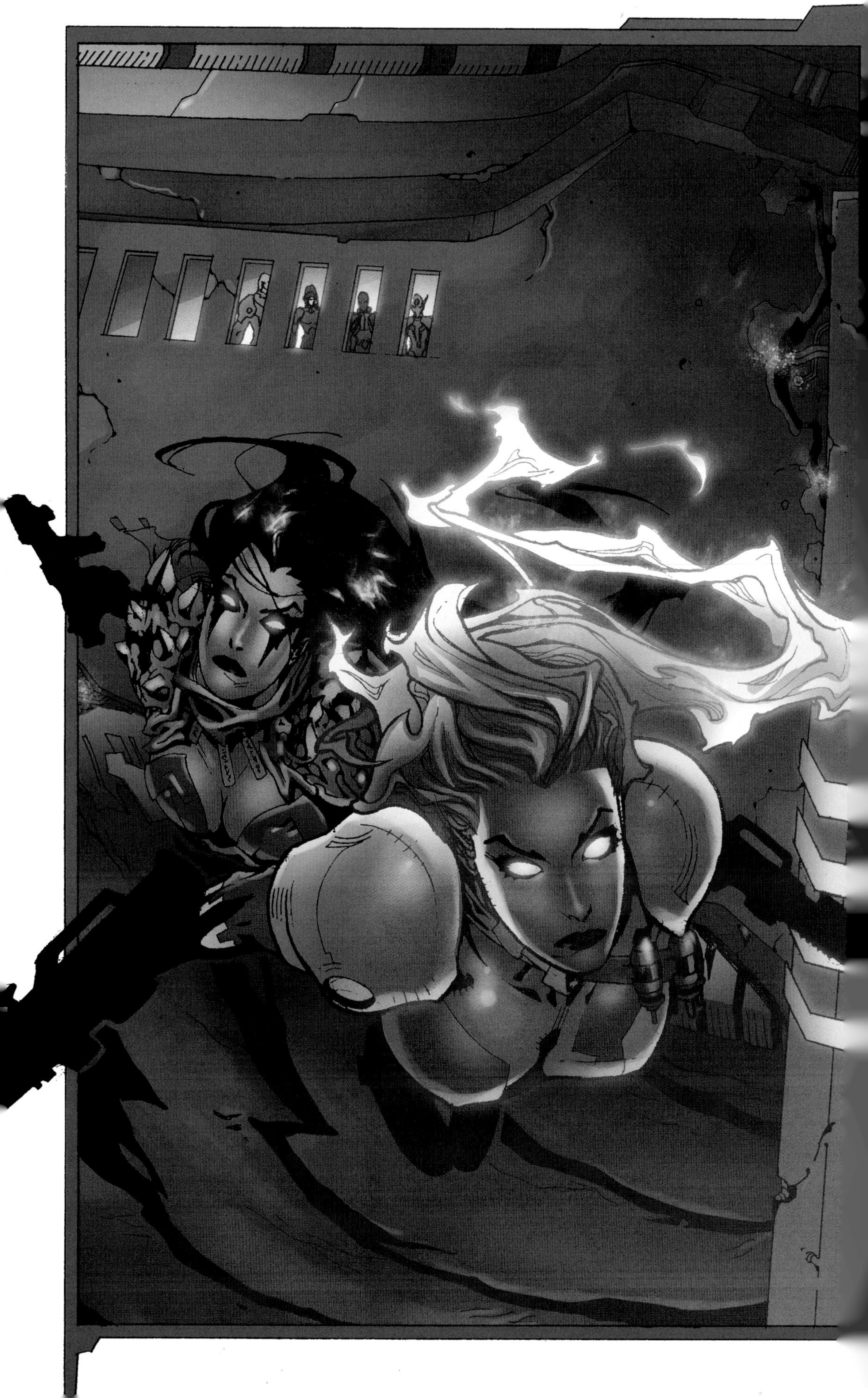

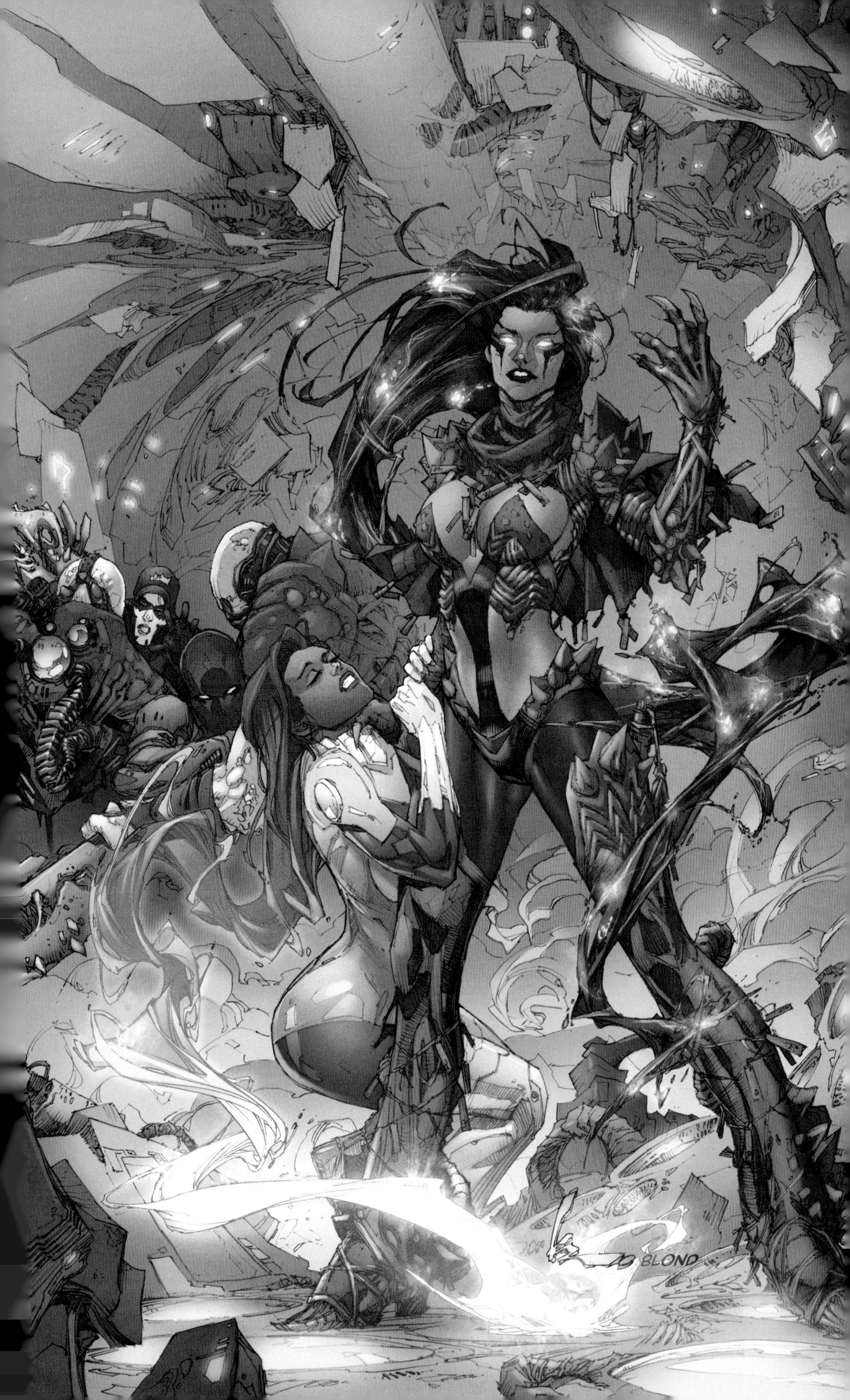
BLOND

SCOTT LOBDELL writer TIMOTHY GREEN II artist cover art by KENNETH ROCAFORT & BLOND

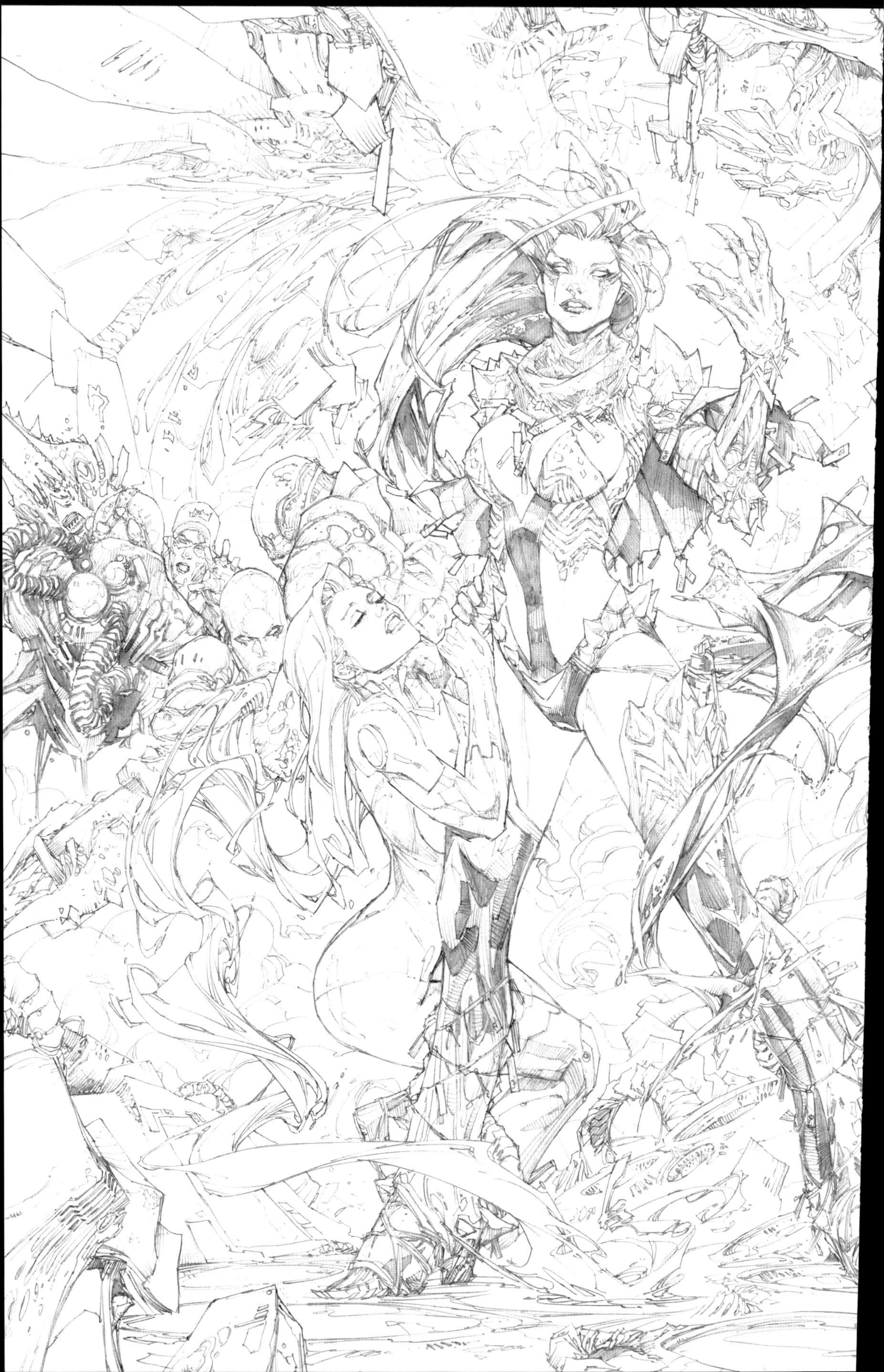

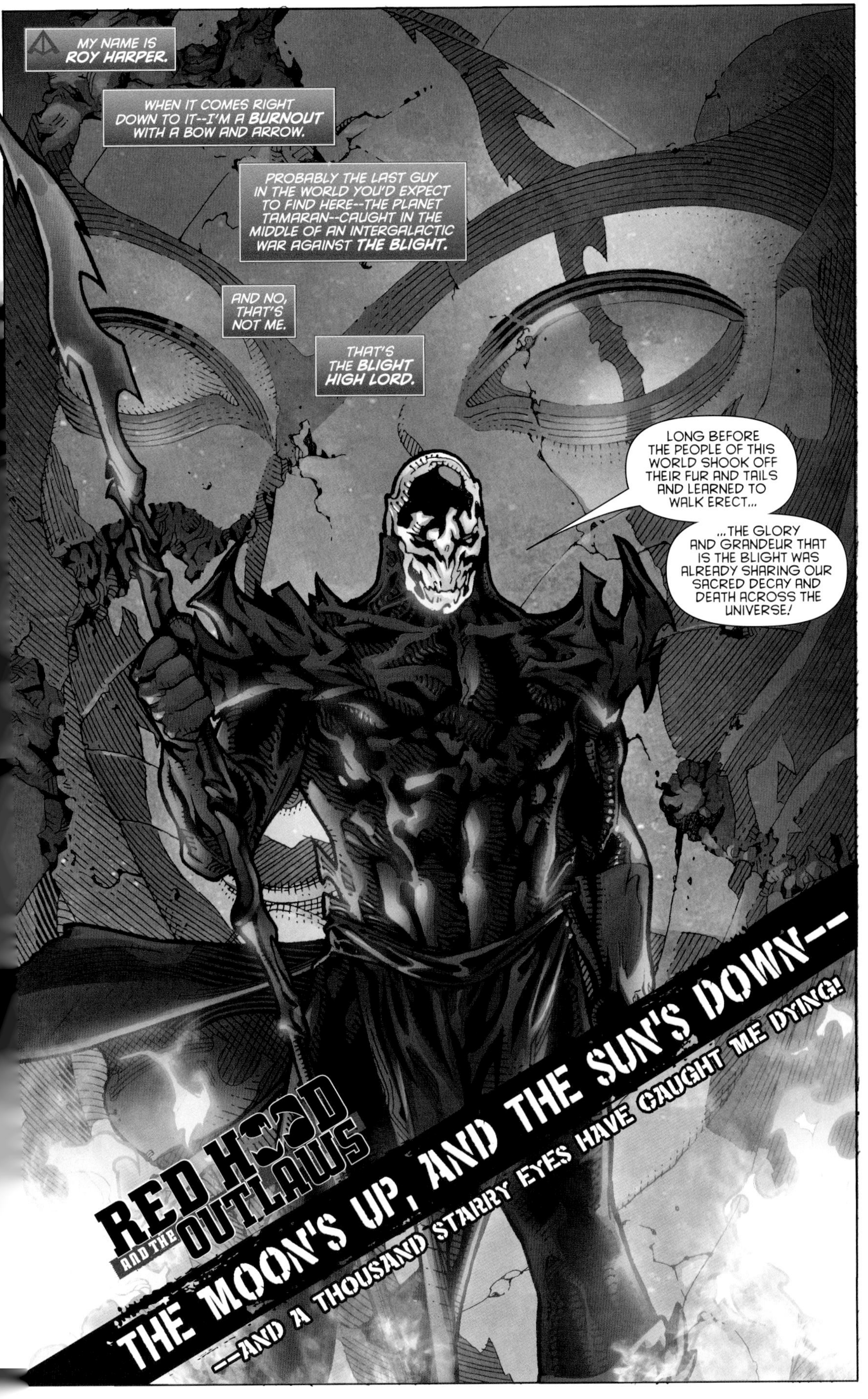
MY NAME IS ROY HARPER.
WHEN IT COMES RIGHT DOWN TO IT--I'M A BURNOUT WITH A BOW AND ARROW.
PROBABLY THE LAST GUY IN THE WORLD YOU'D EXPECT TO FIND HERE--THE PLANET TAMARAN--CAUGHT IN THE MIDDLE OF AN INTERGALACTIC WAR AGAINST THE BLIGHT.
AND NO, THAT'S NOT ME.
THAT'S THE BLIGHT HIGH LORD.
LONG BEFORE THE PEOPLE OF THIS WORLD SHOOK OFF THEIR FUR AND TAILS AND LEARNED TO WALK ERECT...
...THE GLORY AND GRANDEUR THAT IS THE BLIGHT WAS ALREADY SHARING OUR SACRED DECAY AND DEATH ACROSS THE UNIVERSE!
RED HOOD AND THE OUTLAWS
THE MOON'S UP, AND THE SUN'S DOWN--
--AND A THOUSAND STARRY EYES HAVE CAUGHT ME DYING!

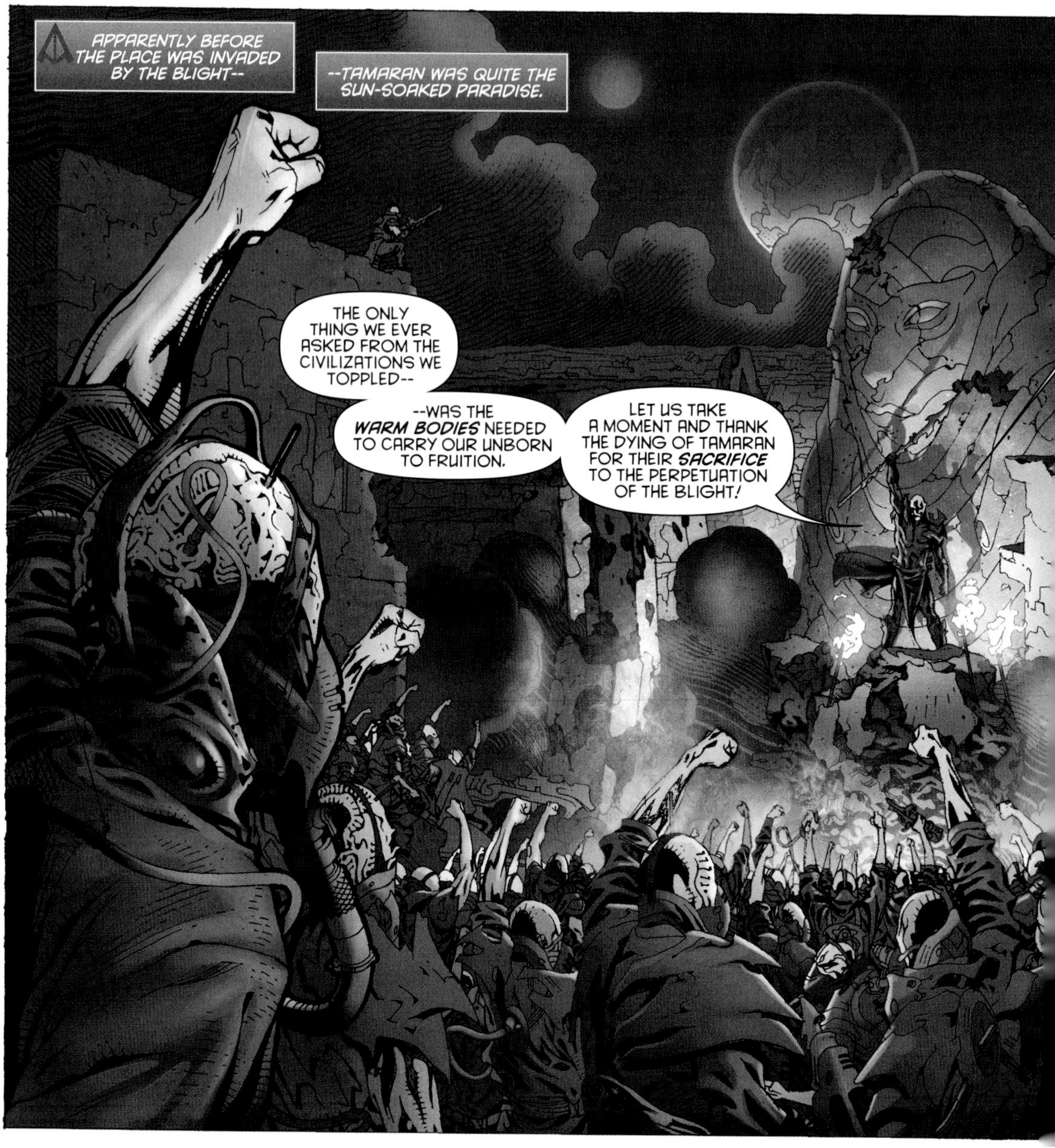
APPARENTLY BEFORE THE PLACE WAS INVADED BY THE BLIGHT--
--TAMARAN WAS QUITE THE SUN-SOAKED PARADISE.
THE ONLY THING WE EVER ASKED FROM THE CIVILIZATIONS WE TOPPLED--
--WAS THE WARM BODIES NEEDED TO CARRY OUR UNBORN TO FRUITION.
LET US TAKE A MOMENT AND THANK THE DYING OF TAMARAN FOR THEIR SACRIFICE TO THE PERPETUATION OF THE BLIGHT!

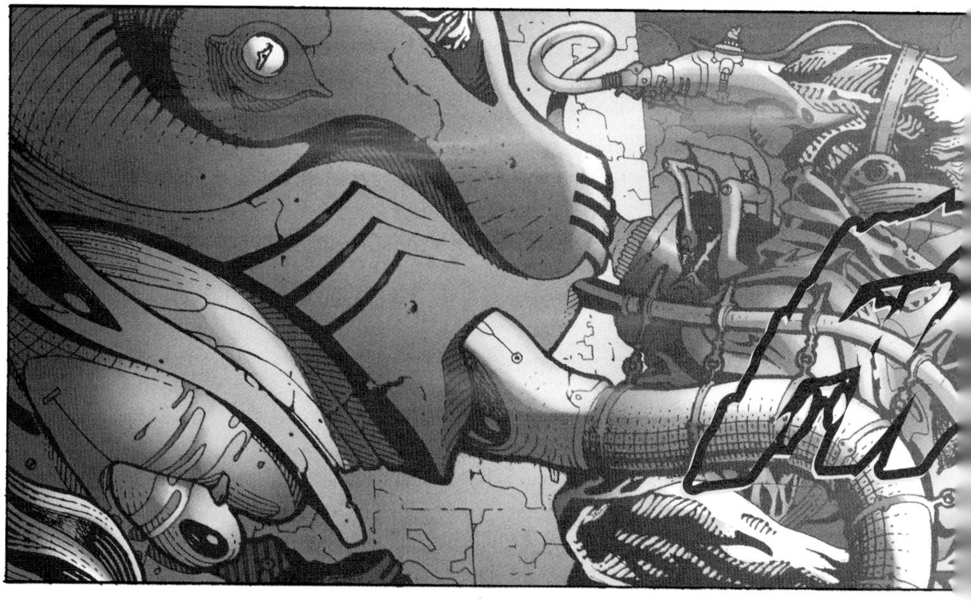

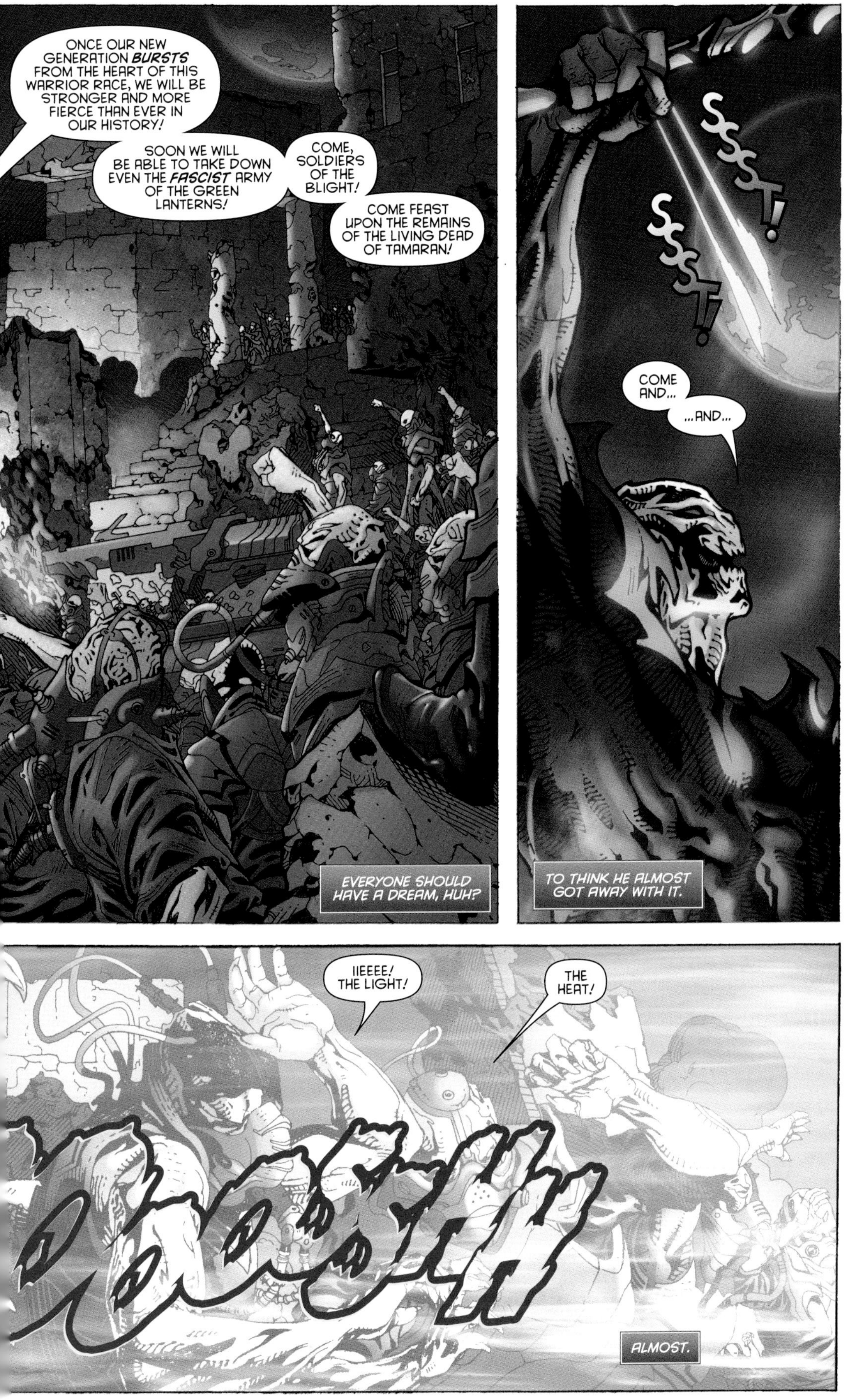
ONCE OUR NEW GENERATION BURSTS FROM THE HEART OF THIS WARRIOR RACE, WE WILL BE STRONGER AND MORE FIERCE THAN EVER IN OUR HISTORY!
SOON WE WILL BE ABLE TO TAKE DOWN EVEN THE FASCIST ARMY OF THE GREEN LANTERNS!
COME, SOLDIERS OF THE BLIGHT!
COME FEAST UPON THE REMAINS OF THE LIVING DEAD OF TAMARAN!
EVERYONE SHOULD HAVE A DREAM, HUH?
SSSST!
SSSST!
COME AND...
...AND...
TO THINK HE ALMOST GOT AWAY WITH IT.
IIEEEE! THE LIGHT!
THE HEAT!
ALMOST.

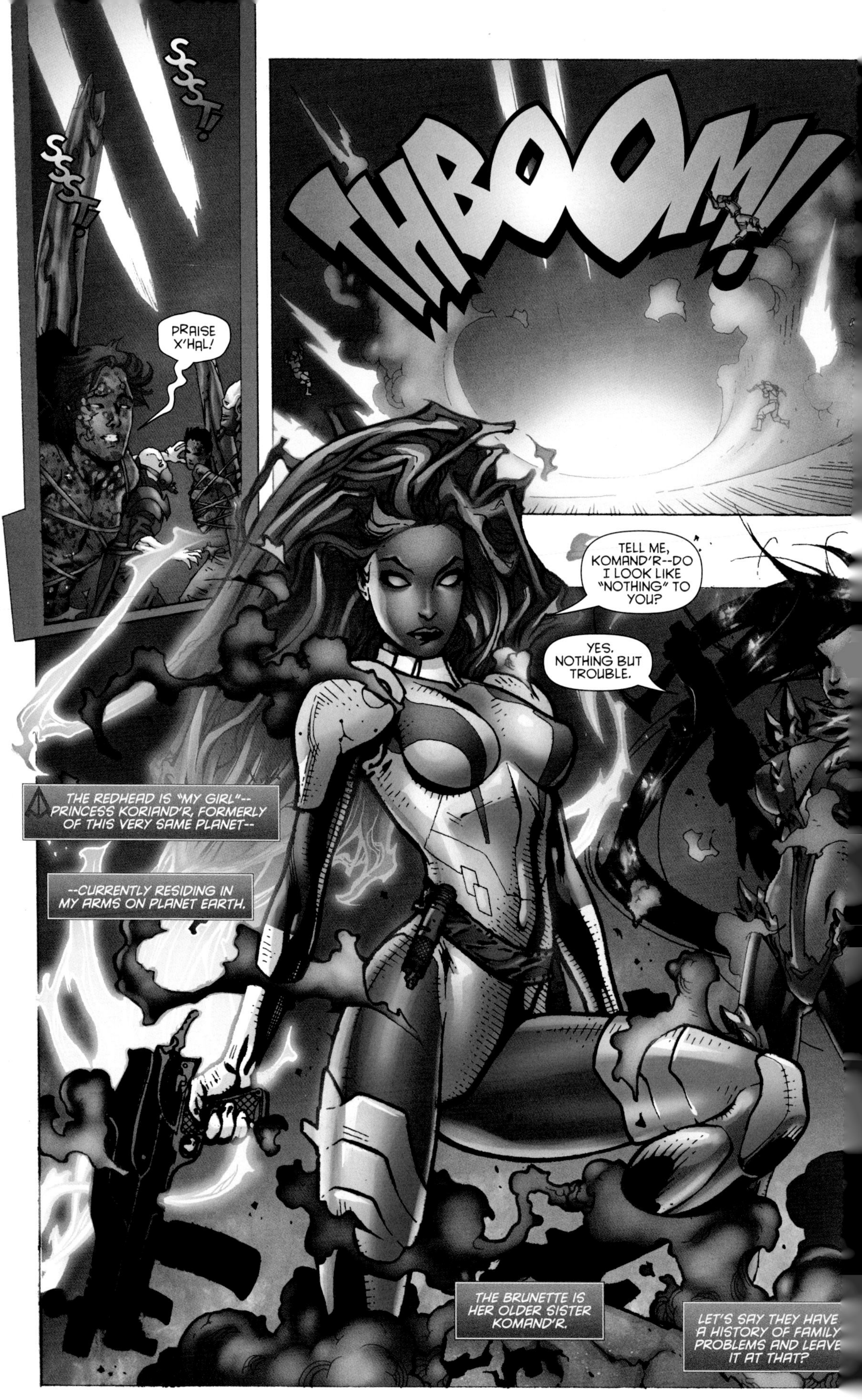
SSSST!
SSSST!
PRAISE X'HAL!
THOOM!
TELL ME, KOMAND'R--DO I LOOK LIKE "NOTHING" TO YOU?
YES. NOTHING BUT TROUBLE.
THE REDHEAD IS "MY GIRL"-- PRINCESS KORIAND'R, FORMERLY OF THIS VERY SAME PLANET--
--CURRENTLY RESIDING IN MY ARMS ON PLANET EARTH.
THE BRUNETTE IS HER OLDER SISTER KOMAND'R.
LET'S SAY THEY HAVE A HISTORY OF FAMILY PROBLEMS AND LEAVE IT AT THAT?

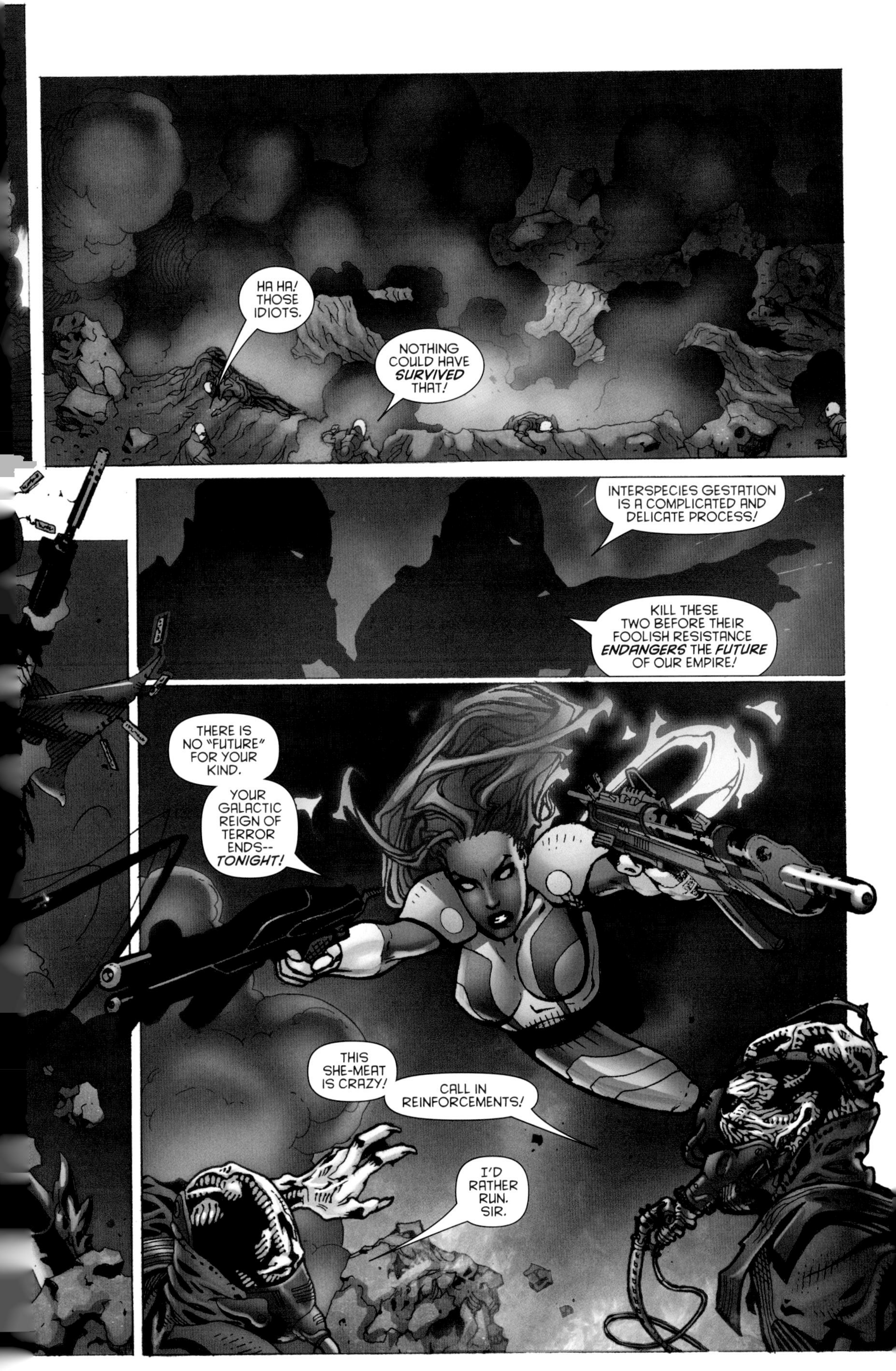
HA HA! THOSE IDIOTS.
NOTHING COULD HAVE SURVIVED THAT!
INTERSPECIES GESTATION IS A COMPLICATED AND DELICATE PROCESS!
KILL THESE TWO BEFORE THEIR FOOLISH RESISTANCE ENDANGERS THE FUTURE OF OUR EMPIRE!
THERE IS NO "FUTURE" FOR YOUR KIND.
YOUR GALACTIC REIGN OF TERROR ENDS-- TONIGHT!
THIS SHE-MEAT IS CRAZY!
CALL IN REINFORCEMENTS!
I'D RATHER RUN. SIR.

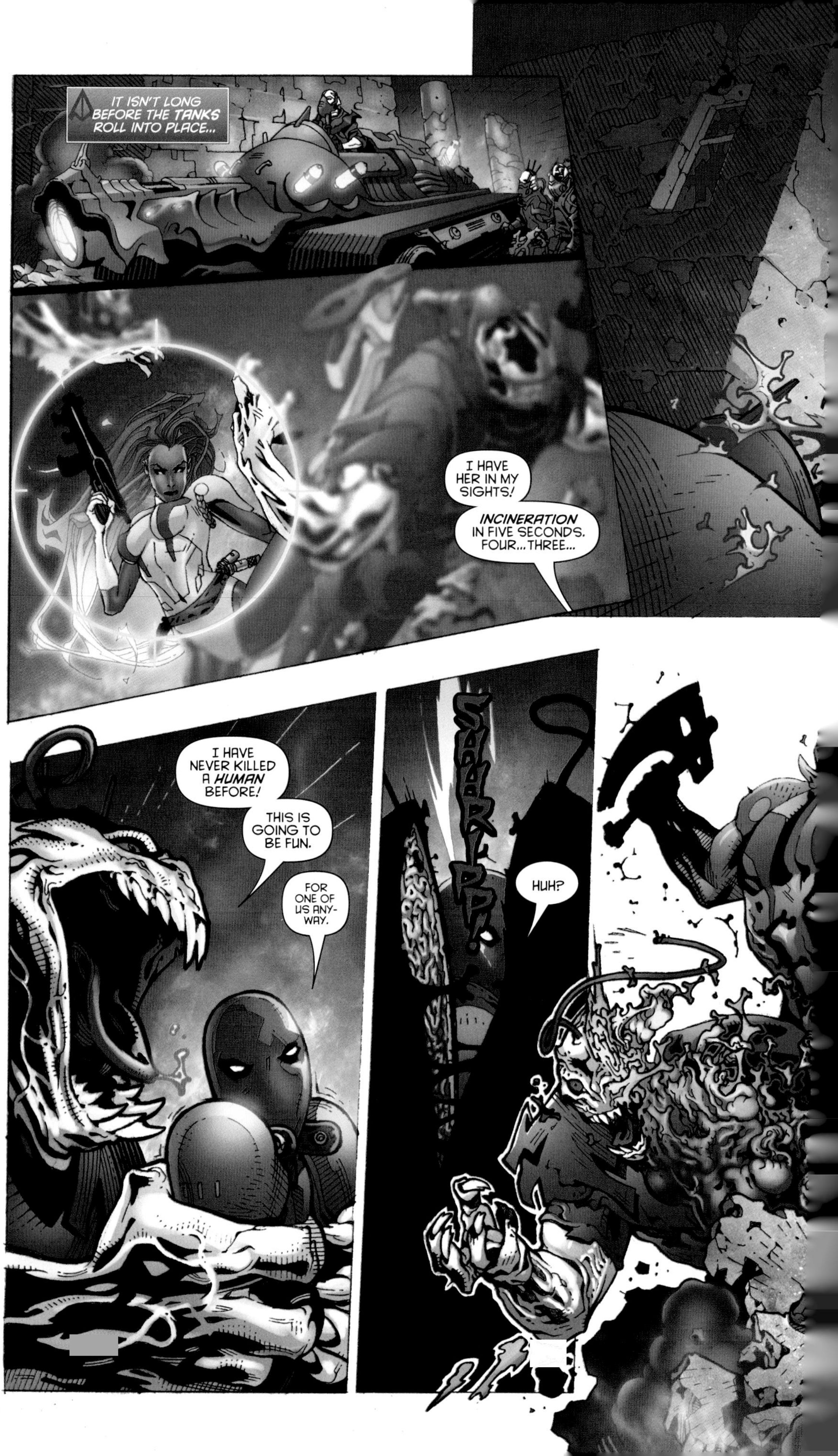
IT ISN'T LONG BEFORE THE TANKS ROLL INTO PLACE...
I HAVE HER IN MY SIGHTS!
INCINERATION IN FIVE SECONDS. FOUR... THREE...
I HAVE NEVER KILLED A HUMAN BEFORE!
THIS IS GOING TO BE FUN.
FOR ONE OF US ANYWAY.
SHRRRIPP!
HUH?

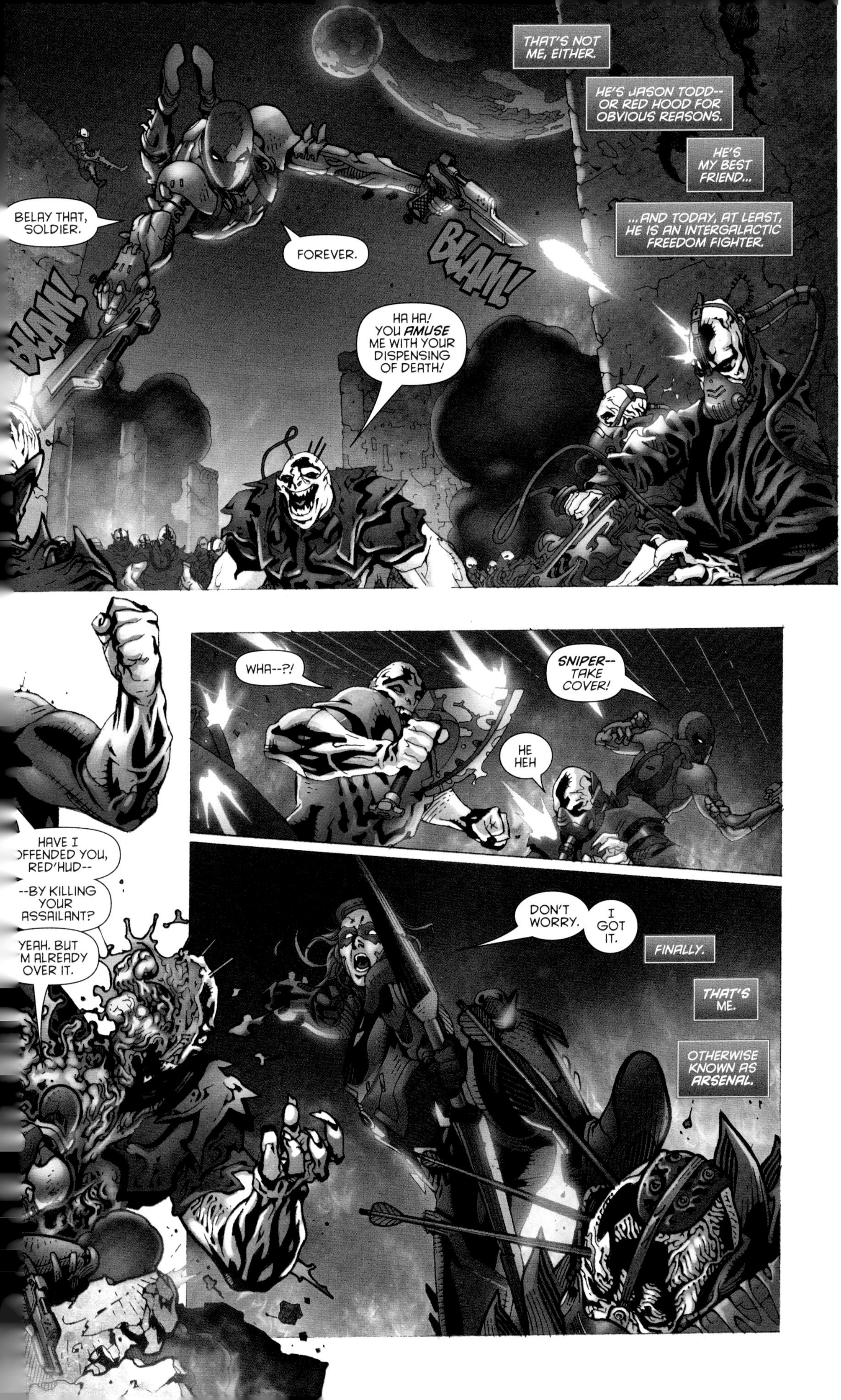
THAT'S NOT ME, EITHER.
HE'S JASON TODD-- OR RED HOOD FOR OBVIOUS REASONS.
HE'S MY BEST FRIEND...
...AND TODAY, AT LEAST, HE IS AN INTERGALACTIC FREEDOM FIGHTER.
BELAY THAT, SOLDIER.
FOREVER.
BLAM!
BLAM!
HA HA! YOU AMUSE ME WITH YOUR DISPENSING OF DEATH!
WHA--?!
SNIPER-- TAKE COVER!
HE HEH
HAVE I OFFENDED YOU, RED'HUD--
--BY KILLING YOUR ASSAILANT?
YEAH. BUT I'M ALREADY OVER IT.
DON'T WORRY.
I GOT IT.
FINALLY.
THAT'S ME.
OTHERWISE KNOWN AS ARSENAL.

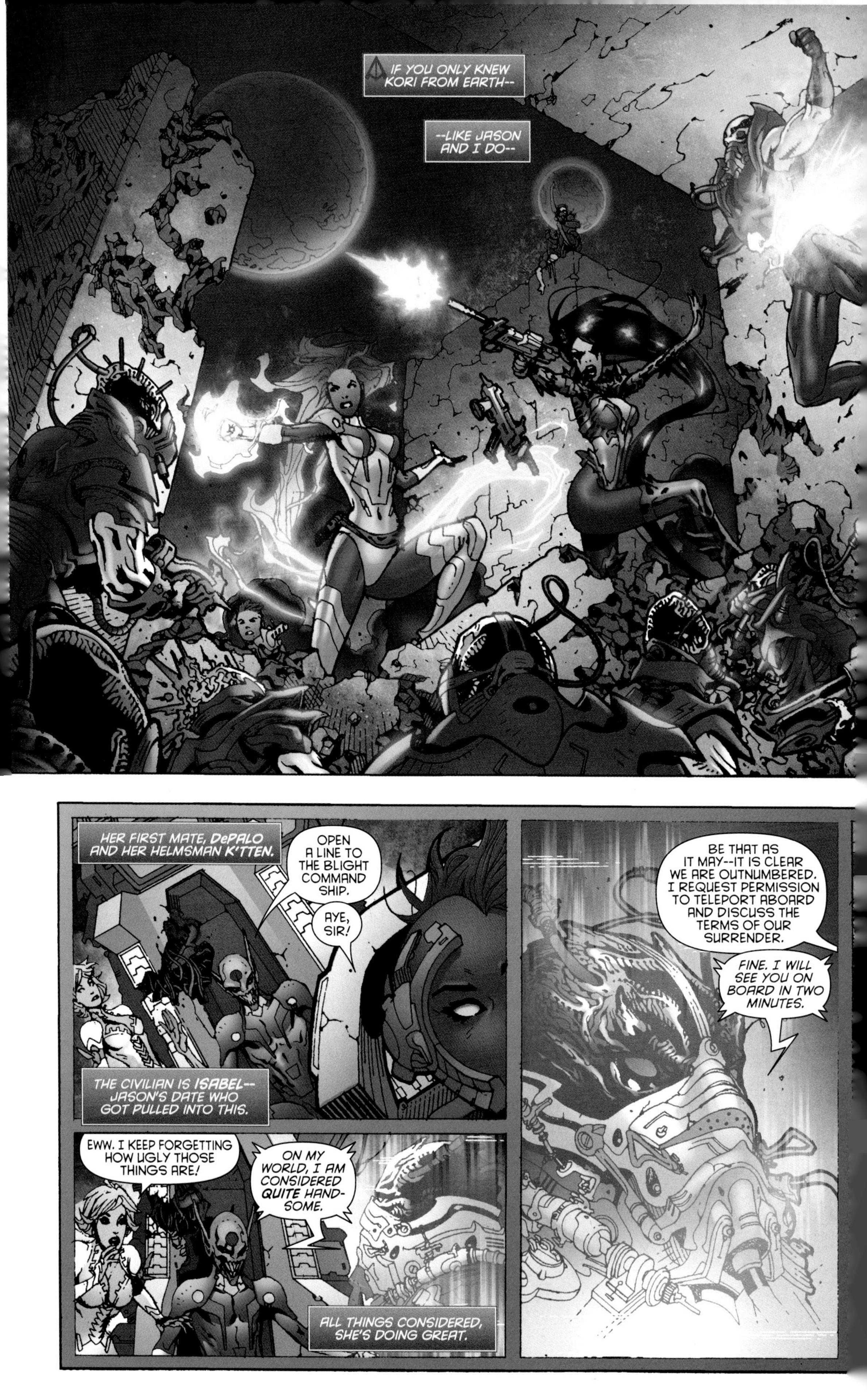
IF YOU ONLY KNEW KORI FROM EARTH--
--LIKE JASON AND I DO--
HER FIRST MATE, DePALO AND HER HELMSMAN K'TTEN.
OPEN A LINE TO THE BLIGHT COMMAND SHIP.
AYE, SIR!
THE CIVILIAN IS ISABEL-- JASON'S DATE WHO GOT PULLED INTO THIS.
EWW. I KEEP FORGETTING HOW UGLY THOSE THINGS ARE!
ON MY WORLD, I AM CONSIDERED QUITE HAND-SOME.
ALL THINGS CONSIDERED, SHE'S DOING GREAT.
BE THAT AS IT MAY--IT IS CLEAR WE ARE OUTNUMBERED. I REQUEST PERMISSION TO TELEPORT ABOARD AND DISCUSS THE TERMS OF OUR SURRENDER.
FINE. I WILL SEE YOU ON BOARD IN TWO MINUTES.

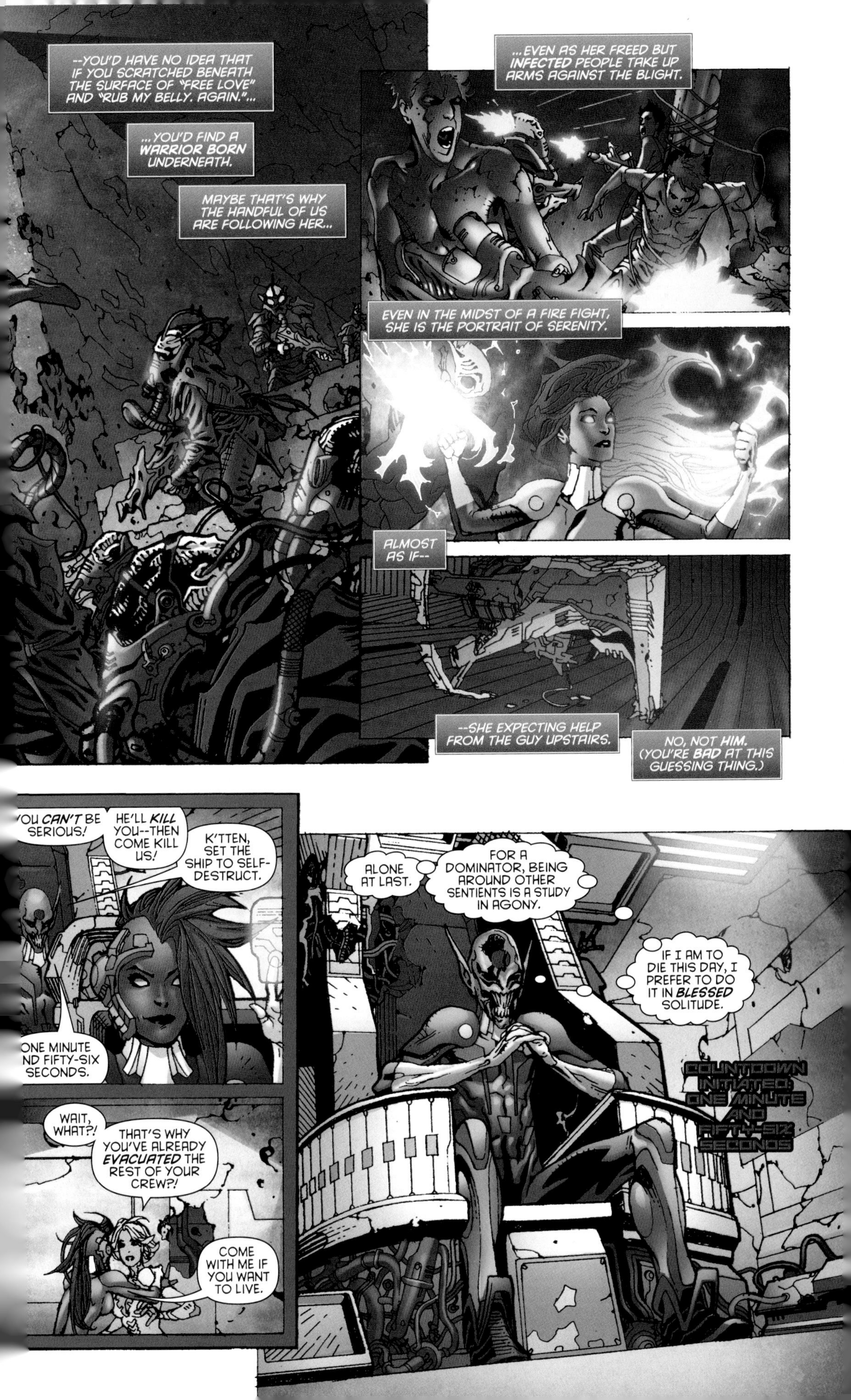
--YOU'D HAVE NO IDEA THAT IF YOU SCRATCHED BENEATH THE SURFACE OF "FREE LOVE" AND "RUB MY BELLY. AGAIN."...
...YOU'D FIND A WARRIOR BORN UNDERNEATH.
MAYBE THAT'S WHY THE HANDFUL OF US ARE FOLLOWING HER...
...EVEN AS HER FREED BUT INFECTED PEOPLE TAKE UP ARMS AGAINST THE BLIGHT.
EVEN IN THE MIDST OF A FIRE FIGHT, SHE IS THE PORTRAIT OF SERENITY.
ALMOST AS IF--
--SHE EXPECTING HELP FROM THE GUY UPSTAIRS.
NO, NOT HIM. (YOU'RE BAD AT THIS GUESSING THING.)
YOU CAN'T BE SERIOUS!
HE'LL KILL YOU--THEN COME KILL US!
K'TTEN, SET THE SHIP TO SELF-DESTRUCT.
ONE MINUTE ND FIFTY-SIX SECONDS.
WAIT, WHAT?!
THAT'S WHY YOU'VE ALREADY EVACUATED THE REST OF YOUR CREW?!
COME WITH ME IF YOU WANT TO LIVE.
ALONE AT LAST.
FOR A DOMINATOR, BEING AROUND OTHER SENTIENTS IS A STUDY IN AGONY.
IF I AM TO DIE THIS DAY, I PREFER TO DO IT IN BLESSED SOLITUDE.
COUNTDOWN INITIATED: ONE MINUTE AND FIFTY-SIX SECONDS

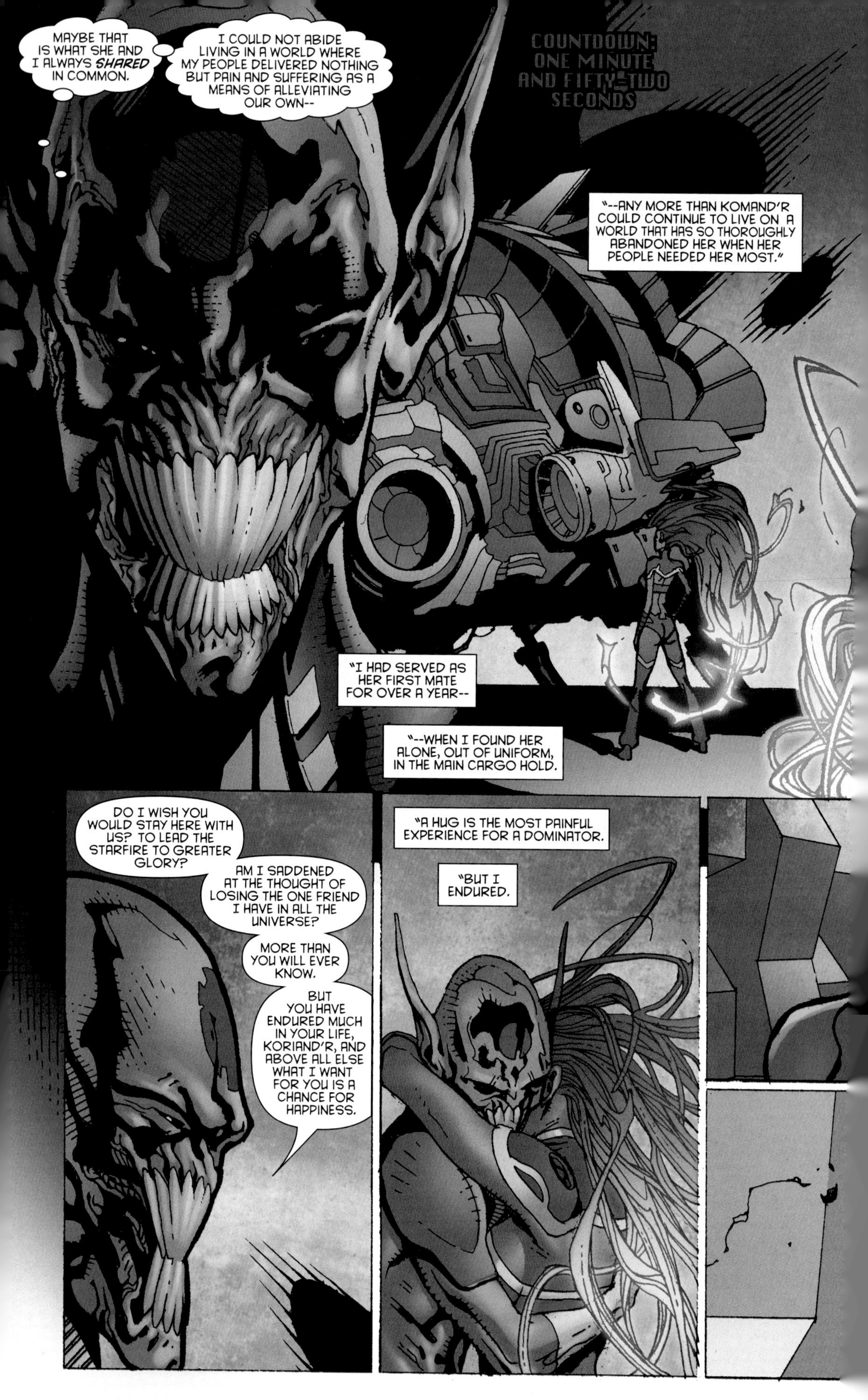

MAYBE THAT IS WHAT SHE AND I ALWAYS *SHARED* IN COMMON.
I COULD NOT ABIDE LIVING IN A WORLD WHERE MY PEOPLE DELIVERED NOTHING BUT PAIN AND SUFFERING AS A MEANS OF ALLEVIATING OUR OWN--
COUNTDOWN: ONE MINUTE AND FIFTY-TWO SECONDS
"--ANY MORE THAN KOMAND'R COULD CONTINUE TO LIVE ON A WORLD THAT HAS SO THOROUGHLY ABANDONED HER WHEN HER PEOPLE NEEDED HER MOST."
"I HAD SERVED AS HER FIRST MATE FOR OVER A YEAR--
"--WHEN I FOUND HER ALONE, OUT OF UNIFORM, IN THE MAIN CARGO HOLD.
DO I WISH YOU WOULD STAY HERE WITH US? TO LEAD THE STARFIRE TO GREATER GLORY?
AM I SADDENED AT THE THOUGHT OF LOSING THE ONE FRIEND I HAVE IN ALL THE UNIVERSE?
MORE THAN YOU WILL EVER KNOW.
BUT YOU HAVE ENDURED MUCH IN YOUR LIFE, KORIAND'R, AND ABOVE ALL ELSE WHAT I WANT FOR YOU IS A CHANCE FOR HAPPINESS.
"A HUG IS THE MOST PAINFUL EXPERIENCE FOR A DOMINATOR.
"BUT I ENDURED.

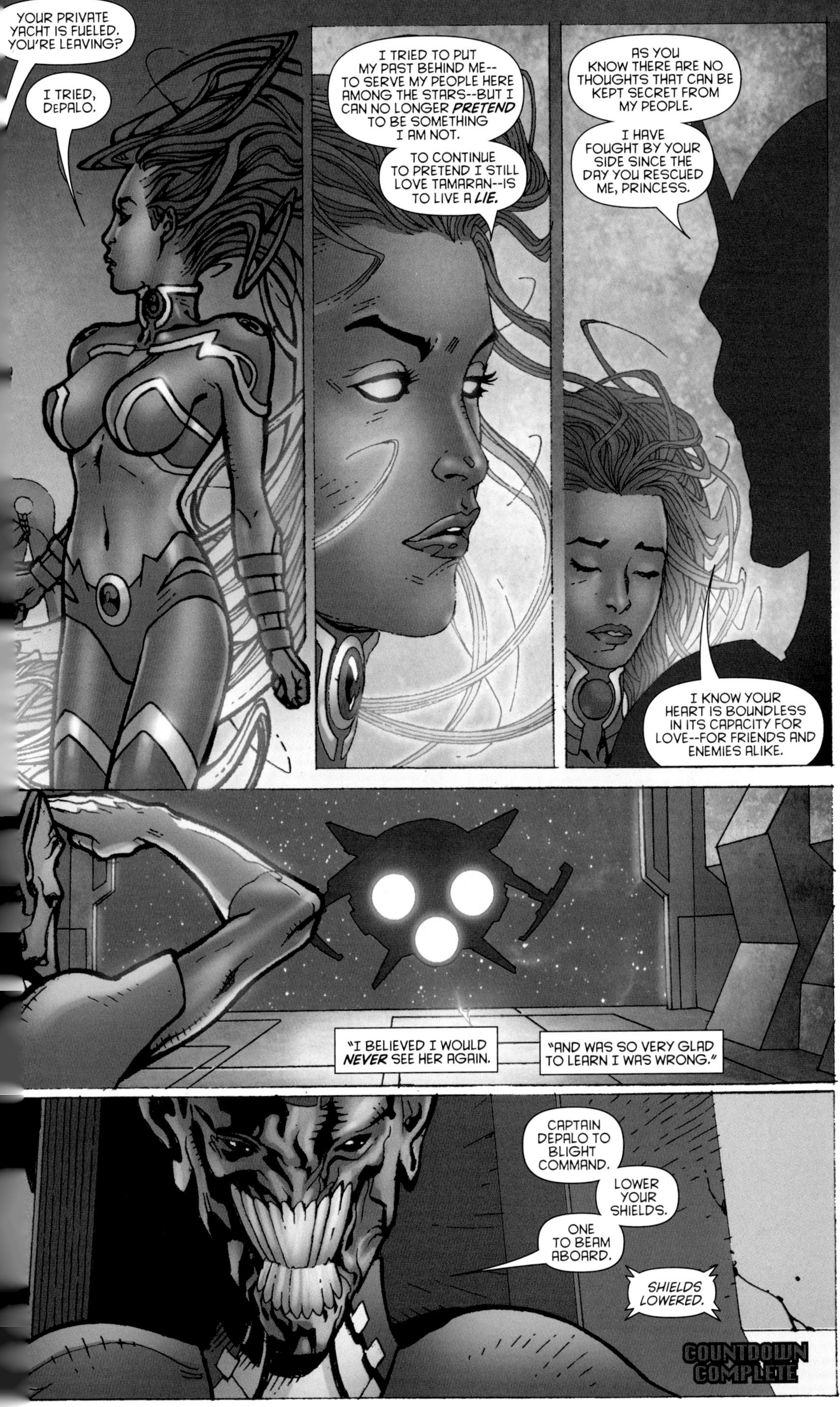

YOUR PRIVATE YACHT IS FUELED. YOU'RE LEAVING?
I TRIED, DePALO.
I TRIED TO PUT MY PAST BEHIND ME-- TO SERVE MY PEOPLE HERE AMONG THE STARS--BUT I CAN NO LONGER PRETEND TO BE SOMETHING I AM NOT.
TO CONTINUE TO PRETEND I STILL LOVE TAMARAN--IS TO LIVE A LIE.
AS YOU KNOW THERE ARE NO THOUGHTS THAT CAN BE KEPT SECRET FROM MY PEOPLE.
I HAVE FOUGHT BY YOUR SIDE SINCE THE DAY YOU RESCUED ME, PRINCESS.
I KNOW YOUR HEART IS BOUNDLESS IN ITS CAPACITY FOR LOVE--FOR FRIENDS AND ENEMIES ALIKE.
"I BELIEVED I WOULD NEVER SEE HER AGAIN.
"AND WAS SO VERY GLAD TO LEARN I WAS WRONG."
CAPTAIN DEPALO TO BLIGHT COMMAND.
LOWER YOUR SHIELDS.
ONE TO BEAM ABOARD.
SHIELDS LOWERED.
COUNTDOWN COMPLETE

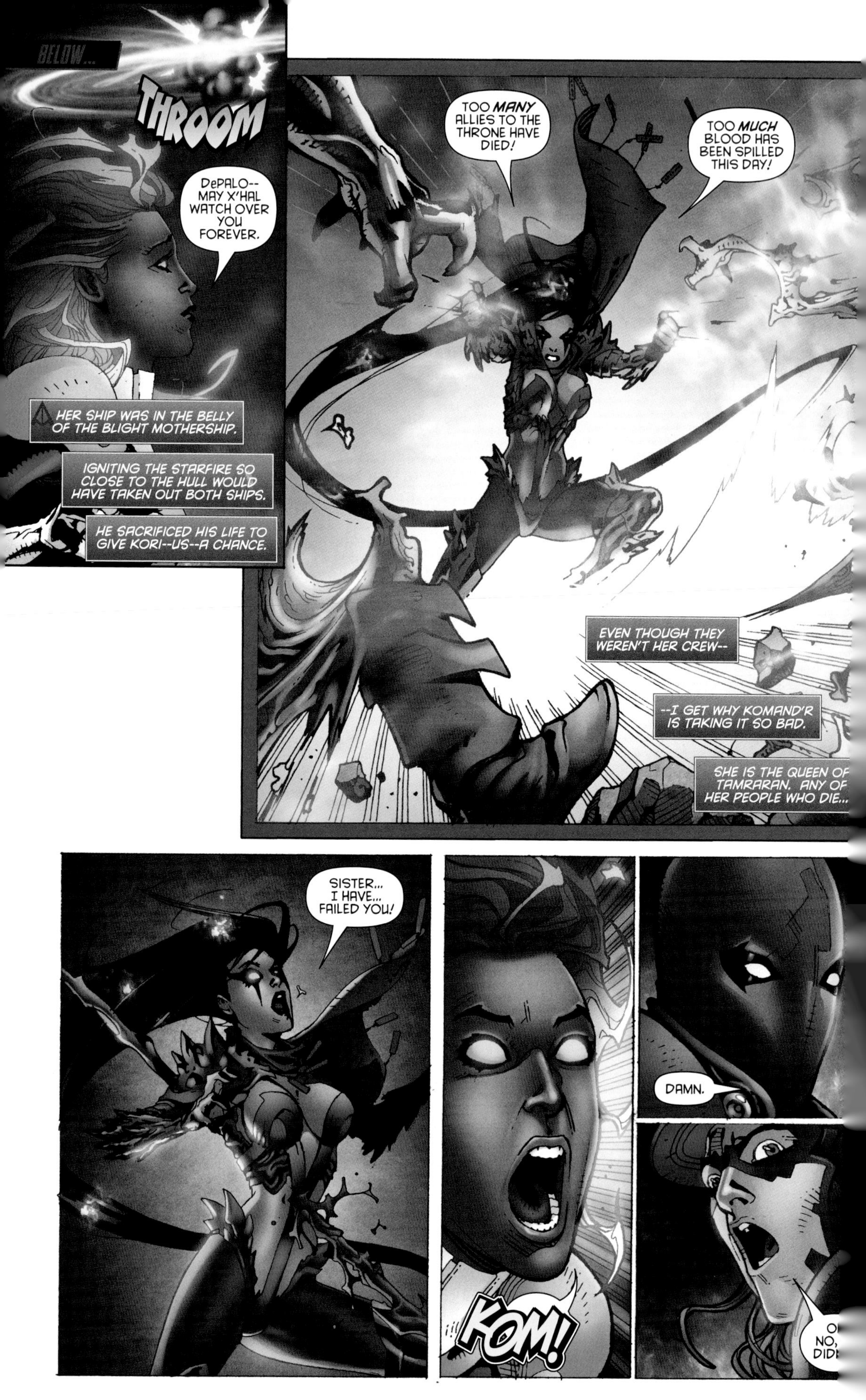
BELOW...
THROOM
DePALO-- MAY X'HAL WATCH OVER YOU FOREVER.
HER SHIP WAS IN THE BELLY OF THE BLIGHT MOTHERSHIP.
IGNITING THE STARFIRE SO CLOSE TO THE HULL WOULD HAVE TAKEN OUT BOTH SHIPS.
HE SACRIFICED HIS LIFE TO GIVE KORI--US--A CHANCE.
TOO MANY ALLIES TO THE THRONE HAVE DIED!
TOO MUCH BLOOD HAS BEEN SPILLED THIS DAY!
EVEN THOUGH THEY WEREN'T HER CREW--
--I GET WHY KOMAND'R IS TAKING IT SO BAD.
SHE IS THE QUEEN OF TAMRARAN. ANY OF HER PEOPLE WHO DIE...
SISTER... I HAVE... FAILED YOU!
KOM!
DAMN.

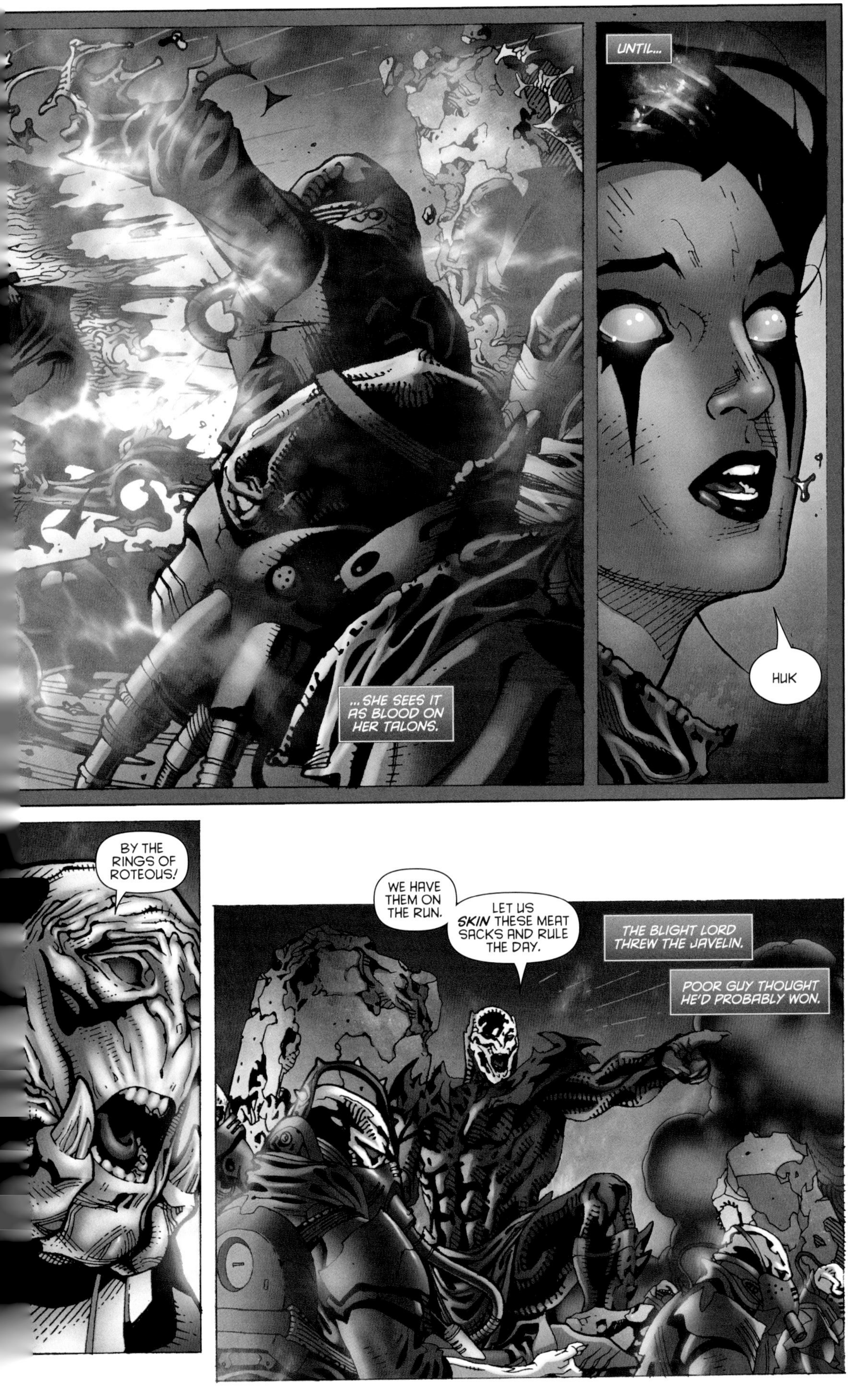
...SHE SEES IT AS BLOOD ON HER TALONS.
UNTIL...
HUK
BY THE RINGS OF ROTEOUS!
WE HAVE THEM ON THE RUN.
LET US SKIN THESE MEAT SACKS AND RULE THE DAY.
THE BLIGHT LORD THREW THE JAVELIN.
POOR GUY THOUGHT HE'D PROBABLY WON.

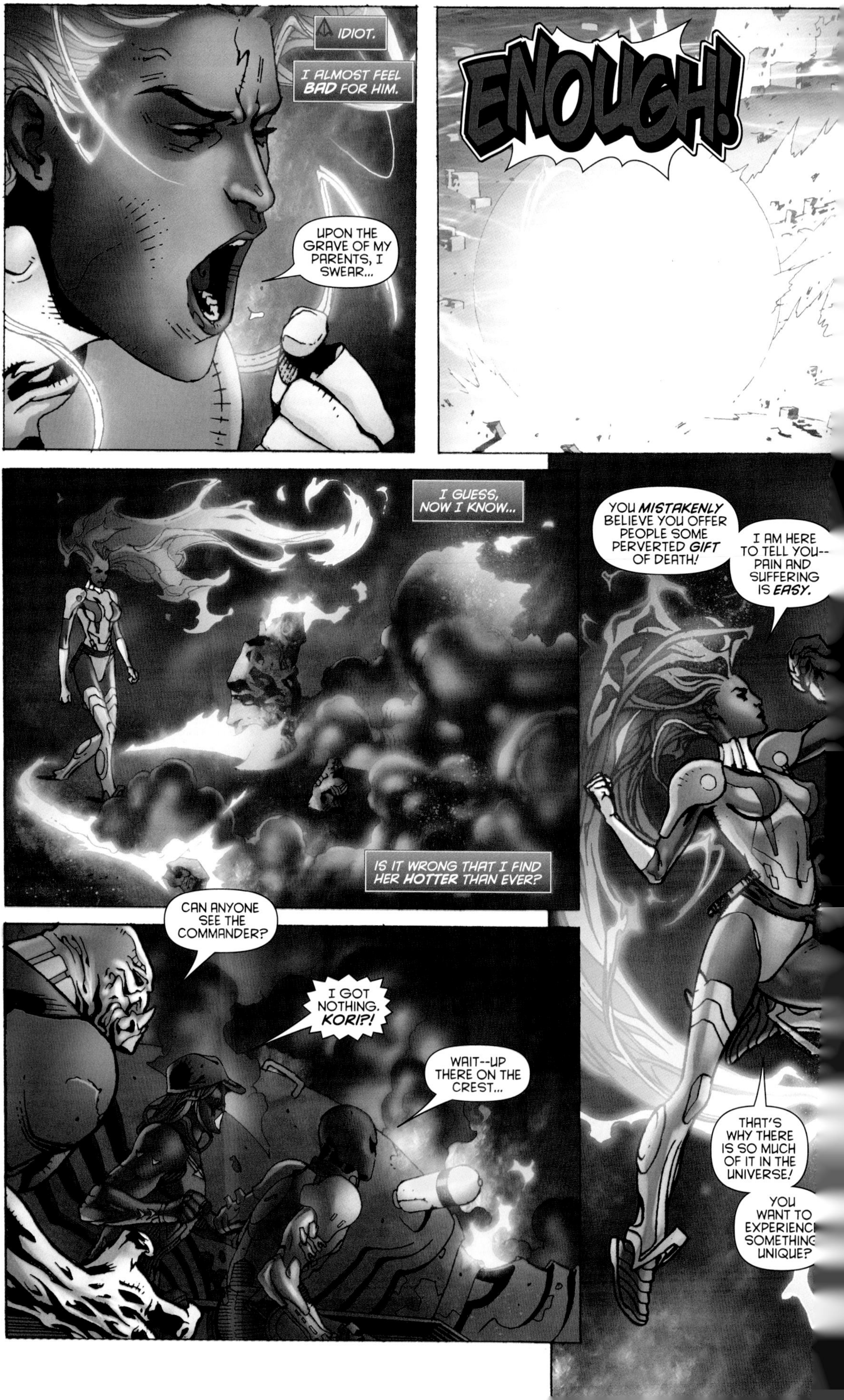
IDIOT.
I ALMOST FEEL BAD FOR HIM.
UPON THE GRAVE OF MY PARENTS, I SWEAR...
ENOUGH!
I GUESS, NOW I KNOW...
IS IT WRONG THAT I FIND HER HOTTER THAN EVER?
YOU MISTAKENLY BELIEVE YOU OFFER PEOPLE SOME PERVERTED GIFT OF DEATH!
I AM HERE TO TELL YOU-- PAIN AND SUFFERING IS EASY.
CAN ANYONE SEE THE COMMANDER?
I GOT NOTHING. KORI?!
WAIT--UP THERE ON THE CREST...
THAT'S WHY THERE IS SO MUCH OF IT IN THE UNIVERSE!

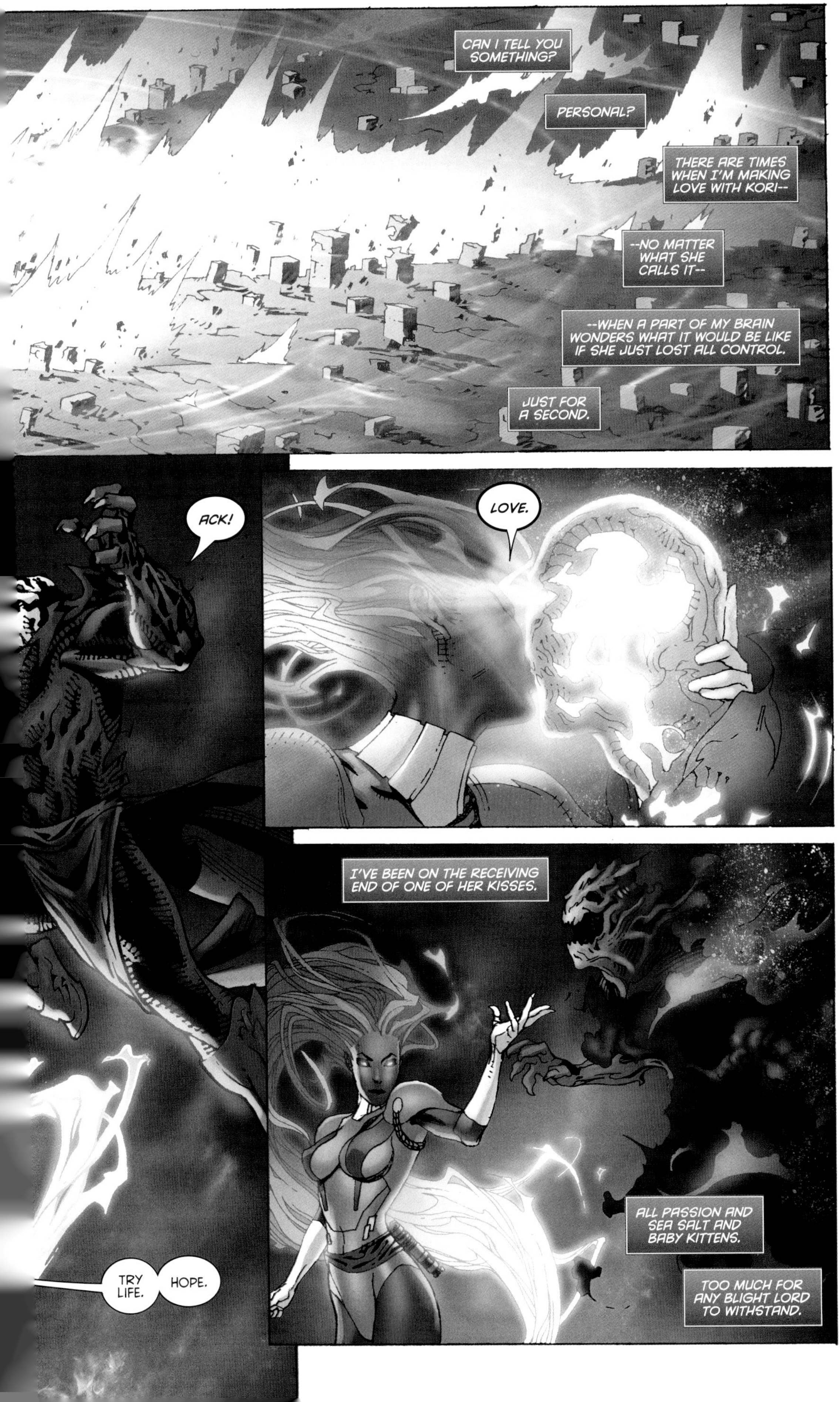
CAN I TELL YOU SOMETHING?
PERSONAL?
THERE ARE TIMES WHEN I'M MAKING LOVE WITH KORI--
--NO MATTER WHAT SHE CALLS IT--
--WHEN A PART OF MY BRAIN WONDERS WHAT IT WOULD BE LIKE IF SHE JUST LOST ALL CONTROL.
JUST FOR A SECOND.
ACK!
LOVE.
I'VE BEEN ON THE RECEIVING END OF ONE OF HER KISSES.
ALL PASSION AND SEA SALT AND BABY KITTENS.
TOO MUCH FOR ANY BLIGHT LORD TO WITHSTAND.
TRY LIFE.
HOPE.

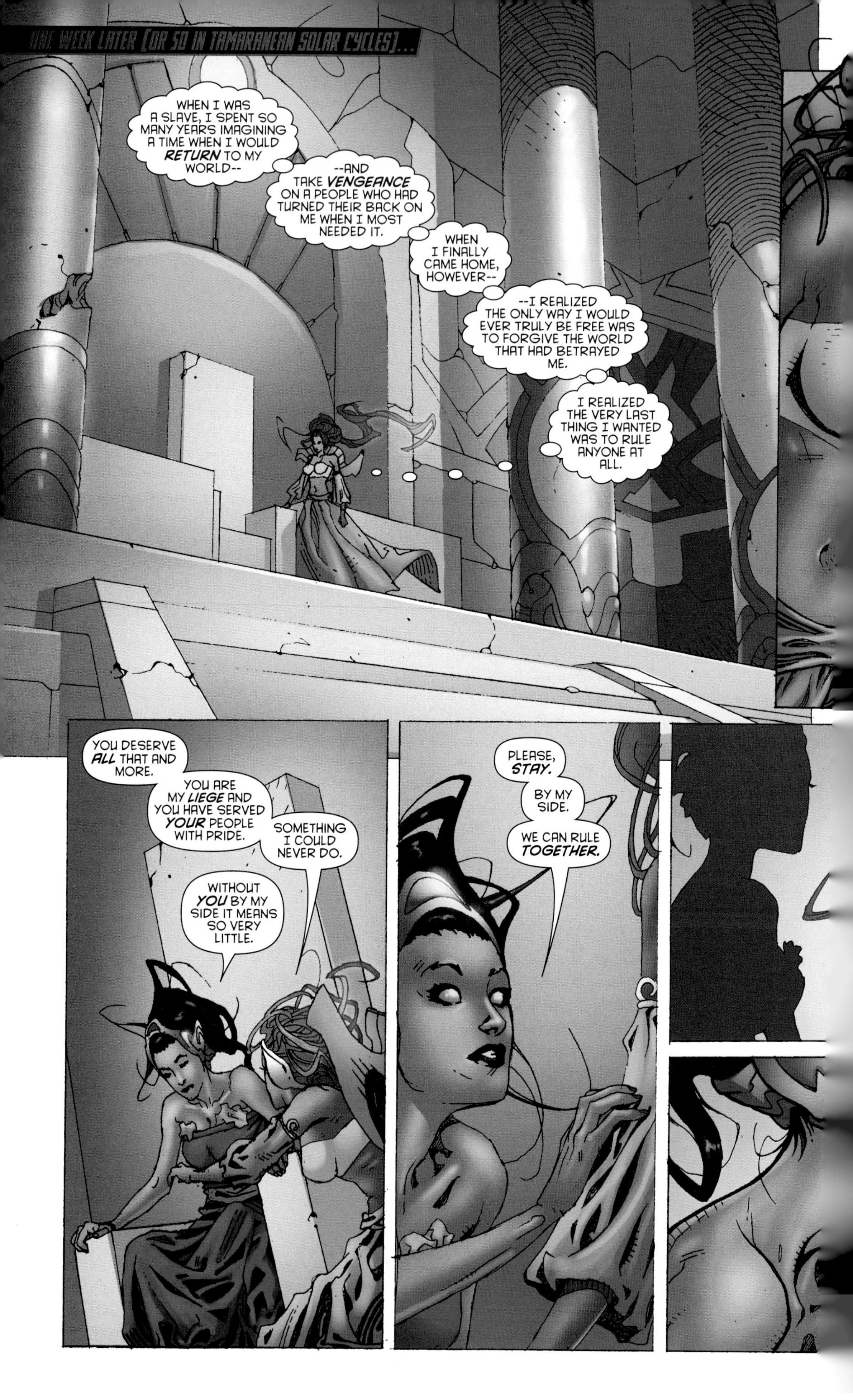
ONE WEEK LATER (OR SO IN TAMARANEAN SOLAR CYCLES)...
WHEN I WAS A SLAVE, I SPENT SO MANY YEARS IMAGINING A TIME WHEN I WOULD RETURN TO MY WORLD--
--AND TAKE VENGEANCE ON A PEOPLE WHO HAD TURNED THEIR BACK ON ME WHEN I MOST NEEDED IT.
WHEN I FINALLY CAME HOME, HOWEVER--
--I REALIZED THE ONLY WAY I WOULD EVER TRULY BE FREE WAS TO FORGIVE THE WORLD THAT HAD BETRAYED ME.
I REALIZED THE VERY LAST THING I WANTED WAS TO RULE ANYONE AT ALL.
YOU DESERVE ALL THAT AND MORE.
YOU ARE MY LIEGE AND YOU HAVE SERVED YOUR PEOPLE WITH PRIDE.
SOMETHING I COULD NEVER DO.
WITHOUT YOU BY MY SIDE IT MEANS SO VERY LITTLE.
PLEASE, STAY.
BY MY SIDE.
WE CAN RULE TOGETHER.

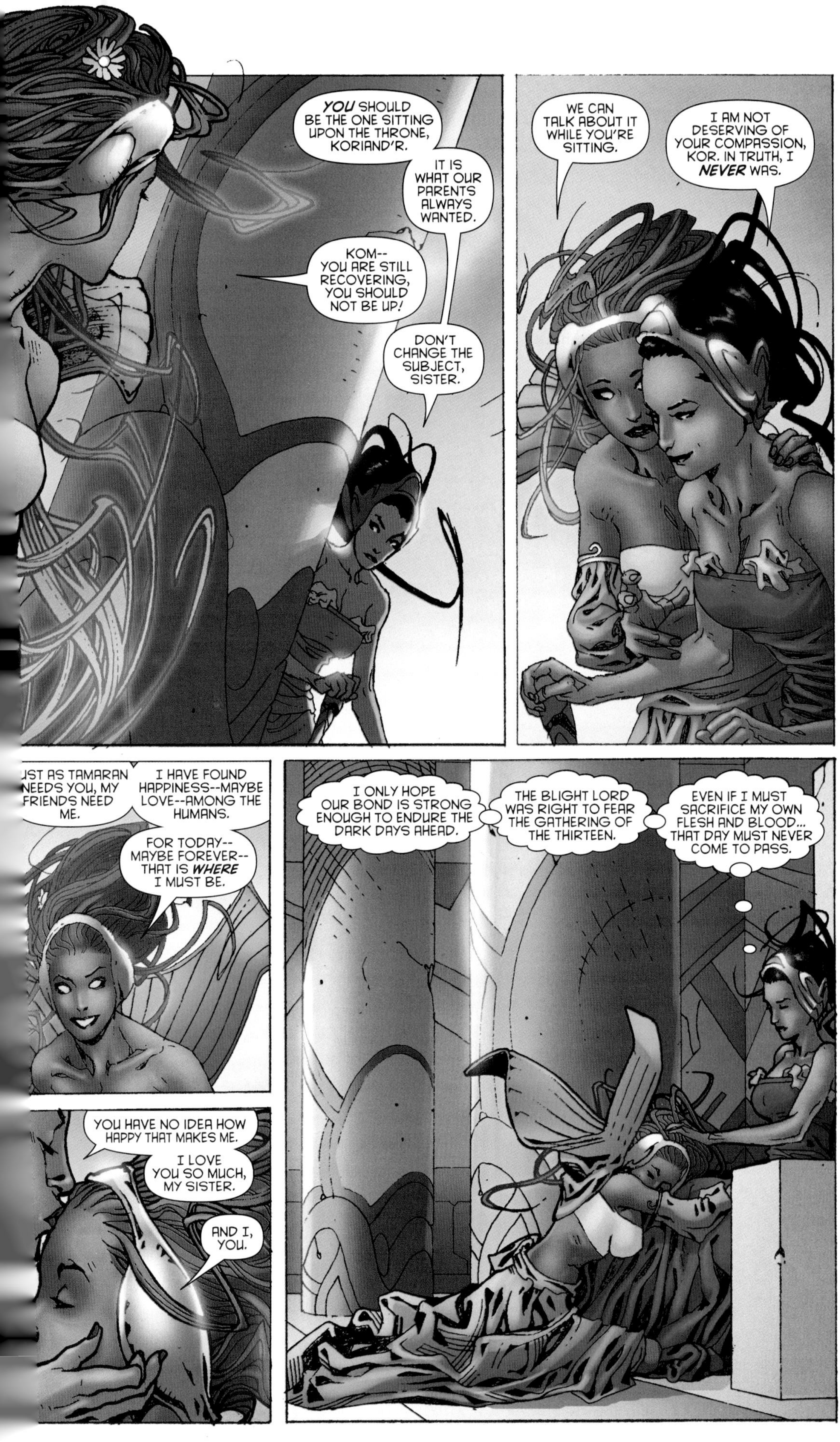
YOU SHOULD BE THE ONE SITTING UPON THE THRONE, KORIAND'R.
IT IS WHAT OUR PARENTS ALWAYS WANTED.
KOM-- YOU ARE STILL RECOVERING, YOU SHOULD NOT BE UP!
DON'T CHANGE THE SUBJECT, SISTER.
WE CAN TALK ABOUT IT WHILE YOU'RE SITTING.
I AM NOT DESERVING OF YOUR COMPASSION, KOR. IN TRUTH, I NEVER WAS.
UST AS TAMARAN NEEDS YOU, MY FRIENDS NEED ME.
I HAVE FOUND HAPPINESS--MAYBE LOVE--AMONG THE HUMANS.
FOR TODAY-- MAYBE FOREVER-- THAT IS WHERE I MUST BE.
YOU HAVE NO IDEA HOW HAPPY THAT MAKES ME.
I LOVE YOU SO MUCH, MY SISTER.
AND I, YOU.
I ONLY HOPE OUR BOND IS STRONG ENOUGH TO ENDURE THE DARK DAYS AHEAD.
THE BLIGHT LORD WAS RIGHT TO FEAR THE GATHERING OF THE THIRTEEN.
EVEN IF I MUST SACRIFICE MY OWN FLESH AND BLOOD... THAT DAY MUST NEVER COME TO PASS.

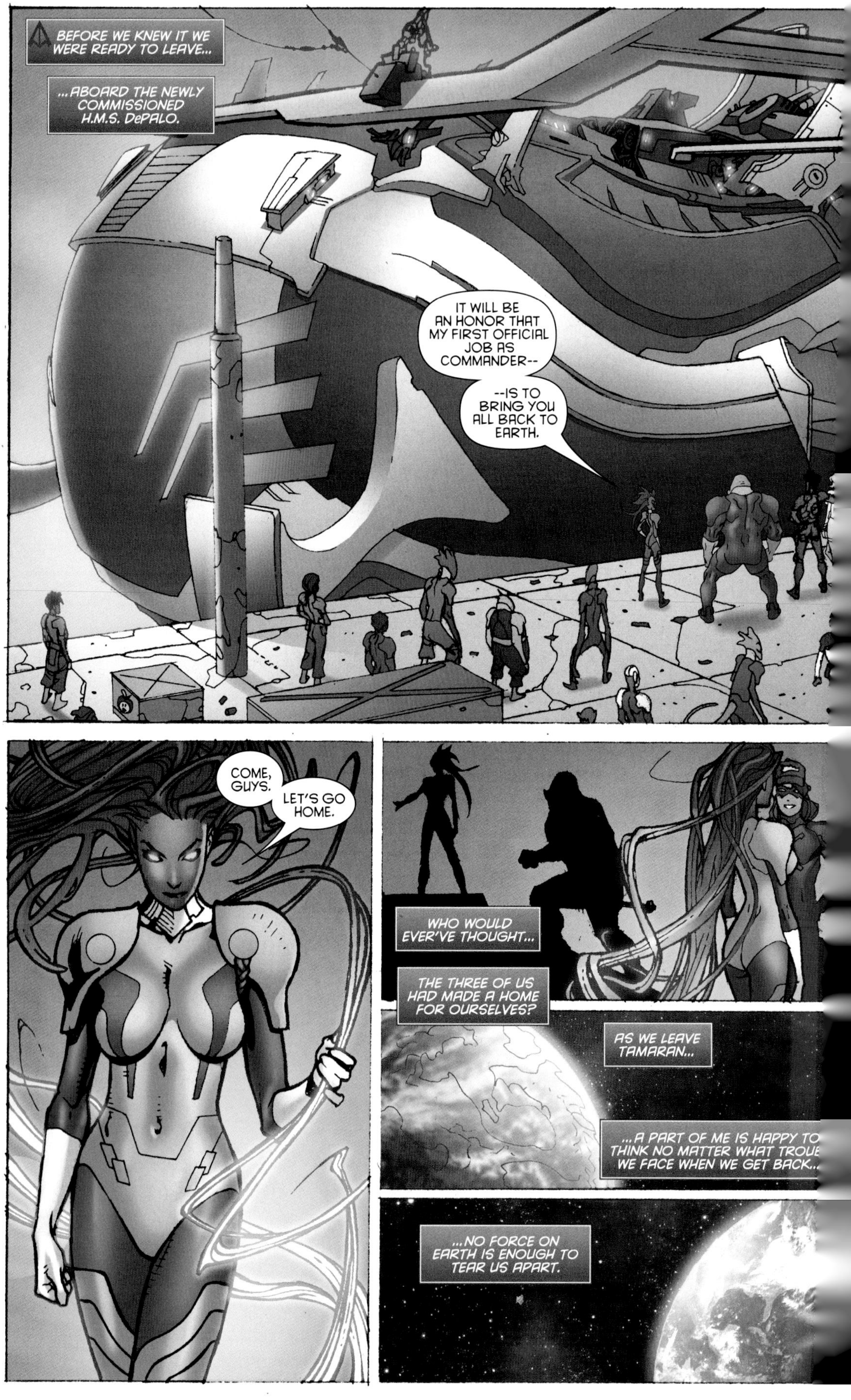
BEFORE WE KNEW IT WE WERE READY TO LEAVE...
...ABOARD THE NEWLY COMMISSIONED H.M.S. DePALO.
IT WILL BE AN HONOR THAT MY FIRST OFFICIAL JOB AS COMMANDER--
--IS TO BRING YOU ALL BACK TO EARTH.
COME, GUYS.
LET'S GO HOME.
WHO WOULD EVER'VE THOUGHT...
THE THREE OF US HAD MADE A HOME FOR OURSELVES?
AS WE LEAVE TAMARAN...
...A PART OF ME IS HAPPY TO THINK NO MATTER WHAT TROU
WE FACE WHEN WE GET BACK...
...NO FORCE ON EARTH IS ENOUGH TO TEAR US APART.

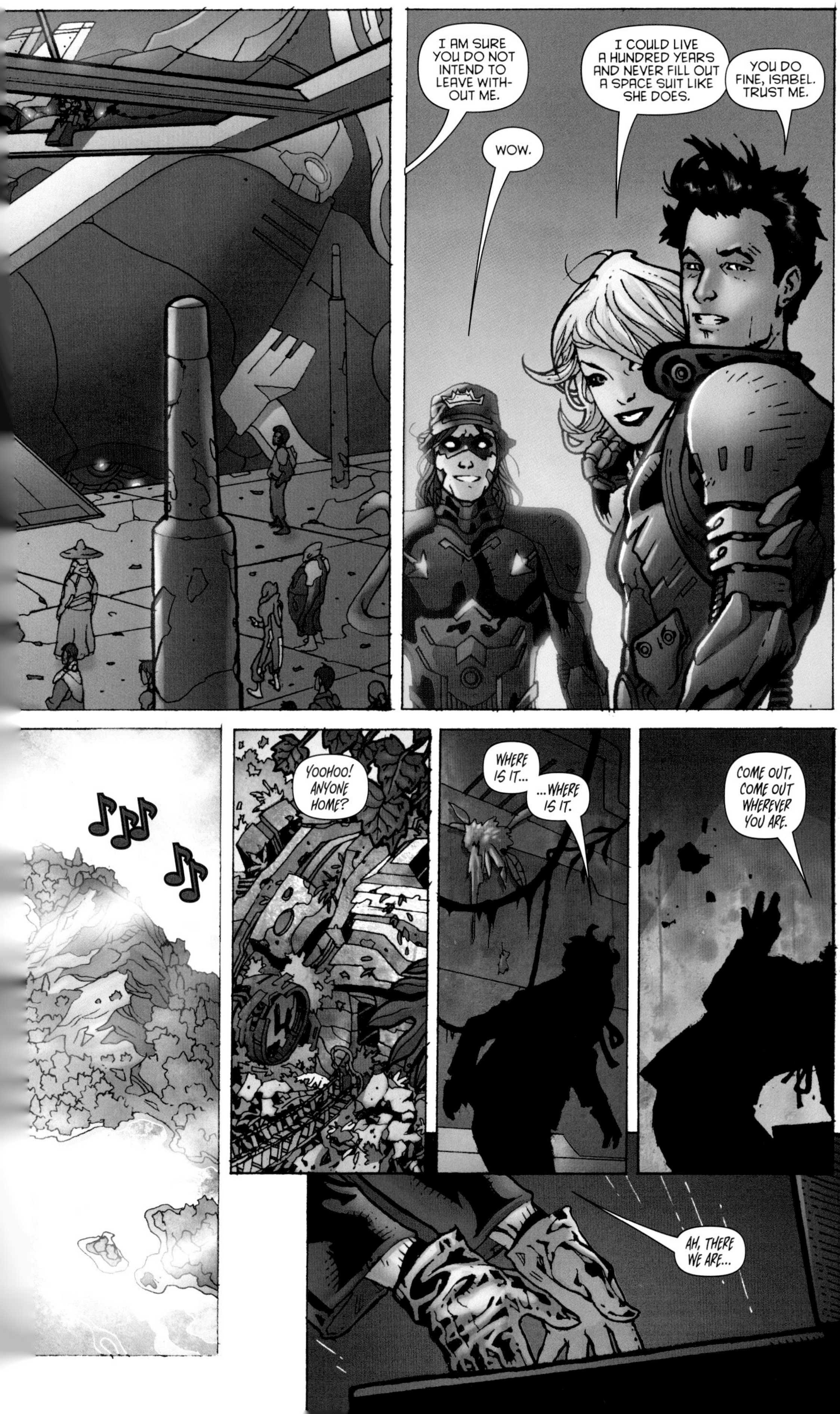
I AM SURE YOU DO NOT INTEND TO LEAVE WITH-OUT ME.
WOW.
I COULD LIVE A HUNDRED YEARS AND NEVER FILL OUT A SPACE SUIT LIKE SHE DOES.
YOU DO FINE, ISABEL. TRUST ME.
YOOHOO! ANYONE HOME?
WHERE IS IT...
...WHERE IS IT.
COME OUT, COME OUT WHEREVER YOU ARE.
AH, THERE WE ARE...

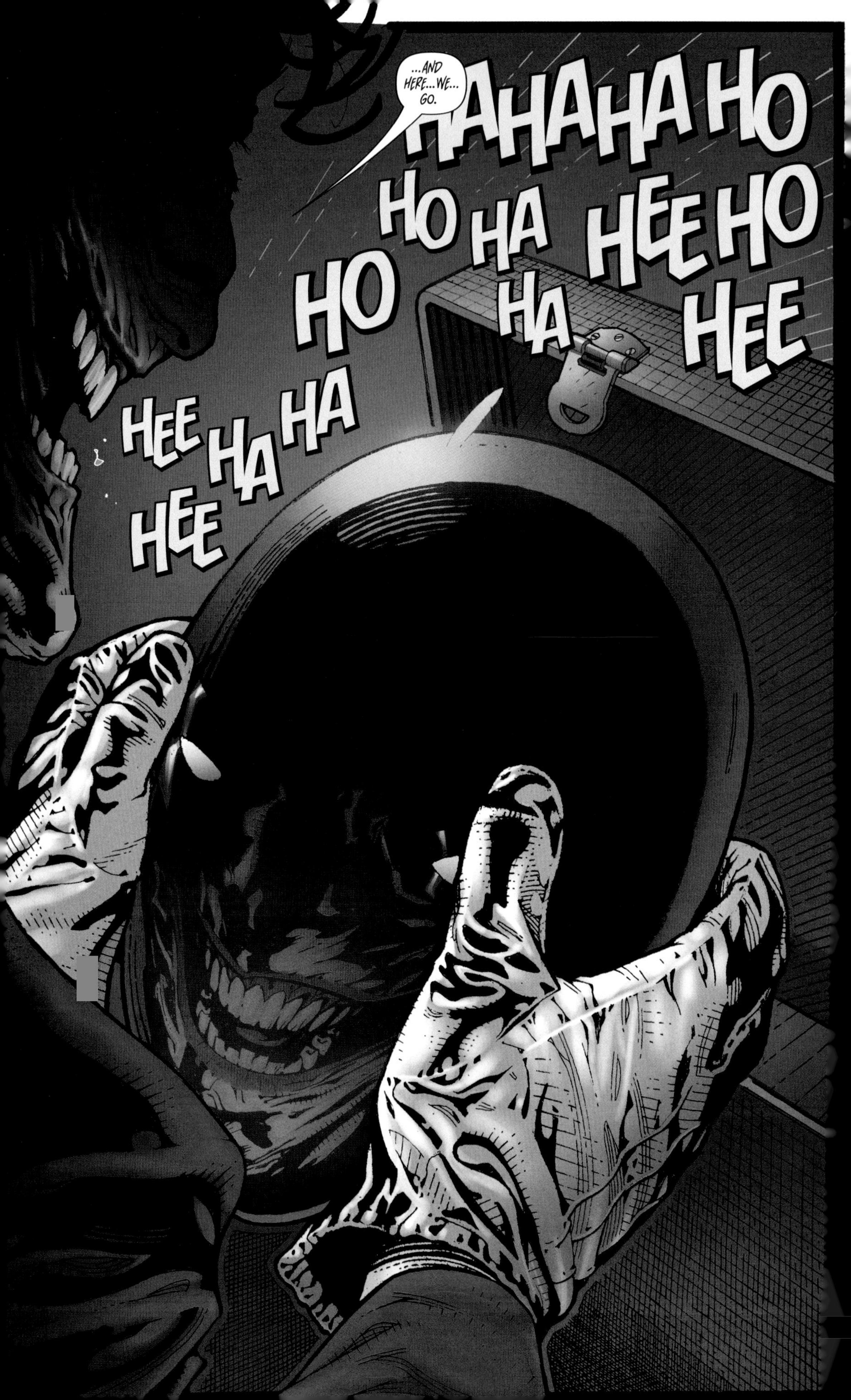
...AND HERE...WE... GO.
HAHAHA HO
HO HA HEE HO
HO HA HEE
HEE HA HA HEE

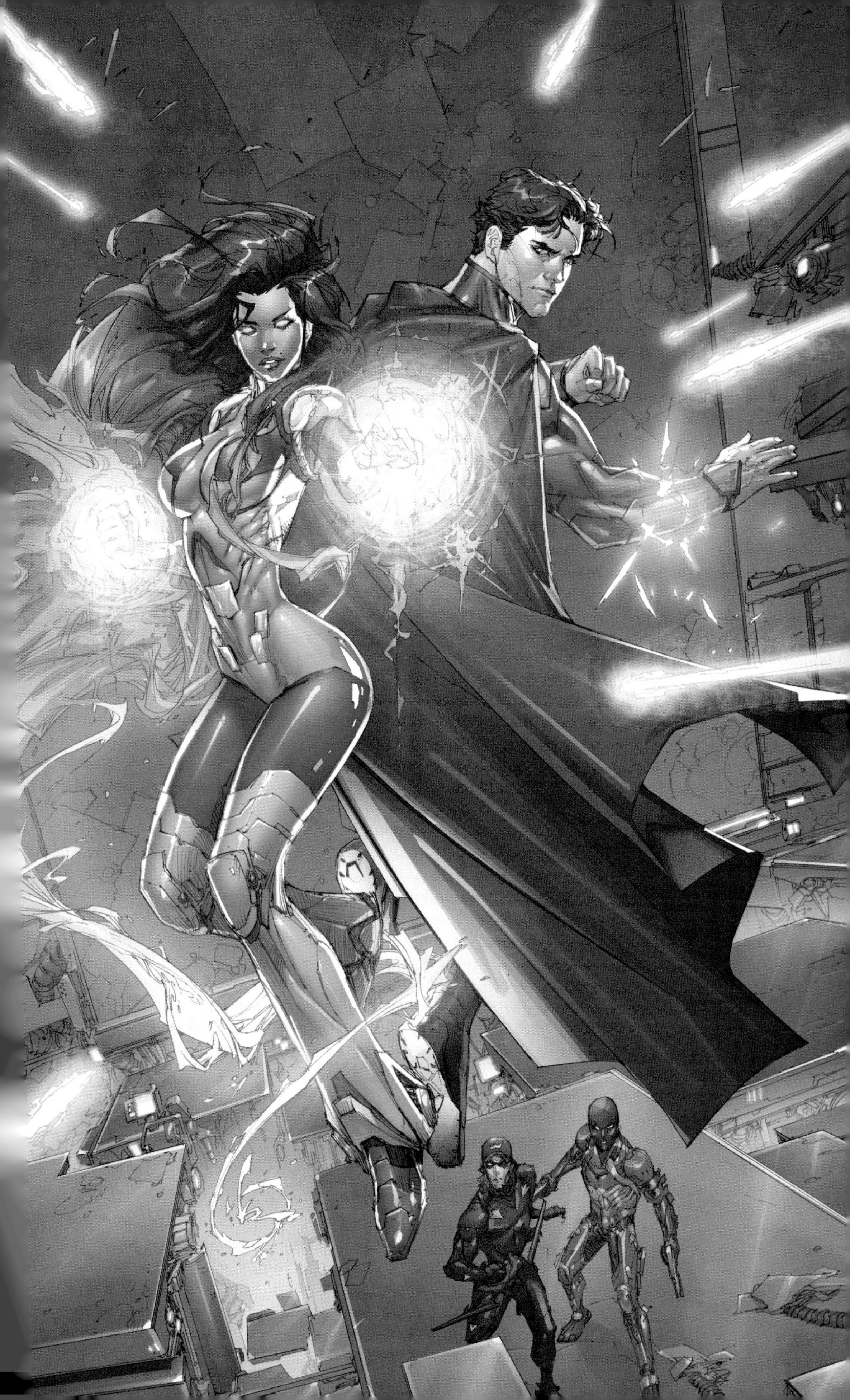

SCOTT LOBDELL writer PASCAL ALIXE artist cover art by KENNETH ROCAFORT & HI-FI

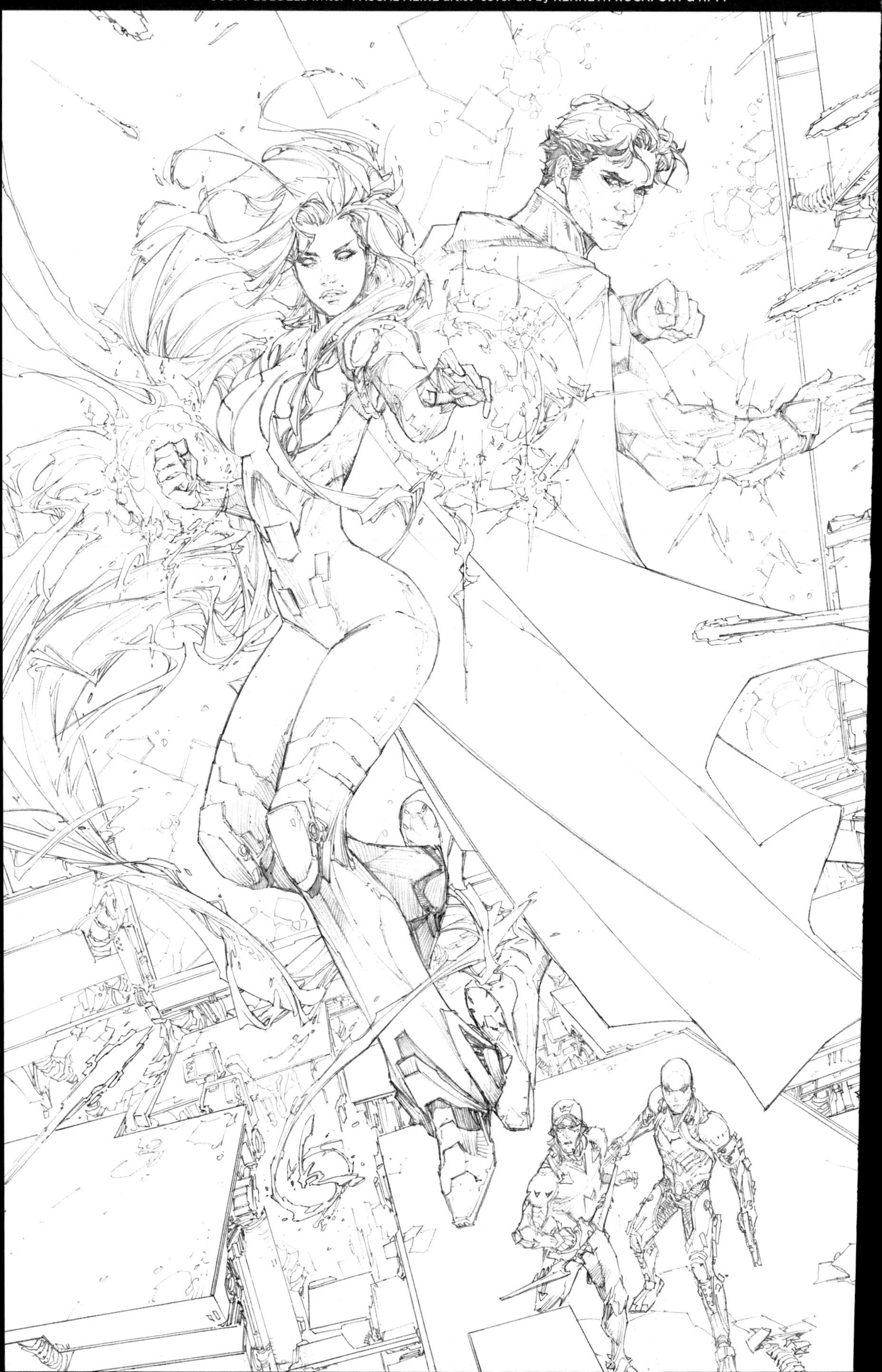

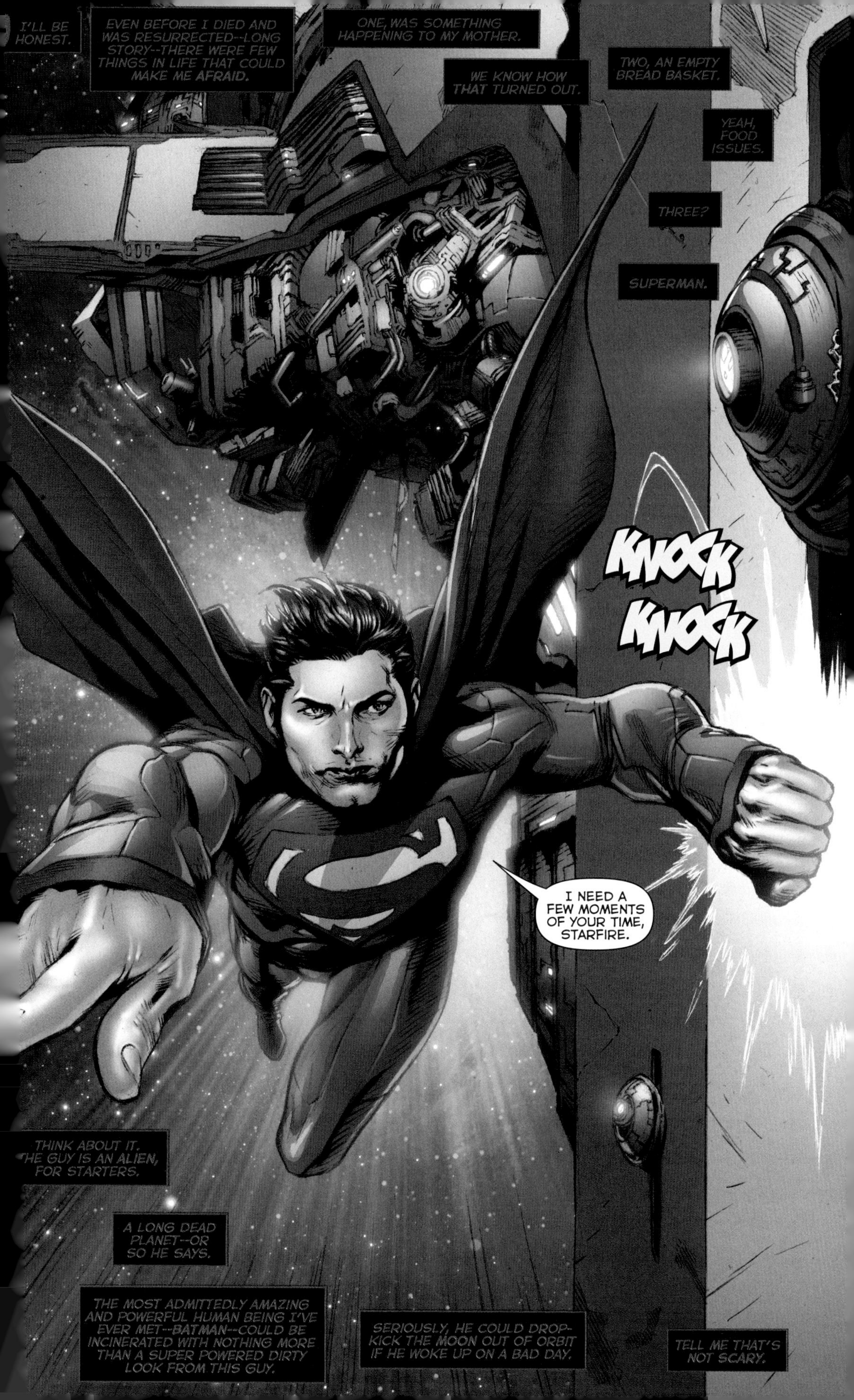
I'LL BE HONEST.
EVEN BEFORE I DIED AND WAS RESURRECTED--LONG STORY--THERE WERE FEW THINGS IN LIFE THAT COULD MAKE ME AFRAID.
ONE, WAS SOMETHING HAPPENING TO MY MOTHER.
WE KNOW HOW THAT TURNED OUT.
TWO, AN EMPTY BREAD BASKET.
YEAH, FOOD ISSUES.
THREE?
SUPERMAN.
KNOCK KNOCK
I NEED A FEW MOMENTS OF YOUR TIME, STARFIRE.
THINK ABOUT IT. THE GUY IS AN ALIEN, FOR STARTERS.
A LONG DEAD PLANET--OR SO HE SAYS.
THE MOST ADMITTEDLY AMAZING AND POWERFUL HUMAN BEING I'VE EVER MET--BATMAN--COULD BE INCINERATED WITH NOTHING MORE THAN A SUPER POWERED DIRTY LOOK FROM THIS GUY.
SERIOUSLY, HE COULD DROP-KICK THE MOON OUT OF ORBIT IF HE WOKE UP ON A BAD DAY.
TELL ME THAT'S NOT SCARY.

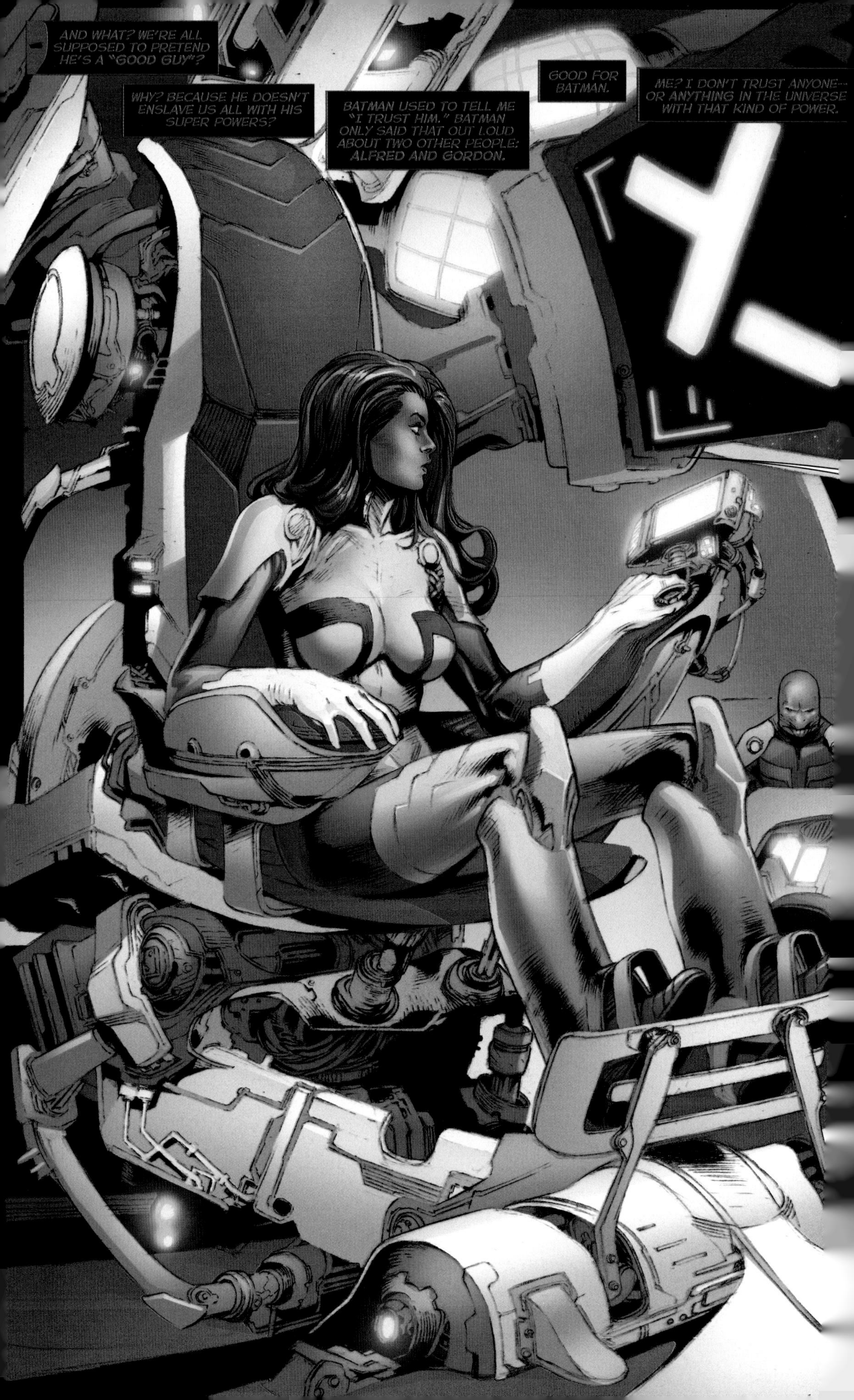
AND WHAT? WE'RE ALL SUPPOSED TO PRETEND HE'S A "GOOD GUY"?
WHY? BECAUSE HE DOESN'T ENSLAVE US ALL WITH HIS SUPER POWERS?
BATMAN USED TO TELL ME "I TRUST HIM." BATMAN ONLY SAID THAT OUT LOUD ABOUT TWO OTHER PEOPLE: ALFRED AND GORDON.
GOOD FOR BATMAN.
ME? I DON'T TRUST ANYONE-- OR ANYTHING IN THE UNIVERSE WITH THAT KIND OF POWER.

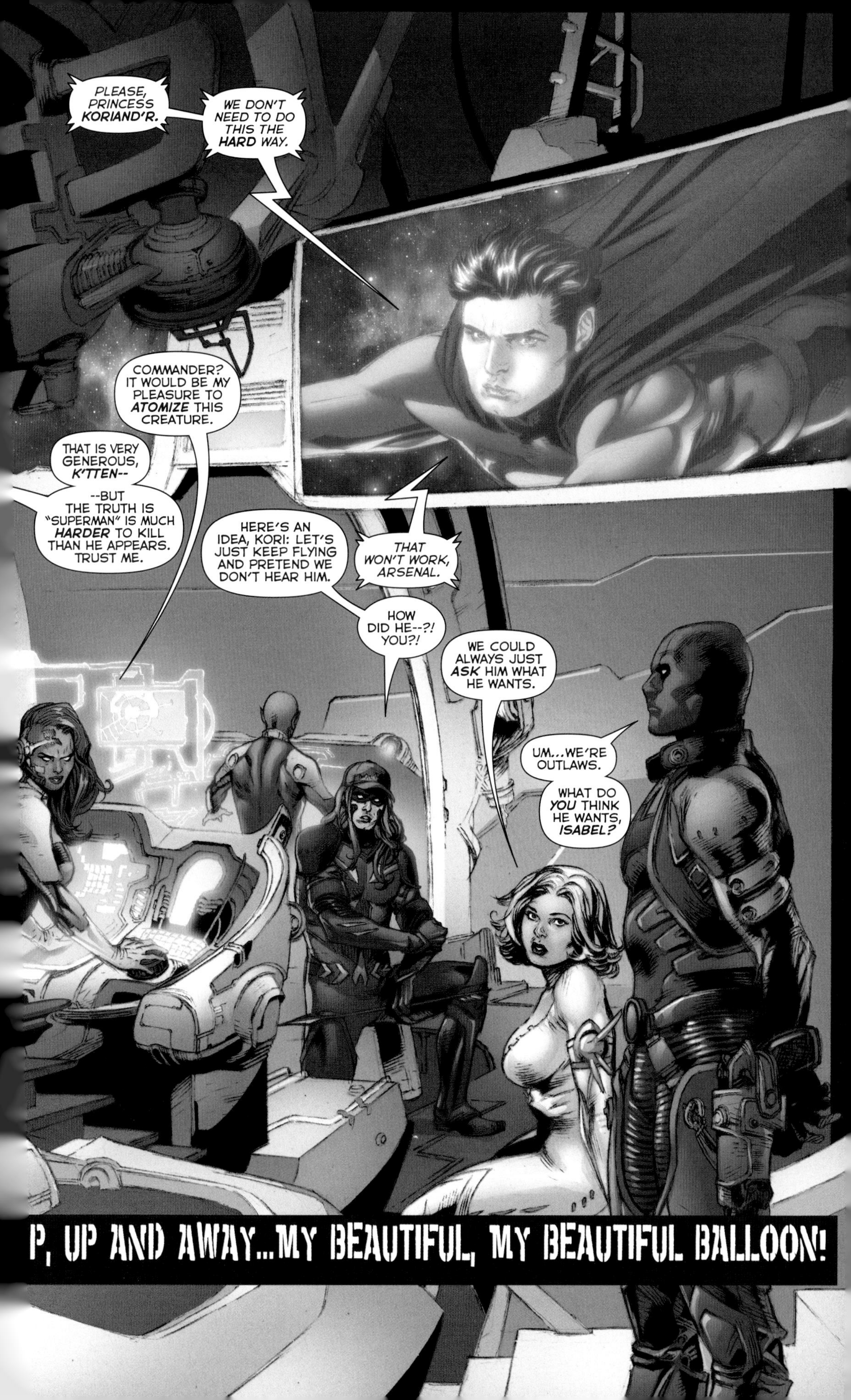
PLEASE, PRINCESS KORIAND'R.
WE DON'T NEED TO DO THIS THE HARD WAY.
COMMANDER? IT WOULD BE MY PLEASURE TO ATOMIZE THIS CREATURE.
THAT IS VERY GENEROUS, K'TTEN--
--BUT THE TRUTH IS "SUPERMAN" IS MUCH HARDER TO KILL THAN HE APPEARS. TRUST ME.
HERE'S AN IDEA, KORI: LET'S JUST KEEP FLYING AND PRETEND WE DON'T HEAR HIM.
THAT WON'T WORK, ARSENAL.
HOW DID HE--?! YOU?!
WE COULD ALWAYS JUST ASK HIM WHAT HE WANTS.
UM...WE'RE OUTLAWS.
WHAT DO YOU THINK HE WANTS, ISABEL?
P, UP AND AWAY...MY BEAUTIFUL, MY BEAUTIFUL BALLOON!

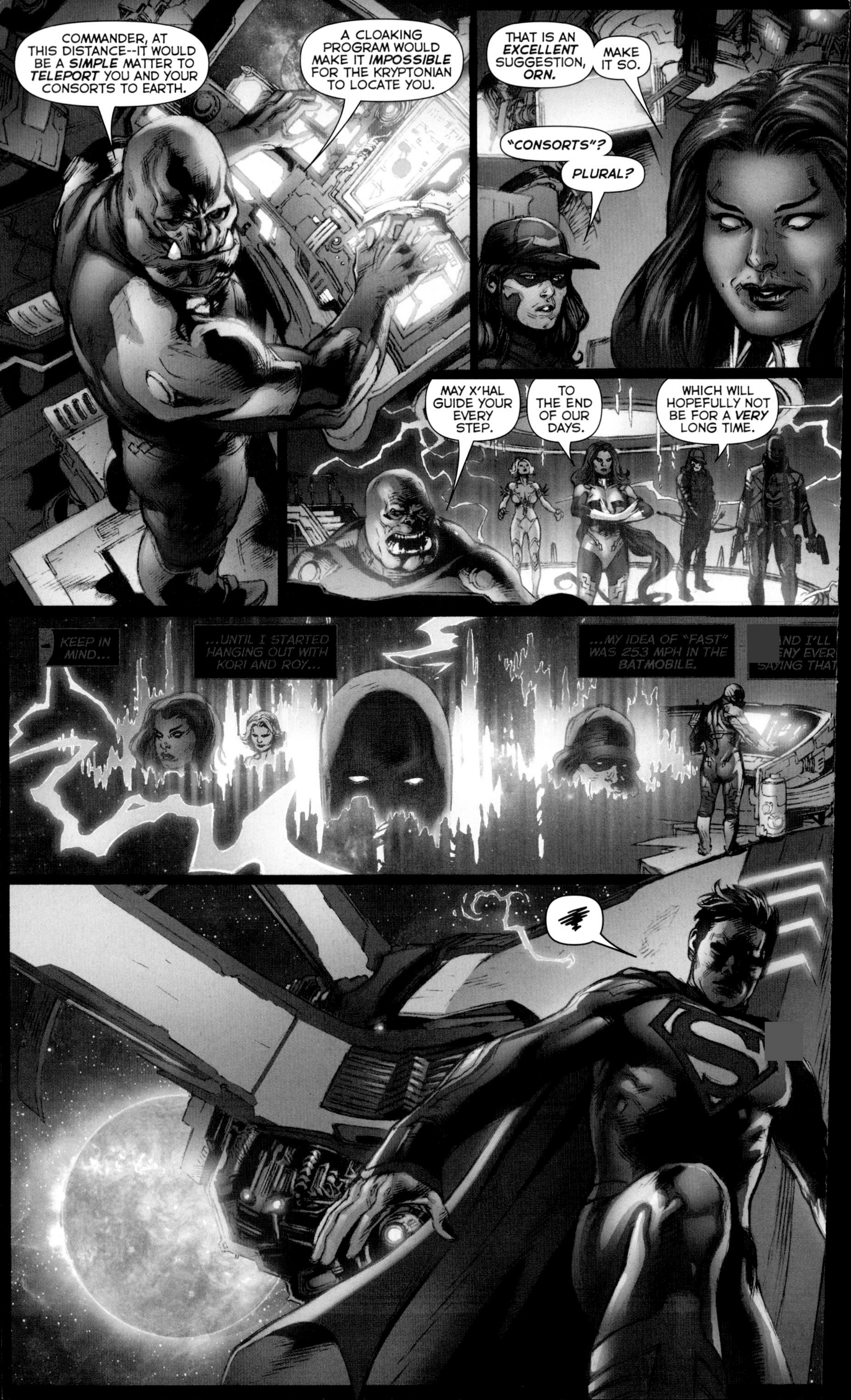
COMMANDER, AT THIS DISTANCE--IT WOULD BE A *SIMPLE* MATTER TO *TELEPORT* YOU AND YOUR CONSORTS TO EARTH.
A CLOAKING PROGRAM WOULD MAKE IT *IMPOSSIBLE* FOR THE KRYPTONIAN TO LOCATE YOU.
THAT IS AN *EXCELLENT* SUGGESTION, *ORN.*
MAKE IT SO.
"CONSORTS"?
PLURAL?
MAY X'HAL GUIDE YOUR EVERY STEP.
TO THE END OF OUR DAYS.
WHICH WILL HOPEFULLY NOT BE FOR A *VERY* LONG TIME.
KEEP IN MIND...
...UNTIL I STARTED HANGING OUT WITH KORI AND ROY...
...MY IDEA OF "FAST" WAS 253 MPH IN THE BATMOBILE.

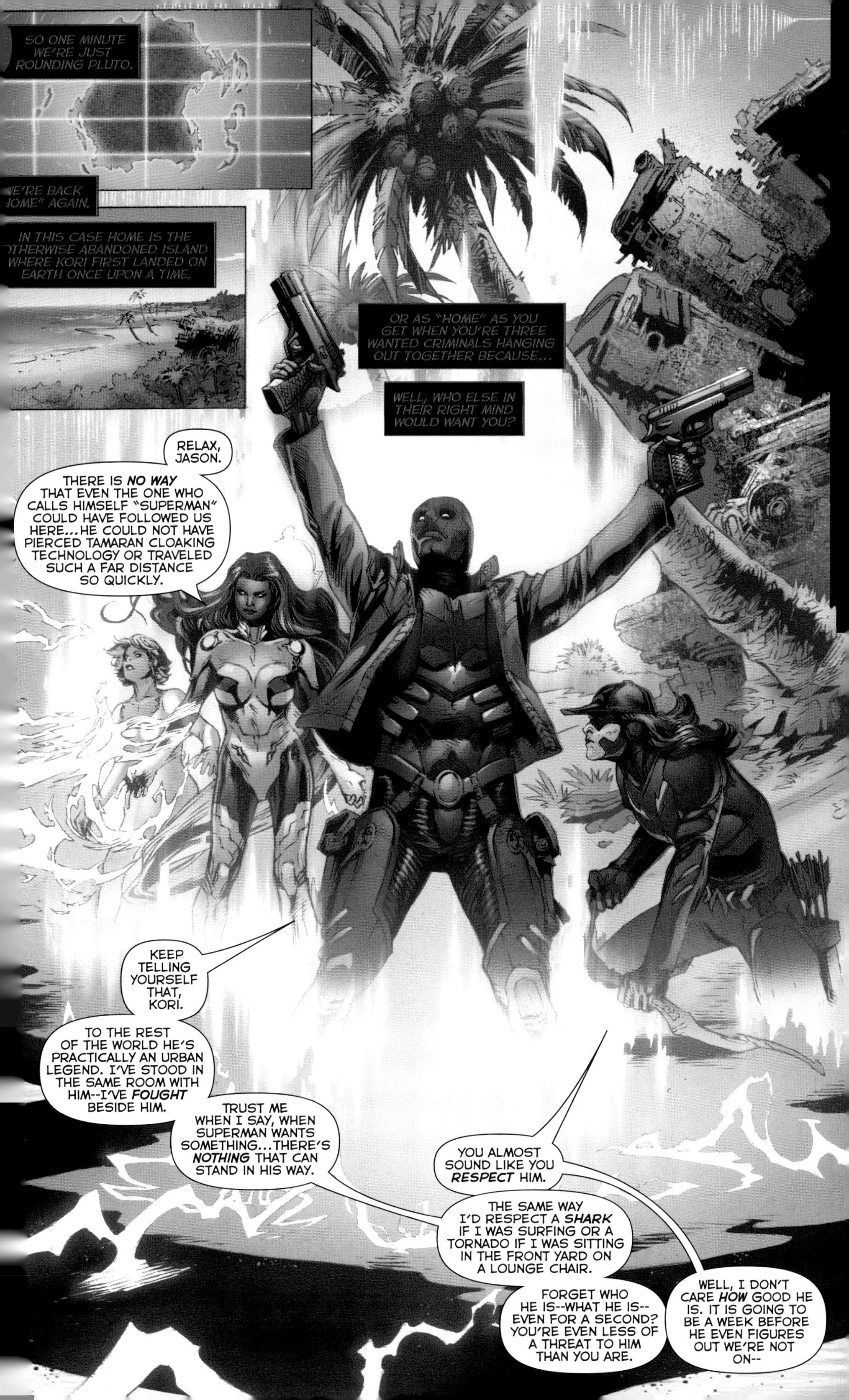
SO ONE MINUTE WE'RE JUST ROUNDING PLUTO.
E'RE BACK OME" AGAIN.
IN THIS CASE HOME IS THE OTHERWISE ABANDONED ISLAND WHERE KORI FIRST LANDED ON EARTH ONCE UPON A TIME.
OR AS "HOME" AS YOU GET WHEN YOU'RE THREE WANTED CRIMINALS HANGING OUT TOGETHER BECAUSE...
WELL, WHO ELSE IN THEIR RIGHT MIND WOULD WANT YOU?
RELAX, JASON.
THERE IS ***NO WAY*** THAT EVEN THE ONE WHO CALLS HIMSELF "SUPERMAN" COULD HAVE FOLLOWED US HERE...HE COULD NOT HAVE PIERCED TAMARAN CLOAKING TECHNOLOGY OR TRAVELED SUCH A FAR DISTANCE SO QUICKLY.
KEEP TELLING YOURSELF THAT, KORI.
TO THE REST OF THE WORLD HE'S PRACTICALLY AN URBAN LEGEND. I'VE STOOD IN THE SAME ROOM WITH HIM--I'VE ***FOUGHT*** BESIDE HIM.
TRUST ME WHEN I SAY, WHEN SUPERMAN WANTS SOMETHING...THERE'S ***NOTHING*** THAT CAN STAND IN HIS WAY.
YOU ALMOST SOUND LIKE YOU ***RESPECT*** HIM.
THE SAME WAY I'D RESPECT A ***SHARK*** IF I WAS SURFING OR A TORNADO IF I WAS SITTING IN THE FRONT YARD ON A LOUNGE CHAIR.
FORGET WHO HE IS--WHAT HE IS--EVEN FOR A SECOND? YOU'RE EVEN LESS OF A THREAT TO HIM THAN YOU ARE.
WELL, I DON'T CARE ***HOW*** GOOD HE IS. IT IS GOING TO BE A WEEK BEFORE HE EVEN FIGURES OUT WE'RE NOT ON--

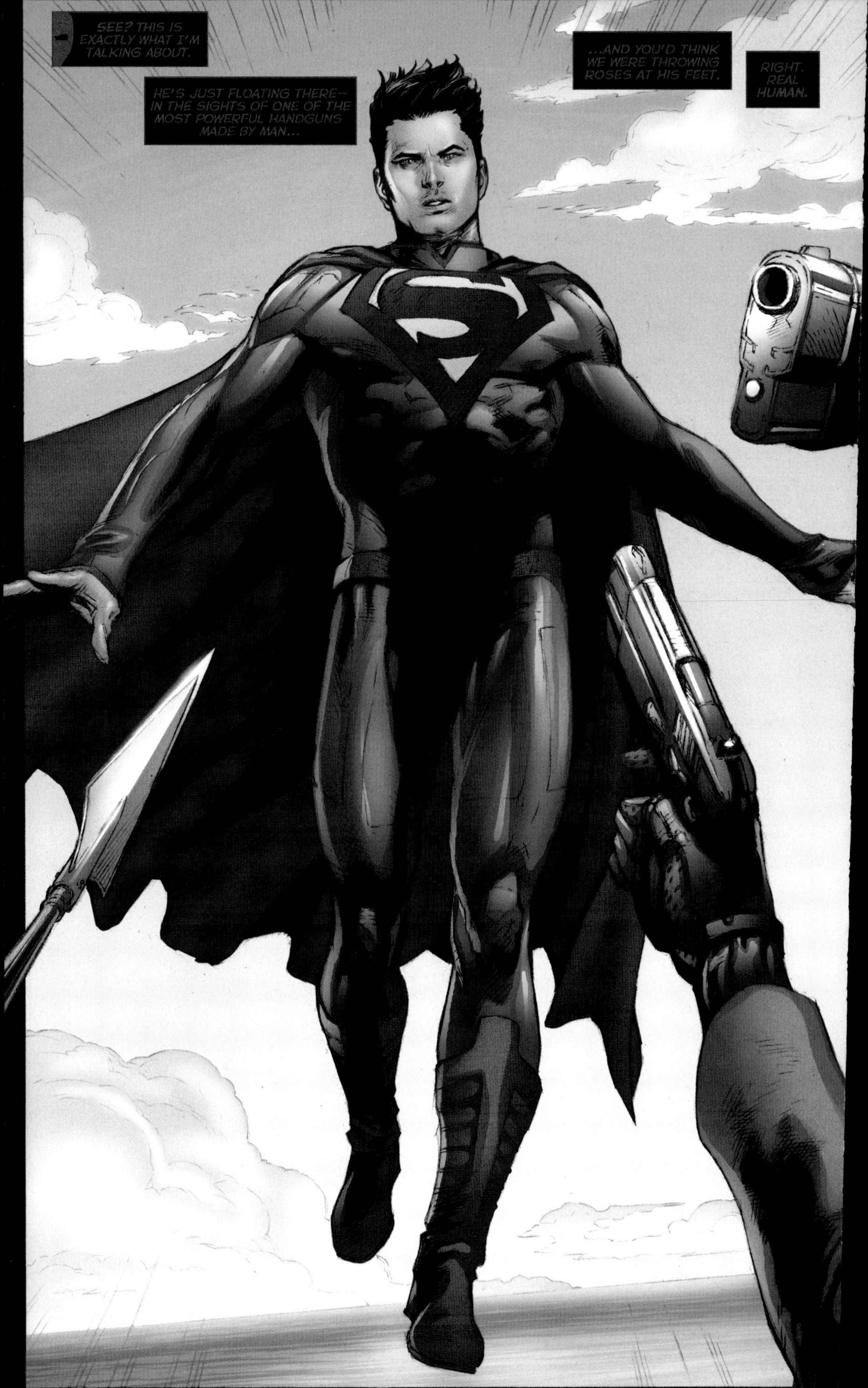
SEE? THIS IS EXACTLY WHAT I'M TALKING ABOUT.
HE'S JUST FLOATING THERE-- IN THE SIGHTS OF ONE OF THE MOST POWERFUL HANDGUNS MADE BY MAN...
...AND YOU'D THINK WE WERE THROWING ROSES AT HIS FEET.
RIGHT. REAL HUMAN.

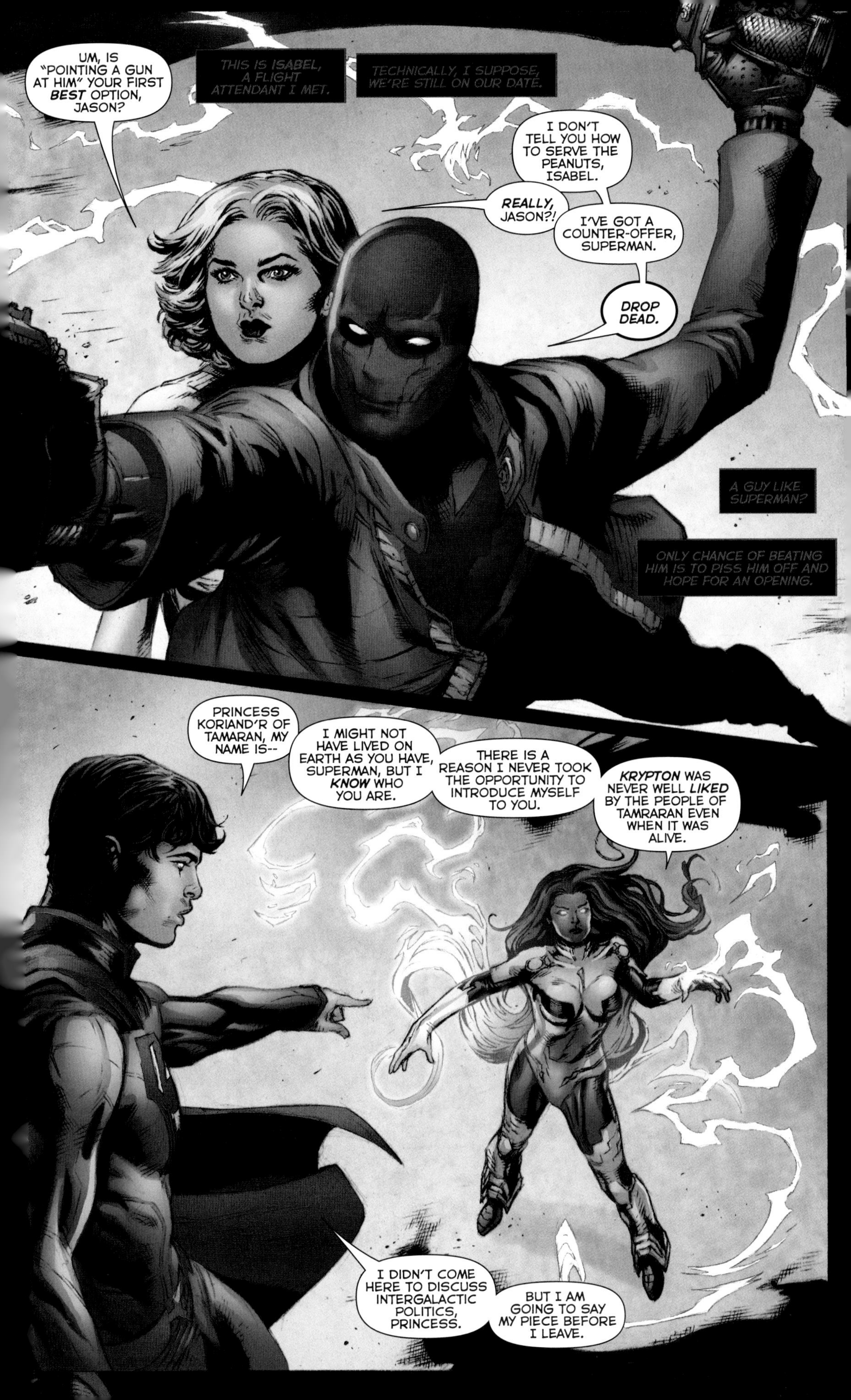
UM, IS "POINTING A GUN AT HIM" YOUR FIRST BEST OPTION, JASON?
THIS IS ISABEL, A FLIGHT ATTENDANT I MET.
TECHNICALLY, I SUPPOSE, WE'RE STILL ON OUR DATE.
I DON'T TELL YOU HOW TO SERVE THE PEANUTS, ISABEL.
REALLY, JASON?!
I'VE GOT A COUNTER-OFFER, SUPERMAN.
DROP DEAD.
A GUY LIKE SUPERMAN?
ONLY CHANCE OF BEATING HIM IS TO PISS HIM OFF AND HOPE FOR AN OPENING.
PRINCESS KORIAND'R OF TAMARAN, MY NAME IS--
I MIGHT NOT HAVE LIVED ON EARTH AS YOU HAVE, SUPERMAN, BUT I KNOW WHO YOU ARE.
THERE IS A REASON I NEVER TOOK THE OPPORTUNITY TO INTRODUCE MYSELF TO YOU.
KRYPTON WAS NEVER WELL LIKED BY THE PEOPLE OF TAMRARAN EVEN WHEN IT WAS ALIVE.
I DIDN'T COME HERE TO DISCUSS INTERGALACTIC POLITICS, PRINCESS.
BUT I AM GOING TO SAY MY PIECE BEFORE I LEAVE.

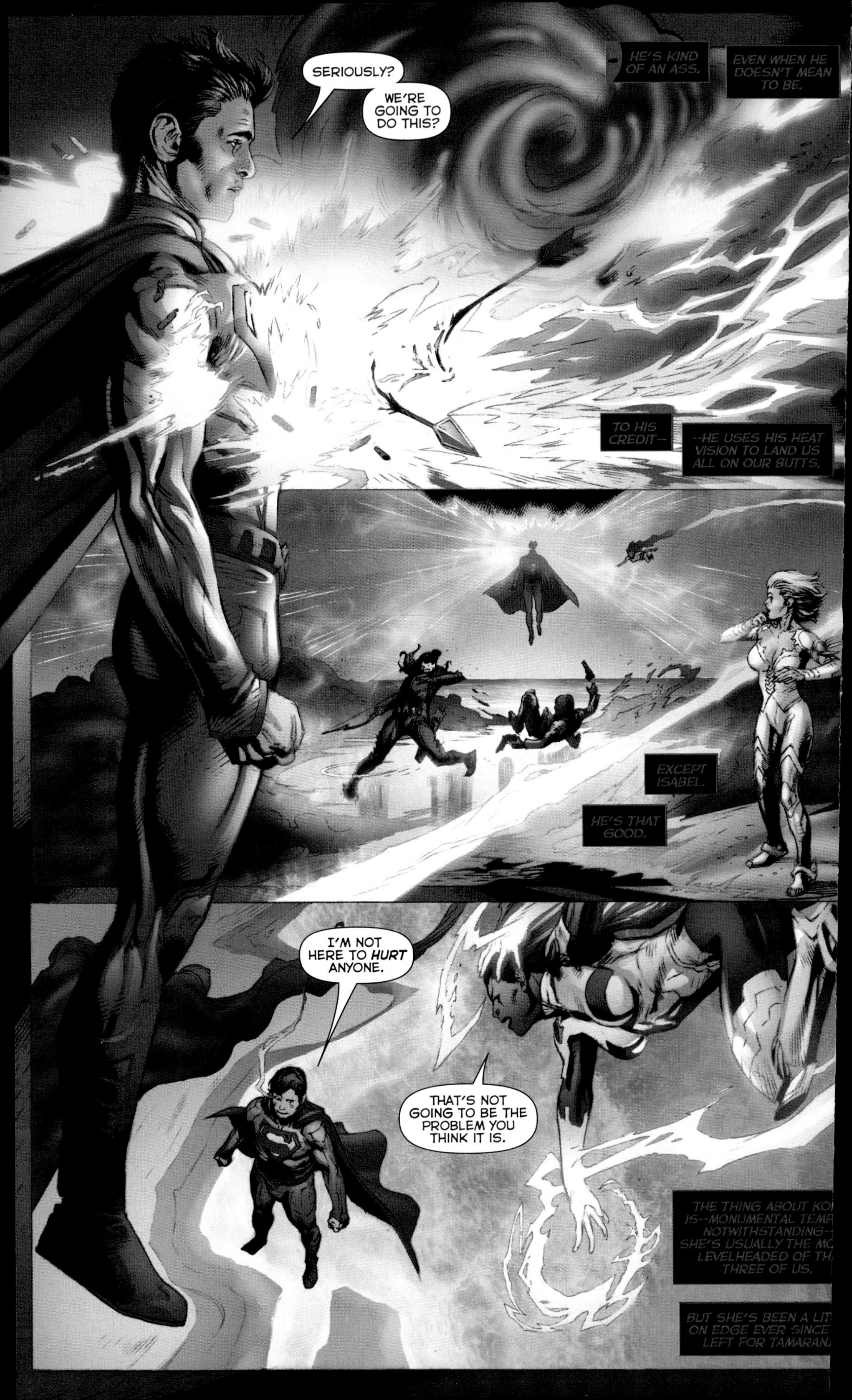
HE'S KIND OF AN ASS.
EVEN WHEN HE DOESN'T MEAN TO BE.
SERIOUSLY? WE'RE GOING TO DO THIS?
TO HIS CREDIT--
--HE USES HIS HEAT VISION TO LAND US ALL ON OUR BUTTS.
EXCEPT ISABEL.
HE'S THAT GOOD.
I'M NOT HERE TO HURT ANYONE.
THAT'S NOT GOING TO BE THE PROBLEM YOU THINK IT IS.
THE THING ABOUT KO
IS--MONUMENTAL TEMP
NOTWITHSTANDING--
SHE'S USUALLY THE MO
LEVELHEADED OF TH
THREE OF US.
BUT SHE'S BEEN A LIT
ON EDGE EVER SINCE
LEFT FOR TAMARAN

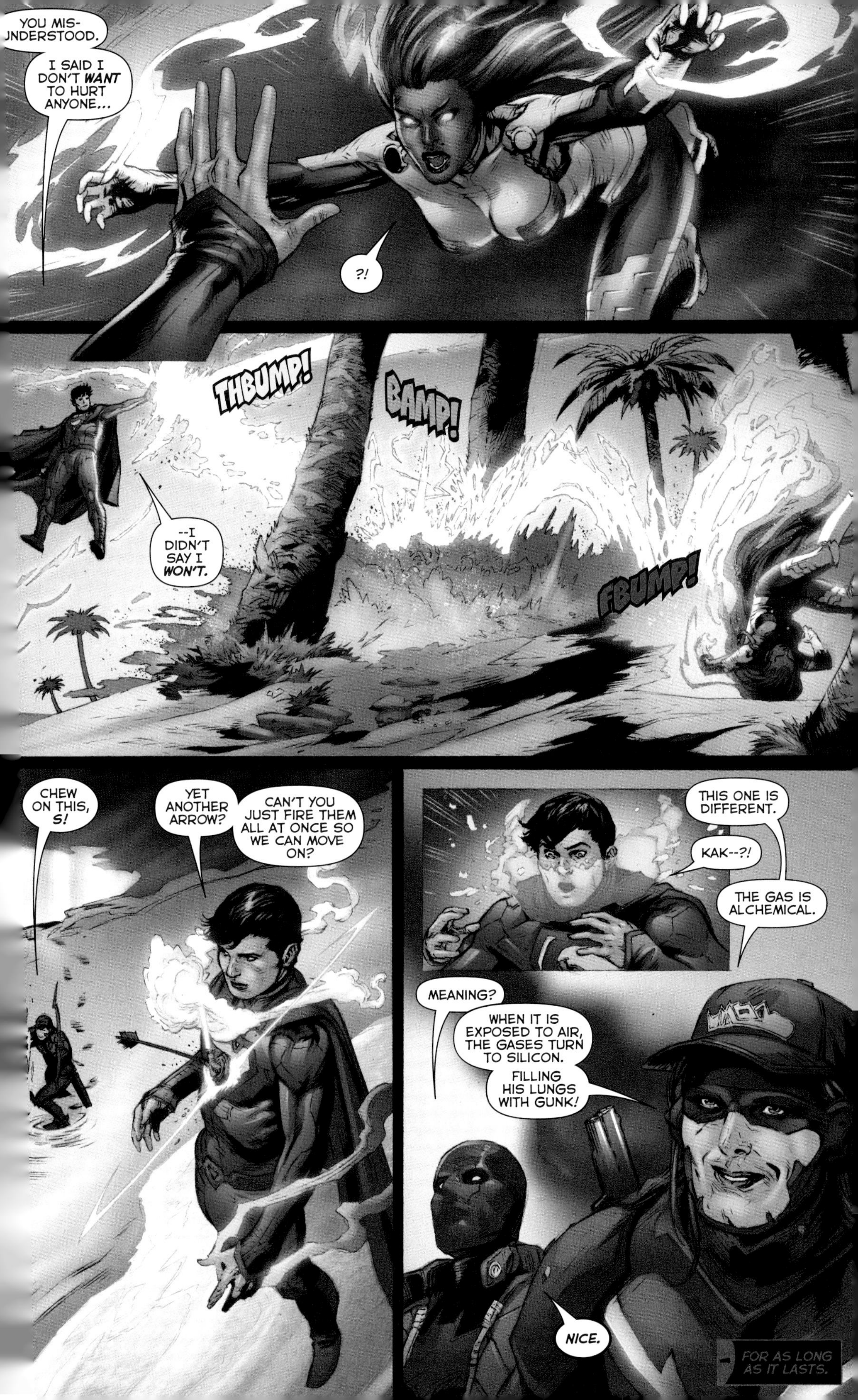
YOU MIS-
UNDERSTOOD.
I SAID I DON'T WANT TO HURT ANYONE...
?!
THBUMP!
BAMP!
--I DIDN'T SAY I WON'T.
FBUMP!
CHEW ON THIS, S!
YET ANOTHER ARROW?
CAN'T YOU JUST FIRE THEM ALL AT ONCE SO WE CAN MOVE ON?
THIS ONE IS DIFFERENT.
KAK--?!
THE GAS IS ALCHEMICAL.
MEANING?
WHEN IT IS EXPOSED TO AIR, THE GASES TURN TO SILICON.
FILLING HIS LUNGS WITH GUNK!
NICE.
FOR AS LONG AS IT LASTS.

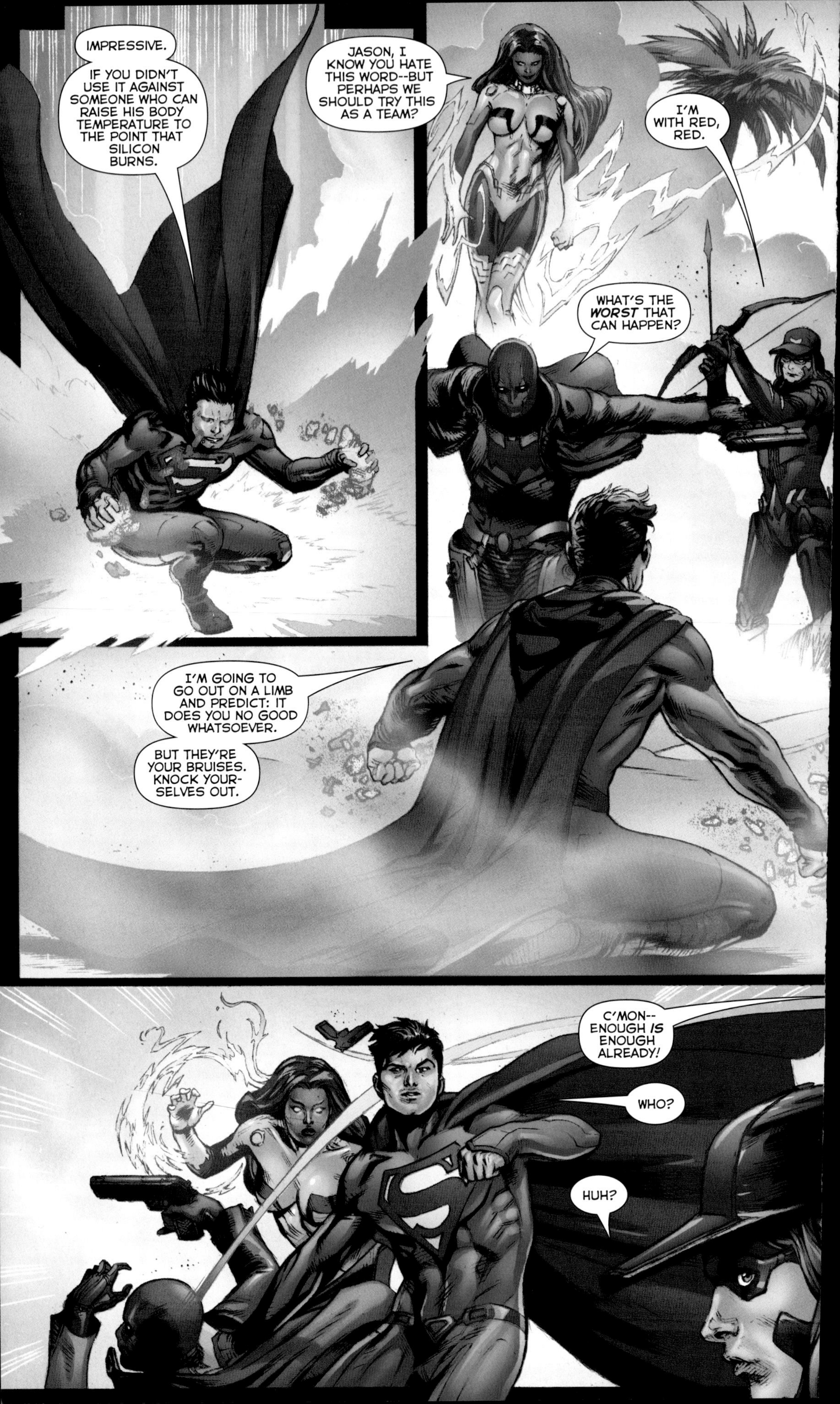
IMPRESSIVE.
IF YOU DIDN'T USE IT AGAINST SOMEONE WHO CAN RAISE HIS BODY TEMPERATURE TO THE POINT THAT SILICON BURNS.
JASON, I KNOW YOU HATE THIS WORD--BUT PERHAPS WE SHOULD TRY THIS AS A TEAM?
I'M WITH RED, RED.
WHAT'S THE *WORST* THAT CAN HAPPEN?
I'M GOING TO GO OUT ON A LIMB AND PREDICT: IT DOES YOU NO GOOD WHATSOEVER.
BUT THEY'RE YOUR BRUISES. KNOCK YOUR-SELVES OUT.
C'MON-- ENOUGH *IS* ENOUGH ALREADY!
WHO?
HUH?

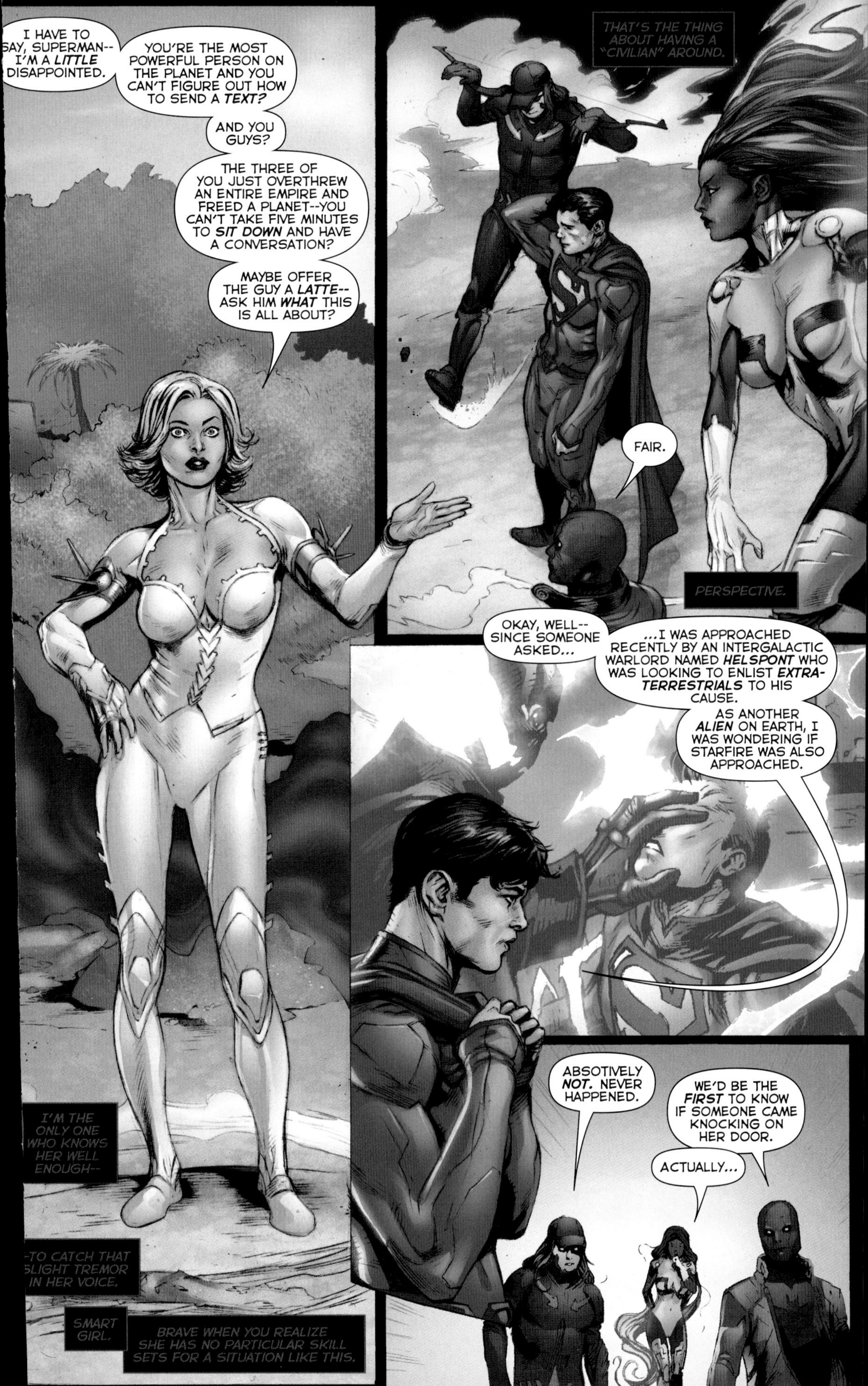
I HAVE TO SAY, SUPERMAN-- I'M A LITTLE DISAPPOINTED.
YOU'RE THE MOST POWERFUL PERSON ON THE PLANET AND YOU CAN'T FIGURE OUT HOW TO SEND A TEXT?
AND YOU GUYS?
THE THREE OF YOU JUST OVERTHREW AN ENTIRE EMPIRE AND FREED A PLANET--YOU CAN'T TAKE FIVE MINUTES TO SIT DOWN AND HAVE A CONVERSATION?
MAYBE OFFER THE GUY A LATTE-- ASK HIM WHAT THIS IS ALL ABOUT?
I'M THE ONLY ONE WHO KNOWS HER WELL ENOUGH--
--TO CATCH THAT SLIGHT TREMOR IN HER VOICE.
SMART GIRL.
BRAVE WHEN YOU REALIZE SHE HAS NO PARTICULAR SKILL SETS FOR A SITUATION LIKE THIS.
THAT'S THE THING ABOUT HAVING A "CIVILIAN" AROUND.
FAIR.
PERSPECTIVE.
OKAY, WELL-- SINCE SOMEONE ASKED...
...I WAS APPROACHED RECENTLY BY AN INTERGALACTIC WARLORD NAMED HELSPONT WHO WAS LOOKING TO ENLIST EXTRA-TERRESTRIALS TO HIS CAUSE.
AS ANOTHER ALIEN ON EARTH, I WAS WONDERING IF STARFIRE WAS ALSO APPROACHED.
ABSOTIVELY NOT. NEVER HAPPENED.
WE'D BE THE FIRST TO KNOW IF SOMEONE CAME KNOCKING ON HER DOOR.
ACTUALLY...

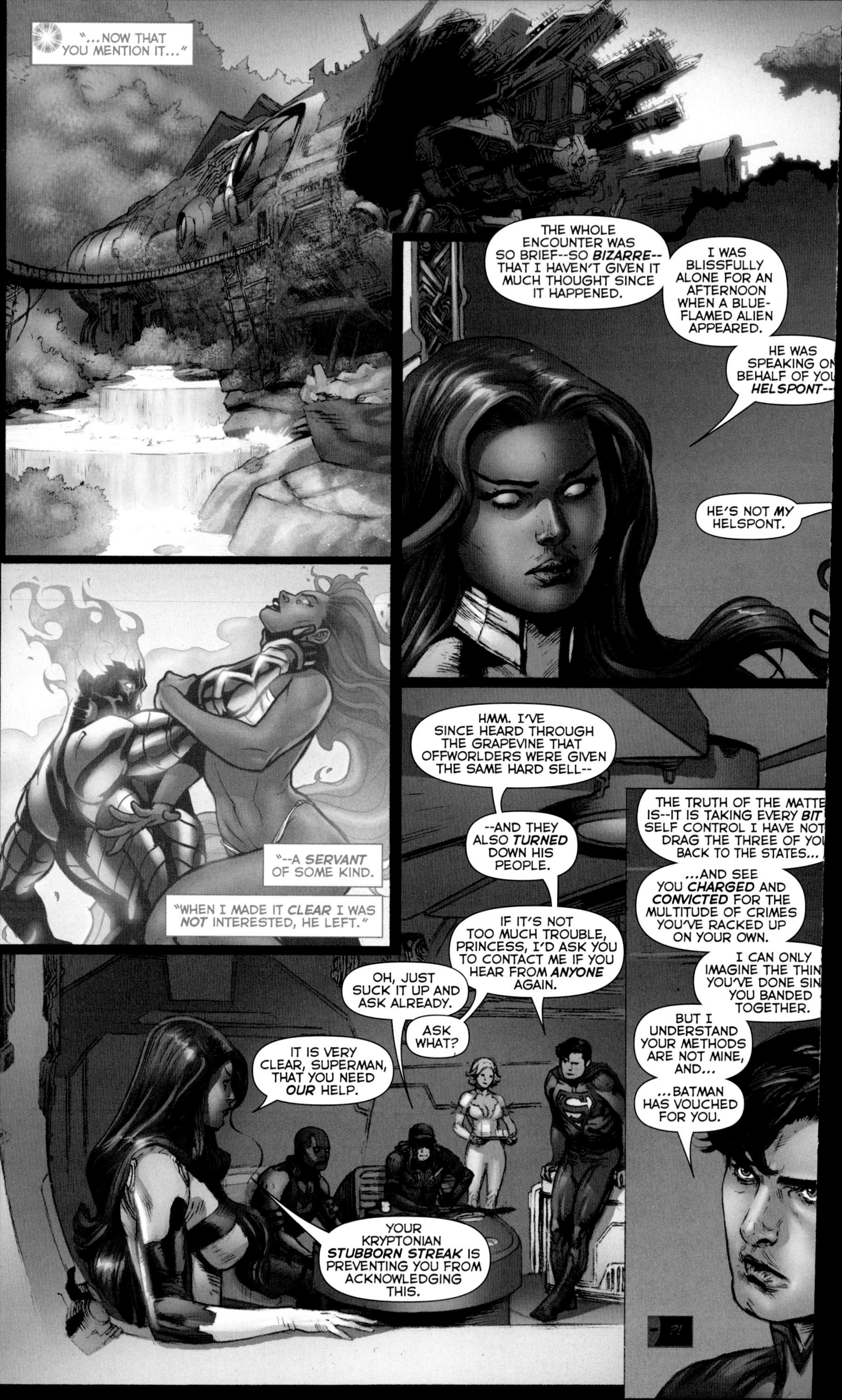
"...NOW THAT YOU MENTION IT..."
THE WHOLE ENCOUNTER WAS SO BRIEF--SO *BIZARRE*--THAT I HAVEN'T GIVEN IT MUCH THOUGHT SINCE IT HAPPENED.
I WAS BLISSFULLY ALONE FOR AN AFTERNOON WHEN A BLUE-FLAMED ALIEN APPEARED.
HE WAS SPEAKING ON BEHALF OF YOU *HELSPONT*--
"--A *SERVANT* OF SOME KIND.
"WHEN I MADE IT *CLEAR* I WAS *NOT* INTERESTED, HE LEFT."
HE'S NOT *MY* HELSPONT.
HMM. I'VE SINCE HEARD THROUGH THE GRAPEVINE THAT OFFWORLDERS WERE GIVEN THE SAME HARD SELL--
--AND THEY ALSO *TURNED* DOWN HIS PEOPLE.
IF IT'S NOT TOO MUCH TROUBLE, PRINCESS, I'D ASK YOU TO CONTACT ME IF YOU HEAR FROM *ANYONE* AGAIN.
OH, JUST SUCK IT UP AND ASK ALREADY.
ASK WHAT?
IT IS VERY CLEAR, SUPERMAN, THAT YOU NEED *OUR* HELP.
YOUR KRYPTONIAN *STUBBORN STREAK* IS PREVENTING YOU FROM ACKNOWLEDGING THIS.
THE TRUTH OF THE MATTE IS--IT IS TAKING EVERY *BIT* SELF CONTROL I HAVE NOT DRAG THE THREE OF YOU BACK TO THE STATES...
...AND SEE YOU *CHARGED* AND *CONVICTED* FOR THE MULTITUDE OF CRIMES YOU'VE RACKED UP ON YOUR OWN.
I CAN ONLY IMAGINE THE THIN YOU'VE DONE SIN YOU BANDED TOGETHER.
BUT I UNDERSTAND YOUR METHODS ARE NOT MINE, AND...
...BATMAN HAS VOUCHED FOR YOU.
?!

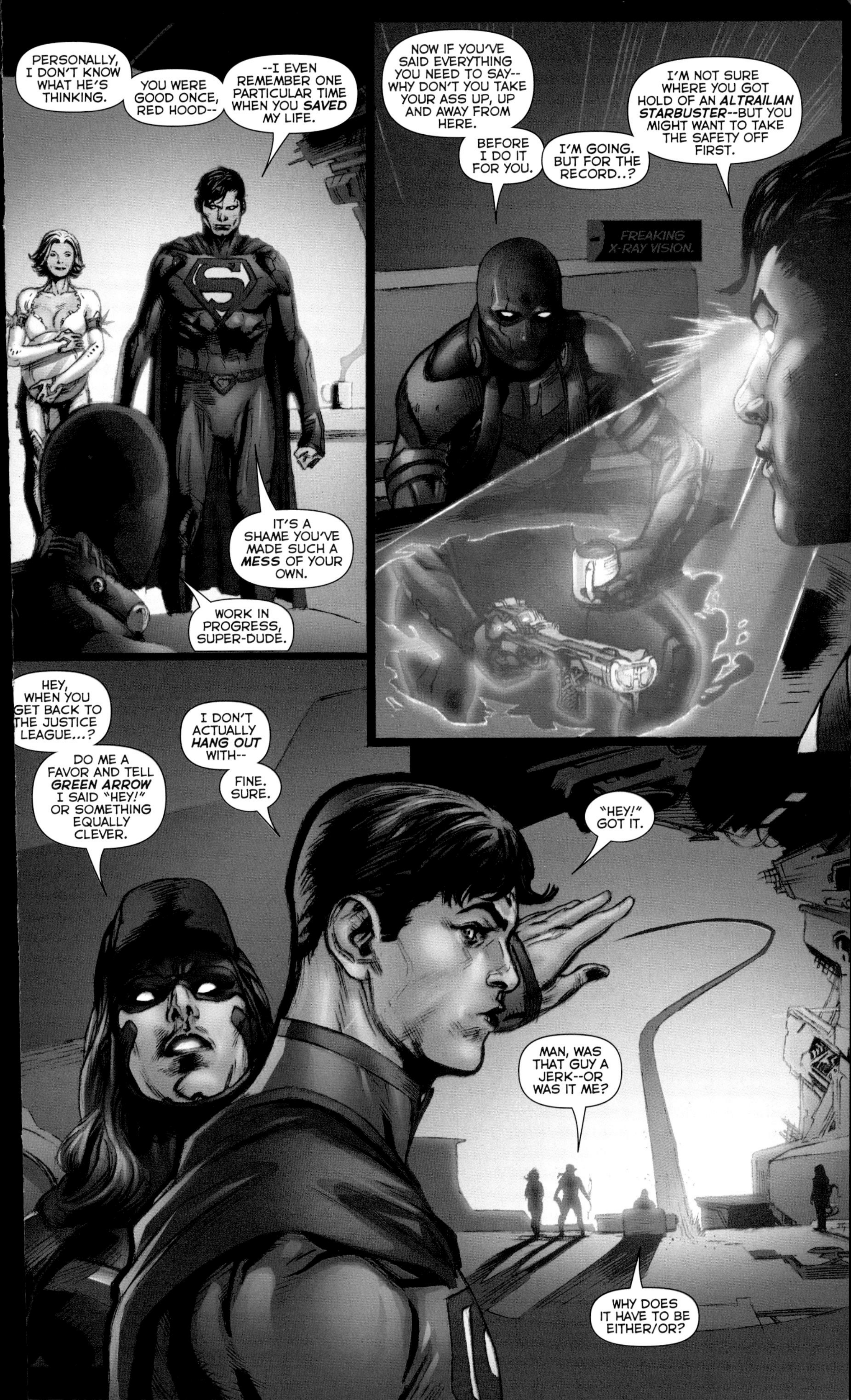
PERSONALLY, I DON'T KNOW WHAT HE'S THINKING.
YOU WERE GOOD ONCE, RED HOOD--
--I EVEN REMEMBER ONE PARTICULAR TIME WHEN YOU **SAVED** MY LIFE.
IT'S A SHAME YOU'VE MADE SUCH A **MESS** OF YOUR OWN.
WORK IN PROGRESS, SUPER-DUDE.
NOW IF YOU'VE SAID EVERYTHING YOU NEED TO SAY-- WHY DON'T YOU TAKE YOUR ASS UP, UP AND AWAY FROM HERE.
BEFORE I DO IT FOR YOU.
I'M GOING. BUT FOR THE RECORD..?
I'M NOT SURE WHERE YOU GOT HOLD OF AN **ALTRAILIAN STARBUSTER**--BUT YOU MIGHT WANT TO TAKE THE SAFETY OFF FIRST.
FREAKING X-RAY VISION.
HEY, WHEN YOU GET BACK TO THE JUSTICE LEAGUE...?
DO ME A FAVOR AND TELL **GREEN ARROW** I SAID "HEY!" OR SOMETHING EQUALLY CLEVER.
I DON'T ACTUALLY **HANG OUT** WITH--
FINE. SURE.
"HEY!" GOT IT.
MAN, WAS THAT GUY A JERK--OR WAS IT ME?
WHY DOES IT HAVE TO BE EITHER/OR?

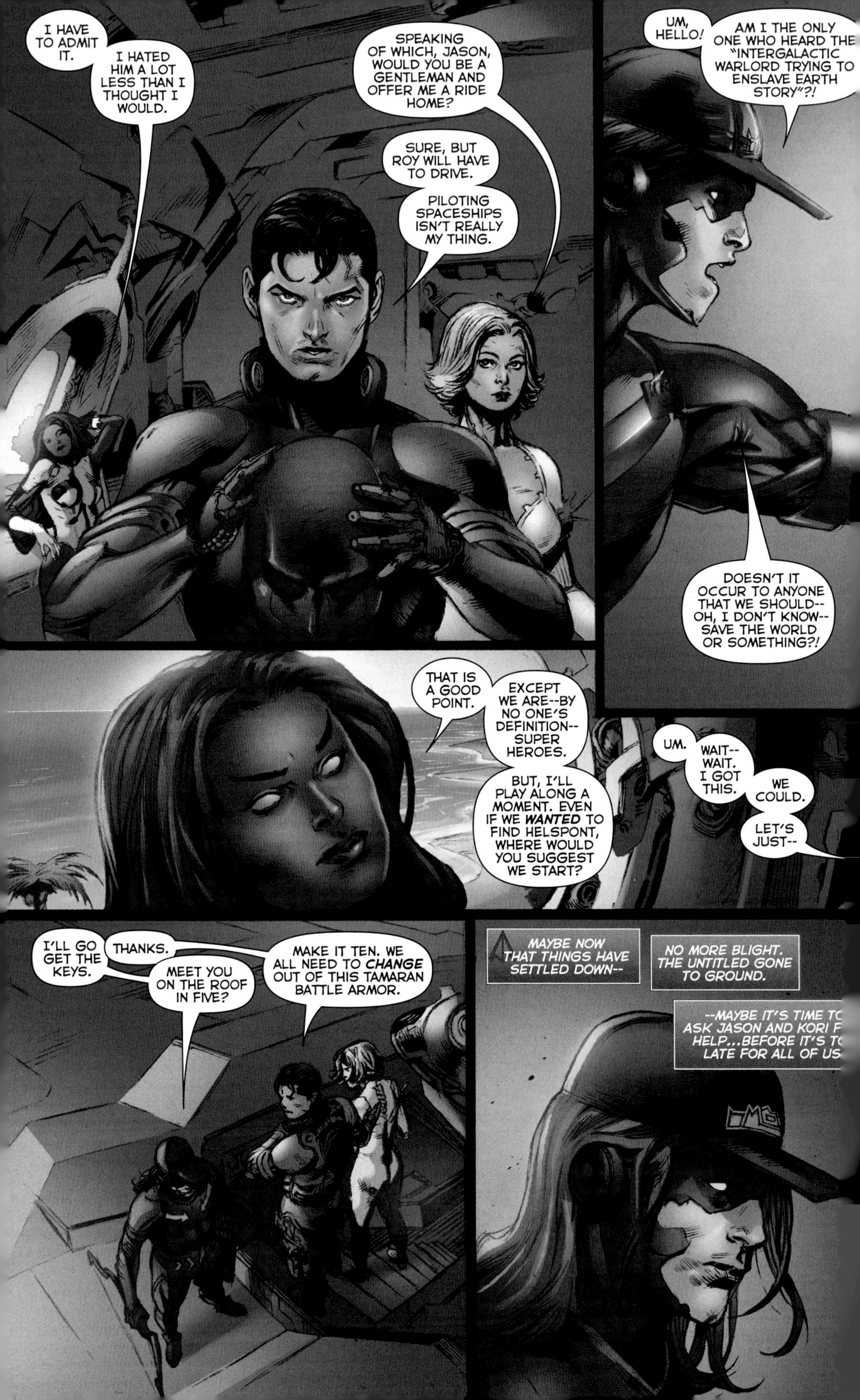
I HAVE TO ADMIT IT.
I HATED HIM A LOT LESS THAN I THOUGHT I WOULD.
SPEAKING OF WHICH, JASON, WOULD YOU BE A GENTLEMAN AND OFFER ME A RIDE HOME?
SURE, BUT ROY WILL HAVE TO DRIVE.
PILOTING SPACESHIPS ISN'T REALLY MY THING.
UM, HELLO!
AM I THE ONLY ONE WHO HEARD THE "INTERGALACTIC WARLORD TRYING TO ENSLAVE EARTH STORY"?!
DOESN'T IT OCCUR TO ANYONE THAT WE SHOULD-- OH, I DON'T KNOW-- SAVE THE WORLD OR SOMETHING?!
THAT IS A GOOD POINT.
EXCEPT WE ARE--BY NO ONE'S DEFINITION-- SUPER HEROES.
BUT, I'LL PLAY ALONG A MOMENT. EVEN IF WE *WANTED* TO FIND HELSPONT, WHERE WOULD YOU SUGGEST WE START?
UM.
WAIT-- WAIT. I GOT THIS.
WE COULD.
LET'S JUST--
I'LL GO GET THE KEYS.
THANKS.
MEET YOU ON THE ROOF IN FIVE?
MAKE IT TEN. WE ALL NEED TO *CHANGE* OUT OF THIS TAMARAN BATTLE ARMOR.
MAYBE NOW THAT THINGS HAVE SETTLED DOWN--
NO MORE BLIGHT. THE UNTITLED GONE TO GROUND.
--MAYBE IT'S TIME TO ASK JASON AND KORI FOR HELP...BEFORE IT'S TOO LATE FOR ALL OF US.

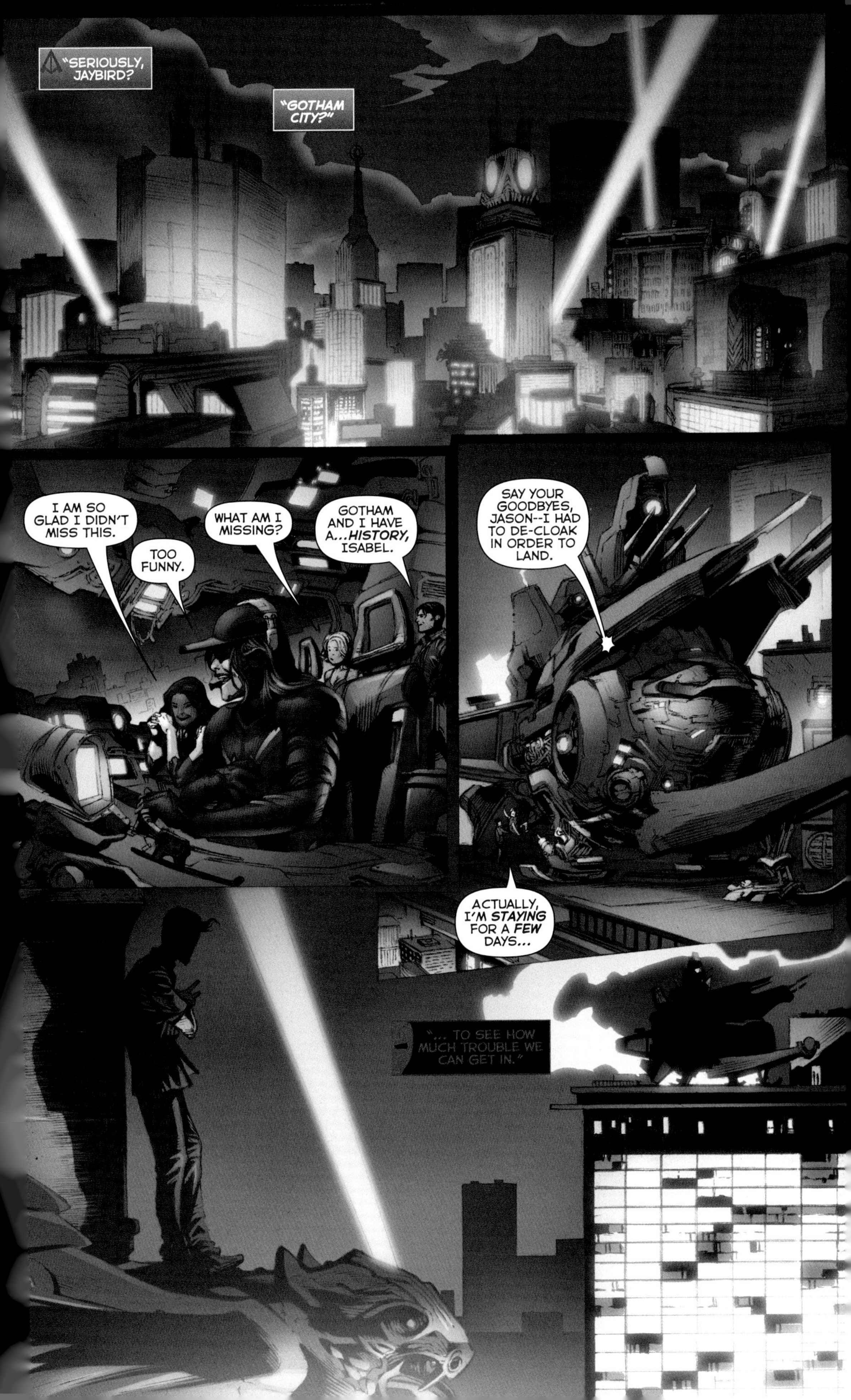
"SERIOUSLY, JAYBIRD?
"GOTHAM CITY?"
I AM SO GLAD I DIDN'T MISS THIS.
TOO FUNNY.
WHAT AM I MISSING?
GOTHAM AND I HAVE A...HISTORY, ISABEL.
SAY YOUR GOODBYES, JASON--I HAD TO DE-CLOAK IN ORDER TO LAND.
ACTUALLY, I'M STAYING FOR A FEW DAYS...
"...TO SEE HOW MUCH TROUBLE WE CAN GET IN."

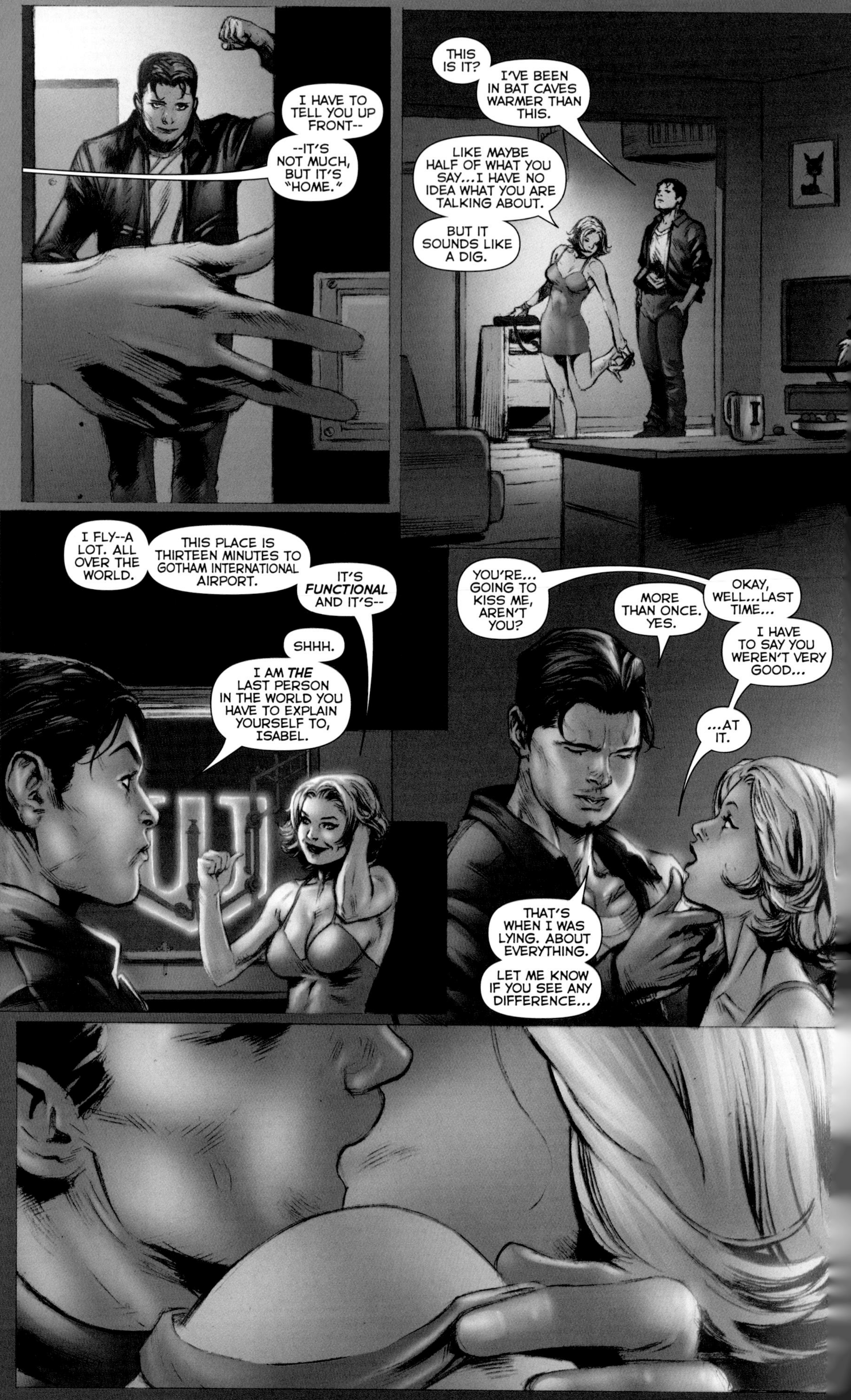

I HAVE TO TELL YOU UP FRONT--
--IT'S NOT MUCH, BUT IT'S "HOME."
THIS IS IT?
I'VE BEEN IN BAT CAVES WARMER THAN THIS.
LIKE MAYBE HALF OF WHAT YOU SAY...I HAVE NO IDEA WHAT YOU ARE TALKING ABOUT.
BUT IT SOUNDS LIKE A DIG.
I FLY--A LOT. ALL OVER THE WORLD.
THIS PLACE IS THIRTEEN MINUTES TO GOTHAM INTERNATIONAL AIRPORT.
IT'S *FUNCTIONAL* AND IT'S--
SHHH.
I AM *THE* LAST PERSON IN THE WORLD YOU HAVE TO EXPLAIN YOURSELF TO, ISABEL.
YOU'RE... GOING TO KISS ME, AREN'T YOU?
MORE THAN ONCE. YES.
OKAY, WELL...LAST TIME...
I HAVE TO SAY YOU WEREN'T VERY GOOD...
...AT IT.
THAT'S WHEN I WAS LYING. ABOUT EVERYTHING.
LET ME KNOW IF YOU SEE ANY DIFFERENCE...

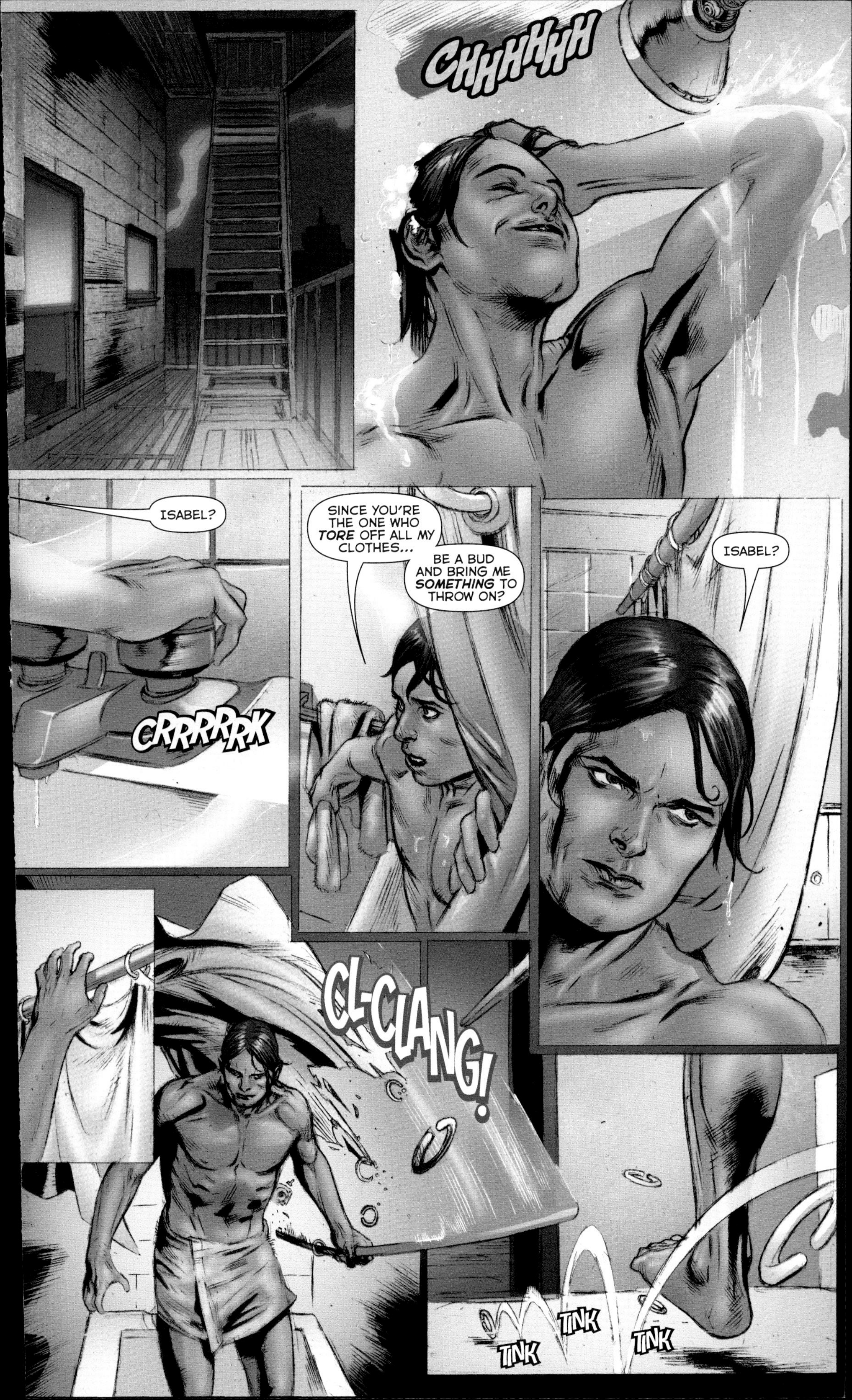
CHHHHHH
ISABEL?
CRRRRRK
SINCE YOU'RE THE ONE WHO TORE OFF ALL MY CLOTHES...
BE A BUD AND BRING ME SOMETHING TO THROW ON?
ISABEL?
CL-CLANG!
TINK
TINK
TINK

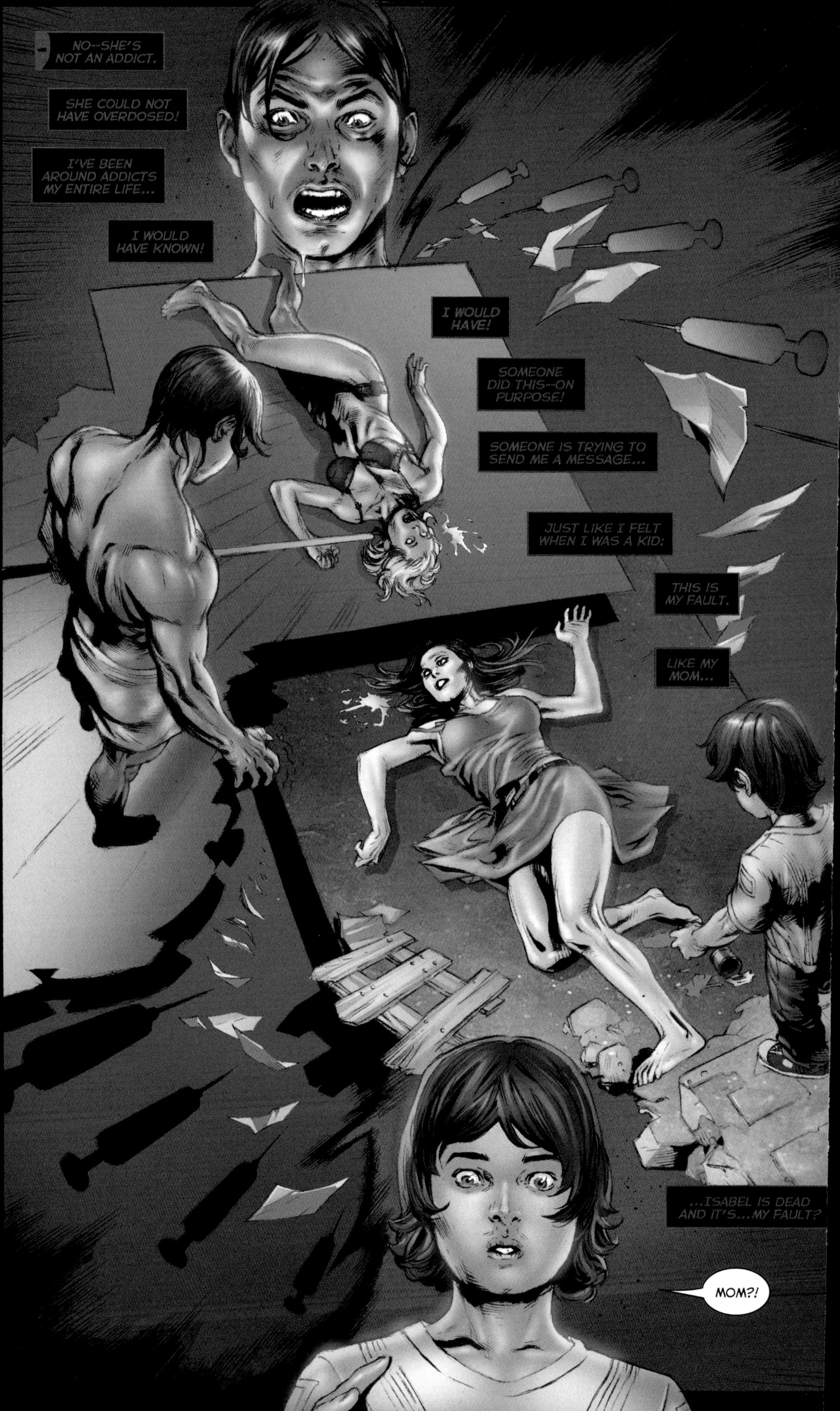
NO--SHE'S NOT AN ADDICT.
SHE COULD NOT HAVE OVERDOSED!
I'VE BEEN AROUND ADDICTS MY ENTIRE LIFE...
I WOULD HAVE KNOWN!
I WOULD HAVE!
SOMEONE DID THIS--ON PURPOSE!
SOMEONE IS TRYING TO SEND ME A MESSAGE...
JUST LIKE I FELT WHEN I WAS A KID:
THIS IS MY FAULT.
LIKE MY MOM...
...ISABEL IS DEAD AND IT'S...MY FAULT?
MOM?!

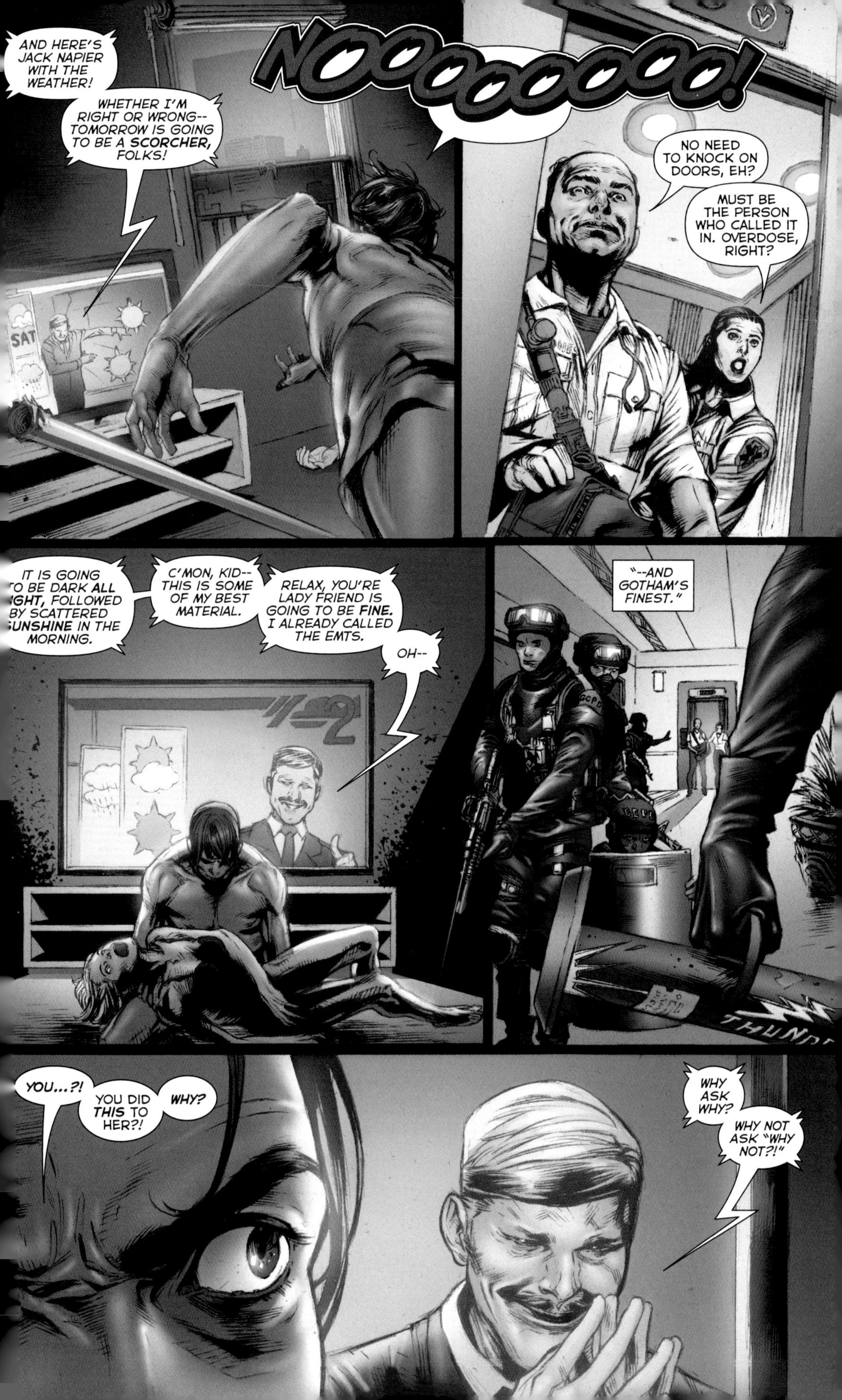
AND HERE'S JACK NAPIER WITH THE WEATHER!
WHETHER I'M RIGHT OR WRONG--TOMORROW IS GOING TO BE A SCORCHER, FOLKS!
NOOOOOOOOOO!
NO NEED TO KNOCK ON DOORS, EH?
MUST BE THE PERSON WHO CALLED IT IN. OVERDOSE, RIGHT?
SAT
IT IS GOING TO BE DARK ALL IGHT, FOLLOWED BY SCATTERED SUNSHINE IN THE MORNING.
C'MON, KID--THIS IS SOME OF MY BEST MATERIAL.
RELAX, YOU'RE LADY FRIEND IS GOING TO BE FINE. I ALREADY CALLED THE EMTS.
OH--
"--AND GOTHAM'S FINEST."
YOU...?!
YOU DID THIS TO HER?!
WHY?
WHY ASK WHY?
WHY NOT ASK "WHY NOT?!"

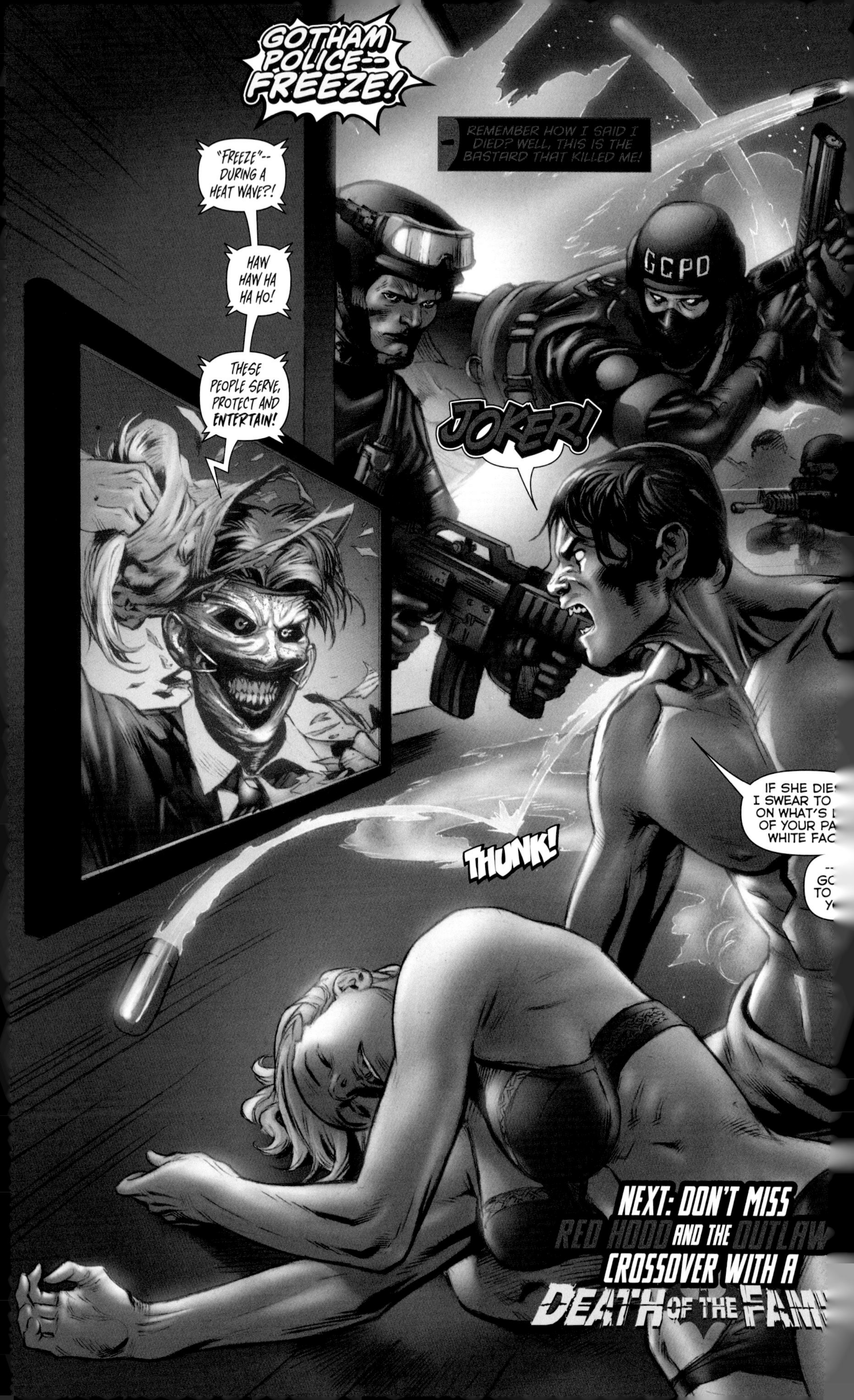

GOTHAM POLICE-- FREEZE!
REMEMBER HOW I SAID I DIED? WELL, THIS IS THE BASTARD THAT KILLED ME!
"FREEZE"-- DURING A HEAT WAVE?!
HAW HAW HA HA HO!
THESE PEOPLE SERVE, PROTECT AND ENTERTAIN!
JOKER!
IF SHE DIE
I SWEAR TO
ON WHAT'S
OF YOUR PA
WHITE FAC
THUNK!
NEXT: DON'T MISS
RED HOOD AND THE
CROSSOVER WITH A
DEATH OF THE

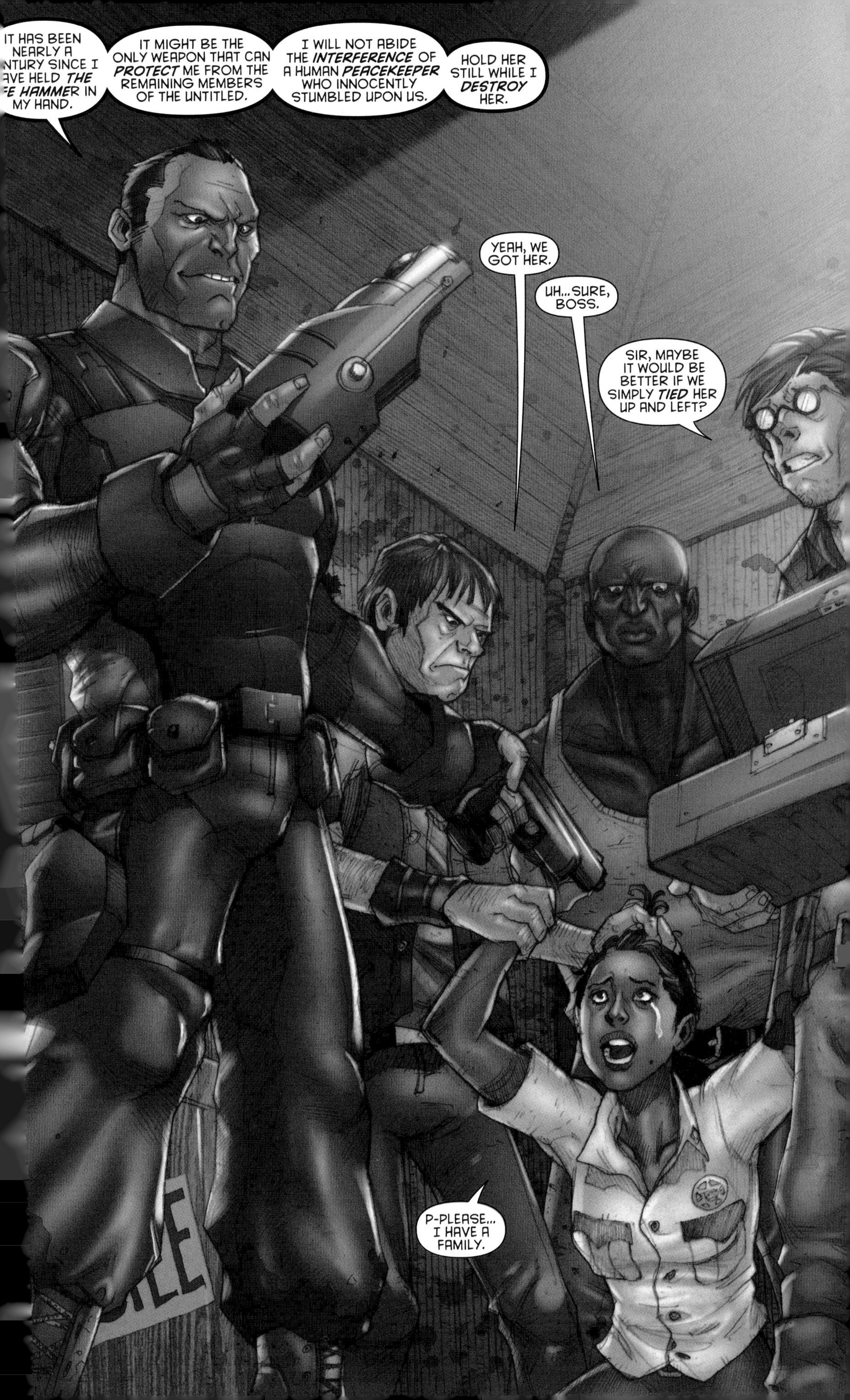
IT HAS BEEN NEARLY A NTURY SINCE I AVE HELD THE FE HAMMER IN MY HAND.
IT MIGHT BE THE ONLY WEAPON THAT CAN PROTECT ME FROM THE REMAINING MEMBERS OF THE UNTITLED.
I WILL NOT ABIDE THE INTERFERENCE OF A HUMAN PEACEKEEPER WHO INNOCENTLY STUMBLED UPON US.
HOLD HER STILL WHILE I DESTROY HER.
YEAH, WE GOT HER.
UH...SURE, BOSS.
SIR, MAYBE IT WOULD BE BETTER IF WE SIMPLY TIED HER UP AND LEFT?
P-PLEASE... I HAVE A FAMILY.

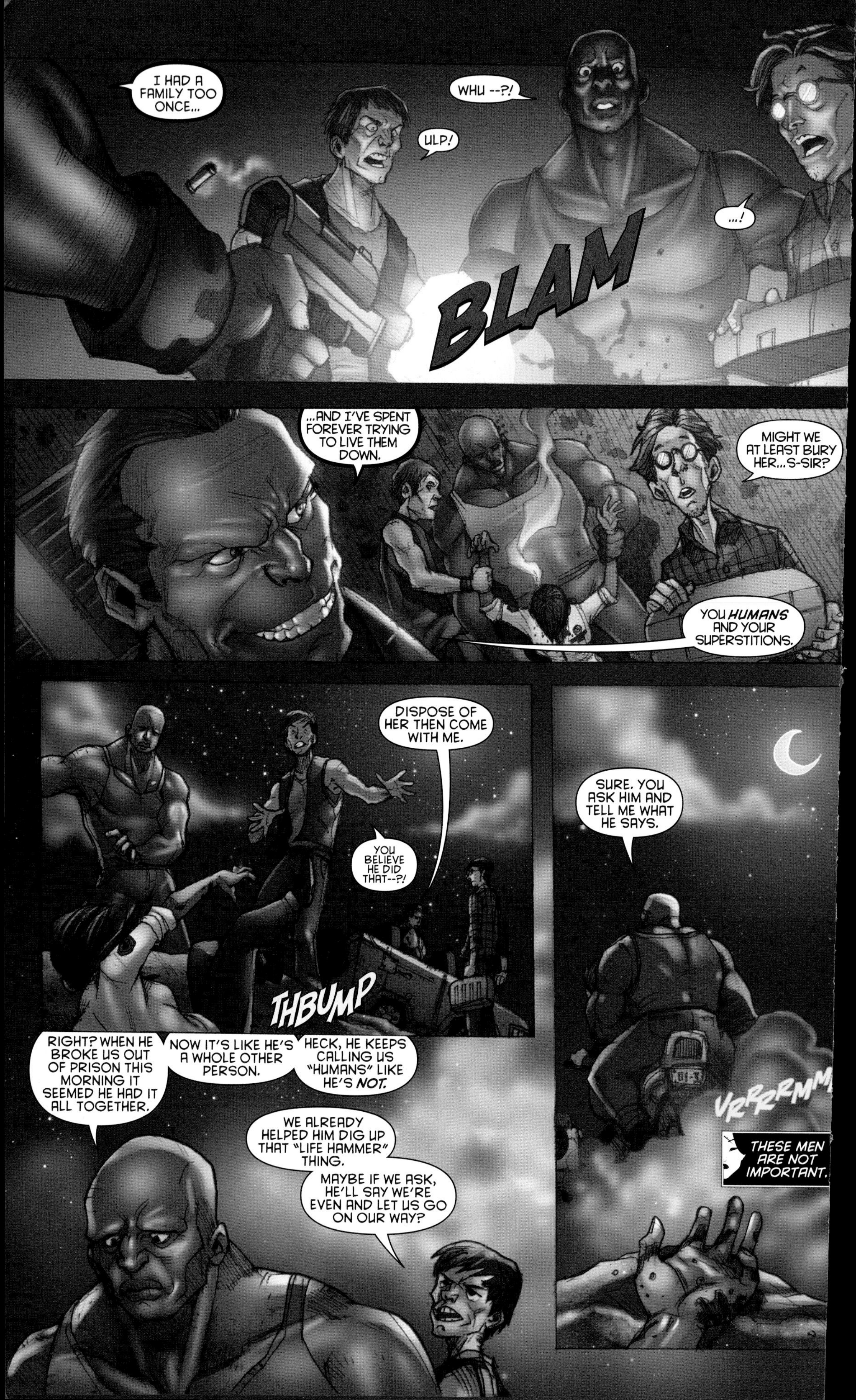
I HAD A FAMILY TOO ONCE...
WHU --?!
ULP!
...!
BLAM
...AND I'VE SPENT FOREVER TRYING TO LIVE THEM DOWN.
MIGHT WE AT LEAST BURY HER... S-SIR?
YOU HUMANS AND YOUR SUPERSTITIONS.
DISPOSE OF HER THEN COME WITH ME.
YOU BELIEVE HE DID THAT--?!
THBUMP
RIGHT? WHEN HE BROKE US OUT OF PRISON THIS MORNING IT SEEMED HE HAD IT ALL TOGETHER.
NOW IT'S LIKE HE'S A WHOLE OTHER PERSON.
HECK, HE KEEPS CALLING US "HUMANS" LIKE HE'S NOT.
WE ALREADY HELPED HIM DIG UP THAT "LIFE HAMMER" THING.
MAYBE IF WE ASK, HE'LL SAY WE'RE EVEN AND LET US GO ON OUR WAY?
SURE. YOU ASK HIM AND TELL ME WHAT HE SAYS.
VRRRRMMM
THESE MEN ARE NOT IMPORTANT.

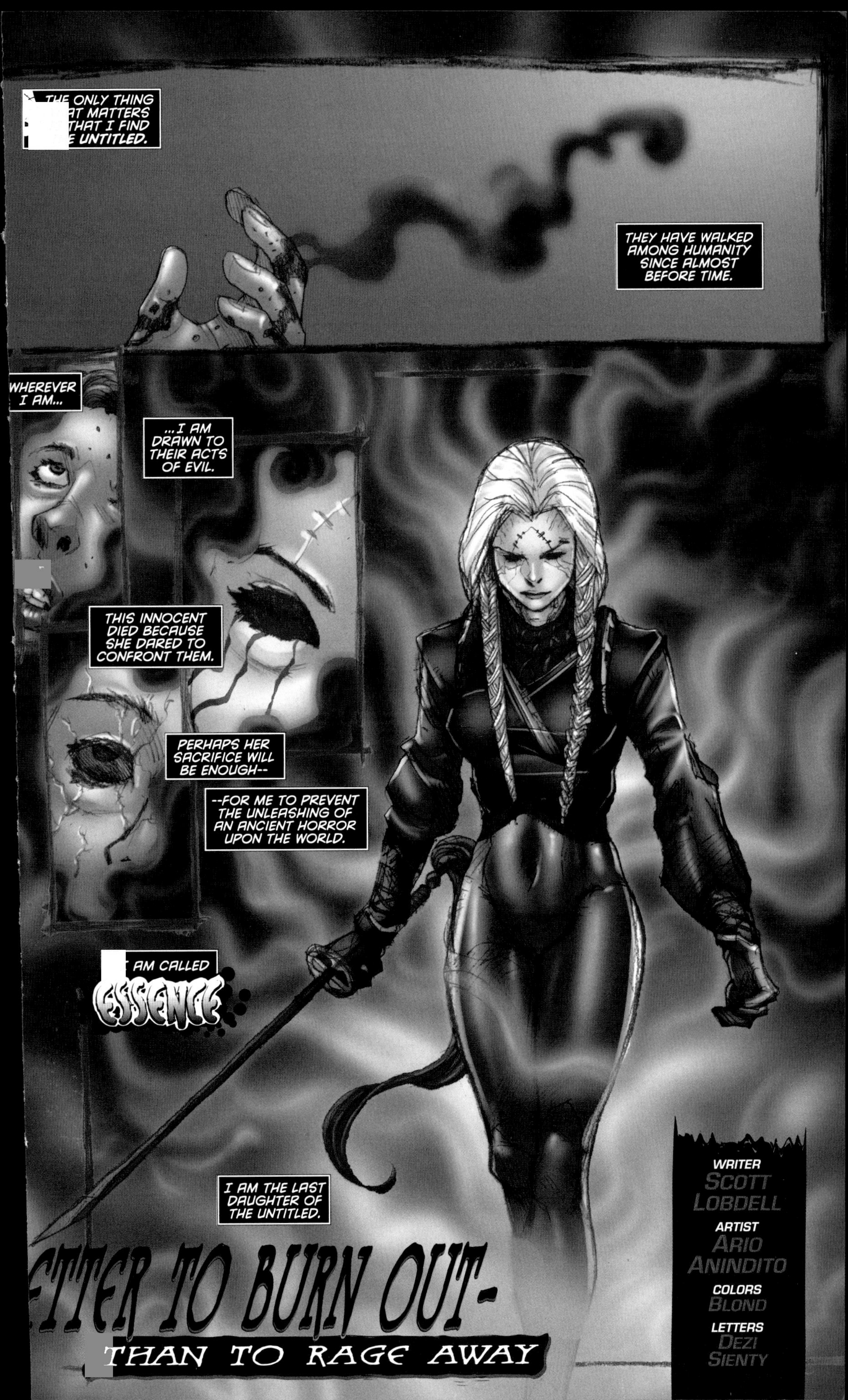

THE ONLY THING
AT MATTERS
THAT I FIND
E UNTITLED.
THEY HAVE WALKED AMONG HUMANITY SINCE ALMOST BEFORE TIME.
WHEREVER I AM...
...I AM DRAWN TO THEIR ACTS OF EVIL.
THIS INNOCENT DIED BECAUSE SHE DARED TO CONFRONT THEM.
PERHAPS HER SACRIFICE WILL BE ENOUGH--
--FOR ME TO PREVENT THE UNLEASHING OF AN ANCIENT HORROR UPON THE WORLD.
AM CALLED
ESSENCE
I AM THE LAST DAUGHTER OF THE UNTITLED.
TTER TO BURN OUT-
THAN TO RAGE AWAY
WRITER
SCOTT LOBDELL
ARTIST
ARIO ANINDITO
COLORS
BLOND
LETTERS
DEZI SIENTY

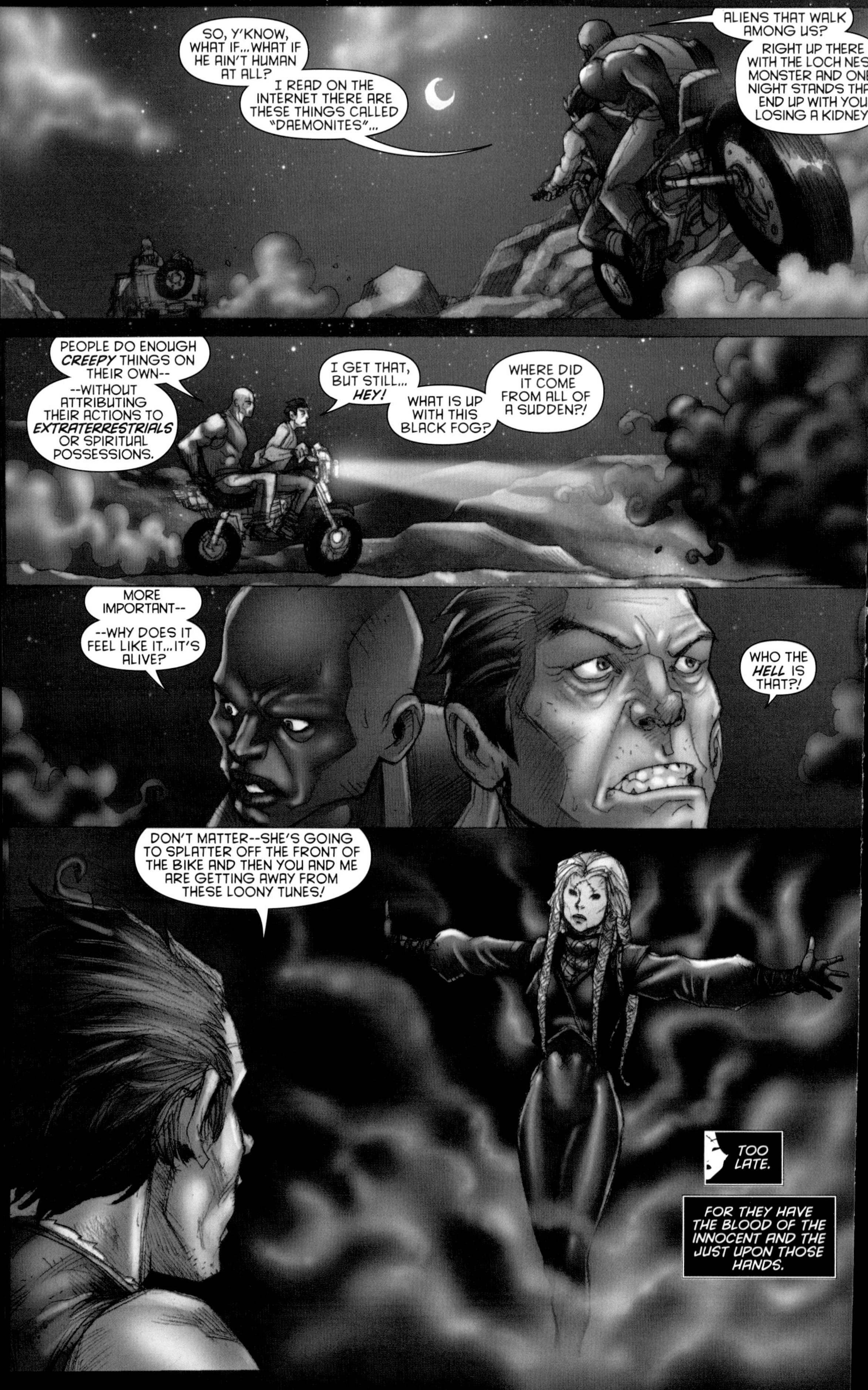
SO, Y'KNOW, WHAT IF... WHAT IF HE AIN'T HUMAN AT ALL?
I READ ON THE INTERNET THERE ARE THESE THINGS CALLED "DAEMONITES"...
ALIENS THAT WALK AMONG US?
RIGHT UP THERE WITH THE LOCH NESS MONSTER AND ONE-NIGHT STANDS THAT END UP WITH YOU LOSING A KIDNEY.
PEOPLE DO ENOUGH CREEPY THINGS ON THEIR OWN--
--WITHOUT ATTRIBUTING THEIR ACTIONS TO EXTRATERRESTRIALS OR SPIRITUAL POSSESSIONS.
I GET THAT, BUT STILL... HEY!
WHAT IS UP WITH THIS BLACK FOG?
WHERE DID IT COME FROM ALL OF A SUDDEN?!
MORE IMPORTANT--
--WHY DOES IT FEEL LIKE IT... IT'S ALIVE?
WHO THE HELL IS THAT?!
DON'T MATTER--SHE'S GOING TO SPLATTER OFF THE FRONT OF THE BIKE AND THEN YOU AND ME ARE GETTING AWAY FROM THESE LOONY TUNES!
TOO LATE.
FOR THEY HAVE THE BLOOD OF THE INNOCENT AND THE JUST UPON THOSE HANDS.

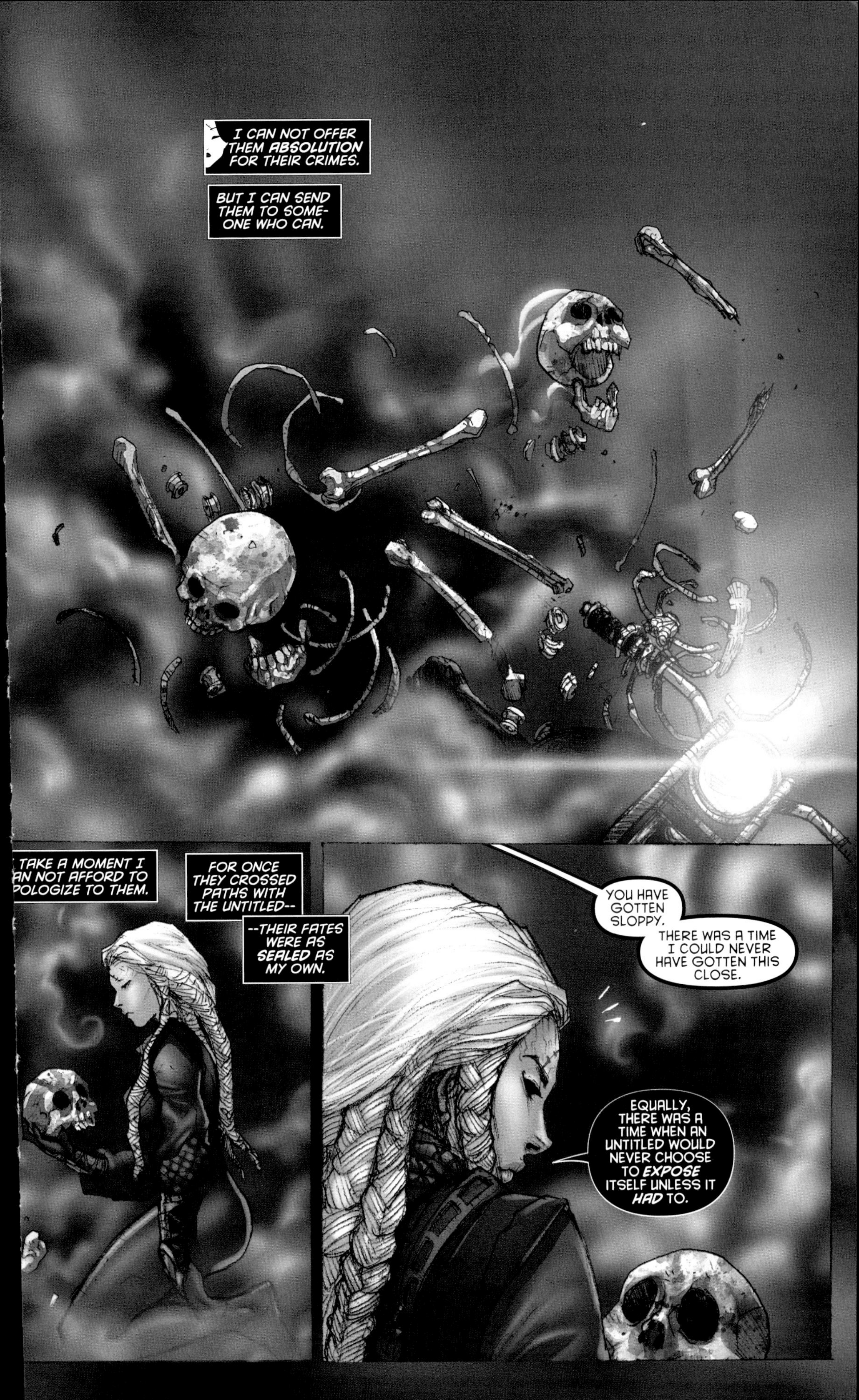
I CAN NOT OFFER THEM ABSOLUTION FOR THEIR CRIMES.
BUT I CAN SEND THEM TO SOME-ONE WHO CAN.
TAKE A MOMENT I AN NOT AFFORD TO POLOGIZE TO THEM.
FOR ONCE THEY CROSSED PATHS WITH THE UNTITLED--
--THEIR FATES WERE AS SEALED AS MY OWN.
YOU HAVE GOTTEN SLOPPY.
THERE WAS A TIME I COULD NEVER HAVE GOTTEN THIS CLOSE.
EQUALLY, THERE WAS A TIME WHEN AN UNTITLED WOULD NEVER CHOOSE TO EXPOSE ITSELF UNLESS IT HAD TO.

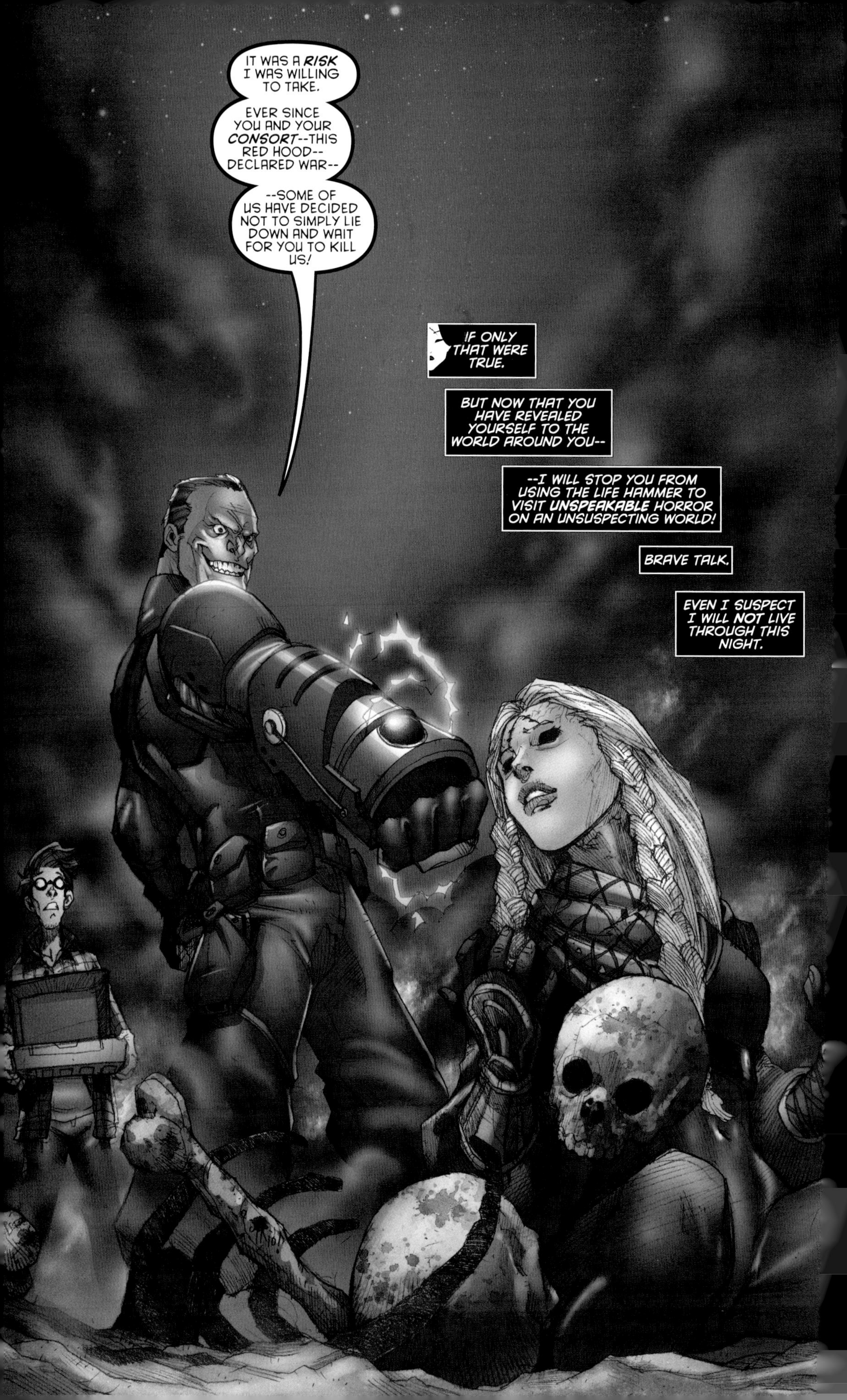
IT WAS A RISK I WAS WILLING TO TAKE.
EVER SINCE YOU AND YOUR CONSORT--THIS RED HOOD--DECLARED WAR--
--SOME OF US HAVE DECIDED NOT TO SIMPLY LIE DOWN AND WAIT FOR YOU TO KILL US!
IF ONLY THAT WERE TRUE.
BUT NOW THAT YOU HAVE REVEALED YOURSELF TO THE WORLD AROUND YOU--
--I WILL STOP YOU FROM USING THE LIFE HAMMER TO VISIT UNSPEAKABLE HORROR ON AN UNSUSPECTING WORLD!
BRAVE TALK.
EVEN I SUSPECT I WILL NOT LIVE THROUGH THIS NIGHT.

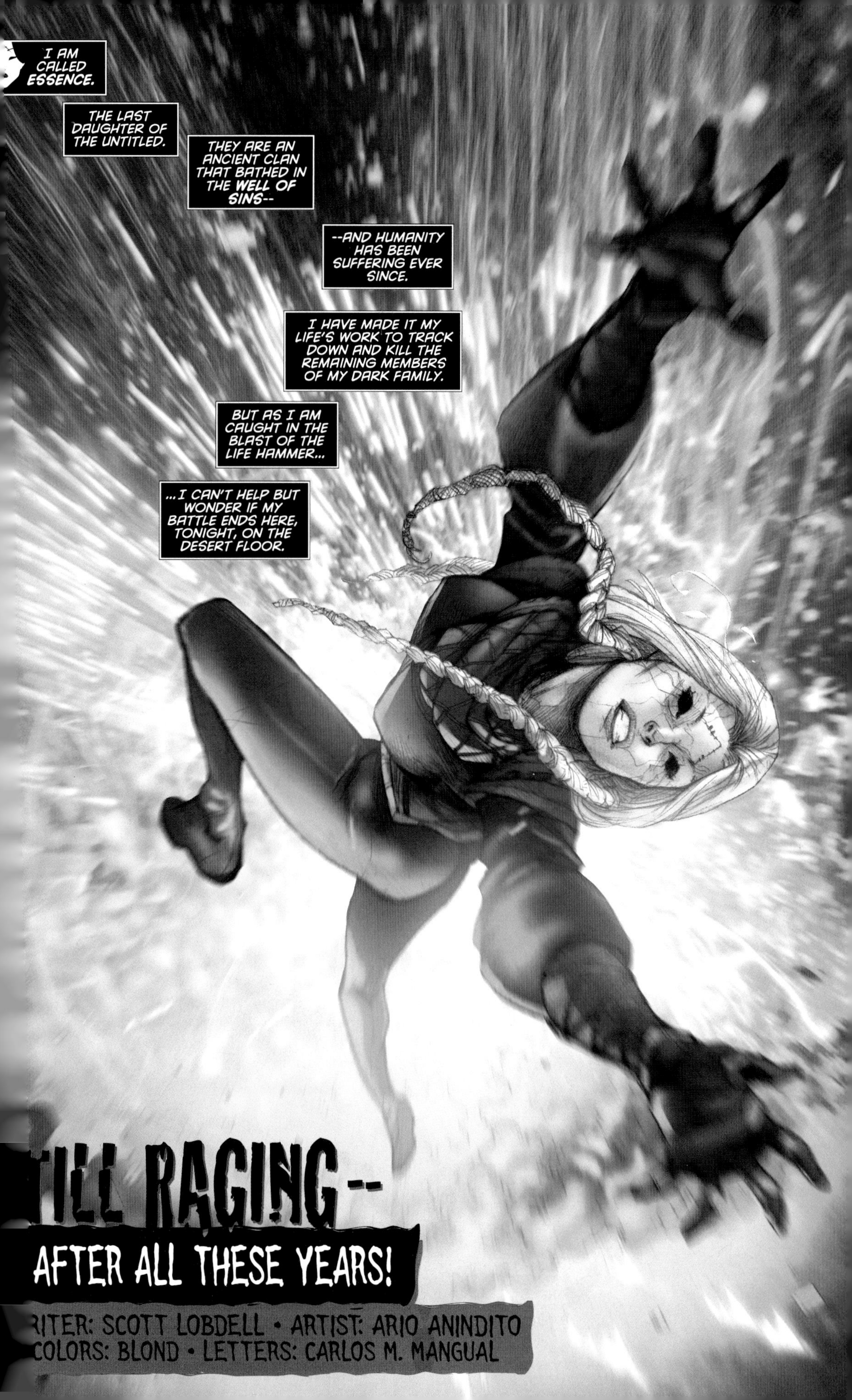

I AM CALLED ESSENCE.
THE LAST DAUGHTER OF THE UNTITLED.
THEY ARE AN ANCIENT CLAN THAT BATHED IN THE WELL OF SINS--
--AND HUMANITY HAS BEEN SUFFERING EVER SINCE.
I HAVE MADE IT MY LIFE'S WORK TO TRACK DOWN AND KILL THE REMAINING MEMBERS OF MY DARK FAMILY.
BUT AS I AM CAUGHT IN THE BLAST OF THE LIFE HAMMER...
...I CAN'T HELP BUT WONDER IF MY BATTLE ENDS HERE, TONIGHT, ON THE DESERT FLOOR.
TILL RAGING--
AFTER ALL THESE YEARS!
RITER: SCOTT LOBDELL • ARTIST: ARIO ANINDITO
COLORS: BLOND • LETTERS: CARLOS M. MANGUAL

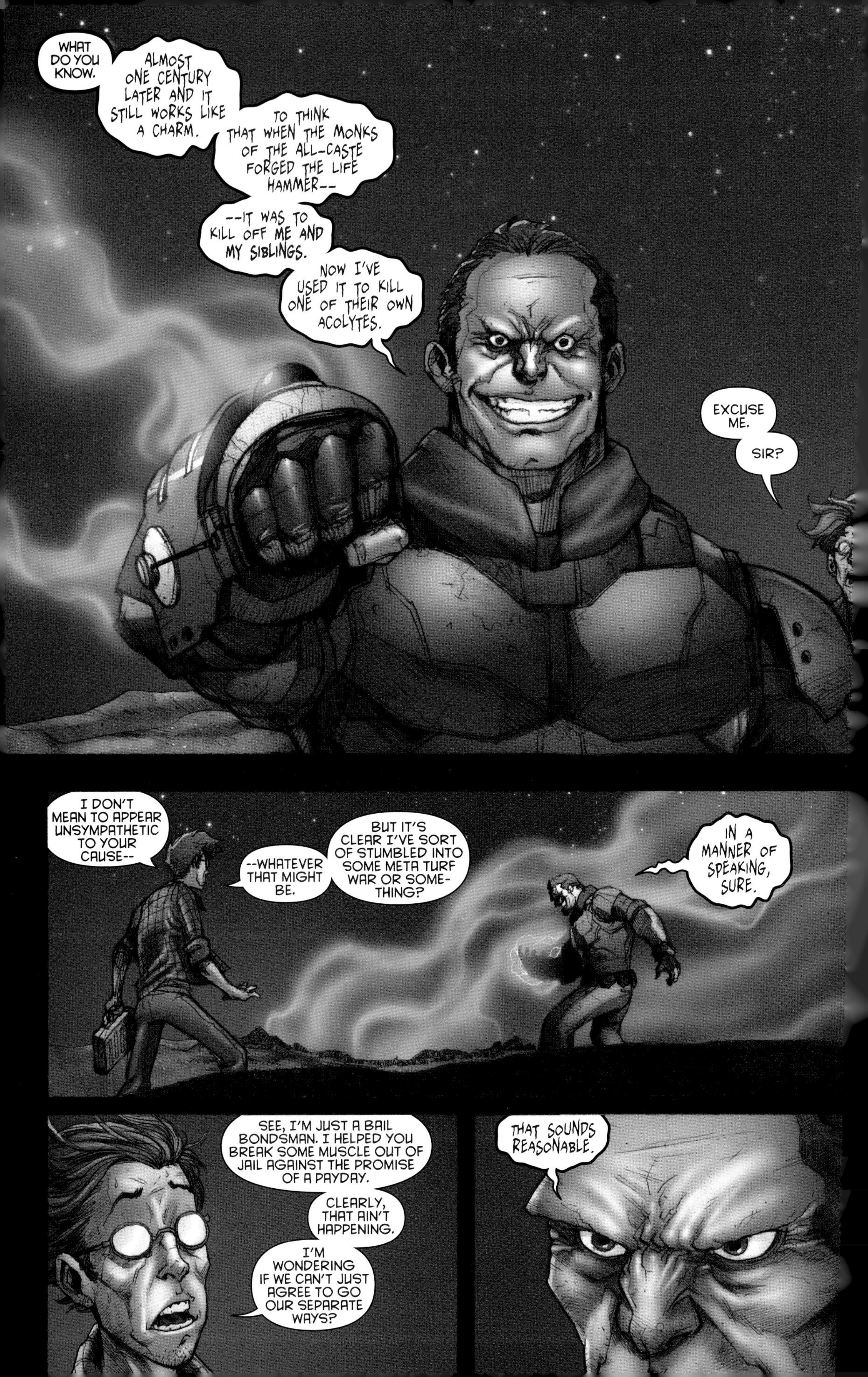
WHAT DO YOU KNOW.
ALMOST ONE CENTURY LATER AND IT STILL WORKS LIKE A CHARM.
TO THINK THAT WHEN THE MONKS OF THE ALL-CASTE FORGED THE LIFE HAMMER--
--IT WAS TO KILL OFF ME AND MY SIBLINGS.
NOW I'VE USED IT TO KILL ONE OF THEIR OWN ACOLYTES.
EXCUSE ME.
SIR?
I DON'T MEAN TO APPEAR UNSYMPATHETIC TO YOUR CAUSE--
--WHATEVER THAT MIGHT BE.
BUT IT'S CLEAR I'VE SORT OF STUMBLED INTO SOME META TURF WAR OR SOME-THING?
IN A MANNER OF SPEAKING, SURE.
SEE, I'M JUST A BAIL BONDSMAN. I HELPED YOU BREAK SOME MUSCLE OUT OF JAIL AGAINST THE PROMISE OF A PAYDAY.
CLEARLY, THAT AIN'T HAPPENING.
I'M WONDERING IF WE CAN'T JUST AGREE TO GO OUR SEPARATE WAYS?
THAT SOUNDS REASONABLE.

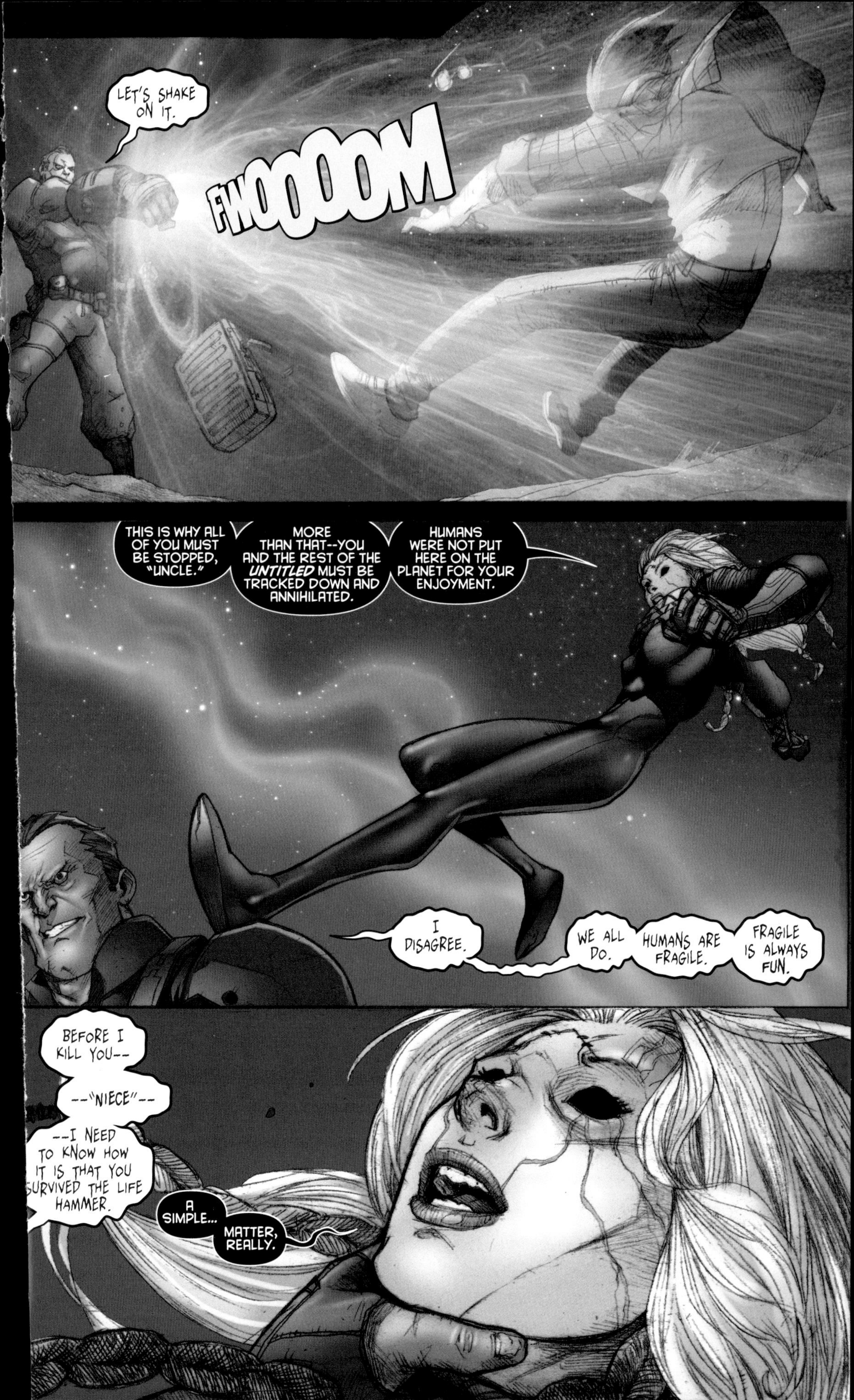
LET'S SHAKE ON IT.
FWOOOOOM
THIS IS WHY ALL OF YOU MUST BE STOPPED, "UNCLE."
MORE THAN THAT--YOU AND THE REST OF THE *UNTITLED* MUST BE TRACKED DOWN AND ANNIHILATED.
HUMANS WERE NOT PUT HERE ON THE PLANET FOR YOUR ENJOYMENT.
I DISAGREE.
WE ALL DO.
HUMANS ARE FRAGILE.
FRAGILE IS ALWAYS FUN.
BEFORE I KILL YOU--
--"NIECE"--
--I NEED TO KNOW HOW IT IS THAT YOU SURVIVED THE LIFE HAMMER.
A SIMPLE...
MATTER, REALLY.

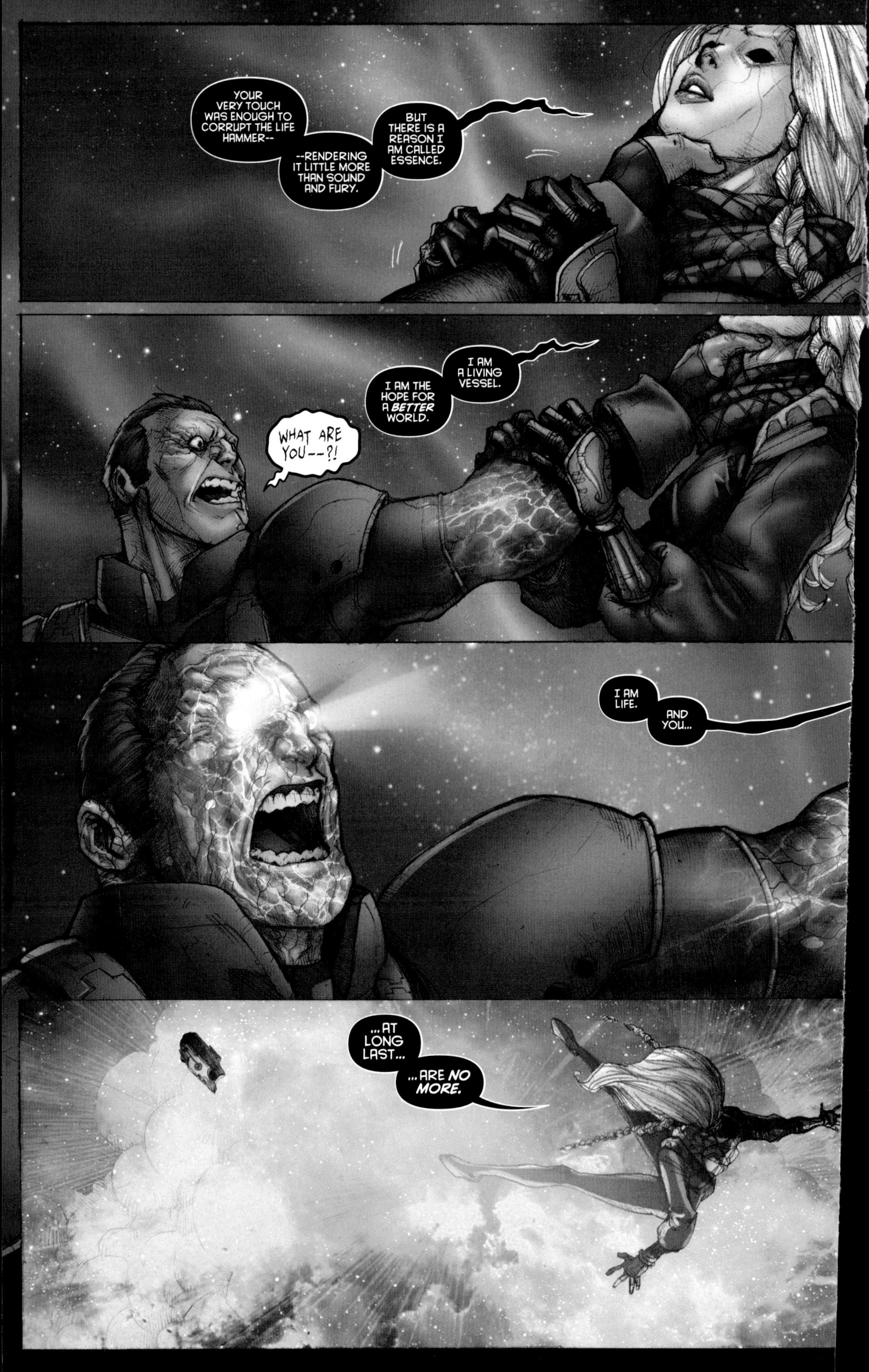
YOUR VERY TOUCH WAS ENOUGH TO CORRUPT THE LIFE HAMMER--
--RENDERING IT LITTLE MORE THAN SOUND AND FURY.
BUT THERE IS A REASON I AM CALLED ESSENCE.
I AM A LIVING VESSEL.
I AM THE HOPE FOR A *BETTER* WORLD.
WHAT ARE YOU--?!
I AM LIFE.
AND YOU...
...AT LONG LAST...
...ARE *NO MORE.*

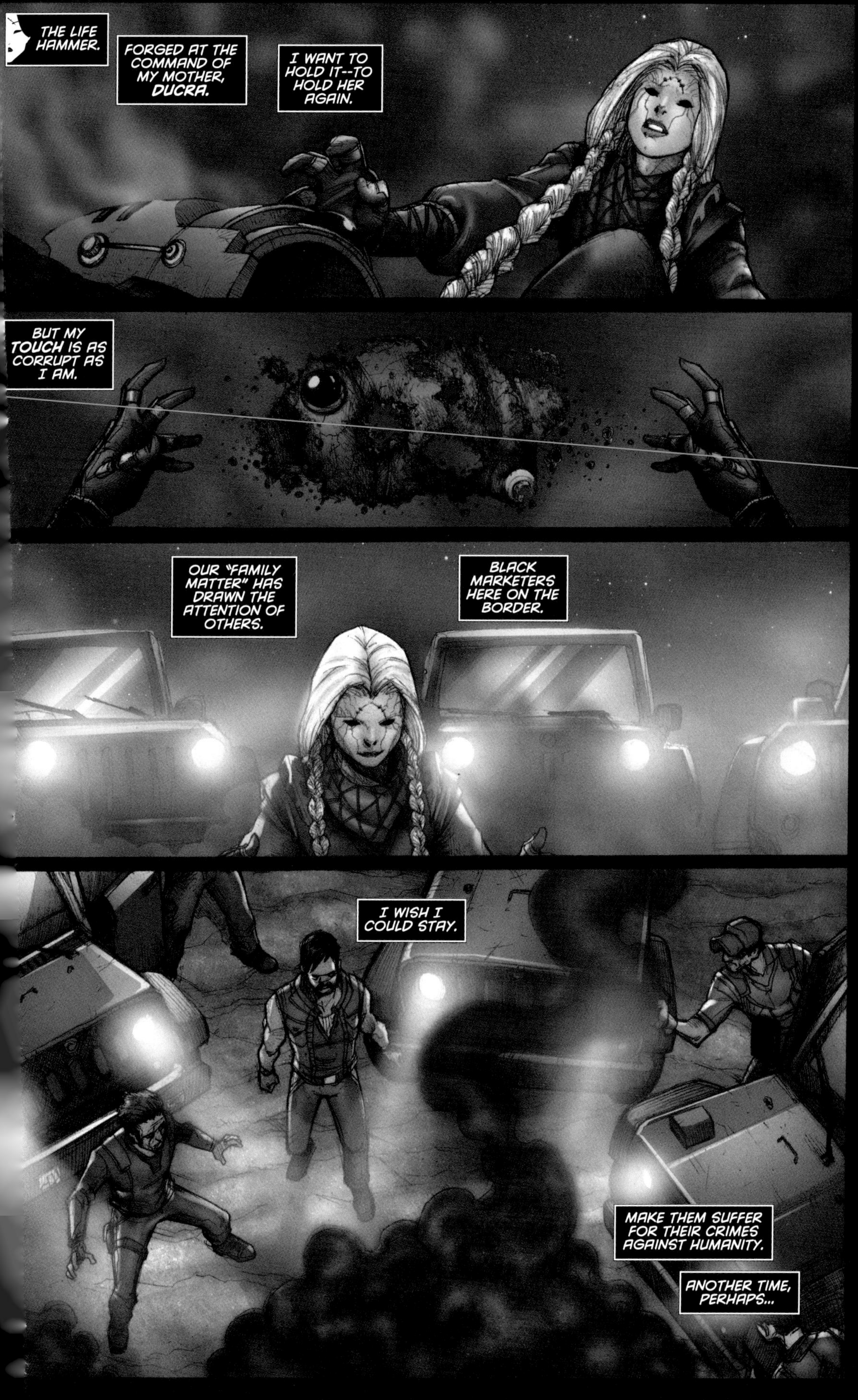
THE LIFE HAMMER.
FORGED AT THE COMMAND OF MY MOTHER, DUCRA.
I WANT TO HOLD IT--TO HOLD HER AGAIN.
BUT MY TOUCH IS AS CORRUPT AS I AM.
OUR "FAMILY MATTER" HAS DRAWN THE ATTENTION OF OTHERS.
BLACK MARKETERS HERE ON THE BORDER.
I WISH I COULD STAY.
MAKE THEM SUFFER FOR THEIR CRIMES AGAINST HUMANITY.
ANOTHER TIME, PERHAPS...

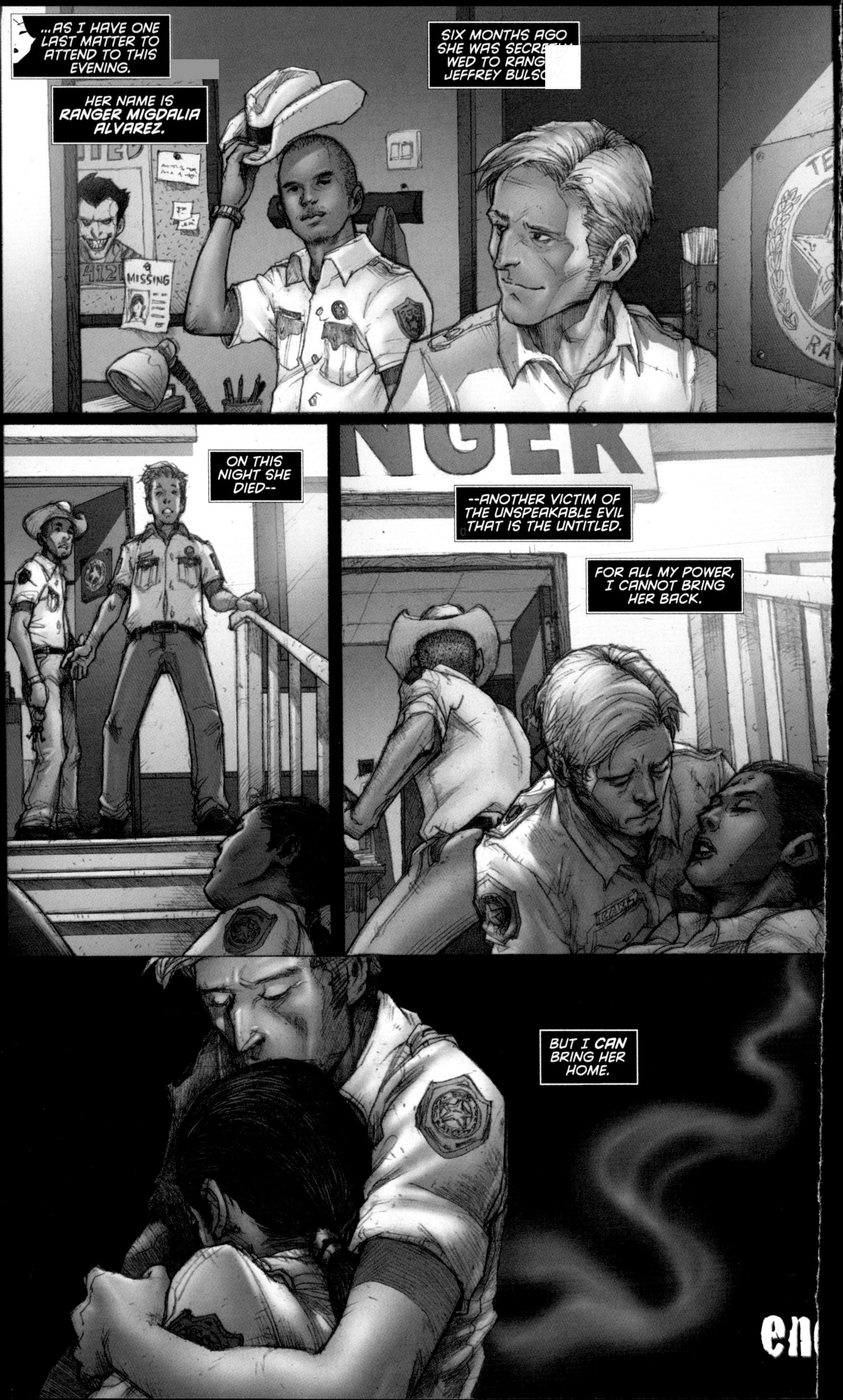

...AS I HAVE ONE LAST MATTER TO ATTEND TO THIS EVENING.
SIX MONTHS AGO SHE WAS SECRE
WED TO RANG
JEFFREY BULS
HER NAME IS RANGER MIGDALIA ALVAREZ.
MISSING
ON THIS NIGHT SHE DIED--
NGER
--ANOTHER VICTIM OF THE UNSPEAKABLE EVIL THAT IS THE UNTITLED.
FOR ALL MY POWER, I CANNOT BRING HER BACK.
BUT I CAN BRING HER HOME.

Suzie Su

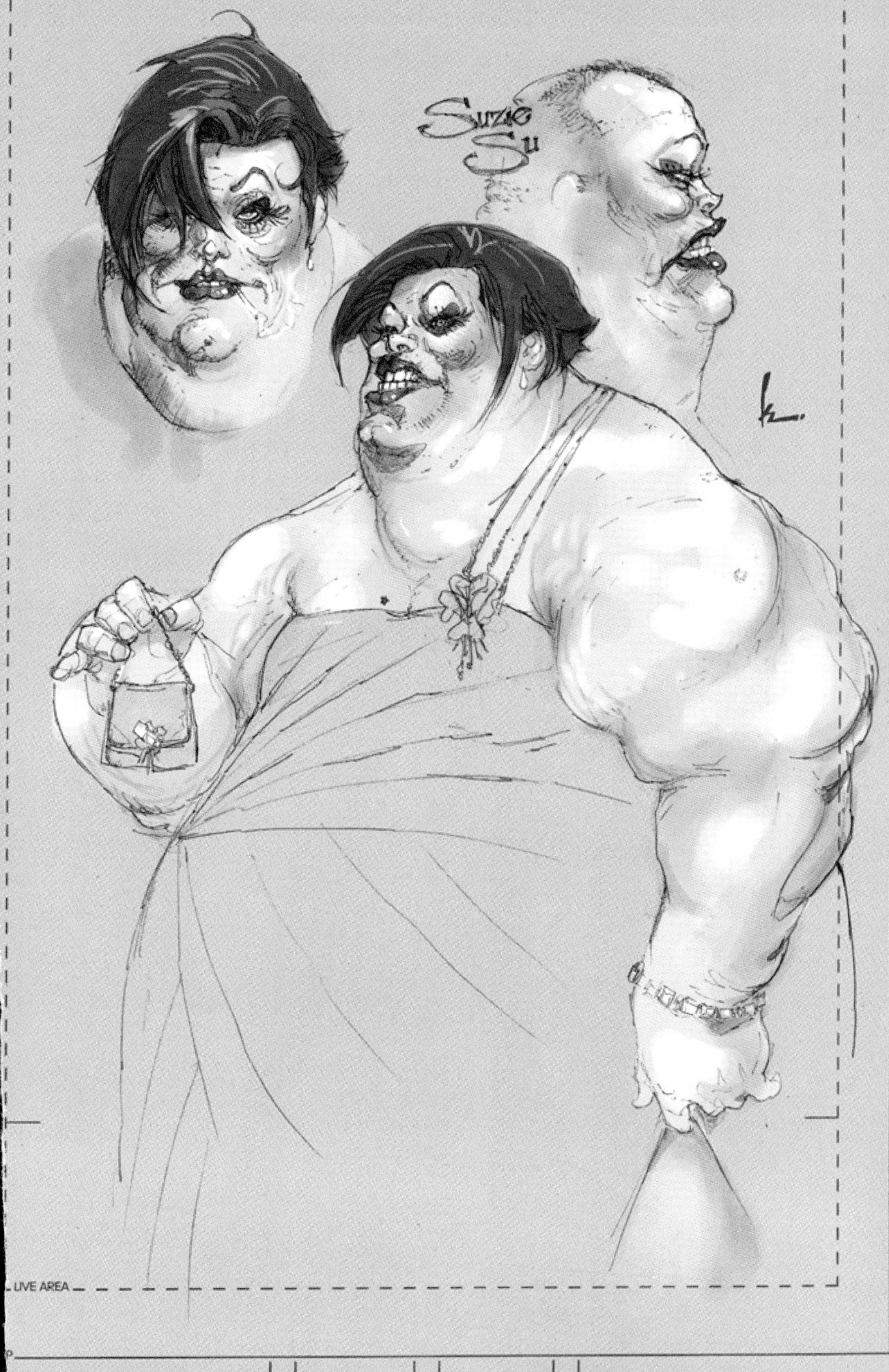
Suzie Su
LIVE AREA

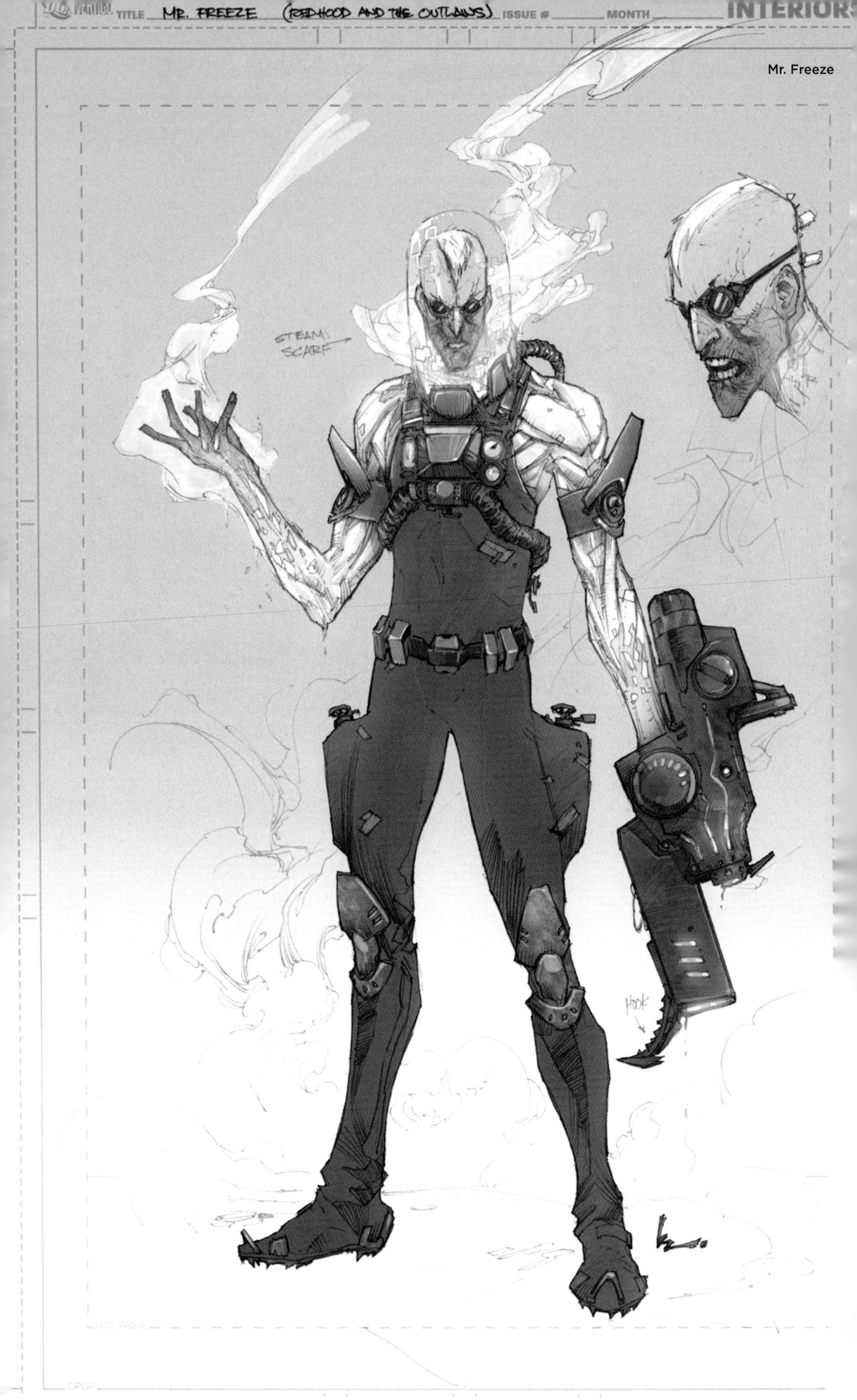
TITLE MR. FREEZE (REDHOOD AND THE OUTLAWS) ISSUE # MONTH
INTERIORS
STEAM SCARF
HOOK

Mr. Freeze